THE ACADEMIC'S HANDBOOK

THE ACADEMIC'S HANDBOOK

THIRD EDITION

EDITED BY

A. LEIGH DENEEF

AND CRAUFURD D. GOODWIN

Duke University Press · Durham & London 2007

© 2007 DUKE UNIVERSITY PRESS

ALL RIGHTS RESERVED

PRINTED IN THE UNITED STATES OF AMERICA

ON ACID-FREE PAPER ∞

DESIGNED BY KATY CLOVE

TYPESET IN MINION BY TSENG INFORMATION SYSTEMS, INC.

LIBRARY OF CONGRESS CATALOGING-IN-PUBLICATION DATA

APPEAR ON THE LAST PRINTED PAGE OF THIS BOOK.

CONTENTS

PREFACE TO THE THIRD EDITION

In the nearly twenty years since the first edition of *The Academic's Handbook* higher education in the United States has undergone significant change. It has also, however, stayed very much the same, at least in one central aspect: most new Ph.D.'s emerge from the nation's premier graduate schools with very little specific knowledge about how colleges and universities really operate or about what academic life in such institutions is all about. This *Handbook*, therefore, like its predecessors, is addressed directly to the beginning faculty member in an effort to provide immediately useful advice to smooth the transition into this complex, demanding, and, we hope, rewarding career.

The first edition of the *Handbook* was heavily indebted not only to the Andrew W. Mellon Foundation but also to the fifty colleagues, both faculty and graduate students, from Duke and elsewhere across the country, who came together over two years in the mid-1980s to talk candidly about their experiences within the academy. The second edition was equally indebted to a group of students and faculty—this time largely from Duke and Guilford College—who participated in a project entitled "Preparing Graduate Students for the Professional Responsibilities of College Teachers," a project developed by the Association of American Colleges and Universities and supported by a three-year grant from the Fund for the Improvement of Postsecondary Education. The present edition builds on these earlier projects, and particularly on the now widely recognized "Preparing Future Faculty" program, funded initially by the Pew Charitable Trusts and directed nationally by colleagues at the AAC&U and the Council of Graduate Schools. For the past decade, Duke's own PFF program has expanded its partner institutions to include not only Guilford College but Elon University, Durham Technical Community College, Meredith College, and North Carolina Central University.

Some of the changes that have taken place on college and university campuses over the last ten years are reflected in essays appearing here for the first time—the rapidly growing number of non-tenure-track positions at major research universities, the impact of various technologies on classroom teaching, the increasing difficulty of publishing research monographs, the dramatic changes in the shape and function of modern research libraries. What remains the same on those campuses—the difference in kinds of institutions and the expectations of faculty who choose to work at each; how to go about getting and keeping an academic job; what makes for successful teaching and advising or mentoring; how to fund and publish research; and what are the standard administrative structures of most colleges and universities—is covered in essays that have been updated for this edition.

Throughout the *Handbook* we have tried to bear in mind that our goal was to produce an essential and pragmatic guide for those planning or beginning an academic career. We hope that the advice we offer here is delivered with both good sense and good humor, and that the volume itself will find a conspicuous place on your bookshelf next to other indispensable and frequently consulted guides.

LOVING THE ACADEMIC'S VOCATION, INSTITUTIONS AND ALL

A Retrospective Appreciation of the Colloquium on

The Academic's Handbook

L. GREGORY JONES

I accepted the invitation more out of flattery and curiosity than anything else. I had been invited to participate in a colloquium about the academic life and academic culture that would culminate in the first edition of this handbook. It sounded intriguing, but I also accepted because I thought it couldn't hurt to have participation in such a colloquium on my cv when I applied for jobs (I had already been acculturated at least that much into an academic vocation!). I could hardly have imagined, however, just how significant that colloquium would be for my own vocation: it helped me see the larger contexts and issues of academic life, to begin to realize that my doctoral education had been increasingly focused on mastery of my field, rather than on acculturating me to a particular profession. To be sure, I had picked up some tips from faculty advisers and other graduate students on practical matters that would help me get a job: reading papers at scholarly conferences, publishing an essay or two in scholarly journals, making sure I had some teaching experience. But the general focus of my graduate education was preparation for a particular field of scholarship. If I thought at all about the institution in which that education took place, it was little more than an enabling structure.

Ironically, one might have thought that I would have been keenly aware of broader institutional issues. After all, my father had spent most of his adult life serving as an academic administrator, including positions as president of a free-standing seminary and then as dean of Duke Divinity School. And while I appreciated my father's academic positions, I discovered through the colloquium that I had very little sense of what he actually did or how academic institutions really operate.

Now, almost two decades after the colloquium, it turns out that I have devoted the last portion of my life to the work of full-time academic administration. Why did I do such a thing? What factors have shaped my own sense of vocation? And what role did the colloquium play in preparing me for my academic career? These were the questions that occurred to me when I was asked to provide a brief retrospective glance at the impact of that initiating colloquium and the volume that followed from it. It seems to me that three broad themes emerged in the original discussion: (1) the significance of the particular; (2) academic life as a shared vocation; and (3) the importance, and the fragility, of institutions.

I

Graduate school, of course, already educates us to attend to the significance of particularity. In part, this is the result of a developing awareness of the perspectival character of all knowledge; one could hardly study in the humanities or the social sciences without becoming aware of how particular identities and histories affected people's perspectives and arguments. Many of us also benefit from having gifted mentors whose scholarly expertise pressed us to pay attention to the subtle details that reshaped disciplinary issues and reframed patterns of inquiry.

Ironically, however, it was precisely because of the scholarly and pedagogical gifts of my mentors that I failed to attend to the particularity of their vocation. They were so good at what they did that it masked the very concrete, practical steps that had enabled them to become masters of their craft.

For example, one of my mentors, Tom Langford, was a masterful teacher who made teaching look effortless, not unlike watching a concert pianist or a superb athlete in performance. He would walk in to class, begin lecturing (without notes), engaging the class for a full hour on the topic at hand. If a student asked a question, whether on- or off-topic, he would pause and typically respond with care and insight. Often his responses drew from a reservoir of reading that enabled him to cite from a dauntingly diverse set of sources. Only later, in the light of the colloquium's discussions about teaching and learning, did I pursue a conversation with him to ask how he had developed his teaching style and his "art" of lecturing. He described how his office hours were crucial to shaping his lectures, as he learned about the questions and issues that were on students' minds. He further described the connections between his reading and his writing and the courses he taught, showing me how one can cultivate an intersection of research and teaching rather than seeing them as alternatives. The colloquium's discussions helped me to think about the academic vocation as integrally connected to learning as well as teaching, to an intellectual conversation as much as conveying information.

Another of my mentors, Stanley Hauerwas, wrote an essay for the handbook. As he prepared that essay, and then as I talked with him about the issues, I found myself engaged with him in an extended conversation about vocation and the skills necessary for wise teaching. He told me about how, as a graduate student interviewing for jobs, he was astounded to discover in his first job interview that his interviewers wanted him to talk about syllabi and his approach to teaching. His description of his failures even to think about these issues was illuminating and both informed my participation in the colloquium and helped me see the importance of syllabi in shaping a scholarly vocation. Yet he also helped me understand that the best teaching is fed by an intellectually vital research agenda. I remember vividly a colloquium discussion in which one of the participants suggested that a fresh research discovery, or reading an excellent new book in one's field, would contribute more to a dynamic classroom than trying to perfect a teaching technique. It is an insight I have verified in my own teaching and have passed on to others.

The colloquium also helped me understand the significance of other particulars: how gender issues shape the dynamics of certain classrooms, how internal political issues shape the culture of different departments, and how the relationships between research and teaching differ in diverse academic disciplines. I also learned, for the first time, the particular expectations of distinct academic job markets and the challenges of getting even to the on-campus interview at different kinds of schools, the realities and differences in tenure expectations, and the vast range of academic salaries and benefits. What became apparent in those conversations, at first only as a faint reality, is the radical diversity of institutions of higher education. The challenge of finding a job that pays an adequate wage seems to most graduate students sufficiently daunting, but a small liberal arts college is a very different context from a major research university, and a publicly supported institution is quite different from one supported by religious commitments.

Yet graduate students are not often encouraged to think about the complexities of institutional particularities. Too often graduate students are expected to focus only on the mastery of their field, and then to think in blunt economic and self-interested terms about the realities of the job market and finding a tenure-track job. The agenda of the colloquium, including the essays that constitute this handbook, fostered an attentiveness that enables us to discover a much healthier way of envisioning our vocation, including even the challenges of finding a good vocational fit amid the realities of the job market. This involves our recognition that the scholarly life cannot be adequately understood or lived apart from attention to diverse kinds of particularity.

II

The colloquium also nurtured a related healthy awareness: the academic vocation is a shared enterprise. Graduate study, especially in the humanities and social sciences, is often a highly individualized activity. As a student moves toward writing the dissertation, the task of graduate study becomes highly specialized, requiring extensive research and writing. As one works increasingly independently, it is often easy to envision the scholarly life in individualistic terms.

Yet the very structure of our colloquium, as well as the topics we discussed, invited us to see how academic life is intrinsically a shared vocation. This is true even of graduate study, and it becomes even more important as people finish their doctorates and begin teaching in diverse institutions.

The first seeds of my discovery of the academic vocation as a shared enterprise emerged within my doctoral program itself. Stanley Hauerwas, who was director of the graduate program in religion at the time, told the graduate students that we would provide for each other some of the most important education and formation we would receive. He was right, and his mentioning it explicitly invited us to be more intentional about educating one another than we might have otherwise been. A group of us, in several different subfields of the program, began to gather together every week to read important works — both in our field and across the disciplines in the humanities. We then pledged to offer one another feedback on dissertation topics and issues, turning even the individualized tasks of research and writing into more of a communal endeavor. Those conversations formed friendships that have continued through the years.

This shared sense of vocation was nurtured more broadly in the colloquium. Here were graduate students from across the university, discovering in conversation that — despite the significance of diverse particularities among us as well as divergence among our fields — we had a lot in common. We were all trying to figure out the nuts and bolts of what it means to be a full-time professor rather than a graduate student, and how we would navigate the complexities of universities, departments, funding agencies, publishers, and personal life decisions.

Through the colloquium, and the discussions that were fostered there, we began to discover that administrative attentiveness is intrinsic to academic flourishing. Whether it is mentoring younger faculty, serving on an editorial board or even editing a journal, chairing a search committee or a department, or serving on universitywide committees and task forces, academic life depends on a shared commitment to collegiality among faculty from diverse fields. The colloquium helped me to understand that, while we must attend to the diverse particularities of the academic's vocation, we also need to attend to the commonalities that cultivate a shared commitment to the academic vocation.

The colloquium's attentiveness to these issues helped me appreciate the gifts I received in my first teaching job at a liberal arts college: an institution that encouraged, and institutionalized a commitment to, collegiality across the disciplines. I was blessed with excellent colleagues in my department. In addition, one of my earliest and best colleagues was a junior faculty member in political science, and another was in English. We were encouraged to read drafts of each other's work, and to talk with each other about teaching and learning.

This sense of a shared vocation developed in a new way when in 1990 I was invited to become the coeditor of a scholarly journal. I learned the mysterious art of accepting and rejecting essays for publication, helping me to discover that to some degree the mystery isn't why some excellent essays are rejected but rather how any essay manages to get through the labyrinth of fallible editors and reviewers. Yet more important was the joy I discovered in working with authors and reviewers to improve essays and then to see the contribution they made to ongoing conversations and debates. I took as much delight in seeing a colleague's essay appear, and in editing an excellent issue, as I would have had I written the material myself. We were involved in a shared enterprise.

Directing a center for the humanities, and then chairing a department, only added to the sense of a shared vocation and the delight of friendships sustained, often amid intense disagreement about matters that matter (and sometimes about matters that didn't really matter that much). As I participated in administrative tasks as a full-time faculty member, my appreciation of the shared life of the academic vocation deepened. The kinds of relationships forged in the colloquium, and its attentiveness to our common vocation, enabled me to see the significance of relationships in ways that would otherwise have remained occluded. I discovered that the tired clichés about "faculty vs. administration" were dangerous and destructive — for even those people entrusted with more, rather than less, administrative leadership were still fundamentally engaged in intellectual work that is fundamentally important to the scholarly vocation.

Eventually, I was faced with a significant decision — should I make a move into full-time academic administration? To be sure, it was not an easy decision in one sense, but in a more profound sense it was an obvious one. For the trajectory of my life had been leading me to understand the intellectual significance of institutional leadership, and to be willing to take on those positions when they presented themselves. The colloquium that led to *The Academic's Handbook* helped me to identify key issues involved in the art and craft of an academic's vocation and also to target crucial issues, thus enabling me to be more successful and attentive than I might otherwise have been.

Yet I suspect that it was at heart a third dimension of the colloquium's discussions, namely, its attentiveness to the importance and fragility of institutions, which helped me understand the critical importance of full-time academic administrative leadership. It is one thing to appreciate that the shared life of the academic vocation requires all of us to participate in administrative tasks as well as those more particular to our own disciplines, fields, and teaching and research. But appreciating the significance of institutions, and of the importance of full-time academic administrative leadership, required a much deeper sense of the academic's vocation. Fortunately, I had been prepared for that deeper sense by discussions with administrative leaders through the colloquium.

III

The colloquium's discussions challenged the familiar but false alternative that a person either becomes an excellent scholar or makes a detour into administration. The latter choice is typically taken to be an implicit admission of a failure to achieve the first rank of scholarship. Several underlying presumptions converge to make these appear to be mutually exclusive options. The first, and most obvious, presumption is that one has to make choices about how time is spent — the more time one spends in attending to administrative matters, the less one has for reading and writing and research. Yet the colloquium challenged this presumption in its starkest form by helping us to see that everyone needs to be involved in administrative tasks if the academic life is to flourish.

There are at least two other, even more dubious presumptions at work in this sense that scholarship and administration are mutually exclusive alternatives. One is that institutions are simply necessary evils, and thus "making the institution work" seems to be a lesser value than "real" scholarship and teaching. Such a view has been a dangerous legacy of some intellectually prominent views in the twentieth century, which in effect equated institutions and administrative work with bureaucracy. This became culturally popular in the "anti-institutional" aspects of the 1960s, with the effect that institutional leadership was devalued as a vocation. This has heightened the level of sneering that often goes on when someone "leaves" the professoriate to become a dean, provost, or president.

The other dubious presumption, closely related to the association of administrative work with bureaucracy, is that administrative work is not itself intellectually demanding or creative. We have too often presumed that making an institution work is a form of low-level paper-pushing, rather than recognizing the ways in which effective administrative work requires a high level of practical wisdom and intellectual creativity.

I began paying more attention to the dangers of these presumptions as I experienced, both directly and through scholarly friends, the consequences of in-effective as well as effective institutional leadership. I have watched in agony as friends' lives, and whole institutions, were torn apart by either bumbling, in-effective leaders or malicious ones. Yet I knew, especially in my early years as a full-time academic, that I was flourishing as a scholar and teacher, in signifi-cant part thanks to a wonderfully supportive department chair and dean who offered the advice and encouragement I needed to grow as a scholar, teacher, and colleague.

I also became acutely aware of the fragility of institutions, and the damage that bumbling or malicious leaders do to people's lives and to the ecology of whole institutions. It didn't take long to damage a person's life or a whole insti-tution, but it would take a very long time to repair the damage that was done. It seemed to me increasingly obvious that providing wise stewardship of institu-tions is important in trying to preserve institutions and prevent damage from occurring in the first place. That involves attention to the themes and issues we had discussed in our colloquium that became *The Academic's Handbook*.

By the early to mid-1990s, I had learned to articulate my conviction that in-stitutions are not merely necessary evils that house scholarly practices. Rather, caring for institutions is itself a critically important practice for sustaining and advancing scholarship, nurturing effective teaching and learning, and support-ing life-giving communities of inquiry and debate. I was learning that I had gifts for caring for institutions, and that it was both a challenging obligation and a life-giving opportunity to sustain and advance the academic vocation to scholarship, teaching and learning, and service.

I began to accept administrative tasks, even as I also continued a vigorous program of research and writing, teaching and learning. To be sure, juggling these diverse responsibilities was made somewhat easier because my first major administrative tasks were both closely related to the research project in which I was engaged.

I also found, as a matter of my own personal vocation, that the questions that had been so much on the table in our colloquium at Duke were issues that I was willing to help address in broader institutional ways. This was in part a matter of my own discernment of gifts and my vocation. But I think it was also, at least in part, a sense of the trajectory of my life and the discovery of the aca-demic vocation as a shared enterprise sustained by friendships, practices, and institutions. In some sense, both my doctoral education and my intellectual re-search—nourished in no small measure by an invitation to participate in a col-loquium on broad facets of life in the academy—set me on a path that would lead to a full-time commitment to academic administration.

IV

Over the past two decades, much more attention has been paid to the issues that are discussed in this book than was typical at the time of our colloquium. Graduate programs now pay substantially more attention to such issues as teaching and learning, the climate of the classroom, interviewing for jobs, and the challenges and opportunities of publishing. Graduate schools and department faculties have intentionally designed programs to prepare students for the transition from their doctoral study to the first teaching job.

We have also become much more explicit and intentional about the importance of mentoring for graduate students as well as junior faculty. Such mentoring, of course, has been going on for years, and master scholars/teachers/advisers have launched many doctoral advisees on to highly successful careers in academia. But in the past, we have not paid as much attention institutionally to the significance of mentoring in initiating people into the culture of the academy.

To be sure, there is much more that needs to be done, and there are complicated issues that need to be engaged. But *The Academic's Handbook* came along at a pivotal time in higher education to frame and reframe discussions that forced us to think more explicitly about the dynamics of academic life. That the colloquium occurred at a formative time in my own academic career is a gift for which I will forever be thankful. I may have begun the conversations because of flattery and curiosity and the offer of some good meals, but they have led me on a trajectory that has been as enjoyable as it has been fulfilling.

PART I

THE ACADEMY AND THE ACADEMIC

All new Ph.D.'s share at least one important characteristic: if asked who they are and what they do, all respond with some version of an *ist* or an *ian*. Biologist, sociologist, political scientist, historian, theologian—the suffixes all announce formal entry into a disciplinary guild. It is likely that new Ph.D.'s have been thinking of themselves in such guild, if not gilded, terms for some time, certainly for as long as they have been in graduate school. With the first job, however, the terms of self-definition suddenly change: now one is a college or university professor, an academic, in addition to a guildperson. What exactly does that addition mean and what obligations or responsibilities accrue to one because of it?

In the essays that follow these two questions are taken very seriously. In fact, it might be said that our authors argue that unless these questions are faced squarely and openly no sense of a university community would develop and no sense of the self as a responsible academic could arise. To all the authors, academics share more crucial obligations than sometimes acknowledged. To be an academic, they insist, is not to withdraw from the more active and pragmatic arenas of social existence but to enter more meaningfully and responsibly into them. To be an academic is to be an intellectual; to be an intellectual is to be committed to the knowledge that academic life is not only educational but also moral and political to its core. Failure to act upon that knowledge is both an abnegation of professional responsibility and a culpable denial of the very mission of the university itself.

A hasty glance at part I might suggest that it is more idealistic than practical, more philosophical than useful. Our authors, however, would object to such distinctions: all would insist, in fact, that the new academic must accept from the start the intrinsically moral and political dimensions of the community he or she is about to enter. Without that commitment, every aspect of his or her university life would inevitably be seriously diminished and ultimately unrewarding.

The individual essays that follow raise this challenge to rethink the roles and functions of the academician from various perspectives. Jerry G. Gaff's taxonomy of the range of institutions composing the academy tries to direct attention to how the new Ph.D.'s conception of professional and personal goals will determine the kind of institution within which employment is sought. Samuel Schuman explains the general topography of the small liberal arts college and the kind of academic career one could anticipate there. Stanley M. Hauerwas argues that the moral activity of teaching is the center and ground of the entire academic enterprise. Emily Toth (with an updated afterword in this edition) and Nellie Y. McKay focus on more specific problems: of women in academia, of minority faculty in academia. As a whole, then, this section may suggest that the development of the budding biologist, sociologist, historian, and so forth both within and without academia itself involves, or should involve, an ongoing confrontation with a variety of *isms*: an amoral objectivism, an apolitical intellectualism, overt or covert forms of sexism, racism, classism. Although none of the essays states this explicitly, the implication is clear enough that all our authors are concerned to emphasize that the academic community you are about to join is as fraught with pressures and demands as society at large. How each of us remains attentive to and acts upon those pressures will define both our own success and the success of the institution as a whole.

2

FACULTY IN THE VARIETY OF AMERICAN

COLLEGES AND UNIVERSITIES

JERRY G. GAFF

One of the hallmarks of American postsecondary education is the wide variety of its approximately 3,900 institutions. They have different missions, offer different types of education, operate by different governance systems, and have different sources of financial support. They enroll different kinds of students and have different expectations for their faculties. They have quite different working conditions, professional responsibilities, and salaries for faculty members.

Faculty members and graduate students like to think that the academy is somehow apart from social and political forces, as it houses faculty members and students to pursue and teach the truth in a disinterested way. But in fact colleges and universities are shaped by historical forces just as much as other social institutions. Starting with the founding of Harvard College in 1636, colonial colleges were established, usually by churches and patterned after the English colleges at Oxford and Cambridge, serving a small elite group of young males who were expected to become future leaders in the clergy, law, medicine, and politics through a classical curriculum. Many of today's colleges and universities are descendants in this tradition, especially liberal arts colleges. Although most liberal arts colleges have now weakened or severed their ties to religious denominations, and most have added practical courses of study to their traditional offerings in the liberal arts and sciences, their roots are still recognizable. Some liberal arts colleges have remained sectarian, catering to a narrow constituency of the faithful and occasionally requiring a faith statement from faculty as a condition of hiring. To broaden access further by serving formerly excluded groups, especially in the latter part of the nineteenth century, some liberal arts colleges devoted themselves to serving African Americans and women, and later in the twentieth century, Hispanics and Native Americans.

The Morrill Acts of 1862 and 1890 supported the creation of public land grant universities that expanded the curriculum to include science and the practical studies of agriculture and mechanical arts and increased access to a wider population of students. The founding of Johns Hopkins in 1876, emulating the German university model, gave rise to the research and graduate university, which especially after World War II contributed significantly to the advance of knowledge and the defense of the nation through the Cold War.

Toward the end of the nineteenth century and the beginning of the twentieth, the United States faced the need to train many more schoolteachers, as the result of increased compulsory school attendance, and normal schools were created for this purpose. These institutions, usually public, eventually became regional state universities offering today a comprehensive array of specialties.

Two-year junior colleges have been in existence for many years, but during the 1950s and 1960s this country engaged in a rapid expansion of these institutions, creating them at the pace of about one per week. The goal was to expand access to higher education by locating schools within a few miles of all members of the U.S. population. Another goal was to expand their missions beyond that of preparing students to transfer to four-year institutions to include serving their local communities through proactive adult and vocational programs, offering support for learning English as a second language, providing rich educational and cultural resources, and engaging in entrepreneurial outreach programs.

Corporate and online institutions are the newest forms of postsecondary education to have been invented, and they serve hundreds of thousands of students. The University of Phoenix alone enrolls 129,000 students, and its faculty members teach undergraduates, graduates, working adults, individuals seeking employment, and immigrants, among others.

In the words of Martin Finkelstein, American higher education "has proceeded through discernable stages in its social role, from the Puritan community's leadership prior to the American revolution, to serve as an engine of industrialization in the late nineteenth century and as an agent of democratization in the post World War II period—and finally, now, as engine of the information-based, globalized world economy."[1]

TAXONOMIES OF INSTITUTIONS

The Carnegie Foundation for the Advancement of Teaching (2001) has identified 1,643 public postsecondary institutions, 1,681 private not-for-profit institutions, and 617 private for-profit institutions.[2] Further, it categorized them as 151 doctoral/research intensive universities that award large numbers of doctorate degrees in many fields, 108 doctoral/research-intensive universities that award doctorate degrees but fewer in number and in fewer fields, 611 masters colleges and universities where the masters degree is the highest degree offered, 606 four-year baccalaureate colleges, 1,669 two-year associate's colleges, and 766 specialized institutions including schools of medicine, law, business, engineering, art, music, and design.

The directory published by the U.S. Department of Education in 2001 identified 103 historically black colleges and universities, 214 two- and four-year Hispanic serving institutions (defined as having at least 25 percent full-time equivalent Hispanic students), 29 tribal colleges, and 63 women's colleges.[3] These various types have distinctive educational missions to serve their special constituencies, and by definition, they tend to include disproportionate percentages of their special constituencies on their faculties. These institutions tend to have an ethos flavored by their distinctive mission that often includes a moral dimension shaped by the values of its constituencies.

A major change has been taking place in the nature of faculty appointments in all types of institutions. Traditionally most faculty members were hired on a full-time basis, and if they were approved for tenure after six years of a probationary period, they enjoyed security that protected their academic freedom. Finkelstein, who with his partner Jack Shuster studied the changing nature of faculty appointments, summarized a major finding this way: "In the year 2001 only about a quarter of new faculty appointments were to full-time, tenure track positions (i.e., half were part-time, and more than half of the remaining positions were 'off' the tenure track."[4]

This trend has played out differently in different types of institutions. The National Center for Educational Statistics (2002) reports that in fall 1999 public four-year (lumping together research/doctoral, master's, and baccalaureate) institutions employed over 302,000 full-time instructional and research faculty, 73 percent of their total faculty. Private four-year institutions employed 174,000 or 59 percent of their faculty full-time; public two-year colleges had 104,000 full-time faculty, 35 percent of their total; and private two-year colleges had 9,300 full-time faculty, 52 percent of their total.

All kinds of four-year institutions usually require a terminal degree for full-time faculty, typically a Ph.D. degree, and most conduct national searches to fill faculty positions. Most faculty at two-year schools have a master's degree, although many of these schools will hire faculty members with Ph.D.'s if they can demonstrate commitment to the community college and effectiveness as teachers of the kinds of students they enroll.

Graduate students aspiring to be a faculty member would be well advised to consider any of these alternatives. All of these institutions are schools, all employ faculty members, and graduate schools prepare faculty for most of them. It is important that new faculty find a "good fit" between their own aspirations, talents, and interests and the characteristics of the institutions that will become their professional homes. Work in any of these settings can be both rewarding and profitable.

This advice might appear to be self-evident, except that it is seldom followed in practice. The powerful role of prestige in shaping academic careers in research universities was documented by Caplow and McGee in their classic 1958 study *The Academic Marketplace*.[5] Given their mission, it is no surprise that prestige in these settings goes to those who are successful researchers and that associated grants, publications, and awards are highly valued, and institutions are compared and judged on these matters. It is not that teaching is not done or valued; indeed, most major universities in recent years have launched initiatives to enhance the teaching of undergraduates. But the mission of research/doctoral universities drives the emphasis on research and graduate education among faculty members.

In such circumstances it is natural for the faculty to transmit their values and the priorities of their institutions to graduate students. The result is that graduate students rarely receive much information or encouragement about careers in the other segments of postsecondary education—or in organizations beyond the academy. In part, this is because their faculty members do not know much about faculty life at other kinds of institutions or organizations; most have spent virtually their entire careers in research universities. The lack of information also owes in part to the fact that faculty members operate in a prestige economy, and they derive prestige from where their graduate students go to work. Graduate faculty whose students work in a community college, where there is little time or opportunity to conduct significant research, derive little benefit, whereas their own prestige is boosted if their students get positions in institutions that have excellent reputations and that expect and support research on the part of their faculty.

Other types of institutions define the terms of the competition in which they engage in ways that are favorable to themselves. They construct hierarchies along other dimensions. For example, liberal arts colleges are very sensitive to rankings, and their leaders are as eager as leaders in any other institution to see how they compare in the infamous listings in the annual *U.S. News and World Report* issue ranking U.S. educational institutions. The elite national colleges and universities claim superiority over the regional ones, while those near the top of the regional rankings look down on their lower-ranked competitors. Although it is common to refer to all liberal arts colleges as primarily teaching oriented, it should not be assumed that they do not expect their faculties to conduct research. Scholarly research is valued at all of these institutions, and a solid track record of research and publication is required at the more selective national institutions.

The prevalence of these competing hierarchies is one of the reasons that faculty (and administrative) careers seldom cross the major types of institutions. While crossovers are not impossible, faculty tend to get "tracked" in public or private institutions, for example, or in a community-college career. Graduate students often think that they can take a starting job at a master's public university and then move up the prestige hierarchy to a research university, but that seldom happens. More likely, they will stay at that same institution, or one like it, for their entire career.

QUALITIES ASSOCIATED WITH DIFFERENT KINDS OF INSTITUTIONS

While generalizations about different kinds of institutions are dangerous, several broad distinctions can be made. In terms of workload and major responsibilities, faculty members at research/doctoral universities are expected to contribute to the advancement of knowledge by conducting research and publishing the results. This is usually acknowledged by being assigned a portion of their workload for research and a lesser number of courses than at more teaching-oriented institutions. Although there is much variation, teaching responsibilities may involve four or five courses a year, fewer at the most well-endowed universities. In addition, faculty are expected to teach graduate seminars, supervise dissertations and theses, and perhaps supervise graduate research or teaching assistants, all expectations that seldom pertain at other types of institutions.

Today all institutions are facing fiscal constraints and are seeking ways to stretch funding by adjusting faculty workloads. The University of Maryland, for example, is an eleven-campus system that during 2002–04 increased enrollment by the equivalent of more than 5,000 students, while state funding decreased by about $120 million and health insurance increased by $100 million.[6] Leaders estimated that enrollment would increase by 8,000 students in 2004–07. In recent years there has been a major effort to provide more support for research, and the flagship College Park campus recently joined the ranks of the nation's leading research universities. The system chancellor has proposed increasing the faculty course load at College Park from 5 to 5.5 courses per year as well as raising costs for students. The proposal at the other comprehensive campuses in the system is to increase the course load from 7 to 7.5 per year.

At the national liberal arts colleges the number of courses taught by a faculty member ranges from four to six, with professors expected to work with students individually and in small groups, both in the classroom and informally. Faculty at the most well-endowed and well-respected of these colleges tend to have course loads in the middle and lower end of this range, while those at the more fiscally limited schools have loads toward the upper end. In the more regional and denominational colleges, the course load tends to be higher, seven or even eight courses per year, and the faculty are expected to participate in the academic, cultural, and social life of the campus and community. Community colleges usually expect their full-time faculty to teach ten courses per year.

Student bodies also differ at various institutions, which creates different conditions for faculty work. National liberal arts colleges aggressively recruit the best students and take pride in students' national scholarships, test scores, and achievements. The regional and many denominational schools tend to be more welcoming to a broader array of student aptitudes, and more of their students need financial aid and work while in school. Most public comprehensive universities tend to have diverse student bodies, and many attract students who transfer from other schools. In states like New York and California with well-developed community college systems and transfer policies, as many as three quarters of the student body may have studied a year or two at other institutions.

The community colleges typically have open door policies, and although they have many very good students and hard-working students, they tend to have larger numbers of working adults, ethnic and racial minorities, students with poor academic preparation, and students needing remediation. Although these generalizations are valid, nearly every institution has some proportion of students exemplifying all these categories. Some Harvard students need tutoring and supplemental instruction in writing and mathematics, for example, just as do some in the local community college.

Many states are trying to cope with a demand for higher education among a wide diversity of students during a time of limited state funding. California developed a master plan that seeks to accommodate this demand from diverse students by developing a three-tier system. Students in the top 12.5 percent of their high school graduating classes may attend one of the 10 campuses of the University of California (UC); students in the top 33 percent of their classes may attend one of the 23 campuses of the California State University (CSU); and any student capable of benefiting from instruction can attend one of the 109 community colleges. Of course, there are transfer policies that, for example, allow students who complete the first two years at a community college to transfer to one of the university campuses.

In addition to accommodating diverse students, the master plan also speci-

TABLE 2.1 Average Salary for Assistant Professors by Type of Institution, 2005–06

	Private independent	Church-related	Public
Doctoral	$71,877	$65,286	$60,440
Master's	54,996	51,411	52,873
Baccalaureate	53,083	45,873	49,546
Two-year with ranks	46,464	n.d.	47,116

Source: AAUP, *Chronicle of Higher Education*, April 28, 2006, A15.
n.d. = no data.

fies the missions of each sector. UC is the state's primary academic research institution and has exclusive authority to offer doctoral degrees and instruction in law, medicine, dentistry, and veterinary medicine. CSU's primary mission is undergraduate education and graduate education through the master's degree, including professional and teacher education. The primary mission of the community colleges is to provide academic and vocational instruction through the first two years of undergraduate education for older and younger students. In addition, the community colleges are authorized to offer remedial instruction, ESL courses, adult noncredit instruction, community service courses, and workforce training services. Faculty have lowest course loads at UC, moderate course loads at CSU, and highest at the community colleges. Not unexpectedly, the amount of per-student funding follows the same pattern.

For years faculty members at all kinds of institutions helped subsidize the cost of a college education by their low salaries and poor benefits. In recent decades, it is fair to say that full-time faculty salaries in most institutions are such that individuals can live a decent middle-class life. The American Association of University Professors publishes an annual survey of faculty by rank at nearly all institutions, and for 2005–06 the average salary over all ranks and types of institutions was $70,333.[7] But among some institutions that have major resource constraints, faculty and staff still subsidize the cost of education.

Not surprisingly, salaries vary by type of institution. At the top, the average salary of a professor at a private independent doctoral university was $131,292, at a private church-related doctoral university $113,740, and at a public doctoral university $101,620. It should be kept in mind that these figures include salaries of highly paid faculty in professional schools like medicine, law, and business as well as other fields.

The average salaries reported for assistant professors at different kinds of institutions are shown in table 2.1, which combines all salaries, from the newly hired through several years of service in this rank.

HOW CAN GRADUATE STUDENTS GET BETTER INFORMATION?

Reliable information about career paths in different types of institutions is difficult to obtain. Important parts of personnel decisions are kept confidential
to protect all parties. In addition, Caplow and McGee noted the existence of
"information screens" that prevent the sharing of accurate information about
academic career paths or even create distortions that make information about
careers unreliable. Such information screens were effected concerning the reasons why a faculty member leaves a position, the terms of the position she or
he takes elsewhere, career progress of departed faculty members, secretive influence wielded by senior faculty, departments trying to hide their hiring practices from administrative inspection, and administrators trying to obscure from
members of departments their criteria for evaluating faculty. Of course, personnel procedures are by law these days more accountable than in the 1950s,
but the details surrounding hiring, termination, and academic career paths remain unclear.

If it is difficult for faculty members to acquire accurate and useful information about faculty careers, it is far more difficult for graduate students who are
just about to enter the academy. And that is exactly what recent research has
revealed.[8] Nerad and her coauthors drew this conclusion from doctorate recipi-
ents ten years after receiving their degrees:

> All in these groups felt that they would have been well-served by better infor-
> mation on the academic market in general, the expectations of potential em-
> ployers, and a candid assessment of their own prospects in particular. For ex-
> ample, one respondent desired "a clear idea of the jobs people in previous classes
> had obtained — we all naively thought [that] jobs at outstanding schools would
> just open up."[9]

The Preparing Future Faculty (PFF) program was created specifically to help
doctoral students understand what an academic career might entail and what
faculty life is like in different kinds of institutions and to develop capacities for
success in different settings. Between 1993 and 2002, programs were created at
twenty-three research/doctoral universities and in forty-four departments. One
unique feature of the PFF was that each participating graduate school assembled
a cluster of different types of institutions to provide opportunities for graduate students to visit for direct and personal experiences with faculty members
and students in those settings. Over four thousand doctoral students enrolled
in one of those programs during the decade. Although the national initiative
has ended, virtually all the campus programs still operate so that graduate stu-

dents in those settings may avail themselves of this opportunity. Their locations may be found at www.preparing-faculty.org.

A four-year independent evaluation of the PFF program concluded that PFF participation enhances the graduate experience by the following:

> Preparing participants for the full range of faculty roles in a variety of postsecondary institutions. Through contact with partner faculty, participants learn about faculty roles and expectations at diverse institutional types, and receive enhanced faculty mentoring. . . .
>
> Helping participants make informed career choices, conduct productive job searches, and achieve early career success. . . . Participants value the demystification of the academic job search process, and alumni credit PFF for giving them an advantage over other new faculty.[10]

Many similar programs have been established at other universities using their own institutional funds. These institutions are as diverse as Claremont Graduate University, University of Michigan, and Vanderbilt University. Other programs have been established through such initiatives as the Carnegie Initiative on the Doctorate at the Carnegie Foundation for the Advancement of Teaching; the Responsive Ph.D. project at the Woodrow Wilson National Fellowship Foundation; the Alliances for Graduate Preparation for the Professoriate at the National Science Foundation; and the Compact for Faculty Diversity sponsored by interstate compacts for higher education in New England and southern and western regions of the country. All of these programs help graduate students overcome the information screens and develop more realistic views of academic careers in a variety of institutions.

Even at institutions and departments with no formal faculty preparation program, there is much that graduate students can do to penetrate the mysteries of faculty careers at different kinds of institutions.

— Many disciplinary societies offer sessions on teaching and learning, faculty careers, and strategies for securing academic positions at their national and regional meetings, and they often involve faculty members and department chairs from a variety of institutions.

— Associations have been formed to represent the interests of different segments of higher education, and their publications and Web sites can provide useful information. They include such public sectors as the National Association of State Universities and Land Grant Colleges, American Association of State Colleges and Universities, and American Association of Community Colleges. Private institutions are represented by such groups as the Council of Independent Colleges, National Association of Independent Colleges and Universities, and a host of religious denominational groups.

— One might also take initiative for developing a professional network by simply starting up an e-mail conversation with faculty members, undertaking informational interviews with professors at different kinds of institutions, and asking a particularly valued professor to serve as a mentor. Most are flattered to be asked and are willing to give you some time to share their experience and wisdom.

None of these strategies is foolproof, but they can help penetrate the information screens to gain useful information about the realities of different faculty careers.

CONCLUSION

It is fitting to conclude with words from the late Robert Gleckner, who wrote this chapter for the second edition of this handbook, citing the most crucial question that new Ph.D.'s must ask themselves: "What *kind* of academic career do I envision for myself? That is to say, if you want mainly to teach, with research and publication decidedly secondary, that desire points you in certain directions for possible jobs and points you away from others—whether in private or public institutions. Contrariwise, for those who conceive of themselves as future publishing scholars, dedicated to making contributions to knowledge (as we say), and who prefer a good share of their students to be graduate students, those desiderata will lead them to seek positions in Ph.D.-granting institutions."[11]

NOTES

1. M. Finkelstein, "The Morphing of the American Academic Profession," *Liberal Education*, Fall 2003, 8.
2. Carnegie Foundation for the Advancement of Teaching. *The Carnegie Classification of Institutions of Higher Education* (Palo Alto, Calif.: Carnegie Foundation for the Advancement of Teaching, 2001).
3. See T. D. Snyder and C. M. Hoffman, *Digest of Educational Statistics, 2002* (Washington: National Center for Educational Statistics, 2003).
4. Finkelstein, "The Morphing of the American Academic Profession," 6.
5. T. Caplow and R. J. McGee, *The Academic Marketplace* (New York: Basic Books, 1958).
6. N. C. Aizenman, "Workload Plan Irks Md. Faculty," *Washington Post*, October 23, 2004, B5.
7. AAUP, *Academe*, March-April 2006, 37.
8. C. M. Golde and T. M. Dore, *At Cross Purposes: What the Experiences of Doctoral Students Reveal about Doctoral Education* (Philadelphia: Pew Charitable Trusts, 2001); A. P. Fagen and

K. M. S. Wells, "The 2000 National Doctoral Program Survey: An On-Line Study of Students Voices," in D. H. Wulff et al., eds., *Paths to the Professoriate* (San Francisco: Jossey-Bass, 2004), 74–91; M. Nerad, R. Aanèrud, and J. Cerny, "So You Want To Become a Professor!: Lessons from the Ph.D.s — Ten Years Later," in D. H. Wulff et al., eds., *Paths to the Professoriate*, 137–58.

9. Nerad, Aanerud, and Cerny, "So You Want To Become a Professor!" 149.

10. S. S. Goldsmith, D. Haviland, K. Dailey, and A. Wiley, *Preparing Future Faculty Initiative: Final Evaluation: Highlights Report Draft* (San Francisco: WestEd, 2004), 9–10.

11. R. F. Gleckner, "A Taxonomy of Colleges and Universities," in A. L. DeNeef and C. D. Goodwin, eds., *The Academic's Handbook*, 2nd ed. (Durham, N.C.: Duke University Press, 1995), 15.

3.

SMALL IS . . . DIFFERENT

A Guide for Newcomers to Small Colleges

SAMUEL SCHUMAN

Many of the academics for whom, I hope, this *Handbook* will prove useful will find themselves, by accident or by design, working in a smaller college or university. For some, this will represent a return to a familiar ambience; for others, it will be an entirely new institutional context. For most, it will be a startling shift from a Ph.D. program at a research university. One effective approach to such a new setting is that of the field-based anthropologist: think of the small college as a self-contained culture, explicable primarily through its own rules. The wise field-worker tries to restrain or suppress the customs and patterns of her own cultural context and seeks the underlying mechanisms of the society under investigation unhampered by prejudgments.

What follows, then, is less a taxonomy than a laboratory manual or field guide. While lacking the specificity of a Peterson's bird guide ("look, chirping over there, it's a Southern, co-ed, Quaker-affiliated moderately selective private liberal arts college!"), it may, at least, help the neophyte investigator distinguish fin from feather, or, to beat the anthropological metaphor into the dust, matriarchal agricultural society from patrilineal industrialism.

I

Small colleges and universities are "different." They are different, as a class, from large universities, and they are different from each other. Much of this discussion will focus on the first of these sets of differences, trying to make useful generalizations that embrace at least most smaller institutions. But it is vital to remember that small institutions may well resemble each other no more than they resemble their larger kin.

This idiosyncrasy is, in fact, one of the chief characteristics of smaller colleges. There is a sense in which the very comprehensiveness of larger institutions guarantees a certain uniformity: one such school is likely to "comprehend" pretty much the same as another. While there are certainly important (and endearing) individual traits that distinguish even our mega-universities, small colleges tend to be far more unique, even quirky. Because they are not even remotely comprehensive, their strengths and weaknesses — indeed, their inclusions and exclusions — are definitive and essential. What languages are taught? Which sciences? How are humanities departments organized?

A concrete example: even in faculties of roughly the same size, departmental proportions, and instructional personnel may vary dramatically. This can be crucial to an incoming faculty member. Thus, a new anthropologist at one small university may be joining a five-person anthropology department; at another she may find herself the sole practitioner of her discipline in a three-person sociology/anthropology department; at a few institutions, such an anthropologist might be the only person in anthropology *and* sociology in a six-person department of social science. My point is not that any of these arrangements is superior to the other but rather the stark importance of ascertaining *which* one is joining before, rather than after, the fact.

Small institutions are more idiosyncratic, too, because they are usually further from the academic mainstream than major universities. As students of language dialects know, isolated societies tend to develop and evolve in highly individualized directions. Many faculty members at small colleges enjoy being somewhat removed from the intellectual fads (or, depending upon one's perspective, the latest developments) which tend to sweep through the disciplines, and they delight equally in what often appears to be a refreshing absence of careerism. Others, though, chafe at what is undeniably sometimes our parochialism and worry about losing touch with mainstream academe. Happily, a good number strike a reasonable and productive middle course: staying in touch with scholarly trends but not feeling compelled to be constantly au courant.

One key way in which small liberal arts colleges are often different from each other has to do with the extent to which they actually practice the "liberal arts," at least in an old-fashioned, curricular sense. Small colleges and universities, private and public, have been subject to severe strains during the past three decades, and often their nature has changed in response. Some would say that missions have "evolved"; other, more cynical voices proclaim defection. The former president of a fine private liberal arts college, David W. Breneman of Kalamazoo College, finds that over the years the number of institutions truly belonging in that category has shrunk dramatically (to 212 by his count in 1994).[1] He disqualifies institutions in which the majority of undergraduate degrees are awarded in "vocational" areas. This is a standard which some (including me) may criticize, but the point remains that at many liberal arts colleges, the traditional subject-matter disciplines have been overwhelmed or at least seriously challenged by career-oriented fields such as management, accounting, computer science, environmental studies, sports medicine, statistics, atmospheric science, administration of justice, music recording technology, and so on. (All of these are areas in which it would be possible for students to major at institutions where I have worked which were, in my opinion, genuine liberal arts colleges.) In practical terms, young faculty members must be prepared to put aside purist definitions of liberal education or confine their job search to a small proportion of smaller institutions.

An important lesson: never assume one small college is like another. It can be dangerously misleading to presume that an idyllic memory of undergraduate days on a small campus is a reliable template for the entire spectrum of institutions of, say, 500 to 3,000 students.

II

Small colleges tend to have small departments, and this is a fact of constant consequence. A professor in, say, a history department of four, or an economics faculty of three, or, for that matter, a music or classics program with a staff of one (I worked at a good liberal arts college which did, in fact, have single-person "departments," complete with full-fledged departmental majors, in these two areas) will face a different kind of teaching load than does the member of a department of twenty-five, fifty, or a hundred. Most teachers at small colleges teach "out of their field," if by "field" we mean the subject specialty in which doctoral research was done. An English professor with a dissertation on non-Shakespearean Renaissance drama will probably teach Chaucer, freshman composition, introduction to the humanities, and British literature survey; an ichthyologist will face classes in introductory biology; an Islamicist might teach courses with titles like "Religion in America," or "The Old Testament," or "Varieties of World Religions." Those of us who love small colleges delight in this demand for generalists. It keeps us alert and learning. But it also tends to mean that we find it easy to drift away from staying current in non-Shakespearean Renaissance English drama, ichthyology, and Islam.

It is also the case that in many smaller institutions, faculty members will teach so far "out of the field" that they are, in fact, out of the entire ballpark. If the institution has a large core or interdisciplinary program, our hypothetical Ph.D. in Jacobean tragicomedy will find himself instructing a course in "Interdisciplinary Studies 101" or "Christianity and Culture," or "Humanities I: Classical

Antiquity." Many thrive on such opportunities to integrate and "stretch"; many others find the experience disorienting, at least at first.

Another obvious implication of small departments at small colleges is the dearth of colleagues in a faculty member's specialty area. The ichthyologist or Islamacist will perhaps find herself or himself the only scholar with such an interest on campus. So, for example, it is often impossible to find a colleague on a small college campus who can give a careful and professional reading to a draft of an article or paper (though increasingly, in the era of e-mail and attachments, this is less and less a problem). It is easy to solicit the response of interested amateurs, or a critique of the style, but the subject matter will usually be foreign to departmental peers. Graduate students are often habituated to deep and intense discussion of the latest research or theoretical development within their subdiscipline. On the small college campus the absence of such interactions may be lamented. It is important, therefore, to ascertain the level of faculty development support available at an institution to fund travel to professional meetings, leaves, and the like.

At most small colleges, the normal teaching load is six to eight classes per year (although some range as low as four per year, and others up to ten), three or four per semester. Usually, these loads are not reduced for unusual research assignments, or other burdens, although course relief may be possible. In a given semester, two or three of the courses taught will have different preparations—for the neophyte faculty member, this may mean three or so new preparations a term for a while. A bizarre but instructive anecdote: at one point early in my teaching career, a sudden illness of one departmental colleague and a failure in the hiring process designed to add another to the college roster resulted in my teaching *six* different courses, each with a separate preparation, in the same semester. I survived; I still wonder if my students learned much that term.

Concatenating the size and the shape of a typical faculty load at a small college, we have a pattern that might manifest itself thus. A member of the biology department, with a Ph.D. in freshwater ichthyology, might teach a year-long introductory course ("Biology 101"), with lab, surveying both botany and zoology. First semester, that instructor would perhaps also have a midlevel course such as "Principles of Animal Biology" and an advanced section in, say, "Animal Physiology." Second term would see the second semester ("Biology 102") of the introductory course, another more advanced offering, say, "Aquatic Ecosystems," and potentially an interdisciplinary contribution, for example., "The Sea in Science and Art." This hypothetical situation is by no means extreme. Add to such a schedule the potential for a dozen major and/or first-year advisees, service on a college-wide committee or two, work on a departmental curriculum review, weekly department meetings, monthly faculty meetings, and nomination to an ad hoc committee preparing for regional reaccreditation. This is a workload designed to combat boredom; it is not one likely to facilitate finishing that first scholarly book, research project, or an article derived from a dissertation!

Most small-college teachers are in their campus offices most of the day throughout the workweek. Many do not even have a functional office elsewhere. Evenings and weekends on campus are not uncommon (the political science awards dinner; a reception for parents on the Saturday afternoon of Family Weekend). The research university model of a division of time between campus office, classroom, private study, and research library or site tends to break down at the smaller institution, with the first two becoming dominant, even all-consuming.

III

Small academic departments also shape the social and general intellectual lives of academics in small colleges. The young academic in a research department of seventy-five, with its own building, parking lot, coffee and mail dispensaries, and the like, will find herself fraternizing mostly with departmental colleagues. In some situations, only the occasional university committee assignment, an accident of residential neighborhood proximity, or a shared school or child-care provider for kids will bring together institutional faculty from different departments or divisions. It may well be possible, at an Ohio University or University of Minnesota, for a French teacher to spend an entire career without the opportunity to interact with professors of electrical engineering or agricultural economics. This is far less likely, indeed, often downright impossible, at a small college. Most institutions with fewer than a hundred faculty members, for example, have democratic as opposed to republican faculty governance procedures: the monthly or weekly "faculty meeting" is a meeting of the entire college faculty. Four or five departments, sometimes with no apparent organizing rhyme or reason, will be housed in the same building; a central campus coffee shop will serve as meeting place for the entire community; and so forth. At one institution where I once worked, one building housed the art department and the campus art gallery, the leadership programs office, the management and accounting department, an outreach program for senior citizens, a small conference center, and the university development office! At many small schools, faculty members make their deepest friendships—and sometimes their most interesting and gratifying intellectual relationships as well—across departmental or divisional barriers. Indeed, those "barriers" are usually permeable membranes.

By way of contrast, at the Twin Cities campus of the University of Minnesota, for example, faculty and students of engineering are across the Mississippi River in Minneapolis from the law school, and those in social work or veterinary science are a pleasant bus ride away in Saint Paul.

Often, the sorts of interdisciplinary or core programs cited earlier will greatly facilitate such diverse patterns of personal and professional association. Many such courses are deliberately staffed and planned by faculty members drawn from the widest possible departmental constituencies, and at some institutions, virtually the entire faculty is, over time, drawn into these curricular ventures.

A good tip-off regarding this dimension of institutional culture for the prospective faculty member is to heed carefully the staffing of the search process. If interviewing for a position in political science involves extended discussion with chemists, economists, theater historians, and professors of sports medicine, it is a pretty good sign that the potential employing institution values and expects frequent and deep extradepartmental contacts.

IV

It is always important for new employees, within and beyond academe, to ascertain with accuracy the standards and procedures by which they will be evaluated. Those standards and procedures will be different between small colleges, and there will probably be pronounced generic differences between small and large institutions. Almost all higher education enterprises affirm that excellence of classroom teaching is an important criterion for reappointment, promotion, and tenure. Some actually mean it. There are still many small colleges in America today where, practically, pedagogical quality is the sole basis for major career decisions. In the majority of small institutions it is the most important factor or at least a very important factor. This means that classroom teaching should and may be evaluated with thoroughness and rigor: student course evaluations will be heeded; classroom visitations by deans or chairpersons will be regular and more than perfunctory.

Note whether or not actual teaching, to actual students, is an important element of the hiring process: if it is, chances are it will also be a significant element in the review process as well.

This does not, of course, mean that research, publication, community service, and other factors will be excluded from evaluative decisions. It is, therefore, very important for the faculty member at an early point on the career path to come to a clear understanding regarding the relative weighing of these criteria in the decision-making process, and the means by which effectiveness — as a teacher, scholar, community citizen, and so on — will be assessed. This under-

standing may not be easily reached. In many institutions, official pronounce-
ments in this area may not always conform to practice. At small, informal, non-
union campuses, the regulatory/descriptive faculty handbook is notoriously
uneven; some are accurate, others flamboyantly unreliable. The wise newcomer
will seek to discuss the evaluation and review process with a few trusted colleagues who have themselves relatively recently been through it, as well as with
those who will administer it. Find out what seems to have made a genuine difference, for good or for ill, and be prepared to find that, more often than not,
teaching makes the biggest difference of all.

Tangentially related to evaluation are salary and compensation issues. Expect the salary scale at most smaller institutions to be demonstrably lower than
at larger and/or public institutions of roughly comparable status. While many
small colleges and universities have generous benefits packages that supplement
base salary, they are sometimes not as comprehensive as state-mandated programs in the public higher education sector, although usually well above the
standards of commercial employers. Expect, too, that (in the private sector at
least) salaries will be formally private but in fact virtually public knowledge,
and the subject of much semi-informed discussion within the campus community. It is rare for a private institution to publish faculty salaries, but it is even
rarer for it to be difficult to get a pretty good idea of individual compensations
levels. In sum, you probably won't be paid much, your benefits status will probably be decent but not spectacular, and most everyone with whom you come
in contact will know it.

It is also often less expensive to live in a small college town than a major university center, and the events — athletic, cultural, intellectual — of the institution are often free, or almost so, to faculty members, a not-insignificant benefit,
especially in smaller, somewhat culturally or recreationally impoverished communities.

V

At the beginning of the twenty-first century, American small colleges exist in
a very wide spectrum of religious emphasis. Given the religious origins — indeed, often, the origins in religious fervor — of very many small colleges, this
is not surprising

At one end of the scale, there are a number of small colleges that are overtly
nonsectarian in foundation and contemporary manifestation. Today's public
liberal arts colleges were created as agents of the state. While public small colleges often do provide outlets for religious expression for students, faculty,

and staff, participation tends to be wholly at the choice of the individual, and usually those voluntary options cover some spectrum of religious inheritance. Certainly public colleges teach courses about religion, as an academic discipline — history of religion, philosophy of religion, and the like. But such public colleges will make no denominational claims, at least officially, on students or employees and keep clear the constitutional barriers between church and state college. Similarly, a number of small private colleges, such as Reed College in Oregon, were created as secular institutions and have remained consistently adenominational.

At the other pole are small collegiate institutions that are wholly or primarily in the business of educating clergy for a specific denomination. So, for example, Columbia Bible College confers 100 percent of its undergraduate degrees in "Theological Studies," or Lancaster Bible College (Pennsylvania) "exists to educate Christian men and women to live according to a biblical worldview and to serve through professional Christian ministries."

Many faculty members at Christian colleges are convinced that they have more academic freedom than their colleagues in the nonsectarian institution. Mary Ellen Ashcroft, in an article about teaching at Christian liberal arts colleges, says, "The teacher's responsibility is to make the classroom a safe place for students to bring out their beliefs and look at them and argue about them and decide what they hold dear."[2] And, she believes, that is far more the case at the Christian institution than at the state university. Comparing sectarian and secular institutions where she had taught, she states, "I feel much more freedom in the classroom, in my office, in the halls at Bethel than I ever felt at the University of Minnesota." She cites James H. Daughdrill, former president of Rhodes College: "Today, research universities are thoroughly secular and comprise one of the few places in America where openly acknowledged religion is not a life option. Consequently, academic freedom has become a casualty at these institutions."[3] It is also the case that many of the evangelical colleges require an affirmation of religious conviction of all students and/or faculty, a condition some might find restrictive of academic freedom.

Between the nonsectarian public liberal arts colleges and the denominational seminaries, there is a full spectrum of religiosity. Some institutions, such as Westmont and George Fox, profess a very strong religious character but offer majors and studies in a wide variety of nonreligious subjects, as well as studies in Christian history, theology, the Bible, and the like.

Many colleges retain some elements or vestiges of their religious origins without affirming an overtly sectarian mission. An institution may retain some seats on its board of control for nominees or representatives of a founding denomination. Some still receive significant or symbolic financial support as a result of historic religious affiliation. Some private small colleges still employ a chaplain, commonly linked to the founding church. Cultural practices of the church may continue to influence life at institutions of religious origin. At Salem College, in Winston-Salem, North Carolina, the traditional Moravian tea ceremony at Christmas time is celebrated. Just a few miles away, Guilford College in Greensboro, a Friends' college (but with fewer than 10 percent Quaker students), practices government by consensus at every level, from student organizations and faculty committees to major decisions of the senior administrative leadership and the board of trustees, and all meetings begin with prayerful silence.

Roman Catholic institutions are a special class of religious institutions (see *The Academic Revolution* by Christopher Jencks and David Riesman, for a full and thoughtful, if occasionally opinionated, discussion of American Catholic colleges).[4] Some Catholic schools (Notre Dame, Villanova, Georgetown) have achieved university status. Others, particularly very small, poorly funded, single-sex institutions, have closed or suffered in recent years (e.g., Mt. Senario College in Ladysmith, Wisconsin, and Sacred Heart College in North Carolina). But there remain many small Catholic colleges, coed and single sex, which continue to play a significant role in the American higher education community. These schools (the College of New Rochelle, St. Mary's of California, Notre Dame College of Maryland, St. Scholastica of Duluth) maintain a strong, overt, Catholic emphasis, in population, curriculum, and mission. While certainly "religious colleges," these institutions seem on the whole less assertive about their religiosity than the "Bible colleges" and the more fundamentalist Protestant institutions.

In the 1970s, when I was a young assistant professor at a Methodist-related liberal arts college, I served on a presidential search committee. Among other questions we put to each finalist was one about the candidate's sense of what the college's religious heritage meant at the end of the twentieth century. The successful candidate, Dr. Phil Secor, gave what struck me then and strikes me now as a profound response. He said that the greatest virtue of working at a college with a religious heritage was that it gave one a sense of humor about that work. What he meant, he explained, is that at such colleges, there is always an implicit understanding that no matter how important the daily business of the college—and that work *is* important—there is a larger theological, cosmological perspective from which the challenges, irritations, triumphs and tragedies of the academic world are little more than a grain of sand.

VI

There is a pronounced difference in the kinds of relationships that develop between teachers and undergraduate students at large and small institutions. At the larger schools, a faculty member may develop a close, mentoring relationship with a handful of strong undergraduate departmental majors. Usually, though, the closer relationships will be with graduate students. In a small college, it is not uncommon for a teacher to teach the same student in courses throughout the undergraduate career, from first semester to graduation. Some such students will not necessarily be majors: it may be, for example, that an accounting major will take two or three theater courses and act in a handful of plays, under the tutelage of one drama professor. Many relationships, with students of varied scholarly bents, will develop at the small college. And often faculty members are deeply involved in student organizations and co-curricular activities. One of the joys of teaching at such schools is the frequent, recurring opportunity to watch undergraduates grow in intellectual and emotional depth during a period of some four years. There is a kind of maternalism about this relationship that some find cloying, but most see as deeply satisfying.

Some of its consequences can be amusing, some touching, and some downright irritating. There are institutions, for example, where it is considered acceptable behavior for students to call professors at any hour of the night and day to discuss out-of-class personal problems, where the pastoral model of the student-teacher relationship is still held by a majority of the faculty, students, and staff. It is also the case that at many institutions the progress and foibles of shared students is a prime topic for faculty conversation. For good or for ill, the passage of higher education privacy legislation has seemed to have little effect upon professorial conversations about students at small colleges around the backyard barbecue cooker.

It is also worth noting that faculty members and students at small institutions will be interacting in numerous ways outside the classroom, on a constant basis. The student one taught in the morning class on *Hamlet* might well be on the Stairmaster next to yours at noon and singing in the concert you attend in the evening. That student whose paper on Plato was really excellent may well turn out to be the school's star quarterback or volleyball shot blocker. Faculty members at small colleges tend to know students as complete persons, not just as classroom personas, and for most of us, that is a great satisfaction.

VII

Faculties at large institutions and at small ones have always played an important role in the governance of institutions of higher education. At small institutions, that role is likely to be sharply different than at larger ones.

A majority of the major institutional governance tasks remain the same, regardless of the size of the school: all colleges and universities need a curriculum committee of some sort, need a personnel review process, need a faculty athletic committee, a library committee, an admissions committee, an academic standards committee, or some general equivalent to these and similar groups. At small colleges, thus, roughly the same number of tasks is distributed among a much smaller pool of workers. While the volume of work is perhaps proportional to the size of the college, the breadth remains more or less constant. Therefore, the faculty member at a small college may find herself serving on committees, study groups, task forces, fact-finding bodies, search committees, and similar institutional extraclassroom organizations in bewildering (and sometimes intimidating) number and range. In one sense, this sort of "community service" often gives to the faculty of small colleges a demonstrable role in directing the destiny of the institution that can be gratifying and educational. (Also, it can be at times frustrating, to faculty and administrators, that small colleges seem to suggest that everyone should have a voice on everything.) On the other hand, such assignments, often contributing little directly to either teaching or scholarship, can be distracting and frustrating. Every small college vows periodically to revamp its committee structure so as to eliminate this problem. The record of permanent solutions is remarkably slim.

On a related tangent, let me also note that faculty members at small colleges will tend to have much more constant and closer contact with others who work at their campuses than might be the case at larger institutions. College presidents and janitors will probably have lunch at the same campus café as faculty members and students fleeing the food service standard fare. Most faculty members I have known at smaller schools have known student affairs staff and often developed close working relationships with them in areas like service learning. Consequently, the level of mutual understanding and respect between diverse campus faculty and staff constituencies is frequently refreshingly high.

VIII

Many of the founding fathers of small colleges sought locations for their institutions that safely removed impressionable young students from the temptations of city life. (Anecdotal evidence suggests those enterprising young people found plenty of quite satisfactory temptations in rural venues.) Garrison Keillor's portrait of New Albion College in *Lake Wobegon Days* is only slightly exaggerated for the purposes of humor![5] There are consequences of this questionable choice, which may face the new faculty member at such schools.

First, at some smaller, isolated colleges it may be necessary—and it is occasionally still required—that faculty live in the small town that houses their employing institution. The informality and potential closeness of such arrangements is inviting, often especially so for young families. It is not, however, without compensatory difficulties. If the college has "anti-nepotism" policies, it can be exceptionally difficult for a spouse or partner to find satisfying employment, especially in a two-academic-career family. Also, these communities are often somewhat homogeneous, especially compared to major cities and large university towns. They do not tend to be culturally stimulating, at least not in the big-city way. If a steady diet of major dramatic and symphonic performances and first-class art exhibits is a necessity, life in Mt. Vernon, Iowa, or Gambier, Ohio, or Collegeville, Minnesota, may seem inadequate. Often the cultural opportunities of a small college community are those provided by the college itself, along with, perhaps, a single movie theater. (A major compensating virtue is the opportunity to become an important player in the cultural life of a small community—community bands, local theater groups, affinity organizations, all are usually eager for participants, and one usually need not be an accomplished professional to be energetically welcomed.) Be prepared, too, for over-the-fence discussions of house painting and plumbing projects, kid's swim teams and the scandal at the local church more often than analyses of the ballet performance last evening. The prevailing cultural and political climate in such towns, at least outside the immediate college community (and sometimes within it, as well), is likely to be more conservative than in major university cities.

It is worth remembering that a good small college library may have 300,000 volumes. If that college is located many miles from the nearest city and/or university, access to significant library resources (or super-computer terminal or specialized laboratory facilities) can be exceedingly difficult. Careful planning and time allocation may be necessary just to accommodate an occasional commute. Many librarians at smaller institutions are exceptionally helpful with programs such as interlibrary loan, but the graduate student who is accustomed to popping into a library of 3.5 million volumes to check an obscure citation will be easily frustrated in Deep Springs, California, New London, New Hampshire, or St. Leo, Florida. Of course, the increasing utility of electronic resources such as the Internet can do much to moderate this bibliographic dearth.

While the cultural connotations of working at a small school in relative geographical isolation are fairly obvious, the implications for personal social life are less clear. At some such schools, a young, single instructor, or one with an unconventional lifestyle, may be uncomfortable. A faculty of, say, ninety members may have three or five members under the age of thirty, and another half-dozen or so between thirty and thirty-five. There may not be many other individuals in this age group in town. A very young faculty member may feel more social affinity with mature undergraduates than with the majority of middle-aged colleagues. But often there will be strict codes or conventions governing social relations between students and teachers that (rightly, in my opinion) will tend to discourage or forbid contacts more intimate than an informal afternoon softball game. Especially in a small pedagogical universe, the real and perceived power differential between faculty and student makes social contact with even a hint of amorous possibility taboo.

Some careful observers have noted, as well, an interesting but sometimes disconcerting phenomenon regarding small college community mores: the pairing of political liberalism and social conservatism. There are those of us still around (albeit, tottering) who can recall settings in which it was acceptable to proclaim one's self a socialist or an anarchist (at least in theory) but still necessary to hide wine bottles in layers of newsprint buried in the weekly garbage set out for collection.

At many more urban schools, and for many individuals, these constraints are inconsequential, but for a few they are real and occasionally devastating. Well-rounded lives extend beyond the classroom and faculty office. Prospective faculty members are wise to ascertain if the extramural conditions of potential employers are a reasonable match with personal needs.

IX

Sometimes those entering the professoriate will ask if it is wise to accept a position at a liberal arts college or a small university, "on the way to" a more desired job at a research institution. This is a difficult query to handle. On the one hand, any academic employment is probably preferable to none at all, at least over an extended period of time. A five-year employment hiatus in a resume will probably be a red flag in any hiring process. Also, many young academics come to a smaller institution intending to move on, find themselves captivated by the attractions and challenges of their entry level post, and stay on indefinitely.

Others, however, for whom a small institution is a clear second choice, are unhappy and consequently do not do very well. Certainly, being denied reappointment and/or tenure will not improve the likelihood of career advancement elsewhere.

Of course, there are many instances of young professors coming to small institutions for a few years, building a good repute as teacher and scholar, and moving on to larger, more research-oriented, schools. There is much variability in the perceived quality of liberal arts colleges, and in the open-mindedness of search committees. Certainly it will be easier in most cases to secure employment at the University of Michigan coming from a job at UC Berkeley than from, say, St. Mary's College of California. On the other hand, the candidate employed at Kalamazoo College may have some advantage based on regional familiarity. The more well-known the institution, the more likely favorable reactions from the search committee: a few years at Reed, Oberlin, or Grinnell are unlikely to hurt a candidate at the state universities of Massachusetts, Ohio, or Iowa.

Naturally, it will be important for those seeking to follow this route to make a substantial effort to maintain personal contacts with the "larger world" of professional scholarship and to keep publishing. Staying in touch with the dissertation adviser is a good idea; attending, even at personal expense if necessary, major professional meetings is certainly helpful, especially as a program participant.

A word of caution: while a lack of candor should never be encouraged, it is important to be very carefully diplomatic about career plans which call for moving to a research setting. Surprisingly often, I have found, beginning college teachers assume that everyone on a liberal arts college faculty would want to be at a major university and is either working diligently to make such a transition or has become resigned to second-rate status.[6] Partially, no doubt, as a defense mechanism, but mostly for more genuine reasons, the majority of us who work in smaller institutions do so, not because we have to, but because we choose to. Indeed, we are not infrequently supercilious and parochial in our proclamations of the superiority of the type of education we profess in comparison with that offered in the research universities.

In sum, it is not unrealistic to envision early career years in a small college setting as a preface to appointment at a research university; it is important for those seeking such a path to build a scholarly resume which will be impressive to recruiters in coming years; it is not wise to make very public proclamations of such intentions.

x

Institutions which place a premium on classroom teaching, which deemphasize research productivity, which are far removed (physically and/or psychically) from major university centers, and which expect a quick and heavy load of on-campus and off-campus community service labor can be difficult places to be while one is simultaneously completing a doctoral dissertation. The "ABD" young academic will need to attempt a realistic and hardboiled assessment of thesis completion very early along the career path. It is not enough to guarantee access to computer or lab resources or major library resources, although these are very important guarantees, indeed. Equally important, and harder to weigh, are time and institutional willingness and understanding of the project. What are the expectations of the college regarding summer work? Are there substantial vacations (fall and spring breaks, midwinter holidays, other breaks) during which real progress can be made? Will the department and/or institution view with favor requests for minimal committee assignments for a few terms while the dissertation is completed? These are probably questions that should be asked before the hiring process is complete, rather than after appointment has begun.

This difficulty can be curiously complicated by conflicting institutional expectations. It is not unprecedented for a college to insist upon the completion of the terminal degree before, say, a review in the second or third year of employment — and simultaneously to make such completion difficult for a very, very busy instructor. Here, as elsewhere, it is sensible to seek the advice of more than one knowledgeable colleague.

XI

"Faculty development" at a small college will have a slightly different connotation than at a large university. Most small colleges focus their faculty development efforts on pedagogical issues. Efforts to introduce new teaching technologies and methodologies will receive significant attention. Funding sources such as the Bush Foundation have supported such teaching-centered faculty development initiatives at small colleges generously.

On the other hand, support for research equipment, especially in the sciences and especially at less wealthy institutions, is often very hard to find. Similarly, most small college faculty travel budgets are considerably tighter than at large research universities, where participation in multiple professional meetings annually is not uncommon.

Potential faculty members at small colleges should also examine closely the congruence between their sense of what kind of leave program they need and what is offered by the institution. Most colleges do have sabbatical or study leaves, but often the number and arrangement for such leaves are more parsimonious than in major research centers.

XII

I have tried to sketch some of the features of academic careers in small colleges with accuracy. I hope the picture that emerges is neither romantically rosy nor forbiddingly bleak. For many of us who choose this version of an academic career, it is the quintessence of the collegiate experience: teaching and learning over a broad area, in intense and close intellectual relationships with diverse students and colleagues. If such a culture calls you, you are invited to doff the objectivity of the observing anthropologist and embrace our customs, conventions, and costumes. Teaching in a small college has never been a more difficult, a more rewarding, or a more important vocation.

NOTES

Portions of this discussion appear in my *Old Main: Small Colleges in America* (Baltimore: Johns Hopkins University Press, forthcoming).

1. David Breneman, *Liberal Arts Colleges: Thriving, Surviving or Endangered* (Washington: Brookings Institution, 1994). Interestingly, the Carnegie Commission classification of 2000 lists a nearly identical number — 228 — of "baccalaureate liberal arts" institutions.

2. Mary Ellen Ashcroft, "Risky Business? Teaching Literature at a Christian Liberal Arts College," *American Experiment Quarterly* (Winter 1999–2000): 24.

3. Ibid., 16.

4. Christopher Jencks and David Riesman, *The Academic Revolution* (Garden City, N.Y.: Doubleday, 1968).

5. Garrison Keillor, *Lake Wobegon Days* (New York: Penguin, 1986), esp. 45–46.

6. For example, "'Coming out of Iowa you're not going to get a job at a research university,' says [a new Ph.D.], who will happily take a job at [a small college in the Northwest] this fall. 'You realize *you're going to have to work your way toward those positions.*'" *Chronicle of Higher Education,* July 27, 1994, A16.

4.

THE MORALITY OF TEACHING

STANLEY M. HAUERWAS

Some time ago I was asked to write an essay on ministerial ethics that, I think, would strike many as a bit unusual. If you cannot trust ministers, who can you trust? That we have to think about the kind of ethic that ought to characterize ministers seems to support those who claim we live in a morally confused, if not corrupt, age.

No less odd, I think, is to be asked to write an essay to help "enculturate" those planning to become university teachers. After all, those who become professors have been around universities for years, and you would think there is nothing they do not know. Just as city kids become streetwise, graduate students become "university wise" — it is a survival strategy. Being asked to write a manual on how to be an academic, therefore, seems analogous to being asked to write a sex manual. What has happened that we now do not seem to know how to do what everyone thought was a matter of nature or a fairly simple learning procedure?

It is not accidental that these concerns are currently being raised, for it seems we have simply lost some of the skills that in the past have sustained the professions and, in particular, academic work. For example, consider the following incident concerning a book written by Timothy Cooney on moral philosophy. Mr. Cooney, in *Telling Right from Wrong*, asserts that while there is such a thing as morality, it is a highly restricted category. Using the refined skills of contemporary philosophy, Cooney argues that morality applies only to those issues that threaten to destroy society. Everything else is simply a matter of taste, manners, or both.

Mr. Cooney, who is not a professional philosopher, submitted his book to Random House accompanied by a letter from Professor Nozick of Harvard University urging its publication. Jason Epstein, the editorial director of Random

House, was not only extremely impressed with the book but also that it was recommended by a philosopher as distinguished and as professionally competent as Dr. Nozick. The publishers therefore accepted the book and started the process of publication. Since Mr. Cooney was not well known, Mr. Epstein thought it would help to ask Dr. Nozick to draft an advertisement commending the book and made such a request. He was shocked to receive a letter from Dr. Nozick saying that he had never read the book.

On investigation the publishers discovered that the letter from Dr. Nozick had been written by Mr. Cooney and that he was not the least bit apologetic about having forged it. After all, he had done nothing wrong since his act did not threaten to destroy society. Mr. Cooney contended that his writing the letter raised no ethical problem but was simply an example of "vigorous game play." Because he was unknown, his manuscript would have been ignored unless it had been accompanied by the bogus letter. Rather than being ashamed of his behavior, in fact, he claimed to be extremely proud of what he had done. The publishers, obviously embarrassed, were not sure whether to publish the book or not. They suggested that they would do so only if Mr. Cooney wrote an afterword justifying on grounds of the argument of the book why he could write the kind of letter he did in the name of Dr. Nozick.

Such an incident would be merely humorous were it not so relevant to our current concerns. Mr. Cooney's attempt to justify his action by appeal to the standards of contemporary moral philosophy, which may be a mistaken view of that discipline, is a haunting reminder of a general unease about the intellectual and moral nature of the contemporary university. Too often the training associated with graduate work in the many disciplines in the university provides no rationale to sustain, and may even undercut, the ethos necessary to maintain the university as an intellectual and moral community dedicated to a common task. What we seem to have lost is any sense that the university is or should be a community that places intellectual and moral demands on those who would be part of that community. Yet I do not believe the university is in so hopeless a condition. Substantial and profound moral commitments continue to shape university life. We may fail at times to acknowledge, articulate, or act on those commitments, yet they remain embodied in our most basic activity—teaching. By focusing on that activity I hope to elicit the sense of common endeavor that continues to inform those who work in the university and that should shape the lives of those attracted to service in the university.

I must admit there are also autobiographical reasons that I take this tack. My own experience has been that I began to appreciate what the university was about only as I came to the realization that my vocation in life was to teach. This came as a bit of a surprise to me for during my graduate work—a professional degree in ministry and a Ph.D. in theology—it never occurred to me that I was training to be a teacher. I was being trained as a theologian who could further the discipline. It was an unpleasant shock for me to be asked in my first interview, What courses do you plan to teach? I began to realize that I was going to earn my living by being a teacher. Nothing in graduate school had prepared me for my beginning awareness that most of my life would be consumed by the effort to learn to teach.

While I in no way want to dismiss the possibility that my naïveté was unique, I think that my surprise on discovering that I was to teach is not all that uncommon today for young graduate students. Of course, graduate students have often assisted in courses and know that it will probably be necessary for them to teach in order to further their research. But the fact that they will spend most of their time and life teaching is seldom fully acknowledged. After all, graduate training is meant largely to initiate us into a discipline and to teach us that this is where most of our future rewards are to be found. People do not enter Ph.D. programs in order to teach; they see the Ph.D. as the only way to become a sociologist, a botanist, or a classicist. Our primary hope, even if we teach predominantly at the undergraduate level, is to find a few undergraduates who may become interested enough in our discipline so we can send them off to do Ph.D.'s in what we have been trained to do.

The idea that we have a responsibility to train students to embody the skills necessary to make the general life of our society better never occurs to us. Not only do we not think of the university as a community that places demands on us, we also fail to see that the university is responsible to other communities in order to sustain its activity, responsible not just materially but for sustaining the moral purpose that legitimates freeing many from labor in order to be scholars. Having been given the privilege to spend most of our lives reading books is a reminder that our task as teachers is to ensure that we pass on the hard-won wisdom of our forebears by instilling in our students a passion for the good.

Commitment to a discipline, of course, is often justified on intellectual grounds. After all, is that not what knowledge is about, extending the boundaries of a field? If this were not the case, then teachers would have nothing to teach. We rightly distrust colleagues who seem more interested in teaching than research, suspecting they are no longer "keeping up" in the field. Good teachers are not those who know how to interest students but those who teach what is interesting because it is crucial to their disciplines. Such arguments are not to be taken lightly as they are also moral claims about the task of the university.

In more realistic terms, however, we also know that loyalty to a discipline is keyed to the ways we will be rewarded as members of a university. Indeed, if we are to be respected at our university, we must first of all acquire reputations in our discipline. For anyone who is so unfortunate as to be stuck in a first teaching job in a college or university that does not live up to personal ambitions, acquiring a reputation in one's field is the only hope of moving. The more we think about the profession in these terms the more likely it is that we will assume that the university exists to serve our discipline, not vice versa.

As a result, most of us seldom feel like members of a university faculty. Instead we are members of departments—those people who come the closest to understanding what we are about. After all, what do we have in common with someone in sociology, biochemistry, or theology? This feeling may well lead us to believe we have no responsibility to serve, for example, on university committees, except as such service is necessary either for tenure or the goodwill of our chairperson (which may be the same thing). Any sense that we are members of a community dedicated to the exploring and passing on of the wisdom of our culture seems to have been lost. What I am suggesting is that such a sense of community will not be regained unless we are able to recover the obvious, but no less important, realization that our first vocation as university people is to teach. That is what we share in common and what makes us part of a cooperative endeavor.

I am aware that to emphasize the importance of teaching will not make the life of the young academic any easier, for those who are beginning their teaching careers often find they are caught in not easily reconciled tensions. The tensions begin as early as the first job interview. We approach that interview thinking the interviewer will be concerned about our views on Rawls's account of the original position, and we discover that she could care less about such matters. She cares only about whether we will be able to teach a course that can attract undergraduates in areas that are not required by the curriculum. Without students the department has no case to make clear to a dean or provost about why it should have that faculty slot rather than sociology or microbiology. Confronted by this degradation of the academic enterprise, many despair at the thought that they must now try to please a bunch of eighteen- to twenty-two-year-olds rather than being concerned about their disciplines. How will we ever get time to do the kind of research we need to further "knowledge," not to mention "our careers," if we have to be worried about whether undergraduates are actually interested in the courses we teach?

This kind of tension tends to create a good deal of cynicism on the part of young instructors. They know their careers depend upon being able to publish beyond the confines of the university, and yet the very demands that they should be popular and interesting local teachers tend to undercut that ambition. Indeed, it might be argued that the fundamental task of the young instructor is to negotiate this tension — teaching just well enough to get by, but primarily working in the disciplinary field.

This tension, of course, can easily be overdrawn. I am not suggesting that we become so concerned with teaching that we let our own work languish. No one can or should teach teaching. We teach about this or that; or rather, we initiate students into skills necessary for them to be continual learners. Put concretely, if you have to choose between reworking a lecture for class or reading an important book just published, read the book. Read the book because the enthusiasm that it generates in you will infect your students. The first rule for being a good teacher is to teach only what (and in a way that) sustains your interest and enthusiasm. That is as true of the most introductory course as of the most advanced, for if teachers do not believe in what they are doing, we can hardly expect students to take it seriously.

Yet I want to make a more substantive claim about the importance of teaching for sustaining intellectual growth. Teaching is not just the way we get paid in order to sustain our research but our most important intellectual resource to challenge the current captivity of the university to the "disciplines." Graduate school, after all, is an extended initiation into a guild through which one is taught to think the way the masters of that guild would have us think. In the process we often fail to notice the limits of the craft, either in our particular school or in general. We know that what it means to be a literary critic is different from one school to another, but we are sure that the way we are being trained is right and feel a bit sorry for those people at other schools who are wasting their time learning cultural studies or queer studies and so on. As a result we do not notice, indeed we are trained not to notice, the limitations of our own graduate training, discipline, or both. We assume that we really do not need to know much about other disciplines as long as we are good sociobiologists, psychologists, physicists, and so on — at most, we ought to subscribe to the *New York Review of Books*.

Teaching, however, can be a rich resource to challenge the limits of our discipline. Through teaching we discover that there are other people in the university who can enrich our work — that is, we discover those most blessed of people, colleagues. Even students bring with them what they have learned elsewhere in the university, and other universities, and through them we learn new perspectives and interests that can throw new light on what we are about. We can learn through our teaching, that is, if we can restrain our temptation to intimidate students with our "expert knowledge." Our task is to give students confidence, to empower them to take themselves seriously as people who would rather know than not know. In this way we free them not simply to give back what they have learned from us but to refract their work with us through what they have learned elsewhere.

This understanding of our task is but a reminder that teaching at every level is a profession—that is, teachers are joined in the common endeavor to respond to a basic human need. Just as medicine and the law are ideally attempts to meet the needs of health and justice, so teaching is a way to enhance our society through knowledge and wisdom. The moral authority of the teacher derives from this commitment and is the reason why the society as a whole feels betrayed when it is not honored.

In this respect, it is interesting that many professors in universities no longer think of themselves as intellectuals. Rather, they think of themselves as academics, as people who have become technically proficient in a subject. Academics are those who have learned the ins and outs of university life and who know how to negotiate those in order to secure a place within the university for themselves and others loyal to them. It is generally a compliment when we refer to someone as a "real academic," for we usually mean such a person is a "professional." By "professional," however, we do not mean one who has committed his or her life to pursuing tasks for a good commonly held; rather, we mean someone who has become an exhort whose expertise gives power over others. When teaching becomes solely a matter of expertise, the very nature of scholarship is perverted.

Too often today teachers do not think our task is to entice our students to be intellectuals because we do not think of ourselves in that way. We do not hold ourselves accountable to have intelligent views on a wide range of subjects and to be able to defend those views among equally thoughtful people. Even when we are intellectuals, we do not understand ourselves as such, preferring to take refuge in our disciplines. Thus we say "speaking as a sociologist" or "from the perspective of my discipline," as if we do not exist at all as thinkers. Such formulas are well known and may voice appropriate intellectual humility, but too often they reflect a defensive, if not cowardly, attitude that is the death of the academic enterprise. Moreover, when we use such formulas, we are tempted to abdicate our responsibility to serve our social order through sustaining the discussion of the true, the good, and the beautiful the university is pledged to sustain.

Nowhere is this ambivalence about our roles as teachers and intellectuals more powerfully displayed than in our self-defensive denial of our task as moral educators. The modern university, uncertain of its mission, claims moral neutrality and professes no, or at least very limited, interest in any substantive attempt to shape the moral life of students. We lay out information for our students, and they can use it in whatever way they wish. By common testimony, undergraduates have taken a wide range of courses, all of which have introduced them into a remarkable range of views about this or that, from which they learn they should never be dogmatic about anything. In other words, contemporary university education is an extended training in cynicism. We teach students never to care about anything too strongly, as otherwise they may not have treated the subject fairly. We call this "objectivity." We ignore the fact that our mission is a moral one or self-deceptively hide that fact from ourselves by openly denying it.

I am aware many will resist this point because they fear they lack the resources to be moral educators, or some may see this as an attempt to sustain the importance of my own "discipline" of ethics. In spite of that danger, I maintain that there is no way for those who teach in the university to avoid morality. To teach Shakespeare or to insist that economics majors learn the history of economic thought is a moral endeavor, for it says to the student that this is not only worth knowing but that by knowing it you will be a better person. The failure of the modern university is not that those teaching in it fail to shape students morally, but that they fail to take responsibility for doing so. As a result our students mimic our fears rather than what we care about — that is, those convictions that have led us to spend our lives believing it is better to know than not know.

There is no way as teachers we can or should avoid being moral examples for our students. We often ignore or dismiss the fact that some students choose courses more by who is teaching than by what is being taught. There is no doubt that students do so at times, and that can be a mistake when they are attracted to the "flashy" rather than to the patient and disciplined scholar. Yet on the whole I think students are right to want to learn from those who manifest in their lives the lessons they have learned from their scholarship.

I think such issues, moreover, are not unrelated to the more mundane and concrete matters that confront new teachers. For example, one of the shocking discoveries many of us made when we began to teach was that there is no such thing as a university qua university. Universities come in many different shapes and sizes, largely determined by their past histories — for example, that the college was founded by Swedish Lutherans and now serves upper-middle-class students from north Chicago. One of the challenges for beginning teachers is how seriously they will let both the limits and possibilities of that particularity shape their intellectual agenda. Will they, for example, try to come to terms with the fact that they are teaching students from either rural or urban backgrounds and what that means for the presentation of their subject matter? Such matters may appear trivial, but they are at the heart of what it means to become a teacher. For if the university is doing what it is meant to do, there is no way to avoid critically confronting both positively and negatively the morality of our society that comes embodied in our students' lives.

I cannot pretend, of course, that a recovery of our vocation as teachers will not cause problems. It certainly can cause a tension in how we have been formed by our Ph.D. work. A Ph.D. too often is the way that we make sure that our knowledge of the past is appropriately fossilized in living representatives who continue to underwrite that knowledge by passing it on through the contemporary university. We thus are hesitant to challenge assumptions about where things are in our disciplines. Nowhere does that become clearer than when we look at undergraduate curricula that are oftentimes relics of the past. What is required is an ongoing attempt to make our curricula live up to the best that we currently know. Otherwise we end up continuing to teach the errors of the past as the truths of the day because we simply lack the ability to think of any alternative.

One of the implications of this is that intellectual life often has as much to do with courage as with being smart. It means we must be willing to act on what we know in a way that will have an effect on other people's lives. We cannot rely on the achievements of the past to avoid making decisions about how a curriculum should be organized and what ought to be read that once was ignored. No issue is more central to the university than whether faculties will find the courage to determine the "classics" that make any curriculum intelligible.

An appreciation of the university as a moral community requires a return to politics as essential to the university's intellectual mission, for the politics of the university must be governed and shaped by the common purpose to educate and form students to know and desire the right things rightly. Put simply, it is our moral task to help students love to read on the slim but real hope that by being serious readers they will be better persons. Politics is not the unseemly side of the university, but the essential conversation that must go on about what it is students should read and how they are best taught to read. Whether to hire someone in American rather than Asian history can and should provoke the kind of discussion necessary for the university to be an institution that stands for something.

One oftentimes gets the impression that many in the modern university fear acknowledging the moral significance of such decisions. We know that such matters are seldom black-and-white but involve judgments about which we are less than certain; still, they must be made. Because we tend to fear the necessity of having to make and defend our judgments, there is a tendency in the university to rely on authority. Nowhere is this better seen than in the continuing temptation of many universities to assume whatever is done at Yale or Harvard is the standard for everyone. We fail to notice that often Yale, Harvard, or Stanford know no better than we what they are doing. What we must acknowledge is that there is simply no ideal of a university that currently exists or ever has existed. Therefore we must, as faculties of universities, trust our own judgments, and working with our colleagues try to do the best we know how to further our task as teachers.

It may be objected that I have presented a far too idealistic description of the modern university. In fact, the university is not the kind of community I have described. Rather, it is a loose confederation of departments that jealously protect their turf against one another. They cooperate only in the face of the common enemy—the administration—but even then their cooperation is more a matter of self-interest than genuine concern about the purpose of the university. The modern university, in other words, has tended to look more and more like a modern corporation, the only difference being that the university lacks the clear purpose of a business since we are sellers of that most ambiguous of products, education.

I have no reason to deny such an account of the university has descriptive power. I have tried, however, to suggest that if we allow our lives as teachers to be shaped by such forces, we will fail to live up to the purpose of our calling as members of the university community. Moreover, to the extent that that happens, we cannot help but produce more people like Mr. Cooney who cannot recognize the difference between being smart and being wise. If we acknowledge, however, that first and foremost, we are at the university because we are committed to teaching, we may well discover that there is a richer and more sustaining community present there than we had thought possible.

5

WOMEN IN ACADEMIA (WITH UPDATED AFTERWORD)

EMILY TOTH

We like to think that women who choose academia tend to be among the best, the brightest, and the most idealistic. They believe in the life of the intellect; they want to be mentors and molders of young minds; they want to make genuinely original contributions to knowledge.

Often they've made their vocation in their twenties, choosing academia over a traditional personal life. They've resisted the push to marry (only half of female Ph.D.'s are married), and they've consciously *chosen*, rather than fallen into, their careers—as opposed to many men, now occupying tenured slots, who entered graduate school to avoid the Vietnam-era draft. Long before graduate school, academic women were resisting social pressures to lower their aspirations: most girls' grades still suddenly sink in seventh grade, when they get the message that boys don't like "brains." Most academic women will have avoided the football-fraternity scene in college: public achievers among women are much more apt to have attended women's colleges. If they're in psychology, at least 20 percent of academic women have endured sexual harassment in graduate school; if they're in technical fields, academic women have refused all their lives to believe that "girls can't do math."

They come into their first academic jobs believing that things will be different now—that they will pursue knowledge for its own sake and be rewarded with acclaim from their colleagues. And in academia the new faculty with the stunning academic records (national grants and prizes, book contracts, novels already in print) are frequently women—who expect their profession to be a citadel for souls devoted to the pursuit of truth and learning.

Of course I'm writing about myself, two decades ago when I finished grad school, as well as about younger women. Yet all of us have been trained to refer to women as "they," as if to distance ourselves from other women. We've been trained to think of ourselves as unique individuals—not as women. That is a deadly tactic.

Among academic men, women are still regarded as outsiders—or interlopers. The messages are more subtle than they were a decade ago, when the men in one academic department crowed that they'd hired "two chicks from Berkeley." But there's still a common assumption that real professors are male (and white): only a few years ago, an assistant dean at my former university suggested establishing a library school, "so professors' wives will have something to do." Universities have been turtle-slow in creating child-care facilities. And women entering all-male departments are still apt to be told the story of the last token woman in that department: "We used to have Z——, but she didn't work out." Z—— is usually a woman who couldn't or wouldn't play the academic game. Often she was a woman of great integrity and brilliant promise—but she didn't get tenure. What went wrong?

The standards by which academic women are judged are not the same ones applied to academic men.

The overt criteria—university tenure and promotion policies—are usually written down, and ideally, all new faculty are told what's expected of them from the start. Will research or teaching be more important? How much service (committee work, advising, community speaking engagements) will be expected? How will their teaching and research and service be evaluated, and by whom? The last question is a critical one—because academic women are also judged by criteria that are not openly acknowledged. An academic woman has to be aware of hidden agendas—and that task can be difficult, painful, and infuriating.

Unless she's had an extraordinarily candid mentor in graduate school (and it's more difficult for women than men to find such mentors), the new assistant professor is not apt to know much about academic politics—and, after all, she entered academia believing that it was above sordid power plays. Some fledgling faculty members will find it consoling to recall George Santayana's famous comment that in academia the fights are so fierce because the stakes are so small. But for the untenured woman the stakes are not really small—for she's often staked much more than her male counterpart has on her choice of the academic profession. And to stay in her chosen profession, she needs political savvy.

Information is power, and so is collegiality—and a new assistant professor should immediately get to know all the faculty in her department. Over lunch with tenured professors, a new faculty member can get tips on research funding, publications, and conference opportunities—but she must also learn about department workings, lore, and feuds (every department has them). She can get advice about teaching, and she can (and should) discuss her research agenda.

Self-promotion is a vital component of an academic career, and something many women find difficult to do, because we've been socialized to depreciate our own achievements.

Dinner parties are also opportunities for collegiality, although for women professors they can be (as one of my colleagues says) "fraught." If the new faculty woman is an excellent cook, her male colleagues may think of her as fitting more appropriately in a kitchen than in a classroom; if she's a poor cook, she'll offend everyone with her food. (If her husband happens to be a good cook, though, everyone will be delighted.) But a single woman inviting a male colleague to dinner at her home will be sending a mixed message (is it academic? is it sociosexual?) — and that may complicate her life. (Erica Jong has written, in "The Bait," about a one-time lover who "attacked/my poems & cooking — / which he'd got confused.") Lunch is easier.

And, in fact, lunch is politically essential for women, who are excluded from most of the channels of male communication. Drinking parties, sports talk, squash games, and poker clubs are all opportunities for academic male bonding — including cementing friendships and sharing vital information. Some department heads, among them a man chairing a communications department on the west coast, have tried to get their colleagues to abolish poker clubs, as discrimination against women — but few other administrators acknowledge that such groups are not just boys' clubs but power centers. Men become allies through their informal networks, but academic women are often both alone and in a fish bowl.

Academic women have to learn to walk on eggshells, playing two contradictory roles: the woman and the professor. Female assistant professors must present themselves as neutral professionals — wear toned-down, frumpy outfits, discuss the latest scholarly discoveries — while still being faced with demeaning or peculiar requests. They may be asked to pour the tea at a faculty reception, to do the photocopying for the department head whose secretary is away, to bake cookies for a departmental gathering. They may be asked for advice about sewing, interior decoration, and gift giving.

And except for nuns, no academic woman ever has quite the right marital status. If she's single, her colleagues may either expect her to decamp for better romantic opportunities or assume that she's either shriveled (and perhaps deserving of sexual overtures from married men) or lesbian. If she's married, she'll be asked constantly (chronically) what her husband does and whether he's happy at it — with the apparent assumption that if he's not, she'll decamp. If she becomes pregnant, everyone's embarrassed (she's a woman after all), and if she has children, her male colleagues may imply, or even say, that she should be at home taking care of them.

The traditional academic career expectations do not, of course, take into account reentry women or people without wives to do their entertaining and errands or people who have responsibility for children. In twenty-five years in academia, I've seen countless forms asking for faculty members' scheduling preferences (courses, times), but only one form has ever offered to accommodate child-care schedules. That form was created by a woman department head.

A woman who is an assistant professor has high visibility (even more so if she's a woman of color, or an "out" lesbian). Her presence or absence is always noted. Especially in her first year, she should regard departmental colloquia, visiting speakers, teas, and receptions as unbreakable obligations. They are her chances to meet people and to shine. Women have been taught to handle small talk and social graces, but rare is the academic male who was not a nerd in high school. Academic men, left to their own conversational devices, may awkwardly take turns, one lecturing while the other waits. But women are assumed to be good listeners, and men love to perform and orate in front of women, so it's easy to make oneself popular by smiling and saying very little — although a woman also has to insist, firmly, that her ideas be heard.

Ideally, of course, one would rather be respected than be popular, but popularity may do at least as much to get a woman tenure. She must let her colleagues know what she's published and presented at conferences, and she must tell them personally: department newsletters are not enough. But unless her colleagues also find her personable, they will not want to keep her.

A tenure decision is senior academics' way of answering the question, Do we want this person to be around for the next thirty years or more? They are most apt to want someone like themselves: a white male squash or poker player. Most academic men are still not very comfortable with women as colleagues.

And so every academic woman also needs at least one mentor. The best mentor will be a full professor with a national reputation who's been in the department for years, has the respect of department members, and is in the would-be protégée's field. From her mentor, a protégée can find out how the department really runs, how decisions are really made, and who makes them. And since her mentor is apt to be on committees that judge her, he can help her negotiate many treacherous slopes, if he likes her and admires her work.

But finding a mentor can be tricky for a woman. Most often a new faculty woman's chosen mentor will be male, and he may misconstrue her friendly overtures. Also, he'll usually be sympathetic, in the abstract, to the cause of women's equality. But he's not apt to be very knowledgeable. He may overestimate — wildly — the number of women in the university and their power; he may think — in spite of the statistical evidence and the evidence before his eyes — that affirmative action is overturning university merit policies and that unqualified women are everywhere being given preference over white males. (In fact, academic women tend to have considerably better records than their male counterparts.) A senior faculty male may also think women are being paid the same, or even more, than comparable men (in fact, academic women earn 85 percent of what men with the same rank and qualifications earn). In short, a male mentor can help a new faculty member as a colleague but not as a woman.

And so a new woman faculty member should also find herself a female mentor. If there are no senior women in her department, she should look around the university administration for a senior woman. (Usually there's one token.) Often there's a commission on the status of women; usually the affirmative action officer is a woman; and sometimes a dean's administrative assistant will welcome the opportunity to advise women. A new woman faculty member should join whatever women's faculty groups exist: whatever her field, she'll almost certainly need them. She needs a support system: women who'll tell her honestly what goes on at the university, for women.

But to remain in academia, an academic woman also has to be able to say no.

New women faculty tend to be overwhelmed with service work: one young assistant professor dreamed that her whole body was covered with bites. New assistant professors are put on committees as the token women — and if they're women of color, their committee burden is doubled. (A white woman I know was put on seven committees during her first year; an African American woman was put on *eighteen*.) A new woman must decline to be on committees not involved in useful work (for example, committees setting up procedures for other committees; committees devising endless variations on degree requirements; committees ratifying decisions already made about the campus radio station or the newspaper or the student union). She should restrict herself to committees that make her academically visible or put her in touch with powerful people; she should serve on committees controlling personnel or money only if her votes can't be used against her when she comes up for tenure. If she is untenured, she must do everything she can to avoid what I call the Early Administration Trap (EAT): running language labs, composition programs, or area studies programs. That kind of work can eat up all of a junior woman's time and energy, keeping her from publishing and getting tenure. She must say no, for her academic survival.

Early in her career an academic woman should, tactfully, enlist her department chair to help her distinguish among service requests: which ones are really important to her career? which ones should she neglect or decline in order to concentrate on teaching and publishing? One of my department chairs once, kindly, withdrew my name from the department's most controversial committee — and probably saved my tenure in the process.

An academic woman must also resist the compassion trap: being always available to everyone. Universities are full of needy students, and we do what we can for them, but no one person can be the adviser for all the women students. We must close our office doors and do our research. Otherwise, we won't be around to open the doors for other women to share our responsibilities.

Sometimes academic women have to be silent, for survival. Most educational systems, in fact, actively discourage girls and women from speaking. Many kinds of classroom behaviors keep women down. Professors call on male students much more frequently. Professors ask women students simple, recall questions but ask male students critical ones — and give the male students more time to answer. Professors and fellow students are much more apt to interrupt women (some 80 percent of interruptions are men interrupting women); professors still use sexist jokes to "spice up" their lectures, especially in technical and business fields; academic men even make more eye contact with men than with women.

Many of these sexist classroom behaviors—including judging women by looks and men by ability—spill over into the professoriate. An untenured woman sometimes has to swallow insults to preserve her energies. Occasionally, she may also have to stifle laughter about the posturings around her: new academic women are often bewildered or astonished by the academic male's preoccupation with what other men think of him.

Questions of "reputation" surface in particular among men in the liberal arts, whose sense of their own masculinity is often a little bit uneasy. ("Real men" go into science or business.) Men in literature give enormous attention to deciding who is a "major" or "minor" author; they continually discuss how writers measure up against one another — comparing the "thrust" of one versus the "seminal" and "penetrating" qualities of another. Scientists, whose sense of worth comes through the size of their grants, seem to be less prey to playing this grown-up version of "Whose is bigger?" (Kenneth Burke has called this preoccupation "The Little Man Afraid for His Widdler.") Women can't play this game and ought not to try.

In graduate school an academic woman is often faced with a political choice her male counterpart hasn't had to make: whether to do her research on women. In most fields in the humanities and social sciences, the excitement is in feminist research. In American literature the ferment over who belongs in the literary canon — and whether there should even be a ranking of "major" and "minor" — comes mostly from feminists, queer theorists, and people of color. In history, "history from the bottom up" is being written by women and some male allies — and more than half of the most prestigious national fellowships are going to women (including women of color) who are writing women's history.

In political science feminist scholars have spent nearly two decades challenging the definition of what is "political"; in art history feminist art historians have pointed out gaps, errors, and distortions in the historical record, so that few surveys of art history would, today, leave out women entirely. In psychology feminists have taken on Freud and his biases; in communications they've shown how women's speech is different — less pompous, more engaging; in religious studies they've analyzed matriarchies and madonnas.

In the "real world" two thirds of the employees in publishing are women. Nearly half of law and medical students are women. Women buy 70 percent of the books sold in this country and write more than half of them. At university presses a majority of copy editors are women — so that academic books often display much more awareness of sexist language than do academics as a whole.

Still, the picture of the world given in graduate school is, with rare exceptions, white and male and phallocentric. (As late as 1985, of the more than thirty thousand courses offered on women in the United States, only a handful were at the graduate level.) And the impact of feminist research has not been translated into greater career opportunities for women: the professoriate remains largely male and white. Only some 10 percent of full professors nationally are women, a figure that hasn't changed in more than twenty years.

Women in academia are more and more clustered in the low-paying, temporary, academic-gypsy end of the profession. Of the women receiving Ph.D.'s in English, more than half are now hired for non-tenure-track, temporary academic jobs; the rest are either outside academia or unemployed. The academic temps are most likely to be women teaching freshman composition — a field now called "the kitchen." Nor are women on the tenure track faring as well as their male counterparts, despite better publication records: men are judged on "promise"; women are expected to have books already in print.

When productive, publishing women faculty are turned down for tenure, often their work turns out to be highly original feminist research — although it's also possible that feminist scholars are most apt to know their rights and insist on getting them. Most feminists, for instance, follow the recommendation of Committee W of the American Association of University Professors: they keep tenure diaries, documenting what they've been told about expectations and evaluations, and jotting down any comments that do not seem to derive from professional expectations, such as a chair's repeated discussion of a candidate's clothes instead of her research agenda. So far, feminist researchers may be the most vocal and best prepared to file complaints if they are denied tenure or promotion. They also have the most commitment to staying in college and university teaching: it's what they want to do with their lives.

Some women graduate students believe that working in mainstream areas (that is, working on white men) will benefit their careers more than working on women. That may be true for some entry-level jobs, and it is valuable for a job candidate to have another field besides women's studies: I have American literature and nonfiction writing, for instance. But a woman who decides to write on, say, Herman Melville rather than Margaret Fuller is putting her energies where they don't matter: she's digging out minutiae and chewing old cud, instead of discovering something new. "I spent eight years of my youth on one dead general," says one well-known feminist historian who wishes she'd pursued Susan B. Anthony instead.

For studying women there are archives never opened, papers never read, manuscripts never discovered, oral histories never recorded. As social historians have noted, one can't simply "add women and stir" in the historical record: putting women into the scene changes the scene. American history, in fact, looks better with women in it: it's about making homes and raising families and working for social betterment, not simply about wars and violence, genocide and slavery.

Doing feminist research means studying genuinely original materials—a dancing through the mine field, a diving into the unknown that too many young women are told they shouldn't do.

Some young women are advised to postpone childbearing and feminist research until after they have tenure. They're told to write on subjects to which they're not committed, to wait in silence and cunning until the tenure decision is made. And then, somehow, everything will flower: the academic woman's life will become her own.

But she may not have a soul left. She's apt to be in her thirties or even her forties, with an ingrained habit of deference and fear. When I wasn't yet a full professor and did outspoken things—such as writing the original draft of this article—someone always warned: "You're going to do damage to yourself." That can still be true—I could get eight o'clock classes or a distant parking space—but I went into academia for academic freedom, not to sell my soul for tiny payoffs.

A woman who waits until after tenure to write on women has given up a decade or more of intellectual life. She won't have done the years of feminist reading and writing one needs to be knowledgeable in the field; she'll be taking baby steps, when she should be making adult strides. A woman who sacrifices her intellectual integrity throughout her twenties won't suddenly get it back in her thirties. No one demands that kind of sacrifice from men and no one should.

Still, I'm a survivor, part of the first handful of tenured women who were always out-front feminists doing feminist research: my first book, *The Curse:*

A Cultural History of Menstruation, both embarrassed and intrigued job interviewers — and I still have one or two colleagues who can't mention it without
blushing. I've since published two biographies of women writers (*Inside Peyton
Place: The Life of Grace Metalious* and *Kate Chopin: A Life of the Author of "The
Awakening"*), along with a Civil War novel (*Daughters of New Orleans*), and
two edited academic books (*A Kate Chopin Miscellany* and *Regionalism and
the Female Imagination*). In 1997 I worked on an advice book, *Ms. Mentor*, for
women professors, graduate students, recovering academics, and people who
love them — and the book was pursued by half a dozen eager publishers.

Still, all of us academic women make sacrifices and compromises: we're
forced to. We have to pick our battles and (before tenure) try to avoid public
ones, such as those at department meetings. We have to conform in dress and
behavior and speech — but we should not compromise on our research interests
or in our treatment of our students, who deserve the best. The women students,
in particular, still rarely get to see a woman intellectual in action. Anne Firor
Scott, the only woman professor I saw in graduate school, showed me how to
teach as a woman: not as a tweedy, pipe-smoking, elbow-patched lecturer, but
as the leader of a community of fascinated, engaged scholars and critical spirits.
I'm grateful to her every day when I step into the classroom.

To most of our male coworkers, we are women first and scholars second.
That will happen no matter how "mainstream" our research may be. And so it
behooves women to make alliances with each other. Academic women should
create departmental caucuses that include women faculty, graduate students,
and secretaries — who have access to valuable information and can use our help
in their own job struggles. (I know many things my male colleagues will never
know simply because I share the bathroom with the secretaries.) We should be
sharing each other's successes, fighting together against the same obstacles, and
making sure that hiring committees include women and hire women.

Outside our own universities, we should be active in women's caucuses in
our fields, we should join the National Women's Studies Association (NWSA),
and we should help one another. In one recent case, a literary scholar was denied tenure on the grounds that her work — on women — was not "substantial."
But she had published in nationally known women's studies periodicals and
had made contacts through women's caucuses and NWSA. Some fifty letters of
support flooded her university, attesting to her national reputation — and she
has her tenure.

The myth of meritocracy still pervades academia: the belief that the smart
and the hardworking will always be rewarded. With women in particular, that's
often not the case: what is forthright and bold in men is considered aggressive

and bitchy—and noncollegial—in women. In academia, the myth of individualism is still strong: the belief that we're judged solely on our individual merits and that our sex or our race has no relevance.

Women must see through the myths but retain our integrity; we must work hard and be smart, but the smartest thing we can do is to reach out to other women, both in our research and in our professional lives. Even in the individualistic halls of academe, sisterhood is the most powerful weapon we have.

AFTERWORD

When I first wrote this essay, nearly twenty years ago, I expected that the lives of women in academia would change.

There are more of us in academia than before, and in more visible roles. Female provosts and deans are no longer rare, and even college presidents can be women. There are also more women teaching—although the greatest growth has been in adjunct (part-time, non-tenure-track) jobs. Women coaches are getting better pay, and women's studies programs are established everywhere. There are active women's caucuses in every discipline, including engineering (the most male profession two decades ago). And because they've grown up with Title IX and with mothers who've had independent careers, academic women today are physically stronger and more professionally self-confident than we were twenty years ago.

My fortunes have also improved. When I wrote, I was mired in a department that would not promote me to full professor, although I had four published books, a top teaching record, and a national reputation. I was in fields that ruffled feathers (women's studies and popular culture), and—I realize now— I was an abrasive personality. I changed jobs, was immediately promoted, and am very contented in a diverse and appreciative English department, at Louisiana State University. I've also mellowed, and my book that was most disparaged as "trash" in 1981 (*Inside Peyton Place*, the biography of Grace Metalious) has been bought by Sandra Bullock and Twentieth Century Fox for a feature film.

And yet—there are still not enough happy endings for women in academe. We are still systematically underpaid, earning about 90 percent of what men earn in the same ranks. That kind of information, hard to gather two decades ago, is now instantly available on the Internet. Women may need to bargain better and to gravitate toward better-paying fields, such as engineering—but at every level, women are routinely offered lower starting salaries than men are. Women are less apt to be nominated for, and receive, national fellowships and research awards, and while women are now 22 percent of full professors, we tend to fill the bottom quarter in salaries. There are also, still, horrific cases of sexual harassment, and the challenges of child care and dual career couples are running sores. And I, as it turns out, have a unique window into the problems.

A decade ago, once I'd figured out the system, I yearned to share the knowledge with younger women, who mostly didn't want to hear the bad news. (This is not an uncommon phenomenon with academics, as well as with "real people.") And so I found myself writing a grandiose question-and-answer style advice book, *Ms. Mentor's Impeccable Advice for Women in Academia* (1997), which led to a monthly advice column for all genders on the *Chronicle of Higher Education's* new Career Network site (http://www.chronicle.com/jobs, and then click on "Ms. Mentor," or go directly to Ms. Mentor's archive: http://chronicle.com/jobs/archive/advice/mentor.htm). The column debuted in September 1998.

Since then Ms. Mentor, who never leaves her ivory tower and channels her perfect wisdom through me, has received thousands of letters. They come from troubled, angry, and bitter academics—over half of them women. Happy people rarely write for advice, of course, and those who write often do so to rant and ventilate, since Ms. Mentor guarantees anonymity and writes answers only in her column. And yet . . . what she and I get are occasional stories of triumph, but many more of betrayal and justice delayed or denied.

Some of the problems women face are universal, such as the rigidity and crudeness of teaching evaluations. All teachers are sometimes misunderstood or underappreciated. But when evaluations are used to decide whether an adjunct should be kept, or an assistant professor should be tenured—then it's time to suss out how to get good scores despite some truly bizarre questions ("How much did the instructor increase your interest? Rate 1 to 7").

Many new Ph.D.'s struggle with the feeling that they're watering down what they know, and many resent knowing that they must be popular and well-liked to get high scores. And lest the new professors start to feel confident, the notorious Web site called Ratemyprofessor.com allows anyone to post an anonymous evaluation of any professor, including rating whether the professor is "hot."

Moreover, students tend to have strong and contradictory expectations for women faculty, as Susan Basow's research (1994) has shown. Students want their female teachers to be nurturing, motherly, and all-giving; students enjoy class discussions conducted by women teachers. And yet—when it comes to scoring teaching effectiveness, students give higher ratings to men who lecture. Students also feel free to write judgments, often negative ones, about the clothes and appearance of women teachers. Women still must dress more soberly and professionally than men do, and being frumpy (in Ms. Mentor's opinion) works better than being chic. It connotes seriousness—and if students are thinking that a teacher looks "hot," they're not listening to the lesson.

Irked by these inequities, Ms. Mentor produced a column titled "The Torment of Teaching Evaluations" (March 24, 2003). It was, as she announced, a completely cynical set of tips for getting better evaluations: give everybody high grades, and be cozy, dramatic, and humorous. Ms. Mentor expected a fire cloud of criticism for being—well—Machiavellian, and for talking about better scores rather than better teaching. Instead, she's received the most kudos and requests to reprint for that column, and it is routinely taught in graduate schools of education.

Not only is the system flawed, but women aren't being mentored about how to work it.

Meanwhile "contra-harassment," a term that did not exist two decades ago, is becoming more common. Rebellious students have always been with us, and so have objectors and stalkers who harass those above them (contra) in rank or status. But the incidents are common enough today that some schools, especially in big cities, have security guards available for faculty. Many have policies about expelling students who are disruptive in classes.

As in the outside world, women are more often the victims, and men more often the stalkers.

Standard sexual harassment is more recognized than it was two decades ago. The law professor Anita Hill's vivid 1991 testimony against Clarence Thomas's Supreme Court nomination was a national shocker, and it was also her greatest teaching moment (although some University of Oklahoma trustees tried to yank her tenure for it). And while there are some famous poets who still get away with groping their students, enough faculty have been dismissed for sexual harassment that word usually does get around, even to the most crass. Every campus has policies against sexual harassment, while many also ban dating or fraternization between students and faculty, or at least where faculty are supervising the students' work.

Ms. Mentor believes that all such relationships should be banned, for dignity and fairness. She is also pleased that bad behavior is condemned more openly. Students do snicker at the midlife professor who gets a red convertible and starts chattering incessantly about sex. It may even be better for students to believe James Kincaid's rather wild assertions in Regina Barreca's and Deborah Denenholtz Morse's *The Erotics of Instruction* (1997). As academics move up the power chain, Kincaid claims, they become more and more physically repellent. Indeed, "it's a wonder the highly-educated propagate," especially since sex for deans and presidents is "reptilian" (86).

But knowledge and snickering do not always bring about change. In a 2005 North Carolina case, for instance, a professor was finally fired for sexual harassment. But he had been harassing women, verbally and physically, for some fifteen years, and only two were willing to risk filing charges (because there are often reprisals). In those fifteen years, he was even promoted twice. There is no way of knowing how many women's careers were stalled or destroyed.

Such cases should be much rarer than they are, and Ms. Mentor is troubled by the fact that many men (and some women) still do cover up for sexual harassers: "He didn't mean it" or "That's his culture" or "He's just a randy old goat." That, in her view, is not sufficient, and people of good will should stop others from doing wrong.

And then there are the issues which were mostly nonissues two decades ago. One is child care, because women professors rarely had children. (I was almost forty before I ever saw a pregnant professor.) Now professors do have children, and universities have scrambled—or refused to scramble—to make it possible to have a full career and a full family life. Schools have dragged their feet about campus child care centers, and most have long waiting lists. Women are still more often the ones to make compromises, or leave meetings early, or devise crazy-quilt arrangements that can easily collapse, making teaching or lab work impossible for that day. Constance Coiner's and Diana Hume George's book, *The Family Track* (1998), tells much more than I can about the heroic and difficult struggles of academic parents, despite what would seem to be flexible schedules and "summers off."

And thanks to the difficult job market, especially in the humanities, some parents cannot even share the same household.

Two decades ago, academic couples at the same rank were rare. It was considered routine for a woman to drop out of her Ph.D. program to follow her husband in his career. (Same-sex partnerships were mostly invisible.) A wife would do part-time teaching or be an associate in her husband's lab. But she was rarely on the path to tenure or grant getting, and she was far more often a "captive spouse," taking whatever work was available and sacrificing her own talents and skills. (Sometimes, too, she wrote her husband's books, as the biographer Lynn Z. Bloom discovered when she delved into the lives of the baby care doctor Benjamin Spock and his unacknowledged ghost writer, his wife Jane.)

But now, women want to be full professors and equal partners, and it's rarely possible. Wrenching commuter relationships are commonplace, and dynamic academic duos—like children in joint-custody divorces—have learned to pack quickly, keep lists, wait patiently, and cherish time for cooking and socializing. The issue of "spousal hires"—should a spouse be hired over outside applicants?—infuriates nearly everyone. And every university town still harbors a cadre of "trailing spouses" without jobs—but now they're fuming malcontents, and more and more of them are men.

It is still unusual for a husband to follow his wife to an academic job, though less unheard-of than it was twenty or thirty years ago, when my husband bravely relocated with me to New Orleans, North Dakota, Pennsylvania, and Baton Rouge. Then, as now, there are traditional souls, both young and old, who feel it's somehow improper for a lady to go first—as Ms. Mentor discovered.

She received a letter from a young woman, a new Ph.D. who'd landed her dream job in the rural Midwest. Her husband, "Peter," came with her and hated it, because he couldn't do the things that he'd done in the big city. Evidently he nagged quite a bit and had already made up his mind: "No matter how much he loves me, he can't stay." The letter writer wondered if she should give up her job, and would she resent him later?

Ms. Mentor answered in a column called "He Doesn't Like the Midwest," which the *Chronicle of Higher Education* archived as "Sullen Spouses" (April 21, 2003). Petulant Peter, she wrote, was a drag on his wife, and Ms. Mentor thought of many good and fulfilling things he could do in the town where fate had cast him. Since he did not have to be the breadwinner, he could follow his artistic bent, work in political or social endeavors, consult or create a small business, or otherwise discover what he most wanted to do. Thanks to the Internet, few creative or interesting jobs outside of acting or music actually require one to be in the same city all the time.

Ms. Mentor also put forth some "ice-veined" calculations: that the average career lasts thirty years, but the average marriage under seven. Half of U.S. marriages end in divorce. Given the odds in the humanities, where two hundred or more people apply for one tenure-track job, it might be easier to find a new husband than to find a new job.

But Ms. Mentor concluded with a mild suggestion, that they try a commuter marriage.

"He Doesn't Like the Midwest" netted forty-five angry letters, almost all from men. Some were funny, perhaps inadvertently: "You know nothing about marriage. No wonder you're a Ms." and "Family is the most important thing. If you print this letter, don't use my name." Many recommended counseling for the wife who wrote the letter; scarcely anyone thought the husband might need improvement. And half a dozen attacked Ms. Mentor for recommending divorce—which she had not done. (Ms. Mentor was reminded of the male professors in Virginia Woolf's *A Room of One's Own* [1929]: so angry that they could not read.)

But Ms. Mentor and I have the luxury of turning away, or laughing, or writing another exposé. Many newer academic women do not. Ms. Mentor can say that no woman should sacrifice her dreams for someone who will not take equal responsibility for her happiness—but she's not sure young women will necessarily believe her.

Still, we all have a rich and very diverse pool of resources for fighting the system, or for deciding which battles needn't be fought. Especially in community colleges, where most of the growth is taking place, we have teachers who are Latinas, Asians, Arabs, Israelis. We have greater numbers of older women who've raised children, and we have women with disabilities who've fought valiantly for their accommodations and opportunities. Lesbians in academia are much more visible, and domestic partner benefits and hirings are the norm at many schools. Students who are lesbian, bisexual, gay, or transgendered can usually find mentors, on the Internet if not in person.

Meanwhile women, as in the past, know how much we can learn from each other. Wise faculty women support secretaries, maintenance workers, and staff members, and we share information. Women have created countless writing and support groups. We also share lunches and compare tips about which opportunities to pursue, which time-wasting committees to avoid, and which sexual harassers to shun or expose. As we've done for centuries, women are using our wits to figure out what men are up to, and when to confront and when to laugh and sigh.

Wise women do not allow themselves to be portrayed as each other's enemies. If two women are competing for the same job, it is not a "cat fight." It is a "tournament of champions."

What I wrote two decades ago, that sisterhood is our most powerful weapon, is still true. Although the pay gap in academia persists, it is smaller than the gap in other professions. Male lawyers, for instance, earn 44 percent more than female ones. What's made the difference? Donna Shalala, president of the University of Miami, says that academic women have come closer because "women faculty members have brought it up." Tenure gives us the power to speak, and to keep speaking, with a security and authority that other professionals do not have. And so, Shalala says, "As women got to be full professors, women looked out for their sisters."

Ms. Mentor and I trust that we will continue to do so. We have nothing to fear except our own silence. As Anne Firor Scott taught me in women's history class over thirty years ago, the women in the suffrage movement lived much longer and healthier lives than most of their contemporaries, because they had a purpose and a passion. She was so right.

6.

MINORITY FACULTY IN [MAINSTREAM WHITE] ACADEMIA

NELLIE Y. MCKAY

*The problem of the twentieth century is the problem of the color-line, — the relation of
the darker to the lighter races of men in Asia and Africa, in America and the islands
of the sea.* — W. E. B. Du Bois, *The Souls of Black Folk*

Thus intoned the famous W. E. B. Du Bois in 1903 as he looked out across the
unknown years of an infant century with hopeful dreams for the future of his
race.[1] More than sixty years later, Martin Luther King Jr. expressed Du Bois's
understood wish in his own vision of an America in which all people would be
judged by their characters and not by the color of their skins or their national
origins.[2] And while Du Bois (as did King) spoke as a black man for black people,
he also knew that the problem — racism — pervaded every aspect of American
life and conduct, extending far beyond his country's complex relationship to
the generations of its ex-slaves. If its harshest manifestations were more easily
discernible in black/white relations throughout the 1900s, nevertheless, by the
time the century reached its midpoint, most of the world recognized that it
had equally wide implications for relations between Anglo-Europeans and the
vast "majority" of non-Anglo-European peoples around the globe.[3] Today, the
sentiments of Du Bois, King, and others find echoes in the cries of peoples
of many colors, races, and cultures in many places, who, ironically, although
far outnumbering the dominant white group, have come to be known as "minorities." We know, too, that the Anglo-American academy has been a strong-
hold for this intellectual, cultural, and social problem, which remains the most
serious issue affecting the lives of minority faculty in the white mainstream
academy.

In 1903, when he published *The Souls of Black Folk*, Du Bois was a young
black intellectual with a lifetime of struggle for human rights ahead of him. He
was educated at Harvard University at the feet of men like William James and
Josiah Royce, who respected and praised his mind, and under their influence
he earned his undergraduate degree there and later became the first black to
receive a Ph.D. from that institution. He also studied sociology, history, and

economics at the University of Berlin before completing his doctoral dissertation. In spite of his superb training and brilliant promise, few Americans of any color were more qualified for the academic offers that never came his way because of his race. What might he not have contributed to the intellectual coffers of Western civilization had he not been forced to concentrate his brilliance and energies on problems of race and human rights? Still, this inequity did not paralyze and keep him from an active career. As a young man, he saw his life's mission as a call to full commitment to the future welfare of all black and oppressed people, far more than to fulfill his personal ambitions. The battle for black faculty to gain access to the white academy fell to those who followed him. He worked and hoped for basic solutions to the problem of the colorline, toward resolving the duality of identity that he and all black people felt. His hopes were never realized. In 1963, when he died, disillusioned and in self-exile in Ghana, black and white Americans were engaged in the most widespread violent racial confrontations in this country's history, and black intellectualism was in a struggle for recognition as an aspect of American life and culture. Du Bois's life remains a poignant symbol of the infamy of Western racism and the concomitant waste of black (minority group) intellectual power.

Unfortunately, in this new century, the problems Du Bois called to our attention still occupy enormous dimensions in our national life. I focus my contribution on minority faculty to *The Academic's Handbook* specifically on minority faculty in mainstream white academia. I begin with the recognition that in addition to having the difficulties of faculty of Anglo-European racial and cultural heritage (hereafter called "mainstream faculty" for conciseness), minority group faculty members in dominant white colleges and universities continue to encounter racism and classism, and for women in this group, sexism and racism together constitute a unit even more corrosive than each by itself. I note, too, that the term "minority" has internal problems for me. As used by the dominant culture, it embraces and erases, simultaneously, any distinctiveness between people of different races and cultures, with different lengths of stay in the country, or reasons for coming, and who had different receptions on arrival. Thus it subsumes all who appear to be outsiders in the eyes of dominant white American culture. As a result, any discussion of problems of "minorities" in the academy, especially by a black woman who feels the tensions between race and gender oppression, cannot accurately represent the concerns of the multiple groups included in the term. At best, I address the subject broadly as the interrelations between white male dominant (privilege) versus the "other" (powerlessness) in the mainstream Anglo-American academy. My essay on black women in the mainstream academy would be significantly different.

The special problems that confront minority group faculty in mainstream white colleges and universities are rooted in the premises that informed Western culture's white, male-dominated, closed intellectual system for hundreds of years. This system originated in the self-serving dictates of race, class, and gender. Its perpetrators, a small group of privileged men, claimed exclusive right to define accepted knowledge based on their opinions as exclusive knowers. So closed, exclusive, and elite was this system that for centuries it excluded everyone outside of its designated knowers, including Anglo-European women. Clearly, it had no place for other races and cultures. In regard to black people in America, racism, which spawned classism, and as Maya Angelou once noted, erased black female experience,[4] was so deeply embedded in the system that after the abolition of slavery, the intellectual tradition continued to reinforce the economic framework in dehumanizing people of African descent. Segregated inferior education, the denial of social and economic access, and the refusal of the powerful to acknowledge the existence of the black intellectual tradition that developed outside of the dominant tradition were means to this end. Before the 1860s, literacy was largely forbidden to blacks; in the 1860s two separate educational systems came about on all levels: one white, the other black, separate, and deliberately instituted to offer unequal training and fewer opportunities for social and economic advancement to the descendants of the slaves. In addition, the scholarship of whites overwhelmingly produced only ancillary and negative images of Afro-Americans until beyond the middle of the twentieth century.[5] For all of these impediments, an Afro-American intellectual tradition had existed for more than two centuries.[6]

Pressure by blacks to end their intellectual subjugation to whites culminated in the 1950s and 1960s in the struggle to integrate white educational facilities. First, there was the *Brown v. Board* 1954 Supreme Court decision, which overturned the hypocritical doctrine of separate but equal in public education and, later, black political confrontations for civil rights. But legal mandates have not improved the attitudes of many white Americans toward the "others," and, since the 1960s, issues that once affected only blacks in their relationship to the dominant educational system have extended to other groups of minorities as they have come into the mainstream academy.

My assignment implies both the positive and negative realities of life for minority faculty in the white academy. On the positive side, for all of the peculiar problems they face within these spaces, there are now blacks and other minority cohort groups in the white academy where almost none existed thirty-five years ago. Their presence has changed the face of American education and revised the premises of accepted knowledge in material content, philosophical approaches, and interactions with and between students and faculty. On the negative side, the lingering problems associated with race, class, and ethnicity that minorities in the academy experience denote the tenacity of the "problem" and the distance we have yet to go. The mistakes of history, like a recurring nightmare, haunt us even in the daylight of our best intentions to dispose of them forever.

For the remainder of this essay, I will attempt to delineate some attitudes that black and other minority group faculty can take toward some of the difficulties they will encounter, as "other," in the mainstream academy. I have no definitive answers to any of the problems and only suggest, from my observations as a black woman survivor in the academy for more than thirty years, my own strategies that may be helpful to others. My approach is philosophical and reflective, and I look at broad, generally observable phenomena especially associated with blacks in the academy over the past three decades.

In launching efforts to integrate the white mainstream academy in the 1960s and 1970s, black students and faculty, as "others," were violently opposed to the system that denied their human and intellectual worth. They determined to change the demography of the institution with their presence and to alter the premises of previously perceived knowledge to take cognizance of their racial and cultural experiences in America. Predictably, the system responded by resisting changes to its long-held authority. But resolute outsiders fought well, and when the dust settled, around the middle of the 1970s, African American studies, as a field of inquiry, had taken firm hold in white colleges and universities across the country; a generation of black graduate students were completing their work in traditional disciplines in major universities; and for the first time in our history, there was a recognizable group of black faculty in a variety of fields (most in areas of African American studies in-the-making) entering white colleges and universities as peers of their white colleagues. They were the vanguard, and their successes paved the way for women's studies and other ethnic studies programs that followed in the closing years of the 1970s. By then, too, the first group of black students and faculty on the front lines of the action, and the whites who had supported them in their struggle, had absorbed the worst of the system's resistance to change. It was time to look toward building a unified intellectual structure that was not a closed system of knowledge controlled by a privileged group of knowers.

In the first stages of the black struggle in the mainstream academy, political considerations were foremost for everyone. This was one avenue along which black students, and the black populace in general, were claiming their moral and legal rights to equal opportunities within a society they and their forbearers had helped to build and for which many of them gave their lives. In their insistence on the recognition of the black American experience as a subject for intellectual inquiry, not simply that black people should assimilate into white

Western culture inside of its academies, they publicly claimed the worth of their identity for themselves and all Americans. To the degree that the numbers of blacks and other minority group people have moved into the mainstream academy within these last three decades, the early political pressures need no longer occupy all of our energies. Most colleges and universities that are serious about diversifying their faculty and student bodies are well aware of how important it is for new minority faculty to discover themselves in a community of other minority faculty, and new faculty should not hesitate to take full advantage of the experiences of those who were there earlier. New faculty need not feel obliged to take their advice, but seeking it out is a good idea. Besides, most are willing to make themselves available for unofficial mentoring of their junior colleagues. In knowing that they have the support of others like themselves who are familiar with the institution, new faculty now have more time to consider their personal goals and ambitions as equal priorities to our political responsibilities. New minority group faculty can now ask themselves why they chose to enter the mainstream academy in the first place, what would they like to achieve in the short term, and, finally, how they perceive their long-term goals.[7] The opportunity to ask such questions in a serious manner represents a new dimension in our relationship to the mainstream academy. In spite of the history, such questions help us to maintain a posture of optimism, openness, and receptivity to others as we explore our possibilities in these places.

This does not suggest that full equality and respect for minority group differences are within our grasp. Racism, classism, sexism, and elitism are rampant in the mainstream academy, in spite of major changes in the makeup of student and faculty bodies and drastic revisions of curriculums in most colleges and universities. But the game is different from what it was a quarter of a century ago. Although some white mainstream scholars continue to resist the new trends, minority experiences are now valid areas of intellectual study in most institutions of higher education. Resistance remains because it is more difficult to change human attitudes, values, and irrational thinking than external elements like curriculum or faculty and student representation. To complicate matters, the negative behaviors are more sophisticated than they were before the system was disturbed. While we should not look for or borrow trouble, minority group faculty in the mainstream need to be aware that on a day-to-day basis they are likely to encounter insulting behavior in a variety of ways, including:

1. Overt hostility on the part of individuals or groups of mainstream faculty members and students toward minority group faculty members and/or minority studies or minority group students.

2. Subtle and less easily detected expressions of prejudices or biases that occur in (1.), on the same issues.

3. Unconscious racism, classism, and elitism toward minority group faculty colleagues or minority studies or students by otherwise well-intentioned mainstream faculty.

At whatever level these are encountered, they are humiliating and unsettling, and we do not always handle them with self-assuredness. No one should beat up herself for feeling unnerved by willful or even accidental hurtful actions. Bigotry is unnerving and degrading to those to whom it is directed, although in actuality, it makes a greater comment on its perpetrators. We should keep in mind, however (as unfortunate as this is), that how the minority group faculty person deals with such situations often determines her/his future career in an institution. We fare best when our dignity appears untouched; otherwise, among colleagues, we are typed as overly sensitive, without a sense of humor, or uncollegial. Try to remain outwardly calm. Concentrating on one's personal and individual goals at these times can be a means of deflecting abuse and using time to devise strategies to cope with these negative behaviors. The offended person should try to see beyond the immediate affront to a larger plane of future action and find it easier to avoid internalizing the problem. Numbers of black and other minority group faculty, who would otherwise succeed, have failed inside mainstream white colleges and universities because of the energies they expended on anger toward bigots and/or the dehumanization they experience because of the repugnant behavior of their white colleagues. The more the minority group person is able to separate the self from immersion in self-consuming rage and a need for righteous vindication, the less the personal distress and the greater the chances of self-defined success.

To the offenses in the first two categories named above, in dealing with obnoxious students, it behooves you to act firmly and to make it clear that you will not tolerate unbecoming behavior on their parts. Take whatever measures (short of physical ones) are necessary to establish this stance at the first sign of an offense. At times, I have invited students to drop my course or change their attitudes. Firmness and decisiveness in these situations is the only way to retain both self-respect and the respect of the students. Do not permit them to test you. Stand firm and assert your authority.

For colleagues who offend you deliberately, a useful ploy is to behave in a manner that the offender might not have expected. This involves the ability to think and act quickly.[8] In cases where the likely response is "sounding off," silence is golden. Whenever possible, walk away from situations that are actually or potentially explosive in their racial, class, gender, or ethnic properties.

Avoid the company of those whom you know or suspect to hold antagonistic feelings toward you or the work you are doing. Aside from the waste of psychic energy these involve, in most instances, confrontation now proves unproductive. Choose open struggles carefully and selectively. It is wise to assume that we will encounter more battles than we can fight in public and emerge triumphant. It is wiser to enter no struggle without intending to win. Instead of frequent open challenges to others, discuss the circumstances with other minority faculty if that seems appropriate or seek advice and/or comfort from friends you can trust, in letters and on the telephone. The cost of long-distance telephoning (if necessary) is well worth it. For, sadly, you will discover that your minority group faculty friends in your and other institutions are having similar experiences. Writing is also an excellent way to get a manageable perspective on these situations. But if you wish to discuss these matters confidentially, I don't believe it is wise to use e-mail. Make the time to use other means of communication.[9]

While overt hostility toward the minority group person is the easiest to detect and deal with, the subtler forms cause greater frustration. The minority person is often unable to be absolutely sure that offense is intended. It is easy to understand the prejudice behind the statement that labels black or other Third World literature as polemic and "not real literature," more difficult to know how to respond to the sighted colleague who says to an African American: "I never think of you as a black person." Sending him/her Pat Parker's "For the White Person Who Wants to be My Friend" (which you might be inclined to do) is too obvious.[10] Even more difficult are the times when well-intentioned mainstream colleagues, who are usually aware of the dangers of their unconscious negative biases toward others, are unknowingly guilty of speech or action that reflects the pervasiveness of the malady. For example, a popular black female instructor, under review for tenure in a major research university, had this experience with a young white woman professor friend. The latter, attempting to be supportive in a difficult period in the black woman's life, assured her that "the administration would not *dare* to deny your case." The black woman knew that support was intended. But more than once in recent history, that administration had denied tenure to worthy young minority professors. The black woman also knew that, unconsciously, the implication was that because she was a popular *black* teacher/scholar, she would get preferential treatment, regardless of the merits of her case. Inwardly, she cringed at the remark but said nothing at the time. Several days later, at lunch with her friend, she calmly pointed out the offense in the remark—the hidden racist and sexist assumptions. By handling the situation tactfully, the black woman saved a friendship and, hopefully, increased the sensitivity of the white professor.

In the cases in which a minority group faculty member finds her/himself exposed to derogatory remarks *about* minority group students, similar treatment as above is the best strategy. Be prepared to defend students against racism in a rational way and, if appropriate, explain some minority group behaviors that might be unfamiliar to the nonminority faculty person. Be particularly alert to racism that emerges in preferential treatment and low expectations of minority group students. In your own classes make it clear that you have one set of standards for all students.

Understandably, minority group faculty often complain that they are the ones on whom fall the burdens of being tactful, of causing no offense, and of "educating" (sensitizing) their mainstream colleagues. When they do not accomplish this successfully, they are penalized, sometimes losing their positions. The situation is indelicately balanced, the unfairness of it indisputable. Yet, the reality we face in attempting to gain our due still means we must often wrest it from those who hold it against our will. Malcolm X's adage, "by any means necessary," takes on new meaning in this struggle. The price of achieving long-term goals, for ourselves and our groups, means extra work and will. The difficulty is in knowing when to be calm and when to mount open challenge. There is no blueprint to guide us each time. As seventh sons and daughters of seventh sons and daughters, we must train our seventh senses toward this end.[11]

However, there are ways in which new minority group faculty members can take the offensive against prejudices or hostilities on the part of mainstream faculty. These approaches may be useful in other kinds of situations for all new faculty, but they are even more important for minority group faculty members. One is to avoid the "chip-on-the-shoulder" attitude. Entering the mainstream white academy with an openness to both minority group and mainstream colleagues, and a genuine wish to become a member of the "team" without compromising the self, increases chances of finding supportive relationships. It often takes a long time to develop close sustaining friendships in a new environment, even with other minorities, but that need not preclude more casual relationships with different kinds of people in the beginning. There are genuine friendships to be made with mainstream faculty, as well as with faculty from other groups, including one's own. Do not make hasty judgments on the nature of political alliances in your department. For instance, minority group individuals may seem less powerful or influential than others, yet many have been effective as mentors or confidential advisers while others are equally so as gatekeepers in mainstream colleges and universities. The wise new faculty member listens attentively to everyone and everything, even (perhaps especially) gossip, but repeats nothing. In short, during the first weeks and months of settling in, hold an open mind about everything and everyone in your department and beyond. Be the best student you can be of people and situations. Your professional life may depend on it.

One of the advantages of being open and receptive to many people as a new colleague in the academy is that one appears less emotionally needy and more socially attractive without giving the impression of being a prima donna, a stance to avoid. Do not ignore invitations to faculty social gatherings. These offer chances to discover what people are like when they are away from their classrooms and offices and give the new person useful information about the institution and his/her new colleagues. In a short time, the natural processes by which friendships form will eliminate many early acquaintances from one's close circle, but not necessarily from one's support group. An open, confident demeanor goes a long way in diffusing ambivalences toward a new member of a department. Even those who did not vote for the appointment of the new colleague (and you *do not* want to know who those were) are willing to give that one an opportunity to show that she wants be a good citizen of the department. The early months are the ones in which a new faculty member should aim to win friends and influence people into believing that she/he is someone everyone will want to have around for a long time. In the nebulous category called collegiality, one can never earn enough credit to ensure tenure or promotion, but many excellent young scholars and teachers have suspected that they failed to make the grade because members of their departments found them uncollegial. Aside from that, a sense of harmony with one's colleagues greatly reduces the inevitable stress that accompanies the first years of a new career. Ask other faculty members, senior and junior, about their work in a manner that expresses interest on your part; talk with recently tenured and/or promoted faculty about their experiences during the process; welcome advice from others; be enthusiastic but not effusive; show that you are pleased to be in the institution.

Committee assignments and formal and informal student advising are the bane of the minority faculty person's life in the mainstream academy. Every committee wants "one." Talk over the merits of the committee assignments outside your department with your chair before you accept them. Listen and learn to say no. You do not want to appear unwilling to be a good team player, but no one was ever promoted or granted tenure on the volume of committee work she/he accepted and did well. Be protective of your time, especially if someone wants you to spend it in ways that will not have beneficial results for you. There is a thin line between selfishness and survival on this score. Formal student advising, if done in moderation, is the quickest and most efficient way to learn about the new institution and about many aspects of academia that one never hears about in graduate school. If possible, accept all committee/formal advising appointments for a specified time. Indeterminate lengths of service can be dangerous for a new faculty member.

Minority students often automatically gravitate toward a minority group faculty member for informal advising and even for counseling on private matters. Take an interest in these students (few other faculty do) and in their group activities. Some may need extra academic help from you, but do not assume that without proof. Be alert lest the minority group student expects that your concern for him/her will translate into undeserved good grades. Set standards and offer help where necessary and when advisable. In every possible way, students will take as much as you will give to them and then some more. Set limits and insist that students respect them. It is advisable not to encourage them to call you at home; much easier on you to make an extra hour of office time than to be harassed by phone calls at midnight or on weekends. Our jobs depend on having students, and we owe it to minority group students to be even more available to them than others, but always within reason. As faculty, you are a role model for them in different kinds of ways. At the same time, you may be the only minority group authority figure that many Anglo-American students come into contact with at close range. You have a good deal to teach this group as well, and what they learn from you (consciously or unconsciously) will influence their future in ways neither you nor they can predict. A black woman friend of mine once discovered that a South African white student in her writing class was so profoundly affected by her handling of racial issues in discussions of literature that his attitudes toward the conflicts in his own country changed. By the end of the term he wanted to work toward a humanitarian resolution of the racial problems in his homeland. What astonished my friend most was that she had not consciously attempted to impose her political views on the class; it had just happened. We affect our students much more than we know.

If racism, sexism, and classism, for all their devastating effects on minority group faculty, are almost always hard to prove, and if in the final analysis collegiality is a matter of personality, teaching and scholarship can be documented. And on these hang the most important index of a junior faculty member's career. While all faculty need to be extremely aware of this, minority group faculty must do so even more. If the job is potentially permanent — one in which the new faculty person expects to earn tenure and promotion — it is absolutely necessary for him/her to understand clearly department and college or university expectations of him/her at specific times on a step-by-step basis. The faculty member needs to know exactly when she/he will be reviewed (as teacher and scholar), the nature of the review, and the value of each review in the total process. Also ascertain, if this was not done during the job interview, the role that teaching versus scholarship plays in promotion and/or tenure.

In the area of teaching, the do's and don'ts are fairly clear, and most graduate students know them well before the end of their degree work. I continue to be nervous (after thirty years) whenever I meet a new class. Many of my friends report similar feelings each term. This is nothing to worry about and may well indicate how seriously we take our work and students. Minority group instructors, like all others, new ones or veterans, should aim to do their best in the classroom: they should always be organized, prepared, and meet classes on time; they must not condescend to students but challenge them and entertain high expectations of them. Good teachers are firm but fair, do not require what the students cannot deliver, and do not play favorites among them. The best teachers gain the respect of their students; they are not in a popularity contest. New instructors can take heart in knowing that everyone, even the best teacher, has bad days. Expect them, and do not be too upset by them.

When scholarship is the most important criterion for advancement, obtaining information on how to proceed with a research agenda is crucial. Minority group faculty often feel tripped up by words like "standards" and "quality," which they often see as euphemisms trivializing them and their work, especially if the latter is in minority studies. On the other hand, "how much" is "enough," or "how good" is "good enough" are impossible to know. Still, one need not feel completely helpless. Aside from having a clear sense of the review timetable, new faculty need to understand, among other things, how an institution views the various stages through which a completed article or book manuscript goes: under review for publication; accepted for publication, no release date; in press; released but not reviewed. In some fields, especially in the social and natural sciences, articles and essays in prestigious journals receive high rewards; in others, especially in some humanities disciplines in some universities, one is judged almost solely on books. One needs to ask whether, for a new professor, edited volumes are worth the time and energy they require. To the great joy of many, new reprints of minority group texts, women's texts, and other long-neglected materials are making our teaching richer and easier. Some of us are involved in editing new collections, reprint series, and/or writing new introductions for reprint editions. A new faculty member must ask to what extent activities in editing count for or against her/him in quantity of work produced and which area of scholarship she/he should best focus on at this stage of the career. In some universities, they count *after* your own book and are no substitute for your own work. Ask too about the value to you of doing book reviews as publications. In some institutions even a hundred of these mean *nothing*. But whatever their value, do not review books you would not otherwise read in conjunction with your teaching or research. There are more profitable ways to spend your time. Whenever possible, the faculty member should secure all information on institutional expectations in writing from the department chair. Ask for it; do not expect that you will get it as a matter of course. It is also important to keep a personal record of all meetings with everyone involved in the evaluative process. If nothing else comes of it, such vigilance and care on your part will convince your colleagues that you are serious about the job and your future in the profession.

Whether a new minority faculty member is a scholar in a traditional field or engaged in inquiry blazing trails in a new field, the first rule of the game is to take one's teaching and research seriously. We ought to enjoy what we do, but the importance of our work far exceeds our individual satisfactions. Institutional considerations prod us to do as well as we can for the rewards they offer (increased salaries, job security, released time to continue research). But beyond external validation, we owe our primary responsibilities for our work to ourselves. We are knowers, revising centuries of misperceptions of knowledge. As outsiders in traditional disciplines or insiders in our special cultural areas, we bring fresh perspectives to learning. The new areas we open up revise the entire structure of this civilization's knowledge base. Without us, this work would not get done. We are very important in our time and in the places in which we work.

Needless to say, the foregoing includes considerations of minority group women in the mainstream white academy. Emily Toth's essay "Women in Academia" also addresses issues relating to minority group women. However, it bears repeating that this group, especially black and other Third World women, faces unique difficulties in these institutions because of their race and gender. Their presence, as bearers of knowledge, is in direct contradiction to Western concepts of accepted knowledge. Of all groups, as bona fide intellectuals, they are the furthest removed from society's expectations of their "place" in it, the least expected to succeed on merit, and the most vulnerable to insult. White male students are more likely to verbally abuse a minority group woman than her male counterpart; minority group male students expect her to be sympathetic to (excuse) their failings because she is aware of their previous deprivation in the white male world (she represents mother, sister, and friend—Zora Neale Hurston's "mule" of the world; Toni Morrison's "hem" of Jude's garment—rolled into one);[12] she is vulnerable to sexual and other kinds of harassment from male students and faculty of all groups; and Third World women faculty also find themselves faced with white female student and faculty hostility at times. While white female faculty also face more student hostility than their male counterparts, more minority group faculty appear to have this problem. My advice remains the same as that which I gave earlier: stand firm and refuse to let any student direct disrespect to you. If the behavior persists, report it to the proper department authorities. Minority women scholars in the academy are piercing the silences of their foremothers and giving them voice in spaces they could not have expected. The recovery of these voices is making the kinds of contributions to knowledge that makes our work some of the most exciting of our times. These efforts must proceed.

Achieving success in the competitive world of today's academy is difficult, and sometimes what seems like personal failure may be unrelated to the individual. Minority group faculty entered the profession at a time when most institutions had little room to expand their instructional staffs. Political pressures, affirmative action, and, at times, moral conviction have made possible minority group representation in colleges and universities across the country. These changes often created hostilities between mainstream and minority group younger faculty. White men, in particular, perceive themselves victims of reverse discrimination. We reject such efforts to undermine our presence in these spaces because many minority group faculty do not succeed in white mainstream colleges and universities no matter how hard they try, and the same is true of many nonminority faculty. However, as newcomers to these fields of endeavor, we stand by our right to share space with all others. We, like all others, need permanency and stability in our lives, institutions in which to work and grow, and colleagues with whom to interact and to support us. This makes it more crucial that we take what we do seriously, that we do the best we possibly can to meet the standards we set for ourselves, and that we understand and value our contributions to knowledge. Minority group faculty have many hurdles to overcome in the mainstream white academy; the most effective way of dealing with them is to remain true to ourselves and to do our work to the best of our abilities.

NOTES

1. Unfortunately, more than one hundred years later, Du Bois's statement remains as true as it was in 1903, except for our now knowing how much deeper the reasons for this than he did then.

2. Martin Luther King Jr., "I Have a Dream," Speech at the Lincoln Memorial, Washington, August 1963.

3. Western civilization's negative attitudes toward groups of people have not been confined to "dark" races but essentially include peoples whose cultural roots are other than those of the Anglo-European tradition.

4. Maya Angelou, *I Know Why the Caged Bird Sings* (New York: Random House, 1970), 51.

5. With few exceptions, studies by white Americans on black Americans from the eighteenth through the first half of the twentieth century revealed only negative characteristics about the group and completely ignored the role that racism played in the black experience. Exceptions to such racist materials include Gunnar Myrdal, *An American Dilemma* (New York: Harper

and Brothers, 1944); Melvin Herskovits, *The Myth of the Negro Past* (New York: Harper and Brothers, 1958); and Lawrence Levine, *Black Culture and Black Consciousness* (New York: Oxford University Press, 1977).

6. Although most scholars accept the existence of this tradition in the writings of men like Frederick Douglass and W. E .B. Du Bois, the beginnings take us back to the eighteenth century with men like Richard Allen (b. 1760), the first bishop of the African Methodist Episcopal Church from 1816 to 1831; William J. Simmons (b. 1849), whose *Men of Mark* (1877) was an early history of African American men of high achievement; and women like Anna Julia Cooper (b. 1858), whose ground-breaking *A Voice from the South, by a Black Woman of the South* (1895) was one of the nineteenth century's strongest feminist tracts. The institutionalization of this intellectual tradition came in 1897 when eighteen men in Washington inaugurated the American Negro Academy to promote black intellectual activity among African Americans.

7. These questions help us to better understand what we expect to achieve within the mainstream academy. We all need not have the same reasons for being there, but it helps to be clear on what we want as individuals.

8. Suppressing enormous rage, I once "swallowed" an insult directed at me by my white male colleague's belittling of a black woman writer's work. Almost immediately afterward I wrote an essay incorporating the insult and my rage. A few months later I presented it at a professional meeting, to the applause of many of my colleagues. The essay found its way into a women's studies journal and was later reprinted in a collection of women's experiences in the academy. You can't help getting mad, but sometimes there are ways to get even as well.

9. Although we seem not to have time for it these days, letter writing is especially useful, enjoyable, worthwhile, and sustaining, once the habit is formed. Since 1975, a black woman friend from graduate school and I, separated because of jobs in different places, have engaged in the kind of letter writing that astonishes most people. In fact, we recreated the nineteenth-century tradition *a la typewriter* first and then by computer. Writing an average of three or four letters each per week, we shared much of each other's lives, including those things that caused us joy or anxieties in the academy. We seldom needed to talk to each other on the telephone. This habit took us both through several rough times when we felt especially vulnerable as black women in the white academy. In moments of fantasy, we imagined graduate students in the twenty-first century reconstructing our lives through our letters even though we did not write with our eyes on posterity—in our letters we shared a sustaining and supportive, meaningful friendship. Unhappily, increased professional activities and their attendant stresses have interfered with that routine in recent years. On occasion she still writes letters that come by snail mail (and what a delight!). I no longer seem to manage more than an e-mail message once or twice per week. I mourn the loss of the letter-writing years.

10. See Pat Parker, "For the White Person Who Wants to Be My Friend," *Women Slaughter* (Oakland: Diana Press, 1978), 13.

11. As W. E. B. Du Bois wrote, "The Negro is a sort of seventh son, born with a veil, and gifted with second sight in this American world." *The Souls of Black Folk* (New York: New American Library, 1969), 45.

12. See Zora Neale Hurston, *Their Eyes Were Watching God* (Urbana: University of Illinois

Press, 1985), 29. In Hurston's novel, the grandmother, who lived through the horrors of slavery, tells her granddaughter to accept, gratefully, her marriage to an older, financially secure man she does not love. Grandmother notes that this arrangement will make up for the years when black women, the "mules" of the world, were forced to bear the burdens of life for every one else. Janie, the granddaughter, rejects her grandmother's advice and goes on to become the first black female heroine in black women's fiction. Also see Toni Morrison, *Sula* (New York: New American Library, 1982), 83. Morrison approaches the theme from the perspective of the black man. When Jude, husband of Nel, a central character in this novel, contemplates marriage, he thinks of a wife as someone to give him the solace he needs to survive in a world that denigrates black men. She will be the "hem" of his coat, keeping him from raveling away. Black male students, especially, often see black women professors as their "safe harbor," to borrow another Morrison term, to protect them from the "burdens" of their "blackness" in the white college and university.

PART II

SOME ISSUES IN THE ACADEMY TODAY

Over the past decade, at least, the academy has seemed anything but a serene space for disinterested study and thinking. Attacked from the outside as either irrelevant to today's world or wasteful of public resources, colleges and universities have found themselves very much on the defensive. They have had to defend their curricula, their hiring and firing practices, the workloads of their faculty, their treatment of nonacademic employees, their policies on sexual and racial harassment, and the integrity of their scientific and research enterprises. Individual faculty members have felt that their grant proposals to national agencies were being increasingly subjected to political rather than scholarly agendas. Indeed, "political" is exactly what the academy became over the last ten years—at least, it became politicized in a way that was open and unmistakable.

The politicization of the academy is perhaps most evident in the internal factionalism that has spawned sometimes acrid arguments over the canon, over the goals and meanings of diversity, over modes and methods of teaching. Formation of the National Association of Scholars is perhaps the most obvious sign of a faculty feeling somehow under siege, and the reactions of faculty opposed to the agenda of the NAS an equally obvious sign of the deep divisions among today's professoriate. We have probably weathered the most extreme versions of this internal debate but, as the arguments over "intelligent design" suggest, the academy still faces serious and sometimes complex challenges. It is not likely that the new Ph.D. will be oblivious to these issues, but it may not be clear what role he or she should adopt in relation to them. In the essays to follow, therefore, we have tried to articulate not only what some of these issues are but what you, as a new faculty member, might expect to encounter on campus as a result.

Craufurd D. Goodwin discusses both the challenges and the risks for new faculty pursuing interdisciplinary or internationalizing projects. Ronald R. Butters explores the principles of free speech and academic freedom, and explains the continuous vigilance required to maintain these core values. Judith S. White gives detailed advice on how to avoid situations that could be perceived as harassing. And P. Aarne Vesilind offers a thoughtful account of the increasingly important issue of academic integrity, particularly as that relates to the responsible conduct of academic research.

7

FADS AND FASHIONS ON CAMPUS

Interdisciplinarity and Internationalization

CRAUFURD D. GOODWIN

Like most human institutions, colleges and universities are swept from time to time by new ideas about practices, about rules of behavior, and about almost everything else. In the early-twenty-first century these new ideas have become more pervasive, primarily because of improvements in communication. A novelty that is stirring a college campus in, say, Seattle, Washington, is very likely today to be active in Florida as well (just check the home pages of newsletters available on Google). Sometimes the novelty is based on intellectual ferment (for example, application of the concept of postmodernism to conventional disciplines); sometimes on technical change (Ipods and blogs); sometimes by strengthened moral purpose (affirmative action); sometimes by government prescription (provisions for the handicapped); and sometimes by developments far from academe (the war in Iraq). One possible response to these novelties is to resist their intrusion: to insist that scholarship must be protected from the impurities and distractions of the external world. But in most cases, the result of this strategy is like that of King Canute's command that the tide not rise. He got his feet wet! Similarly, campus dwellers have no real choice but to deal with the novelties that wash over them. Rejecting change simply forecloses opportunities to benefit from new ideas and new approaches.

The most sensible posture for a young faculty member to take toward fads and fashions as they arrive on campus is cautious interest and careful response. In this essay, I will demonstrate that point by exploring the nature and consequences of two waves of innovation still breaking over American higher education: interdisciplinarity and internationalization. I say "still breaking" because I do not believe we have yet seen the final permutation of either of these movements despite the fact that both began nearly twenty years ago. Certainly the number of interdisciplinary and international study programs (both graduate and undergraduate) has continued to explode over the last decade and into the post-9/11 world. Many of these programs and centers, in fact, have available lines for faculty working "outside" their own disciplines. Should you consider applying for a position in one of these free-standing centers? That is just one question you might bear in mind as I try to explain what these two movements are, what they imply for higher education, and how the young scholar might deal with them.

INTERDISCIPLINARITY

There has been rapidly increasing discussion in recent years on the American campus about the need to "break the tyranny of the disciplines" and to encourage scholars in their teaching and research to move beyond the narrow disciplinary or subdisciplinary borders within which they were trained. Why these proposals? Would it not be just as reasonable to argue the reverse? That in intellectual life, as in the economy, division of labor and specialization rather than eclecticism lead to efficiency and greater productivity? Scholars therefore should cherish and protect disciplinary boundaries. The flaw in such an argument will be readily apparent to academics in the biological or medical sciences, where it is becoming increasingly difficult to tell just what the "disciplines" really are. What distinguishes cell biology from cellular and molecular biology or molecular cancer biology? Botany and zoology departments are rapidly giving way to biology departments: have they, then, ceased to exist as "disciplines"? Beyond these realities of disciplinary change, there are several reasons that could be cited concerning why interdisciplinarity is not merely happening but desirable.

First, the increasing division, subdivision, and sub-subdivision of scholarly inquiry in recent years may have led to rapidly diminishing returns in some areas. Moreover, the ever-smaller boxes in which some scholars work seem increasingly to be impervious to movement through the walls either way. Many departments, curricula, and research groups have suffered from sclerosis imposed by scholars protecting a small piece of turf that is the only ground where they know to stand but that has now become irrelevant. The implications of this situation for scholars and for scholarly inquiry are serious. The division of knowledge into disciplines and subdisciplines that now prevails is not inherently natural; it responded to contemporary conditions and when conditions change, so should the disciplines. Interdisciplinary activity is one way to explore new formations and to remain on the frontier. Much of the progress in many disciplines has come through research on topics that were at one time thought to be in other disciplines. Mathematical economics was once considered to be in mathematics, not economics, psychohistory in psychology, not history. Now what were formerly interdisciplinary adventures have become mainline disciplinary endeavors.

Second, as the burgeoning growth of higher education in the post–World War II years came to an end, to be replaced by widespread stagnation, and even some decline, many institutions found that they could ill afford the growing particularism of the disciplines. The major research universities might be able to afford a specialist who works only on mathematical models of economic growth, but the smaller institutions, and the liberal arts colleges in particular, need someone who can not only teach a survey course in economic principles but can also contribute with scholars from other disciplines to a sequence on Western civilization and take part in a program on Third World development. In the aftermath of 9/11, colleges and universities are scrambling to meet the demand for courses on the history, cultures, and languages of Middle Eastern, particularly Islamic, countries. With insufficient faculty expertise in traditional disciplines, curricular developments have been largely interdisciplinary. In these ways, some interdisciplinarity has been market driven.

A third pressure for interdisciplinarity comes from beyond the professoriate and administrative leadership of the institutions; it comes from the student body, alumni, employers of students, and the wider community. Outside the academy, mounting interest in a range of urgent public policy problems, from hardcore poverty to environmental degradation, has led to calls for multidisciplinary approaches. Some academics have responded to these calls by saying that the way to understand the elephant is in fact to study the tail separately, then a toenail, and then the trunk. However, neither students nor the public, those who pay for higher education, find this response deeply persuasive, and they tend to vote with their feet and their dollars for courses and research projects which, at a minimum, look at tail and toenail in some kind of juxtaposition or which place tail studies and toenail studies together. Hence we have the growth of interdisciplinary teaching and research programs and projects dealing with women's studies, the environment, the urban crisis, cultural studies, and numerous other rubrics that do not correspond to the conventional disciplinary map.

So what should the young scholar do when confronted with a fashion like interdisciplinary studies? The first thing is to figure out just what is meant by the term. In this case, considerable confusion is injected by the bountiful rhetoric that surrounds it. Administrators, funding agents, public figures, and some faculty colleagues are all likely to applaud the concept of interdisciplinarity without ever explaining or perhaps even understanding what it is.

For your purposes, as a young scholar, it may be suggested that there are three principal meanings of the term. The first (which might better be called "multidisciplinarity") refers to arrangements through which scholars from many disciplines come together collaboratively to address a topic that transcends any one. They may do this informally or formally, in a program or a center. But each scholar does not abandon disciplinary practices or loyalties. The environment is a case in point. Here there are puzzles aplenty for biologists, physicists, economists, sociologists, psychologists, ethicists, and a good many other disciplinarians. In this kind of interdisciplinary collaboration, each disciplinarian typically remains firmly rooted in the mother discipline but addresses a piece of the puzzle that is susceptible to that discipline's tools. Someone on the team may attempt to integrate the disciplines and their findings to produce an aggregate understanding of the problem, but this need not affect the research of any one contributor.

This is the form of interdisciplinary activity that is least problematic and potentially most rewarding for the young scholar. You may discover the joys of team teaching and that your course offerings are enlivened by the challenge of contrasting viewpoints. You will discover that some of the brightest students will resonate to this multidisciplinary orientation in a way that they do not to your specialized subdiscipline. Some funding agencies, especially private foundations and problem-oriented parts of government (for example, departments of energy, education, labor), may be more sympathetic to this approach than to conventional science. In addition, the stimulus of interaction with unfamiliar colleagues, as well as institutional gratitude for "community service," may be significant. For some future employers, participation in multidisciplinary projects may demonstrate an admirable imagination and openness of mind. The scholarly costs of such interdisciplinary activity are the amount of conventional disciplinary work that is sacrificed thereby and—in some cases a not inconsiderable factor—the displeasure of some senior colleagues who may perceive even the most productive interdisciplinary activity as frivolous, and consorting with certain "disreputable" other disciplines as particularly reprehensible.

The second form of interdisciplinary activity involves scholars who are firmly rooted in one discipline reaching out to another for tools and other devices that may be helpful to the borrower. In some cases where the benefits to the importing discipline are well established, this kind of reaching out is well regarded by the importing discipline, as in the case today of botany taking from cell biology, political science taking from economics, or literary studies borrowing from anthropology. When all of these particular borrowings began, they were considered dangerously heretical. Now they are routine. But there are other cases where borrowing is quite new; where it is from disciplines that are viewed with suspicion within the importing discipline (for example, economics from psychology or political science from history). Here young scholars must be sensitive to the professional image of dilettantism that may be created and also to whether they really have command of the "borrowed" tools or are going to appear simplistic.

The third kind of interdisciplinarity is the most hazardous to the health of a young scholar. This is where adherence to a single discipline is essentially abandoned by a scholar and use is made of tools and materials from whatever disciplines or professions seem most appropriate for the occasion. This is the case where the physicist decides to teach science through biography, an engineer gives a course in the novel in order to demonstrate the two cultures, and the physician teaches about Third World development based on experience in the Peace Corps. Any of these experiments can have high payoffs. But they can also fall very flat. Except for the most exceptional individuals, this approach requires the sacrifice of commitment in any one discipline or profession and therefore invites the contempt of strict disciplinarians. Despite the excitement it promises, this essentially "nondisciplinary" stance is better attempted by a scholar near the end of an academic career who has little to lose from the wrath of peers.

This brief summary account has not covered all the complexities of interdisciplinary interactions by any means. For example, a scholar's place on the landscape of a particular institution may be highly relevant. Interdisciplinary activities may be easier in the liberal arts college than in the large research university and within a single professional faculty or one arts and sciences "area" (for example, social sciences, or arts and literature) than across faculties and areas. In some institutions, administrators construct friendly interfaces for interdisciplinary interactions, in others they could not care less. As noted earlier, many institutions have created formal interdisciplinary centers which have their own faculty lines quite separate from traditional disciplinary departments. At times, faculty in such positions have very close and supportive relations with their disciplinary colleagues; at others, they may feel not only isolated but also rejected as a true scholarly peer. Here, as in all the situations I have been discussing, interdisciplinarity is a condition that should be well understood by the young academic before being attempted and should be entered into only after the complex costs and benefits have been carefully scrutinized and found to yield a positive balance.

INTERNATIONALIZATION

The second fashion that I wish to explore is for "internationalization" of the campus. Like the pressure for interdisciplinarity, it is based on solid ground but is surrounded by various swamps and quicksands. Some leaders and observers of American academe believe that higher education has been in the vanguard of the national conversion from isolation to cosmopolitan involvement in world affairs. They point to the enormous increase in foreign students on campuses, the impressive but more modest growth of study abroad by Americans, the involvement of academe in overseas development programs, area studies, and the establishment of numerous schools and centers and institutes devoted to international and security affairs. Skeptics respond, however, that these developments have affected the campuses at large remarkably little other than to construct ghettos within which international activities can be segregated and ignored. Fifteen years ago, with the end of the Cold War and a seeming loss of commitment to the developing world, the prewar provincialism and isolation of American campuses seemed to be returning once again. After 9/11, many conservatives on and off the campus have come to associate interest in other countries with lack of patriotism, and "multicultural" has joined "liberal" as an epithet of the right. Not many American scholars, indeed, have ongoing interactions with their counterparts overseas. Today, with foreign enrollments under increasing pressure and with fewer faculty seriously engaged in cross-cultural research or other international collaborations, the so-called globalization of the American campus is more of a veneer than a reality. Here, the "flat world" model does not seem to work.

Why should it matter to the American academic community, and to you in particular, who are just beginning an academic career, that understanding of the world on the campus is limited. At least three reasons are typically suggested. First, isolation to a single nation's culture cuts a scholar off from the richness of the intellectual life of a majority of humankind. For a few years after World War II, it might have been argued that in some fields at least this isolationism was not very costly. In the sciences especially, the frontiers of scholarship were squarely in the United States and foreign innovations were certain to come to the United States so that Americans would not have to seek them out. If this situation was ever true, even in the sciences, it is surely not true today, and above all, not in the humanities, social sciences, or professional areas. The incapacity to communicate effectively abroad for an academic is a scholarly as well as a cultural obstacle. In some research areas like aquaculture or civil engineering, you simply may not be able to remain on the scholarly frontier without a command of Korean or Spanish or of the Korean and Chilean cultures where research is under way. As a young scholar, you should always entertain the possibility that scholars halfway around the globe may be as relevant to your work as those in the next office, if not now then soon.

The second reason for a new emphasis on internationalization of the academy is that almost all college graduates today are required by circumstances to understand the world. Whether they become businesspersons, engineers, journalists, public officials, or enter almost any other occupation, they will be faced inevitably over their life spans with a host of people and things that are not American. To the degree that they remain unfamiliar with this "difference," they will be unable to cope. Indeed, recognizing this reality ahead of their teachers, students (both American and foreign) have formed one of the most strenuous forces pressing for the introduction of international material into the curricula of the liberal arts college and the professional schools. They demand that you prepare them for a world they will face that is already highly diverse and is becoming more so.

The third reason to internationalize the campus is because so many of the problems that we face today within the United States are multinational in their origin and solution. Not only do the traditional international relations problems of war and peace know no national borders, but environmental degradation, ethnic conflict, AIDS, and a host of other issues span the globe. If we are to attack these problems through our research, and as citizens, we must understand other places and other peoples. Like it or not, the rest of the world, as 9/11 and its aftermath have clearly shown, is part of each problem and each solution.

So what will the American campus do in the years ahead to internationalize itself? First, there is likely to be a premium on well-traveled faculty and students — those who can move comfortably in a culture other than their own. This is evident already in professional fields such as business and law. This premium may be reflected even more widely in appointment and employment. Second, curricular material will reflect contributions from abroad in languages other than English and with more description from the experiences of other nations. Third, interinstitutional exchange of students and faculty is bound to increase, with regular exposure to a foreign environment expected to be routine. Finally, the presumption will continue to grow that the world community of scholars is the appropriate reference group for American scholars, rather than a regional or even national one. Employment, student selection, peer review, and audience identification all may become global with their reference sets perhaps extending first throughout the developed, industrialized countries and then into the developing ones.

How should the young scholar react to the pressure for internationalization in higher education? The best answer seems to be "with a positive attitude but with care." The particular circumstances and attitudes of home disciplines and institutions must be attended carefully, first of all. For example, in some disciplines, like political science, civil engineering, and literature, and at some liberal arts colleges, the wave of internationalization is in full flood and the young scholar is probably safe to ride it with abandon, to visit abroad, to publish abroad, and to develop a coterie of colleagues abroad who will testify when tenure review comes along. One means to get overseas for the first time, that is open to practitioners of almost any discipline, is to join the faculty of an overseas study program and use the opportunity to sample the cultural and scholarly life of another country. In some disciplines, like chemistry, economics, and electrical engineering, and especially at major research institutions, international activities in these areas are likely to generate only muted applause, and even a few boos. International involvement in these areas and places may be interpreted as frivolous and lacking in seriousness ("why wasn't he back in the lab?"). Young scholars should determine the special circumstance they face in a department and on a campus and gauge the individual implications of international circumstances. You must take stock of the manifold benefits of joining in the internationalization of your discipline and institution. But at least until tenure has been gained, you must appreciate that this may be a controversial path with costs and dangers that you need to take into account. The optimum position for the young scholar is squarely on top of an academic wave, not too far in front where drowning awaits or too far in the rear where the action has already passed and the water is merely stagnant. This advice holds for internationalization as well as for interdisciplinarity and other fads and fashions.

CONCLUSION

These two examples of fads and fashions on the American campus have been described only as representative of a well-populated and evolving species to which young scholars will inevitably be exposed and with which they should routinely become familiar. Other examples might include gender studies and ethics in the disciplines and professions. Fads and fashions may be the source of stimulation, intellectual enrichment, and support for the new scholar. They can also be dangerous traps for the unwary. The challenge is to make sure they are the former and not the latter.

8

FREE SPEECH AND ACADEMIC FREEDOM

RONALD R. BUTTERS

For several years now, it has seemed to many observers that free speech and academic freedom — two of the institutions most cherished by members of the professoriate — have been under fairly constant attack. Recent high-profile free-speech cases would certainly include the anthropologist Ward Churchill at the University of Colorado and the computer science professor Sami al-Arian at the University of South Florida. The current climate is further evident in the increased influence of the radical right in curricular matters at public and private universities, in the resistance to the suddenly increasing numbers of Holocaust deniers in the academy, in potential effects of the Patriot Act, in government subpoenas to various online entities such as Google and America Online, in government wiretapping of citizens, and in the publication in student newspapers of the hugely controversial Muslim cartoons. The relatively new online academic site Inside Higher Education (www.insidehighered.com) already has a substantial archive on these post-9/11 matters. Despite these ominous signs, I believe that academic freedom and free speech are alive and well in the groves of academe — more so, I believe, than ever before. Academic freedom and free speech can stay that way if students, faculty members, and administrators remain dedicated and vigilant.

Let us distinguish first between the two institutions.

Free speech is a political right to unfettered expression granted to all citizens by the First Amendment to the United States Constitution: "Congress shall make no law . . . abridging the freedom of speech, or of the press." No one has ever seriously suggested that these rights to expression, extended by judicial interpretation to limit the powers of all branches of government as well as Congress, should be absolute; indeed, despite the First Amendment's seemingly unambiguous wording, the list of kinds of speech that the U.S. government has successfully "abridged" is long and includes criminal solicitation, perjury, sedition, assault, conspiracy, incitement, commercial fraud, obscenity, and talking out loud in the public library. Other linguistic acts, such as slander, libel, copyright infringement, and breach of promise, though not violations of criminal law, are nonetheless punishable by government through civil penalties assessed in the courts as the result of lawsuits brought by the aggrieved parties. In deciding how to go about limiting the seemingly unlimitable constitutional right to free speech, the courts quickly settled upon instrumental criteria that judges inferred to have been in the minds of the authors of the First Amendment: roughly that, to be constitutionally protected, the function of the expression in doubt must be to help at arriving at truth — particularly political truth; and to be excluded from First Amendment protection, the expression must be seriously dangerous or disruptive — or both — to society. Obviously, lots of what today are voguishly called "judgment calls" have arisen in the application of such vague and potentially conflicting criteria.

Most important for our purposes here, free speech is specifically protected constitutionally only against *government* "abridgement." As far as the First Amendment is concerned, private employers may fire their employees for linguistic acts that displease them (though there are growing exceptions to this that stem in large part from legislation and other parts of the Constitution), churches are not constrained from excommunicating those who utter heretical doctrines, and parents may order their children not to say taboo words (and punish them if they do not comply). *Academic freedom* therefore carves out additional rights for persons who study, teach, or do research within an educational institution. It relates both directly and indirectly to constitutionally protected free speech.

Directly, academic freedom derives legal power from the fact that many schools are publicly supported and hence arms of government. For example, when (in 1969) the U.S. Supreme Court ruled that public high school students in Des Moines had the right to wear black armbands to class (so long as they did so in a nondisruptive manner) as a protest against the government's Vietnam War policies, the courts felt empowered to so rule because the schools in question were in a real sense branches of the government of the state of Iowa (and because the protest was "political" enough in nature that it seemed to be exactly the sort of speech that the authors of the Bill of Rights intended to protect in creating the First Amendment). But even the right to academic freedom that this landmark case represents is legally tenuous, complicated by the fact that (again) the protection of free speech is not absolute: when a federal judge ruled (in 1992) that the public schools of Norfolk, Virginia, had the right to prohibit a fourteen-year-old girl from wearing a T-shirt that said "Drugs

Suck" on its front, he certainly took into account the fact that the schools were government-supported and that the purpose of the message might possibly be sufficiently serious and "political" in the broadest sense of the term. He granted that the message might not have been disruptive (though one school administrator argued that the word *suck*, displayed on the precociously endowed chest of a nubile female, could sexually arouse others and hence seriously disrupt classes). But the judge ruled against the suit of the girl and her parents on the ground that teachers have a duty to censor what they in their professional judgment conclude to be ill-mannered, uncouth language—and he declared that *suck*, as used in the message of the T-shirt, if not obscene, is at least a slang usage the prohibition of which amounted to little more than an object lesson in language arts. Some teachers saw this conclusion as supportive of *their* academic freedom. The plaintiffs did not appeal.

Indirectly, academic freedom derives from the putative reasoning that lay behind the creation of the First Amendment: that the prohibition of ideas is dangerous because it runs the risk that truth will thereby be squelched (generally owing to the self-interest of the squelchers); and that truth will emerge only through dialogue and debate, whereby error will be revealed through communal reasoning, and self-interest will be unveiled and neutralized. Because the primary goal of educational institutions was assumed to be the discovery and dissemination of truth, the notion grew throughout the twentieth century that special protection should be given to the expressive acts of academics—teachers and researchers and, to a lesser extent, students—in their pursuit of truth.

Most of us, I think, still believe in the fundamental utility of this classical theory, however empty and corruptible it may seem to some (see, for example, Stanley Fish, *There's No Such Thing as Free Speech, and It's a Good Thing, Too.*[1] True, the critical weaknesses of the theory are clear enough, especially the fact that the interplay of competing viewpoints in the so-called marketplace of ideas is governed not only by dispassionate reason but also by economic forces (even the customary metaphor can be read as a dead giveaway that capitalistic powers are *really* in control), by the inertia of tradition, by kings and desperate rhetoricians. Doubtless, the most common way in which we human beings exercise "reason" is to begin with the conclusion that gives us the most power and satisfaction in the real world and from there work backward to our argument (and finally our basic premises, which are generally vague enough to support any argument that one cares to make). As thoughtful persons discover for themselves at about age fourteen, the fundamental notion of "truth" can be shown to be philosophically vacuous and in practice subject to frustrating manipulation by those more powerful than ourselves.

Well, so what. Despite all the evils that may have been inflicted upon Western culture in the name of free speech and even academic freedom, what alternative is there? As Annabel Patterson asks in responding to Fish's argument, "Whose sensibilities will count for most in . . . arguments, when there are no judges, with First Amendment principles to guide them, to adjudicate between us? None of these procedures, required to replace the current (admittedly imperfect) reliance on ubiquitous protection for speech, are even spelled out [by Fish]."[2] Most of us believe that freedom and fairness and truth are more humane — if not more human — ideals than power, gratification, and rhetorical prowess. Moreover, the icons of free speech, academic freedom, and fundamental truth have an important pragmatic function: they continue to inform our debates, to offer an opportunity to continue to try to "level the playing field" (another term that Fish eschews because his ideological opponents use it in ways that he doesn't approve of). Because of our emotional commitment to the primacy of such ideals, they can be made to give rhetorical advantage to the underdog in any argument — and at any given moment, the underdog may be us. Even Fish, who understands the limitations and perversions of our cultural icons, but not their value, agrees to the necessity of a practice that he finds theoretically impossible: disputants "need not throw up their hands or toss the dice; . . . they must argue, thrash it out, present bodies of evidence to one another and to relevant audiences, try to change one another's mind."[3] Free speech, academic freedom, and fundamental truth are the deeply revered names for the rules of precisely the contest that Fish here advocates, and though the rules obviously keep changing as society changes, to abandon the labels themselves — and with them their emotive and regulating powers — seems as disingenuous and disruptive as claiming that they "preside over the debate from a position outside it" (an idea that Fish rightly debunks).[4]

Despite the traditional (and I hope ongoing) commitment, academic freedom is largely not constitutionally protected (except in such roundabout ways as that of the Des Moines armband case), particularly not in private schools. Faculty members (and students) may enter into legal, contractual free-speech agreements between themselves and their colleges and universities, thereby extending academic freedom through the civil court system, but if Born Again University chooses to fire Professor Snopes for teaching evolution in his biology class or if some hypothetical private Fidel Castro College dismisses its chaplain for condemning abortion in his sermons, there may be little that those who have lost their jobs can do about it (absent an academic freedom guarantee in their contracts or academic freedom rights implicit in the documents of university governance) except complain to the American Association of University Professors, which may then place the schools on its list of censured institutions. While the most powerful and prestigious of universities generally try to avoid

AAUP censure, such condemnation is apparently of least consequence to those institutions most likely to incur it. In the end, although threats of civil action and AAUP condemnation surely act as powerful forces for academic freedom, the most significant incentive in favor of free expression within the academy is the force of evolved and evolving tradition, interwoven in complex, quasi-legal ways into the fabric of university governance: tenure procedures, grievance procedures, departmental organization, powers bestowed on the faculty senate.

Academic freedom is different for students and for faculty members (who have the most of it). For faculty members, moreover, there are different aspects to it: what one can say to students in the classroom (and out); what one has the right to teach and what one has the right to deal with in one's research; and what one can say in the public domain outside the university, particularly outside one's own specific area of expertise. Of this last I shall have little to say here except that the further one gets from one's area of expertise and the further one gets from classroom teaching and academic publishing, the weaker the protection of academic freedom.

ACADEMIC FREEDOM FOR STUDENTS

Until the last twenty-five years or so, the expressive rights of students have been less than a marginal issue not only in high schools but in colleges and universities as well. Student research has always by definition had to meet with the approval of faculty members. The speech of students within the classroom is heavily subject to the control and judgment of the teacher, who has an almost absolute right to assign grades on the basis of what the student says and even how he or she says it. Curricular matters have likewise always been decided by faculty members working through academic departments and faculty senates, though since the late 1960s there has been a tendency (at least in the universities that I have been associated with) to involve students in an advisory capacity, especially at the level of the committees that are considering curricular change. The faculty, however, generally have the final word, not only because the power structure assigns them the bulk of the decision making but also because the faculty maintain the institutional memory. The individual student, after all, rarely stays around more than four years (the same can also pretty much be said for most deans and department chairs), and her effective time usually excludes her first year, final semester, and all of her summers. The faculty, however, endures, perdures, and forgets nothing.

The issue of sanctions upon the nonacademic speech of students has recently become a live issue because some schools have created (1) formal sexual harassment codes that attempt to define in detail the limits of what one student must or must not say or do to another when making romantic overtures; and (2) so-called hate-speech codes (some of which have been tested in the courts and generally found unconstitutionally too vague) that supposedly are designed to protect racial, ethnic, and other minorities from the "psychological damage" of "having their feelings hurt" (as those who oppose such codes generally put it).

There is, however, nothing particularly new about college administrators' attempts to control the sexual behavior of students; whereas today some schools are attempting to deal with the more serious problems by prescribing linguistic and behavioral guidelines, until the late 1960s schools simply kept the sexes apart as much as possible, required them to be fully clothed in loose-fitting garments when they were together, and locked up the women at night under the watchful eyes of housemothers. Homosexual passion was assumed not to exist and severely punished when its reality intruded too obviously. Likewise, there is nothing at all new about attempts at suppressing those student utterances that faculty·members and administrators deem vulgar, cruel, or otherwise objectionable; by and large, all that has changed about "hate speech," if anything, is the nature of that which is deemed objectionable and the greatly lessened severity of the sanctions. In 1954 an eighteen-year-old undergraduate at a major southern university committed what was then a major speech crime: he confided to his roommate that he thought that he might himself be "homosexually" attracted to his fellow. Distraught, the roommate reported the confidence to the dean of students, who summoned the terrified "homosexual" to his office and expelled him summarily from the university. In the 1990s, the distraught roommate would in all likelihood report his roommate's confidence to the authorities only if he wanted to try to get a room reassignment, and no crime would have been committed—unless the roommate should, say, call the gay youth a "disgusting faggot" in front of other students, and perhaps tell anti-gay jokes as well. The sanctions against such harassment would be far milder than the draconian methods of the 1950s and earlier. Typically, hate-speech rules today censure a student convicted of such "insensitive" or harassing acts, and perhaps require him (or her) to attend "sensitivity workshops."

If I have to choose between the 1950s and the beginning of the twenty-first century with respect to the way administrators view and deal with speech infractions, I'll take the twenty-first century. In general, administrators seem to me to be less imperious and more humane today than they were in 1960, when I was an undergraduate. If we *must* continue to have formal hate-speech codes (and again, they are really little more than the watered-down legacy of an earlier era), they should merely be tools of last resort that the local Office of Student Life makes use of in keeping the peace among the disparate and volatile personalities who must live together in the confines of a college campus, especially those who find themselves living with unkindred fellows in the same dormitory or even the same room. Hate-speech codes most emphatically should (and in fact generally do) apply equally to protect all constituencies — not just ethnic and sexual minorities, but political and religious minorities as well.

Even so, in the end I have strong doubts about whether formal hate-speech codes are worth having. The Office of Student Life can generally deal with interpersonal problems among students without resort to such formal sets of rules. The dangers of vague language and overzealous implementation are real. Furthermore, it is hard to believe that mandatory sensitivity workshops or official censure will very effectively alter the mindset of either a vile-tongued hater of the Born Again or a bitter homophobe, both of whom will rebel at being subjected to the "political indoctrination" of "the New Fascism." In the end, such codes appear to me to be impressively self-defeating, for they furnish those who in their secret hearts are most opposed to an end to racism, sexism, homophobia, and religious and political intolerance with a smoke screen (what Stanley Fish rightly condemns as "moral algebra") behind which they can continue to do their nefarious work: if the codes themselves lead to unjust application and "brainwashing" sanctions, so goes the emotional logic, so, too, is the whole "emancipationist" enterprise the work of dangerous hypocrites. Thus I agree with the cultural conservatives who would in this case like to make a break with the draconian past and do away entirely with such codes — so long as we can do away with every code, expressed or implied, that any segment of the political spectrum would find objectionable.

ACADEMIC FREEDOM FOR FACULTY MEMBERS

The late sociologist Edward Shils, writing in the *American Scholar* (62 [1993]: 187–209]) describes what he sees as the expansion of classroom freedom for professors in the decades since the fall of Senator Joseph McCarthy in the 1950s:

> University administrators are nowadays very reluctant to dismiss, suspend, or take any other action against teachers whose conduct falls short of the traditional expectations of morality. . . . Dereliction of duty in teaching, always difficult to prove, is likewise viewed with a blind eye. More important . . . is the abstention of administrators from any sanctions against academics for radical political views or for political agitation in their classrooms.[5]

Like many conservatives, Shils is not entirely happy with this situation; though he cites no cases or other specific evidence, he feels certain that in American universities in recent years ... [there] has been the acceptance of the notion that a person who regards his or her task as a university teacher to make propaganda for socialism or for revolution among the students is not being un-faithful to his academic obligations and is therefore entitled to the protection of Academic Freedom. . . . They think that, as university teachers, they have a unique opportunity as well as a moral obligation to further the cause of revo-lution. . . . The American Association of University Professors never contended that teachers should be assured of a right to conduct political propaganda be-fore their students in class.[6]

Besides what he thus views as a serious abuse of academic freedom by leftist "polymorphous emancipationist antinomians" (his terms), Shils finds a most serious current danger to professors' academic freedom in the classroom—and in their research: "Where administrators do attempt to impose restrictions on verbal or graphic expression, it is usually on behalf of aggrieved and demanding groups of homosexuals, feminists, blacks, and Hispanics in the student body."[7] The sanctions he mentions are not nearly so serious as those of the old days. Professors are generally not fired for expressing their objectionable ideas, but, like students found guilty of hate-speech violations, they are sometimes re-quired to attend "sensitivity training" courses; or the "aggrieved" students are allowed to transfer to another class. Shils ought to have added, however, that complaints from "aggrieved" students can seriously affect promotion, tenure, raises, teaching assignments, access to research funds, even size and location of one's office. He ought to have added as well that the animus can come not only from fellow students but also from "aggrieved" alumni, "aggrieved" adminis-trators, and "aggrieved" fellow faculty members who may find the research of the individual faculty member to be ideologically objectionable.

Professor Shils's arguments here are repeated over and over in right-wing at-tacks on the current academy. As they frame the discourse, who can do anything but agree with Professor Shils that we must somehow stand vigilant against wrongs done to professors who may have their academic freedom infringed upon by "demanding groups" of students and others? And who cannot agree that professors who "conduct political propaganda before their students in class" have no right to do so? Where I *cannot* agree with the right-wing critics is (first) in the typical neoconservative limitations that they place upon the list that follows the passage I have just quoted: "homosexuals, feminists, blacks, and Hispanics in the student body." I would add to this list just about anybody one can think of who might be "aggrieved": moralists who would censure me if I find reason to illustrate my lectures with photographs by Robert Mapple-thorpe, cultural elitists who could not possibly believe that any good reason could exist for my assigning popular song lyrics as a part of the syllabus in a course on poetry, fundamentalists of all stripes who would deny me the right to discuss the literary treatment of atheism or homosexual passion or abortion or Islamic extremism or class exploitation or intergenerational sex or Palestine liberation as topics as worthy of serious and dispassionate and respectful examination as, say, Milton's ideas about marriage or Shakespeare's view of the Great Chain of Being. Though there certainly must be "polymorphous emancipationist antinomian" zealots of the left who are hard at work trying to censure and silence professors with whom they disagree, the left by no means has a monopoly on such zealotry. Indeed, it is members of the radical right that we see attempting by federal and state law to forbid teachers from "displaying homosexuality or the homosexual life-style in a positive light," members of the radical right whom we see attempting to forbid teachers from teaching that "Western culture is in any way inferior to other cultures," members of the anti-pregnancy-termination radical right who try to keep abortion instruction out of medical school curricula. My point is not merely that there are radical-right excesses today that are just as bad if not worse than the putative excesses of the left that so disturb Professor Shils and his fellows. Nor can one dispute the fact that radical-left excesses must be much more widespread than they were forty or thirty or even twenty years ago. In the old days, the academic left had so little power that there was little possibility of much excess from that direction — though there was a plethora of excess from the radical (and not-so-radical) right. With power comes the temptation to silence and exile the opposition, a temptation that must be resisted strenuously no matter which quarter it comes from, even when it comes from within ourselves and our ideological allies.

The second way in which I cannot agree with Shils's assessment of the current situation is in his belief that speech that reinforces rightist values is to be protected as a means to the search for "truth," whereas speech that challenges rightist values is "political agitation" and "propaganda for social revolution." He leaves unasked the hard question of how to distinguish the search for "truth" from the propagation of "propaganda"; his benchmark seems to be that what he agrees with is "truth" and what he disagrees with is "propaganda":

> The confluence of the valiant and long-overdue, if misguided, effort to eliminate discrimination against blacks and women with the emancipationist attitudes which were latent in collectivistic liberalism, and with an uprooted and disillusioned Marxism, has touched the foundations of academic freedom. It has touched the most crucial point in the justification of academic freedom. Academic freedom is only justified if it serves the causes of the discovery and transmission of truth by scientific and scholarly procedures.

An aggressive and intimidating body of antinomian academic opinion has gained in strength. . . .

In its view the equality of "genders," the equality of "races," the equality of "cultures," the normality of homosexuality are the only real values, while the criteria of truthfulness are illusory, deceptive, and fundamentally intended to exploit women, people of color, homosexuals, and the poor. The value of academic freedom is denied; it counts for nothing alongside these other values, since the truth which it would protect is declared to be an illusion.[8]

The passage demonstrates that "political correctness" is at least as much a conservative's failing as a liberal's. Its author assumes that rightist theoretical positions (anticommunism, the "abnormality" of homosexuality, conventional roles for men and women, the superiority of Western culture, even, seemingly, the inequality of races) are "truths" and therefore apolitical and the only valid starting place for any classroom treatment of subject matter. Nonrightist theoretical positions (for example, "the normality of homosexuality"), however, are "misguided, . . . collectivistic, . . . uprooted Marxism," mere "antinomian academic opinion" that is, furthermore, "aggressive and intimidating." For him, the theoretical positions he so disagreeably caricatures do not "serve the causes of the discovery and transmission of truth by scientific and scholarly procedures" and are thus to be dismissed as political and their interjection into classroom discourse justifiably prohibitable as the pure "propagandizing" efforts of a corrupt and deceitful professoriate. (Though it is incidental to Shils's article, such right-wing political correctness colors as well much of the current vigorous debate about what should be taught in colleges and universities—the canon, the nature of the curriculum, the idea of what counts as a proper university course, even the proper goals of a college education.)

I must say that I sympathize with Edward Shils's all-too-human impulses. I feel similar tendencies in myself. When I imagine all those people whom I don't know as individuals and who go into print with such views as Professor Shils's, I, too, tend to summon up images of fools and demons and fascist torturers—just as Shils imagines "polymorphous emancipationist antinomians" who were so traumatized by McCarthyism that they turned thereby against their culture, their heritage, and maybe even their God, and whose "only real values" are "equality"![9] But then I remind myself that there are social conservatives who are good teachers and scholars (who, in Shils's terms, struggle against the tendency to propagandize in their own work), just as I will continue to try to ensure that there are social radicals (I consider myself to be one) who are also good teachers and scholars (who try to educate, not propagandize); although the struggle for equality of opportunity is very important to me, "emancipationist" goals are scarcely my "only real values." Rightist values are in reality no more "traditional" than liberal values—they just emphasize different aspects of the tradition. And I continue to have faith that (as Stanley Fish puts it) only by continuing to "argue, thrash it out, present bodies of evidence to one another and to relevant audiences, try[ing] to change one another's mind" do we ever have a chance of realizing Shils's goal of "the discovery and transmission of truth." Only by continuing to strive for—and exercise—academic freedom (in the sense that I hope Edward Shils *fundamentally* meant it) will we ever get anywhere that is better than where we have been and where we are now.

NOTES

1. Stanley Fish, *There's No Such Thing as Free Speech, and It's a Good Thing, Too* (New York: Oxford University Press, 1994).
2. Annabel Patterson, "More Speech on Free Speech," *Modern Language Quarterly* (March 1993): 64.
3. Fish, *There's No Such Thing as Free Speech*, 10.
4. Ibid., 11.
5. Edward Shils, "Do We Still Need Academic Freedom?" *American Scholar* 62 (1993): 197.
6. Ibid., 199–200.
7. Ibid., 198.
8. Ibid., 209.
9. Ibid.

9.

ANTICIPATING AND AVOIDING

MISPERCEPTIONS OF HARASSMENT

JUDITH S. WHITE

Harassment. The word disturbs people. To start there is the question of how you pronounce it. HAR ass ment? ha RASS ment? I prefer the second. It sounds ugly and harsh to me. That is how harassment feels to people experiencing it. Some people use the word as a joke. Every time someone disagrees with something they have said, they declare "harassment." But either way you say it, harassment is not a joke.

Harassment interferes with teaching and learning. Understanding what it means and how to avoid it are important for you as you make a career in the academy. What I describe is not a list of actions that constitute harassment and thus a list of what to avoid. That is not "understanding" harassment. What I do in this essay is give some background on how we have come to define harassment on campuses today and offer you some advice on how to anticipate and avoid situations in which someone may perceive that harassment has occurred.

For purposes of this essay, I am making some assumptions about you. I assume that you have no desire to exchange sexual favors for academic assistance and no intention of using hostile and intimidating behavior as a pedagogical style. That you have not thought much about what harassment may mean — beyond the horror stories on campus or in the newspapers — and would really rather avoid the topic. I realize that you may be a target of harassment yourself, but in this particular piece I am focusing on situations in which students are the target of harassment. I have chosen this focus in order to address the main issue raised in most of my discussions with faculty — fear that something they or their colleagues have done will be wrongly interpreted as harassment.

In order to avoid situations in which such misinterpretations can occur, you must think about how certain behaviors are likely to be perceived and how you can make your intentions clearer. You cannot do that by avoiding the topic or clinging to a set of rules. Being active about complying with your institution's harassment policy is your best strategy for preventing harassment and harassment complaints from interfering with your work.

UNDERSTANDING WHAT HARASSMENT MEANS ON YOUR CAMPUS

You can better anticipate your responses to misperceptions of harassment if you understand what "harassment" means on your campus. All colleges and universities are mandated to create their own harassment policies and make sure that procedures for investigating alleged violations are fair and accessible to all parties. Policies at different schools vary, but they generally follow certain models and they all have their roots in the evolving discrimination law of the past thirty years.

Harassment discussions generally begin with an understanding of "sexual harassment." In the late 1970s, judges in several important cases ruled that employers demanding sexual favors in exchange for jobs or promotions were not engaged in "courtship"—behaviors that follow "naturally" when people are attracted to each other—but were instead abusing their power as employers—taking advantage of the economic vulnerability of a subordinate to extort unwanted sexual activity. And because these sexual favors were being demanded only of certain employees, targeted because of their sex, the judges agreed that such activity was a form of sex discrimination. The legal terminology for this sort of exchange is *quid pro quo*, this for that. So the first form of harassment to gain recognition by the courts is generally referred to as quid pro quo sexual harassment.

Two major changes have occurred since these early legal cases that complicate our understanding of harassment significantly. The first of these was the evolution of another definition of sexual harassment to add to that of quid pro quo harassment. The Equal Employment Opportunity Commission (EEOC) definition of sexual harassment "by the creation of a hostile environment" is more open-ended than that of quid pro quo harassment. The harasser does not have to be a person with direct power over an individual's job; but rather the person has the power, usually by force of social threat or peer pressure, to make an individual's life on the job miserable. The intent of the EEOC's sexual harassment policy is to stop such behavior that singles out individuals because of their sex, whether female or male.

The second significant change comes from recognizing that people can be targeted for the creation of a hostile environment based on many reasons other than sex. EEOC guidelines define quite broadly what is to be understood as harassment in the workplace. At the same time, the Department of Education and the U.S. Office of Civil Rights also developed guidelines for defining and dealing with racial harassment on campuses. Today it is clear that academic institutions are being held responsible for harassment of many sorts perpetrated by faculty and other employees toward employees and students, and by students against employees.

All of this is pertinent to you because most colleges and universities have used definitions of harassment that closely reflect the language of the EEOC guidelines:

> unwelcome sexual advances, requests for sexual favors, and other verbal or physical conduct of a sexual nature when (1) submission to such conduct is made either explicitly or implicitly a term or condition of an individual's employment, or (2) submission to or rejection of such conduct by an individual is used as the basis for employment decisions affecting an individual, or (3) such conduct has the purpose or effect of unreasonably interfering with an individual's work performance or creating an intimidating, hostile, or offensive working environment.[1]

Early on many schools using this definition focused primarily on sexual harassment, but some extended the language of the EEOC guidelines on "hostile environment" to other forms of harassment as well, thus creating "general harassment" policies. Now that the EEOC and the Office of Civil Rights have published guidelines for other forms of harassment and listed specific responsibilities of campuses for monitoring those other forms of harassment, more campuses have instituted broader harassment policies.

A smaller number of colleges and universities, and some professional associations, have chosen to use a definition of sexual harassment that is not derived from the EEOC guidelines. While the EEOC model focuses on legal definitions of sex discrimination in all work settings, this approach focuses on the professional ethical issues specific to those of us in academic institutions. The 1993 American Philological Society Statement of Professional Ethics reads as follows: "Sexual harassment may be broadly defined as any unsolicited or objectionable emphasis on the sexuality or sexual identity of another person that might limit that individual's full participation in the academic community."[2] Note that no formal element of coercion is required in this definition. Because this policy sets as its goal "full participation in the academic community," it covers the student who is obliged to be in class or to meet an adviser in order to pursue legitimate academic interests and must in those settings unwillingly experience gratuitous sexual attention. The intensity of the behavior does not have to reach a level of "hostility" or "intimidation" — only a level that would divert attention from the academic subject at hand and focus it instead on the sex or sexuality of a specific student.

This sort of definition was originally created specifically to cover sexual harassment. The same format has also served for defining other forms of harassment as well. The intent of such policy statements is to go beyond the current state of the law to address the ethical issue of why professors bring any topic or approach into their classrooms. Such policies avoid the quarrel about what legal curbs can be placed on the speech of faculty because they direct attention to the faculty member's responsibilities and goals. If the subject is gratuitous and potentially harmful to students learning in that setting, then that subject would not meet academic goals and thus would be best left for other occasions.

You should be aware that some universities have written policies to curb behaviors that may not fit legal definitions of harassment but that are deemed to be out of keeping with the responsibilities of a faculty member. Some policies forbid, or strongly advise against, consensual sexual relationships between students and faculty. By definition, truly "consensual" relationships cannot be considered a form of sexual harassment because the first defining characteristic of sexual harassment is "unwanted" sexual activity. However, many would argue that the unequal power and status of the student and faculty member would make equal consent hard to imagine. But even those who argue that equal consensual relationships could exist under these circumstances may agree that such relationships complicate and potentially compromise the sort of attention professors can give a student with whom they are sexually involved, or the attention other students will get while such a relationship is being pursued with a special student. A policy on consensual sexual relationships with students can be added as separate from the sexual harassment definition and still be binding as an expectation of professional behavior.

Your first responsibility in dealing with harassment on your campus is to know your college or university's policy, its definitions and intentions. Once again, you are not likely to find a set of rules. You will find definitions of behaviors that are prohibited because they interfere with the academic mission of your institution and its responsibilities as an employer. If you find these definitions less than adequate for your own understanding of harassment, follow your personal guidelines in going beyond the institution's requirements. If you find the policy too restrictive for your understanding of harassment, speak to those in charge of administering the policy so that you understand the definitions fully. If you still disagree, register your protest and begin working with others to propose alternatives. In the meantime, follow the policy. Your institution has specific mandates to follow state and federal law on discrimination and harassment. Harassment is not an area in which you can simply make up your own rules.

Rules. I find that many faculty are indeed looking for just that—rules. I am frequently asked to give a list of things not to do. Or to ratify someone else's list: "I never touch a student who is crying. I always leave my door open. I never mention how anyone looks." I generally refuse to respond to requests framed in this manner. Too often such requests are only a way of asking, "How can I cover myself and then stop thinking about this topic?" Harassment does not work that way, and neither does your responsibility as a professor. Instead, I offer only one rule, then I have some advice that should help you in most other situations.

First, the rule. *Do not exchange professional attention—or grades or recommendations—for sexual favors.* Such behavior is illegal and unethical. This is true even if you believe a student is offering such activity willingly in order to gain advantage. If there is an advantage to be gained from you for participating in such behavior, the exchange is considered quid pro quo sexual harassment. If you encounter a student whose behavior seems to fit this pattern, try ignoring it if there is a chance you may be misinterpreting something. If it becomes clear that you are not mistaken about the intention, then be clear about your response. Tell the student that you do not participate in such exchanges and that in order for him or her to do better in your courses, you expect harder or smarter work, not bribery!

In this vein, I will also offer some related advice. Don't flirt with your students. I mean do not get into relationships marked by exchanges of bantering or teasing with sexual connotations. None of us ever knows how others will interpret our behavior; helping you think about unexpected responses is what this essay is all about. But it is quite predictable that flirtatious behavior is open to various interpretations and likely to end in misunderstanding about meaning and motives.

Sometimes faculty will raise concerns about students who have "crushes" that turn into harassment charges. If it is true that a student has held you in silent admiration and suddenly imagines that your lack of response constitutes "harassment," then you are facing an unsubstantiated charge and should follow advice I offer later in this essay. It is much more likely, however, that what some faculty members may call a crush is really a flirtation gone sour. And now the faculty member who had enjoyed the low-level titillation of flirtatious conversation will suffer the embarrassment of having witty double-entendre quoted back as evidence of sexual attention. The best defense against that sort of situation is not to get yourself into the situation.

BE ACTIVE IN COMPLYING WITH THE HARASSMENT POLICY

Now some more positive advice: Be active about complying with your school's harassment policy. Do not simply wait, hoping that harassment will not happen to you or to your students, or that no one will perceive your behavior as harassing. It is much better to consider harassment issues right along with other important matters as you set your goals for interacting with your students and your colleagues.

You will note that I have used the phrase "complying with" your institution's policy rather than "supporting" it. I have done that for two reasons. First, I do not expect that every faculty member will be pleased with the harassment policy of every college or university; yours may appear to be too much or too little for your understanding of the problem. So "supporting" the policy may be more than you can do. Nonetheless, you will be expected to comply with it until you help change it.

Second, often well-meaning people will consider themselves "supporters" of antiharassment efforts while assuming that the policy really does not apply to them personally. Thus some "nice people" can find themselves without a clear understanding of the complicated meanings of harassment and the new responsibilities placed upon faculty to prevent harassing situations. "Harassment" is not just blatant stuff that only fools would do. Often harassment comes in quite subtle forms. You need to understand the subtle forms so you can anticipate those situations and avoid anyone's misunderstanding your actions.

ANTICIPATE SITUATIONS

Two guidelines for your own interactions with students and colleagues should go a long way toward avoiding such misunderstandings:

1. Articulate your goals.

2. Offer alternatives for meeting the goals.

I urge you to think right now about your goals for teaching and for being a member of a department and wider university community. What are you trying to accomplish? What sort of relationships do you want to develop to do those things? Once you have those ideas clear for the big picture, practice asking yourself those questions about small encounters. It is the small encounters that make for the bigger relationships.

Let's start with a situation raised frequently in harassment discussions. What if a student starts to cry when the two of you are alone? Should you touch the student? What is your goal in this situation? To comfort the student? To control the episode? To end the conversation? Do any of these goals involve touching the student? Let's say your goal is to comfort the student before determining whether this is a good time to continue the conversation. Touching the student is one way to offer comfort. But are there other ways to do that? You might feel comforted by being touched, but could that make the student feel even more awkward?

I would advise telling the student what your goal is — "I'd like to help you feel better right now" — and offer a couple of ways of doing that — "Can I get you some water or a tissue?" If the student accepts either and is trying to calm down and go on with the conversation, you have achieved your goal. If the student seems unable to calm down, then you might make another pair of offers — "I can sit here with you, if that would help; or I can leave you alone for a few minutes." Either gesture could have the desired effect, depending on whether the student responds well to having another person there for support or prefers privacy in such awkward moments.

By considering your goals, by evaluating your options, by allowing the student some choice, you increase the likelihood that the awkward moment will pass and that you can both get back to shared academic goals. The biggest problem I have observed about a faculty member hugging a distraught student is not an intention or perception of harassment but an inappropriate assumption that the student wants the moment prolonged or escalated rather than contained. Such an unwanted escalation, particularly in the form of unwanted touching, can make future interactions strained and unproductive.

Let's move on to a more complicated situation and try to understand a student's perspective on the matter. In the first situation, the crying episode, many faculty members can imagine that they might feel uncomfortable with a distraught student. But the key to avoiding perceptions of harassment is trying to imagine what could make the *student* feel uncomfortable when you the professor see nothing wrong.

It is important to remember that coercion can be experienced quite acutely in rather subtle situations. Those are the ones to work on avoiding. The element of coercion comes from making someone feel that academic resources are available only in exchange for sexual favors. "Resources" is a broad term meant to convey the wide range of power that can be used to coerce sexual activity. Grades or employment are obvious resources; recommendations, nominations, endorsements are clearly resources, although harder to track in comparing fair and unfair treatment. But time, attention, and energy are also resources that teachers offer students. Offering these based on a desire for sexual activity —

even the pleasure of having a particularly attractive person around more often — is an act of dubious ethics.

Coercion can be explicit or implicit. The professor who makes explicit bribes or threats is still out there; but most coercive behavior is not blatant, it is somewhere short of an open proposition of resources for sexual activity. Most people would recognize the implicit coercion in a remark like this: "Your dissertation defense is only a month away. I think it would go much better if you and I spend more time together between now and then." And most people would be suspicious of an explanation like this: "Well, it would go better. I was only offering a little extra assistance." But few faculty stop to consider how their own "indirect signals" might be read in a similar way.

A professor who was really offering "extra assistance" could surely convey that offer with sufficient clarity to avoid misunderstanding. All of us dealing with students should strive for such clarity. A professor who offers to meet a student "outside of class" — either for coffee or at home or at the student's residence — may well be seeking to be more "accessible" to that student. But if a student's desire is really only for a professor who is more available, who is there when the student needs help, then moving the meeting to an unconventional setting may feel awkward rather than more open. A professor who makes such an offer may well be read as making a "demand" — setting an expectation that extra time and attention will come only on the professor's terms and in exchange for consent to unwanted circumstances.

So what can you do? Avoid all meetings outside your office? No. Concerns about harassment should not be used to avoid your students or abandon efforts to spend time with them in settings you may all enjoy. Instead, go back to first principles: (1) articulate your goal in this particular situation, and (2) offer the student an affirmative alternative for meeting it.

"I am trying to finish grading at home tomorrow. It would be convenient for me to have you meet me there in the afternoon. If you are available the next day, I'll be back on campus and we can meet at my office."

"I think it would be fun to try out the new ice cream place while we talk about this report. Maybe there's someone else from the class who can join us. Or I can bring a cone back and meet you in my office at three."

In either of these examples, the student can decide whether your convenience or your desire for ice cream seems reason enough to depart from conventional settings for student-faculty interaction; the offers include a way for the student to respond affirmatively to a conventional option. Forcing a student to say "no" to an option, to oppose you, while asking you for help can easily be read as coercive behavior, regardless of your intention.

When you articulate your goals for choosing another meeting place and make it clear that they are separable from the student's primary goal—getting academic assistance—then you have kept the focus on the student's needs rather than your own preferences. The student's academic progress is, of course, your primary goal as well as the student's goal.

I have urged you to undertake these responsibilities as part of actively complying with your institution's harassment policy. It is not necessary, or even desirable, that you undertake this responsibility alone. You would be much better off discussing these issues whenever opportunities arise in classes or in situations with colleagues. It would be a good idea to encourage your chair to discuss these issues at department meetings. If you are not eager to be the only one identified with questions about harassment, you can enlist other colleagues to ask for such discussions. If you think the issues need to be raised but do not find support within your department, you can generally find help from the dean or from those responsible for administering your harassment policy. Harassment prevention education is an important part of your institution's mandate under the federal civil rights laws.

I have been talking about being observant of your own behavior and enlisting colleagues to help you avoid potential misunderstandings about harassment. What do you do if you observe what you perceive is harassment on the part of a colleague? The inclination of most people who see inappropriate behavior by a colleague is to ignore it. If you have reason to think the behavior is out of character and perhaps an inadvertent episode, ignoring it may be best. But if you observe the behavior more than once, and the impact on the colleague's students concerns you, you will have to be direct. Most harassing behavior is part of a strong pattern. It is not likely to be interrupted by subtle cues—even less by silence or neglect.

If you are dealing with a colleague with whom you have, for other reasons, an unpleasant working relationship, you may need to seek help in confronting that person about something as sensitive as harassment. But if you have an otherwise functional working relationship with the person, try the "helpful colleague" approach: "I know you meant that as a compliment, but I don't enjoy comments about my figure. It makes me wonder whether that's all you see of me." "I don't know him very well, but I thought that student looked rather uncomfortable while you had your arm around him." Such entrées come from the "I thought you'd want to know . . ." school of confrontation. What if you get a hostile response? Then you have learned that the problem is more serious than you thought, and you need to get someone else to help. If you get a slightly awkward thank you, you may well have helped a colleague avoid unnecessary trouble in the future.

The helpful colleague approach, difficult as it may seem, will probably feel easy compared to your sense of burden the first time a student comes to talk with you about "a problem" he or she is having with one of your colleagues. Although your school probably has deans or others designated to advise students concerned about harassment, experience indicates that students turn to people they trust. Often that is a faculty member rather than a "designated person."

The report coming to you may be about a colleague whose behavior you have wondered about from your own observations. It may be about someone you know well and who you cannot believe would deliberately act in the way described. In either case, your responsibilities are the same.

The key responsibility is to listen with care. Do not make judgments. Do not make promises. Just let the student describe as much as is comfortable. Your responses should indicate you consider harassing behavior very serious, without necessarily affirming any of the specifics you are hearing. If the student has any questions about whether the behavior might be a matter of misunderstanding, encourage the student to keep an open mind and seek clarification. Refer the student to others who are trained to advise complainants. Even a one-on-one informal conversation to clear up the matter will probably go better if the student has a chance to discuss the issues with someone knowledgeable and an opportunity to practice possible approaches to the conversation. If the situation is more serious, it is best for the student to make contact with the appropriate people right away. Invite the student to come back if another conversation would help.

You need to understand, however, that the student may not share any more information with you. Such silence may be the student's choice or it may be a condition of confidentiality once a complaint is formalized. Discussion of harassment investigations is usually limited only to the parties directly involved. You will surely be curious about "what really happened" and concerned that the student is not experiencing any more disturbing behavior. Unfortunately, your curiosity will probably not be satisfied; you should definitely not ask the student to discuss the complaint. You can express your hope that the referral was helpful and that the situation is better. But if the student has gotten help with the complaint, expect and encourage the student to observe confidentiality.

Now, let's consider what you would do if a student confronts you, or more tactfully informs you, about perceptions of your own behavior. If you have accepted the advice from earlier situations, you should be ready. Your responsibility here is the same as that when a student has concerns about someone else's behavior: listen. Your best strategy is the same as in all the interactions discussed here: articulate your goals and offer alternatives for meeting them.

Start with your goal at this particular moment; later you can get to your goals for the episode the student is concerned about. Affirm that you consider harassment a serious issue and you want to understand what is behind the student's concern. You have several alternatives for getting to that goal. The two of you can talk about the problem and try to clear it up right away. If the student describes your behavior accurately but interprets it differently from your understanding, you can consider whether you will try something different. Agreeing to do something different—not expect people to come to your house alone, not greet everyone with a hug, not call this student by a nickname—is not agreeing you have harassed anyone. It just means you are willing to honor someone else's preferences in matters that are not central to the academic mission of your interactions.

If the behavior the student describes seems quite different from what you recollect or quite a bit more serious than what I have just described, then you may suggest that it would be helpful to bring a third person into the discussion. The goal here would still be clarifying the differences between what you and the student think happened. In this case, however, if the student is alleging something beyond what you can readily imagine as a misinterpreted episode, you are probably better off with a witness and facilitator for the conversation.

You may face a student who seems quite adamant about the charge of harassment and unwilling to pursue the options of discussing possible misunderstandings. In that case, you should once again affirm that what you are discussing is serious and suggest that both of you may need assistance from those responsible for administering your institution's harassment policy. If the student wants to handle the concern through a formal process, you are both better off asking the appropriate persons to deal with the allegation within the framework of established procedures.

So now, what if a student makes a formal complaint against you? You will be contacted by those responsible for your institution's harassment procedures. The first thing you should do is seek assistance from those persons. While the harassment "officers" are usually seen as advocates for those making complaints, that is not their full role. Those responsible for overseeing harassment complaint procedures are advocates for the process; they are there to see that the process is handled seriously and fairly for all parties. They will be able to answer your questions about the steps of the harassment procedures and about what options and responsibilities you and the complainant have in the process.

The second thing you should do is try not to be overly defensive. That's a lot to ask. But remember, if you understand the policy and you've been active in complying, you are now in a position to participate fully in a process designed to test allegations and determine as clearly as possible what may have happened. Your best defense is willingness to cooperate in the procedures.

If you have any reason to believe that something else is going on in the complaint, by all means articulate that fear to those overseeing the complaint procedures. Do not assume, however, that naming another possible agenda will mean that the harassment complaint automatically has no validity and thus does not need to be handled through normal procedures.

You may think immediately of seeking the assistance of an attorney. You probably will not need legal *representation* in the institutional complaint process. In fact, at many colleges and universities attorneys are barred from direct participation in an internal complaint procedure. Whether you need legal *advice* depends on the seriousness of the complaint against you. If the complaint is serious, if there is any indication that the outcome of the procedures could result in a change in your contract, then by all means consult legal counsel. Remember, however, that you are still involved in an internal procedure specific to your institution and that even with an attorney's help you must follow the steps expected there.

Usually institutional harassment resolution procedures allow you to have a representative or adviser who is a faculty or staff member at the college or university. If there are trained persons designated for this role, use them. In addition, or in the absence of such designated advisers, you should ask someone else to help you. Do not avoid getting help because you are embarrassed or reluctant to talk to a colleague.

Turn to someone who knows the policy and procedures well, preferably a person who helped create the policy for your institution or has served in an advisory role for other harassment cases. Such a person can help you interpret what behavior a student may have misunderstood as sexual coercion or as the creation of a hostile environment, even though neither was the intended outcome of your actions. If what is alleged does not match any behavior that you could imagine being interpreted in such a way, then someone familiar with the policy and complaint procedures will be able to help you raise appropriate questions about the evidence presented against you.

Understandably, few people have any desire to go through a complaint process, even an informal one. Therefore, respondents sometimes wish to avoid investigation of complaints altogether. The logic in such a stance is that even to be named in such a complaint, regardless of outcome, does irreparable damage to a professional career. This approach has led to abrupt resignations and departures, not necessarily desired but often agreed to by respondents, rather than face charges. In the past, the agreement to resign usually carried an agreement that the institution would not reveal the circumstances of the resignation.

Times have changed so that today institutions are less ready to make such agreements for fear that concealing the circumstances will be interpreted as "passing along" a "known" harasser to another institution. Institutions that are being careful about background checks and find out about abrupt departures are more likely to wonder why an "innocent" person left an academic appointment rather than stayed to finish a process that could have offered official exoneration. Therefore, I do not recommend making a deal to avoid the complaint procedures once they have reached the formal stage.

Informal negotiations or resolutions are a different matter. Discussions of this sort are overseen by those responsible for your harassment policy but are aimed at clearing up misunderstandings and changing behavior rather than determining whether a violation of policy has taken place. Such informal procedures may not be appropriate if the allegation involves serious forms of coercion or a pattern of targeted hostility. But for allegations of a less serious sort, talking through the complaint and reaching an agreement about what will clear up the matter is generally a good option.

Make sure you understand what stage of the procedures you are in and how informal and formal processes may be related. Some negotiated processes are formal—they can result in findings and sanctions. In some institutions, such resolutions may be final and binding; in others, dispute resolutions are attempted but if they fail the complaint can be turned over to a formal hearing.

Whichever procedure you are following, remember that the goal is to determine both what may have happened and what it meant to the people involved. Often in harassment cases, the complainant and the respondent agree on the actions taken; they disagree on the interpretation. Your best stance in responding to a complaint is to be clear about what happened and what you intended, and then be open about how the other people could have interpreted your behavior. That may mean acknowledging the logic of a complainant's interpretation, even if mistaken. That may also mean finding that what you intended to do had unintended negative effects on the complainant. If that is the case, you should apologize for what you did. It is not a bad idea to be prepared to express regret for any harm caused by a misunderstanding—as a considerate person you would feel such regret. You want to be honest in conveying that you meant no harm in the situation being discussed and clear that you mean no harm in the future. You want to get back to teaching. You want the student to be able to get back to learning. A good harassment resolution procedure should help clear the air so you can both get back to work.

Teaching and learning. That is why you chose this profession. Harassment interferes with those professional goals. That is why you should know about harassment and use what you know to anticipate and avoid misunderstandings that can hurt you and your students.

NOTES

1. EEOC Guidelines (29 C.F.R. Section 1604.11), cited in American Council on Education, *Sexual Harassment on Campus: Suggestions for Reviewing Campus Policy and Education Programs* (Washington: American Council on Education, 1986).

2. *The Ninth Edition of the APA Directory of Members* (Worcester, Mass: American Philological Association, 1993).

10.

THE RESPONSIBLE CONDUCT OF ACADEMIC RESEARCH

P. AARNE VESILIND

Modern academic life will, in most instances, demand that you, the young faculty member, participate in research and scholarship: producing new knowledge, contributing to the wealth of our intellectual capital, and stretching the boundaries of human understanding. Having written a dissertation, you certainly have some idea of the imposing nature of this task and probably look forward with some confidence to continuing the scholarly endeavor. What you may not realize, however, is that some dangers lie along the path of a scholarly career.

Academic research and scholarship have a long history, and those of us engaged in these activities zealously guard the integrity of the process. For the vast majority of academic researchers and scholars, this sense of professional right and wrong is so strong, in fact, that we often expel those who do not live up to our frequently unwritten standards. Thus, it is possible to end your career before it has ever begun by doing something that does not conform to the rules of the academy.

In recent years, in fact, the academy has come under intense scrutiny for ostensible violations of the integrity of scientific research. What has happened, various media pundits have wondered, to the pure search for scientific truth and the responsible conduct of objective experiments and accurate reporting of conclusions? Whether the ideal of an objective, unbiased scientific inquiry ever existed in practice, the fact is that pressures of publication, securing external grant support, and making a scholarly name for oneself have turned scientific experimentation into a serious business in which much is at stake. And in such a high-stakes enterprise, it should not come as a surprise that some individuals want to win what they can by whatever means. The problem here is not simply flawed research but research that willfully misleads or misstates, research that subverts the very foundations of the academy itself.

It is conceivable, of course, that concerns about the integrity of academic research are overstated and unwarranted. Still, as a new member of this academy, it is important that you understand both the nature of these concerns and the written and unwritten rules that govern research within the academy. This understanding is critical—to you as a researcher whose career will depend not only on the success of your research but also on its intellectual soundness, and to the academy itself, which will rapidly lose not only the general support of a nonacademic public whose good will it needs but also the more critical financial support of those agencies that look to the academy to conduct the nation's basic research.

These rules that govern academic research can perhaps be divided into three broad categories—manners, regulations, and ethics. In this essay, I first discuss good and bad manners, then the regulations imposed on research, and finally some of the complexity of professional ethics. Under all three categories, I hope to provide you with pointers on how you avoid getting into trouble. Finally, I have tried to suggest what you might do if you ever find yourself in a situation where others are acting unethically.

BAD MANNERS

Here I call good and bad manners in research the seemingly trivial conventions and understandings that scholars have developed among themselves as a community of investigators. Those who want to participate in this community would be well advised to accept its code of manners. Just as you would refrain from telling your host that dinner was inedible, for example, you would probably not intentionally disrupt a professional lecture, publicly excoriate a senior colleague, or bully graduate students. While none of these actions by itself would end your scholarly career, such conduct would certainly not enhance it. At the very least, it is important to remember that colleagues whose scholarship you may intemperately criticize may serve on panels reviewing your work, and those who today are working in your laboratory or in your classroom will tomorrow be your professional colleagues. Future references, recommendations, appointments, and other evaluations depend upon what people think of you as a scholar *and* a human being. There is, in short, a lot to be gained simply by being a polite person. Like all communities, that of scholarship demands minimal levels of human decency and respect. Where these are lacking, there is only interpersonal friction—the true horror of virtually any academic department.

REGULATIONS

Most scientific research is subjected to numerous regulations that are stated in various university policies and often based upon federal laws and requirements. For example, if you intend to do any work with animals, you are required to obtain permission from the federally mandated University Animal Experimentation Committee (or whatever it is called on your campus). This committee, composed of your colleagues, is required to evaluate the purpose, objective, and protocol of experiments that use animals, with the purpose of minimizing the suffering of sentient creatures. There is, of course, an ethical balance here, in that human suffering is placed paramount and animal suffering is condoned if it leads to a reduction in human suffering. Such committees have been mandated because in the past some experiments with animals were clearly not worth the cost in suffering, such as experiments where the skulls of sentient cats were slowly crushed solely in order to study the strength of feline skulls. Although the issues today in animal experimentation are less obvious, they are often no less strident as various groups espousing animal rights have raised serious questions about the reliance of much academic research on animals developed solely for that purpose. At this level of social concern, the University Animal Experimentation Committee is not likely to be of much assistance.

If you are doing work involving other people as subjects, you will also be required to obtain approval from your university's Human Subjects Committee. This committee, also federally mandated, seeks to minimize the detrimental effects that scientific experiments can have on humans. Again, the value of the promised information is judged in light of the potential damage done to the participants. For example, research that places people in stressful situations without telling them that this is part of the experiment is unlikely to be approved by your university committee and may raise among its members serious questions about your own sense of the critical issues at hand.

Your university will also have a conflict of interest policy that you will probably have to sign if you haven't already done so. Simply put, the conflict of interest policy states, among other things, that you cannot use university facilities or resources for private benefit. In recent years, conflict of interest issues have tended to center on instances in which researchers find themselves asked to speak as objective consultants on the risks of products they have helped develop. Obviously, such instances violate not only institutional regulations but also the scholarly codes of conduct. There are, however, many gray areas within the domain of potential conflicts of interest, so it is worthwhile for you to review your institution's policies and to talk with senior colleagues about what those policies mean and imply. It is especially important that you become proactive about such policies before engaging in funded work, particularly in work funded by private corporations.

Another rule in funded research is that the funds are to be used for the stated purpose and not to defray other costs, particularly those of a personal nature. Such use of research money is, to put it bluntly, illegal, and can result in a felony conviction. If you have budgetary responsibility for a grant, it is absolutely necessary to adhere strictly to the budget and not to shift funds without proper approval from the funding agency. Recent cases where researchers have used funds from one project to fund students and research on another topic have resulted in severe penalties. There is no surer way to end your scholarly career than to be caught manipulating grant funds.

Finally, most universities have strict regulations concerning academic integrity, particularly plagiarism. These regulations are intended primarily for students, but they apply equally to faculty, although few faculty realized this until widespread publication of a flurry of reports concerning issues of integrity in academic research. No university will condone plagiarism among its faculty, but even the charge of plagiarism is damaging to young, untenured faculty.

Plagiarism, the use without permission or acknowledgment of intellectual material, might be as simple as lifting several key sentences from a literary work, or as crass as translating papers from a foreign scientific journal and publishing them under your own name. There are different levels of plagiarism, and sometimes it is even difficult to decide if it has truly occurred, or if the literary passage, data set, or musical refrain in question was independently created. In some cases, it is also difficult to decide when to attribute and when not to. For example, if you borrow a new idea or concept from a textbook and use it in your lectures, should you attribute it? What if you use an equation in a derivation that is so widely known that nobody would presume that you developed it yourself?

The rule that governs all these cases is that of "potential deceit." Is it possible that someone will think, rightly *or* wrongly, that the material you present is your own? If there is such a possibility, then cite your source. Apart from the moral principle involved if you do not, some graduate student will, without doubt, find that source, and you will be acutely embarrassed. A good rule of thumb is "when in doubt, attribute."

ETHICS

A wide gulf exists between good manners and regulations. For example, it is not illegal to agree to have your name included in the list of authors for a scientific publication, even if you have not actually contributed to the work. Nor is this a case of bad manners. It is, however, a case of unethical behavior because the inclusion of your name implies that you can take some credit for developing the ideas or conclusions of the paper.

Most of the problems young faculty face in developing their own research programs are these murky, ill-defined, and often deeply troubling ethical dilemmas. In its simplest sense, being ethical is doing the right thing. But what is the "right thing"? Which, among the many alternatives presented in troubling situations, is the "right thing" to do?

Ethics plays into many decisions you will make in your scholarly career, including the very selection of your research topic. If, for example, you feel strongly that sentient animals should not be used in medical research, then an ethical decision would be to reject topics that require the use of such animals. If you feel that the human genome project is going to lead to ethical quandaries that we are unprepared to confront, then you should not work in this area. Many ethical problems can be averted by judicious and careful screening of research topics, although the choices are perhaps not as clear-cut as those I have just posed. If, for example, most of the federal research funding in your area is precisely targeted at issues involving human genetics, it may not be so easy to explain to your chair that you cannot compete for such funding because it violates your ethical principles.

Ethical questions also arise because research and scholarship in the sciences, and increasingly in the social sciences, are not solitary activities but require a full superstructure of support — from the project officers at funding agencies, to administrators at the university, to journal editors, to academic colleagues, to laboratory technicians. All these people must have a sense of right and wrong if this complex process is to function properly.

One of the most ubiquitous problems facing academic researchers is the appropriate citing of collaborative authorship. Since science is a public endeavor, and credit is received for publishing good works under one's own name, questions of authorship may cause serious collegial disagreements. For example, should the senior researcher in a laboratory be included as an author even if she or he has not been involved in the work in any way except to provide the necessary research funds? In some science subcultures, this is acceptable; in others, it is not. In one case, the editor of the journal to which a paper had been submitted insisted on being listed as a coauthor before the paper could be published, and he pressed his point by showing how many times he had been listed as a coauthor on similar papers.

I cannot cover all the problems of authorship in this short space, but my general advice would be to decide the questions of attribution *before* undertaking the study. In this way, if any of the participants feel that they may be badly treated, they have the option not to participate. At the very least, the laboratory assistants or collaborators should have a clear understanding of the policy they are following. In my own case, when one of my M.S. or Ph.D. students finishes a thesis involving one of my own ideas and working within my laboratory, I ask that student to write up the research for an article to submit to a professional journal. If he or she so chooses, I am willing to be listed as a coauthor of the paper, although this is not necessary. If the student chooses not to publish the data, we all agree that I may do so, provided that the student's role in the research is duly acknowledged. Although this may not be a foolproof system, it is one that all my students know from the start, and it has thus far avoided any disagreements or misunderstandings.

Another ethical problem relates to the value of information. Since science is the search for truth, new information has a fairly immediate value or significance to the research community at large. Two problems can arise, however, in the normal flow of this research information. First, it is possible to obtain important data from casual conversations or from questions during professional meetings. Several instances have occurred in which a researcher has voluntarily but unintentionally revealed information during a scientific meeting and has later accused others of unfair competition. The rule of thumb here is that when you present a paper at a meeting or present any scientific data publicly, you are, in effect, offering scholarly evidence to the world at large and should be certain that your material is protected by copyright.

A more important problem with information flow is inherent in the present mode of research funding—the proposal. Since all proposals are peer reviewed, it seems only natural that the people who would be your fiercest competitors are also the ones most likely to read your grant applications. There is a strong element of trust in such a system, in that we all agree that the information so revealed will not be subsequently used. But ethical problems may, nonetheless, arise. Suppose, for example, that you have scheduled a series of experiments and then review a proposal that demonstrates that these experiments have already failed. Should you go ahead with your own experiments, or use the knowledge learned from reading the proposal to shift the direction of your research? If a proposal provides you with an insight about a research direction that you may or may not have otherwise developed, what would be your reaction? Should you call the author of the proposal, even though the system requires strict confidentiality? In my own view, this would certainly be the only way to proceed: *any* appropriation of another's research idea without acknowledgment or consultation is a violation of the codes by which academic research is conducted.

This is not to say, however, that ethical issues are always either straightforward or clear-cut. In fact, some of the federal agencies—especially the National

Institutes of Health—are so concerned about such issues that they now require formal training in the ethical conduct of research for *all* graduate students and postdoctoral fellows in *any* department holding a research grant from that agency. There is no doubt that the National Science Foundation and the National Institutes of Mental Health, among others, will follow suit. The point to be made here is not that irresponsible or unethical research is running rampant in the country, but rather that the conduct of academic research has become increasingly more complicated and more collaborative in recent years, which makes some of the ethical concerns even more complex than ever. The requirements of the funding agencies are but one attempt to help deal with that complexity and to elicit the active collaboration of the academic institution in ensuring that research in the United States continues to be above ethical reproach.

HOW YOU CAN FOSTER RESPONSIBLE CONDUCT OF RESEARCH

Many academic institutions today expect that all faculty will work actively to create in their classrooms and their laboratories both understanding of and appreciation for the ethical issues involved in the responsible conduct of research. Some of these institutions—particularly those that are affiliated with medical schools—offer new faculty formal and informal training in research ethics. Even if such training is not available at your school, the U.S. Office of Research Integrity (ORI) regularly publishes articles and books on these issues. ORI itself formally lists nine instructional areas in the responsible conduct of research: data acquisition, management, sharing, and ownership; conflict of interest and commitment; human subjects; animal welfare; research misconduct; publication practices and responsible authorship; mentor/trainee responsibilities; peer review; and collaborative science. Familiarization with these nine areas, and full discussions of them with your students and mentees, would be an initial step that you could take yourself in fostering a community of responsible and ethical research.

WHAT TO DO IF YOU ENCOUNTER UNETHICAL BEHAVIOR

It's one thing to behave ethically yourself, and to make sure that your students and technicians do likewise. It is a different situation if you encounter unethical (or illegal) behavior among your colleagues. What do you do, for example, if you discover that one of your colleagues has plagiarized a student's paper? Is it your responsibility to make this public? And if it is, how should this be done? How public is public? How should you react if you discover that funds from a federally funded research project are being misspent? Or what should you do when you find widespread manipulation of data? Whom do you talk to, and what do you say?

Most universities have policies regarding the reporting of unethical actions by the faculty. Your first step should be to read this policy, and then to find out what your alternatives are. If the apparent wrongdoing is serious, you should recognize that your whistle-blowing may place you in a dangerous position, and that you must first be able to document thoroughly anything you say to anyone. Remember that careers of others may be affected by what you disclose, and you do not want to damage them unfairly or to destroy yourself in the process.

Once you have decided that the misconduct is serious and that you have a strong presumption that it occurred, most university policies require you first approach the person above you on the administrative ladder. If you suspect one of your colleagues, you should talk to the department chair. It is possible that the situation can be resolved at this level and that nothing more need be done. If, however, you do not receive a satisfactory answer, you should move up the ladder, usually to the dean of the faculty, always remembering that by so doing you are also increasing the risk to your own career. Only in extreme situations, where you recognize that the harm caused by unethical action is truly egregious, and you have not received satisfactory reactions from official contacts, should you *go public*. If you do this, be prepared to be at the center of a storm.

CONCLUSION

When you enter academic life and devote your career to scholarship and education, you carry with this decision a commitment to act in such a way as to bring the greatest credit to your discipline and your institution. The easiest way to do this is, of course, to do good research—but it is also important to be cognizant of academic manners, regulations, and ethics.

Most of the time it is easy to recognize good manners in scholarship, and it is easy to understand the regulations governing your scholarly activity. Most of the difficult questions fall into the gray area of ethics. How do we know with certainty what is right or wrong? How do you discover what, all things considered, you ought to do?

Ethical considerations do not necessarily give you correct answers to moral dilemmas. But thinking ethically can show that some alternatives are clearly better than others. The best piece of advice I know for finding such "better" alternatives is always to behave in such a manner that you will not be embarrassed if whatever you do or say gets plastered on the front page of the morning paper.

PART III

ACADEMIC EMPLOYMENT

In relation to the seemingly leisurely pace of the first three or four years, the final spring to the Ph.D. is often hectic and harrowing. Not only must the "promising" research now bear tangible and readable results and the document itself be subjected to fearful professional evaluation, but the candidate must also find some way to metamorphose from learning pupil to learned professor. Neither dissertation nor defense could be as frightening as this last step. Horror stories abound: how the best student anyone can remember failed to get a single interview at the national convention; how Sarah Wells was forced to accept a job at South Central Tech and was never heard of again; how Joe Simmon's adviser sabotaged his dossier with a less than glowing recommendation; how Jill Adams got her dissertation published by Chicago but was still denied tenure. The entire ordeal is encompassed by two vast unknowns — one real obstacle called the job market and an even vaguer one called tenure. The essays that follow attempt at least to bring some light to these two dark threats. Henry M. Wilbur and Sudhir Shetty offer practical advice on how to negotiate the dangerous currents of the market; John G. Cross and Edie N. Goldenberg try to shed some light on the advantages and disadvantages of non-tenure-track positions; Matthew W. Finkin explains the legal theory and the implications of tenure; Craufurd D. Goodwin outlines the three hurdles to achieving tenure; and A. Leigh DeNeef summarizes some financial aspects of academic employment. The difference in approaches is itself a sign that the transition from Ph.D. to professor is neither a natural chronology nor an easy shifting of academic gears. Getting a job is one thing, but keeping it is many. As the stakes rise, so do the issues. The new academic will have to prepare as thoroughly as possible for the challenges ahead. A major part of that preparation may simply be knowing in advance just what those challenges are about.

11

ON GETTING A JOB

HENRY M. WILBUR

The first task of the new Ph.D. is to obtain an academic position. In the following pages I offer some tactics that may be helpful in locating suitable openings, submitting an application, surviving an interview, and negotiating an offer. My advice is admittedly personal and based upon my own limited experience, which includes successfully competing for positions that could fulfill my expectations and then serving on search committees as a faculty member during the past three decades. On the basis of that experience, I immediately qualify my opening sentence: before you set out to obtain a job in a college or university, you should do some frank and honest soul-searching.

PRELIMINARY CONSIDERATIONS

Not all graduate students are larval professors. Although this handbook is a guide to metamorphosis from graduate student life to professorhood, not all graduate students want to or should attempt this particular transition. There is life outside the university—in industry, in government, and in private foundations—for students in all fields. Of course, the computer scientist or chemist probably has a broader range of options than the philosopher or classicist; nevertheless, it is important for graduate students continuously to question their career goals. Academics are generally not paid very well considering the length of time they have spent educating themselves. The hours are not attractive, particularly in the first few years when you are expected to write three to six term papers (lectures) a week, establish yourself as a research scholar of national repute, and devote hours to committee work you are told is indispensable to the proper functioning of the department and the university. However, the rewards of academic life should be obvious to you by now. If you can't articulate them clearly, then you should investigate alternatives to an academic career. The choice not to become an academic is often difficult; it can seem an admission of failure at the very moment you have achieved significant graduate success. And yet a Ph.D. should never be viewed as a career answer, but rather as an opening of career options. College or university teaching is only one among many. For the remainder of this essay, however, I shall assume that you have decided to try your hand at professorhood.

There is a great deal that can be done as a graduate student to increase your chances of obtaining a satisfactory position in academia. The work ethic remains alive and there is always room at the top. Having a number of scholarly publications before the dissertation is submitted is becoming the norm, as least in the sciences. Attendance at meetings of scholarly societies and the presentation of talks or posters is not only good practice but good advertisement. A high level of intellectual interaction with fellow students and faculty throughout your graduate studies produces favorable letters of reference and propels you to the top of your adviser's list of "promising young scholars." Begin this behavior as soon as possible after entering graduate school. There is a high correlation between early publication and sustained publication. Graduate students who work hard their first year preparing their undergraduate research for publication seem to be the ones who get tenure ten years later. Too many students begin their publishing careers by pushing a series of potboilers off to journals six months before they intend to apply for positions. Today's competition demands that you prepare for an academic position as soon as you enter graduate school. I do not mean to imply here that scholarship should be motivated by employment prospects rather than intellectual curiosity, for without that curiosity all is already lost. There are, however, a number of practical strategies that can help your application rise to the surface of the sea of inquiries a search committee receives. This essay is about those tactics.

An early decision relates to the kind of position that you would accept. Your adviser and peers probably act as if you must get a position at a prestigious research university. Is that what you want? All students, to be sure, tend to get less selective the longer they go without interviews and offers, but you should anticipate this reaction from the start. You will quickly antagonize your referees if you ask for too many recommendations for positions for which you are not appropriate or which you would not accept if offered.

Schools vary considerably in the relative emphasis they give to undergraduate teaching versus externally sponsored research programs. A college that places a strong emphasis on undergraduate teaching may still expect you to have a research program, but one that involves undergraduates. Such a program may not require extramural funding to be successful. Some research universities may not expect you to teach undergraduates at all; rather, it is taken for granted that you will rapidly establish a nationally recognized research program that successfully obtains funds from the highly competitive panels of the National Science Foundation or the National Institutes of Health. Graduate students may come later. Most universities have some intermediate expectation in which a balance between teaching and research is sought. Your task is to discover where on this continuum you would be most satisfied.

The decision of whether to apply for a particular job involves your personal as well as your career ambitions. You may be able to tolerate an urban (or isolated rural) campus for a one-year sabbatical replacement position but would bypass it as a place to raise your family. A different decision is the one between a temporary position at a good school versus a potentially permanent position at a less desirable school. Temporary positions can vary from a postdoctoral research position that will almost certainly enhance your later opportunities to a teaching replacement that will help pay the bills but may impede progress toward your career goals. Temporary positions involving teaching of even a single course a semester are likely to stall your research progress.

Search committees at major universities are going to pay close attention to your scholarly productivity in the few years surrounding your doctorate. On the positive side, the responsibility for teaching a course may provide just the experience and letters of reference required to land a teaching position at a liberal arts college.

FINDING OUT ABOUT POSITIONS

Different fields have different modes of advertising positions. Some scholarly societies have directories or newsletters about openings, and many journals accept advertisements for positions wanted or positions open in the field. In the sciences, especially the biological sciences, nearly all academic positions are advertised in the journal *Science*. Many also appear in the Jobs section of the *Chronicle of Higher Education.*

The "old boy network" is more alive in some fields than others. Many departments will circulate advertisement copy to colleagues throughout the country before it is submitted for publication. The rapid response by a candidate to such a notice assures some degree of attention because it demonstrates both that you are in contact with respected figures in your field and that you are eager. Some departments formally request nominations of promising scholars from established figures to fill open positions. A rapid and enthusiastic response by your adviser to such an invitation is essential. It is therefore imperative that you frankly discuss your aspirations and progress toward completing degree requirements with that adviser. The adviser should have at hand a current curriculum vitae and have read your statement of teaching and research interests (see below). He or she should not have to reach back to your oral preliminary examination for a recollection of your promise.

SUBMITTING THE APPLICATION

The materials you submit in response to an advertisement or nomination are going to determine whether you get an interview. Your application has to attract immediate, positive attention. It has to be brief enough to catch the eye of a search committee confronted with several hundred applications and yet must include enough detailed information to convince the specialist or skeptic. A wide variety of formats for presenting your credentials to a search committee is available, but the following suggestions would be appropriate for most university positions, at least in the sciences. It is important to tailor your application to both the type of school (major research university versus small teaching college) and the specific description of the position (don't dwell on your skill in introductory courses if the department seeks someone to strengthen its graduate program). Perhaps the most important thing to appreciate is that the search committee may be attempting to evaluate several hundred applications in a few weeks. Your application will probably be rejected or passed through the first filter based on one or two minutes of effort. You must present your credentials in a compact form that allows a reader quickly to appreciate your talents and then lures him or her to read the more detailed statements of your qualifications. Be sure your name is on every page of the application and staple each section separately!

Keep an organized checklist of where you have applied, when you sent the application, who you asked to write letters, and when you receive confirmation that materials have been received.

The Cover Letter   The cover letter should be a short formal statement of your interest in the position and a very brief list of the enclosed documents. If you were told of the opening by an adviser or have been contacted by a member of the search committee or department, this too should be mentioned. The cover letter is a good place to drop a name, if that can be done gracefully and with tact. The cover letter should also contain a clear statement of when you will complete your degree requirements, if you have not already done so. It may be important to have your adviser verify this expectation in a separate letter.

The Curriculum Vitae   The curriculum vitae should be a factual outline of your life as a scholar. It will probably be the most carefully read and widely circulated document in your application. Letters of reference are generally considered confidential documents, but your vitae may be widely circulated to faculty, deans, and students. It tells who you are and is a very good indication of what you think of yourself. A suggested format follows.

Personal information: Name, birthplace and citizenship, university address and telephone, home address and telephone, social security number (these last two items may be needed for interview reimbursements). Some choose to include sex, birthdate, marital status, and number of offspring (these data may be considered irrelevant by some departments and very important by others).

Education: List the institution, department, degree, and date of all degrees earned.

Positions held: List employment that is not redundant with other categories. Casual summer jobs are not important, but you should account for significant gaps between your degrees.

Awards: List honorary societies, scholarships, fellowships, and other recognition for academic achievement. For some positions it may be useful to list evidence of good citizenship outside of academics, but don't reach back to high school or Scouts to find it.

Societies: List the scholarly societies to which you belong. Don't stretch this to include hobbies: an ornithologist should include the American Ornithologists' Union (the publisher of a research journal) but not the Audubon Society (the publisher of a lay magazine). If membership is by election, list the date of election as evidence of sustained interest rather than a last minute membership to fortify your credentials.

Professional service: List journals or granting agencies for which you have served as a reviewer and offices you have held in scholarly societies.

Teaching experience: List by title the courses that you have taught and include your responsibilities (lecturer, discussion section, laboratory section, and so on).

Papers delivered: If you have presented papers at meetings of scholarly societies or symposia it may be wise to list them by title, date, and meeting. This section should not be inflated by talks to the hometown crowd; it should definitely include presentations for which you were invited. The main purpose of this section is to establish your stature among the community of scholars outside your home institution.

Publications: This section presents some difficulties. Lists of publications can be seriously diluted by the inclusion of published abstracts, unrefereed publications, or publications in questionable journals. Established scholars vary considerably in what they include in their publications. I personally prefer to see a list of publications in refereed journals (including publications in press) arranged by date, with titles, citations, and order of coauthorship clearly stated. A separate section can be established for published abstracts and technical reports. Titles "in preparation" should also be relegated to a separate section with a note explaining the status of each (for example, in review, rough manuscript, research completed, a good dream).

Statement of Research Interests   The curriculum vitae presents the facts of your research accomplishments. The statement of research interest is a concise presentation of what your research has been about and where you see it heading. This should be a statement that can be read quickly and appreciated by nonspecialists in your field. It may also serve as a sample of your writing skills. Because your success at obtaining an interview may depend on a vote of the entire department or the judgment of a dean trained in another field, you must avoid jargon without being condescending and you must be complete without belaboring the details. The statement should be a page or two.

The application packet should also contain reprints of publications or preprints of work in press. Some applicants include a paragraph or two describing the major results of each publication and each research project in progress. You should include an abstract of your dissertation or an outline of what you have completed. Very few members of the search committee will have time to read any of your publications, but if you pass the first screening they may be read before you are invited for an interview. If, after the interview, there is still controversy about your suitability for the position, your publications may be read in detail.

Statement of Teaching Interests   This statement should be an honest evaluation of your qualifications to teach courses at the graduate and undergraduate levels. It is appropriate to include a statement of your personal approach to teaching. Short course descriptions are more useful than mere titles. It may be wise to include a detailed syllabus if you have designed a course or know what kind of course a prospective employer wants offered. Your interest in and approach to undergraduate independent research projects and graduate students can be described if you are familiar with how the department is structured.

Letters of Reference   Because many search committees are going to put great stock in letters of reference, your choice of who writes for you is significant. You need to pick professors who know you and your work well. Given a choice it is always better to have a letter written by someone known, and trusted, by members of the search committee. If you are known by someone outside your home department, he or she may add a useful dimension: a biologist with a minor in mathematics would profit from a letter from a mathematician. If you did collaborative work or took a course at another institution you may obtain a letter that places you in a national perspective. Respect your referees: they are busy and letters of reference soon become a great burden. The cost of an excessive number of requests is that you will get only a standard form letter. Personalized letters that address your suitability for a specific position are much more useful than the generic EGS (Excellent Graduate Student) letter of platitudes. If the referee knows a member of the department well, a copy of the letter sent directly to that contact may focus the attention of the search committee on your application. Give all your referees copies of your application so they have an updated curriculum vitae and are familiar with how you represent your teaching and research interests. Even more important, give them as much time as possible to write the letter and provide them with a return note to send you when they have written it.

THE INTERVIEW

A completed application is an implicit statement that you are ready to interview on short notice. It is not at all unusual for the first response from a search committee to be a telephone call asking you to come for an interview the following week. A little preplanning can help both your mental health and your presentation. First, let your optimism prepare you for the telephone call; it will not help your case if you sound shocked and request additional time to get ready. Don't make it obvious that this is your first interview. On the telephone ask about the format of the interview: Will you have a chance to talk with students? Will you be able to see special facilities? Does the department expect a seminar? Who will attend and how long a presentation is expected?

Don't be shy about asking explicitly about reimbursement arrangements, but be prepared to pay for hotel accommodations and meals. You may have to tie up hundreds of dollars buying airline tickets and paying for living expenses, because reimbursements from some state universities require a month or even more. Be sure to get directions as to whether you will be met at the airport or if you need to find your own way to a hotel.

Do your homework. Go to the library or the department Web site and learn who the faculty are. Look at their CVs and ask your professors about their work. If you review the names and have a bit of introductory information it will be much easier to carry on a personal or professional conversation. A bit of recognition will flatter your hosts, reveal your awareness of the profession at large, and demonstrate that you are serious about the position. A review of the department's course listings tells about the interests of the faculty and gives you a preview of the character and balance of the department. Such a preview may provide you with questions that you need to ask in order to evaluate the department as a potential home. Prior knowledge of the department demonstrates the sincerity and the depth of your interest.

Most research departments will expect you to present a formal lecture on your research as a focal point for your visit. A department with an emphasis on undergraduate teaching may request that you give a lecture, perhaps on a topic of their choice, to an undergraduate class.

Your seminar should be expertly prepared within the format customary in your discipline. Science departments will expect a forty-five- to fifty-minute paper with perhaps fifteen to twenty minutes for informal questions followed by an open house or reception. The seminar gives faculty a chance to examine both the soundness of your research (few will have read any of your papers) and your skill as a lecturer. Your talk should be pitched at the general audience with a clear statement of how the project contributes to the broader field of your interest. Very meticulously weed out lab-lore and jargon. Excellent slides and a well-practiced delivery are essential. Be sure that you have talked with the projectionist about how the lights and microphone work. Bringing a slide tray ready to go may ensure that your slides are projected correctly; there are seven wrong ways to load a slide and only one correct orientation. If you are using a PowerPoint presentation, make sure that you will have appropriate computer facilities, that you know how to use them, and that you carry a spare CD. The better prepared you feel, the lower the level of terror you will experience when you first stand up. Try not to read notes, but if you have a completely written script at hand you will have the assurance that there is a fall-back position that could save you. Remember, you may get less than a week's warning. Prepare your slides well in advance and practice your talk before the hometown crowd. Include a couple of nonspecialists in your audience and take their criticisms seriously. Coax them into listening to a revision.

Graduate students often seem very concerned about appropriate dress for interviews. The advice varies with both school and department. Urban campuses and humanities departments tend to be more formal than rural campuses and science departments. Note what the professors in your department wear when they lecture and dress at that level or slightly more formally. It is probably wise to be a bit more formal when you present a lecture and when you visit the dean than when you are making the rounds of the faculty. Personal appearance will be used to judge lifestyle. Some colleges are very concerned about the lifestyle of their faculty. If the department wants to know your marital status and number of offspring, it probably wants to see you in business clothes. Be sure you dress for the local climate; it is very important to feel comfortable.

Remember, they invited you; they are interested. But you should also interview them. The chair of the department should tell you about the position. Is it a new position or a replacement for a lost faculty member? What is the department's expectation with respect to teaching and research? You can respond with how you would meet these expectations. If you need research space, ask forcefully to see the space you would occupy. Talk about possible renovations. Ask to tour the facilities and try to find out to what extent equipment is shared. Ask about how the office works; is secretarial and other technical help available for research as well as teaching activities? Ask to see the teaching laboratories. Visit the library; does it have acceptable holdings in your area? Do they appear accessible? How are new acquisitions chosen? What are the computer facilities like? What is the nature of the research and grants office?

The chair should be willing to talk about how faculty are evaluated. When are appointments reviewed? Ask how the tenure system works without sounding accusatory. Ask why faculty have left the department. Now is probably not the time to talk salary or set-up money, but it is the time to talk about facilities and work conditions. Will you be a member of the graduate faculty right away or only after a separate election? Assert your concerns without dominating the interview or appearing too aggressive. Talk enough to demonstrate your intelligence, knowledge, and tact, but don't become a bore or dominate conversations.

You will probably be circulated among the faculty for interviews of an hour or less. Now is when the homework pays off. If you know a little about someone before you are introduced, it may save insulting the National Academy member, and it will certainly flatter the assistant professor. Let them interview you, but ask them about their research and teaching roles in the department. Ask about department facilities and working conditions. Ask the young faculty about how they were received; ask the older faculty how they view the new appointment. Ask about plans for future appointments and try to learn about the age structure of the department. Is it likely that you can become a force in determining the future of the department? It is important to uncover schisms and to learn what the department prides itself on. Asking the same questions of several faculty members independently is a good way to find out if there is a consensus on important issues. When you go to lunch and dinner with faculty try to gauge the familiarity among them as a way of predicting your own social and intellectual interactions.

You will probably be interviewed by a dean or two. This is often a courtesy interview that you need to get through with grace rather than aggression. Save

your tough questions for the department head. The deans are probably looking at your professionalism rather than taking a hard look at your research or
the details of the appointment. They may be interested to see if you can explain your scholarly interest to a lay person. It is probably appropriate to ask
deans about promotion and tenure policies as they are applied to the school
as a whole. It is also okay to ask how they view the future of the department,
but this may be awkward if the department head is attending. Try hard to get a
chance to talk with students in the absence of faculty, especially if the department has a graduate program. Ask them about the strengths and weaknesses of
the current program and how they view the new appointment. Graduate students are likely to be honest, but they too have axes to grind. Making a good
impression with graduate students may exert a strong influence on the faculty.
I think that the current intellectual vigor of a graduate department can be un-
covered in an hour's conversation with a fair sample of students. Learn about
how graduate students are supported with respect to both their stipends and
their research needs. Ask about the fate of recent graduates. Are graduate students housed in faculty space or do they have their own offices?

THE OFFER

There may be a long wait between the interview and the next telephone call.
Don't get pessimistic too early. Many search committees choose a slate of three
to six candidates and interview them all before they make a decision. If you are
pressed by another offer, it is entirely appropriate to call the department, tell
them of your situation, and ask for advice. This procedure can get a bit complex. Do not let yourself be pressured into making a premature decision, but
at the same time be honest with yourself and the departments involved. Never
play games with potential employers. You may get caught.

Some schools will invite you for a second visit once you become their favored
candidate, although this is more likely at senior rather than junior levels. In
some circumstances it could be appropriate for you to request a second visit,
even if you have to pay for it yourself. The tables are now turned and the department is courting you. On a second visit you should work very hard to gather
the information you need to make the decision. This is the time to talk money,
space, equipment, and teaching responsibilities. It is also appropriate to bring
your spouse along and get a feel for his or her employment prospects, housing,
and the community. It would not be ethical to accept an invitation for a second
visit unless you are very serious about accepting the offer.

There is probably some negotiating room when considering an offer, although there is little latitude if the position is temporary or has only a very slight chance of resulting in tenure. There is much more room if you are being hired to strengthen a department or to expand its range of interests. Salary is probably predetermined, but it might be increased if you have more than the usual amount of postdoctoral experience or a firm, and higher, offer from another school. Salary can probably be negotiated every year and good work will be rewarded in time. Now is the time to negotiate space and initial equipment allowance, because once you arrive as an assistant professor it may be difficult to expand your research space. Research grants will generally pay for the direct costs of doing research, but ordinarily they will not pay for renovations and office equipment. Get firm commitments for those file cabinets, bookshelves, blackboards, and computers. The amount of set-up money that can be expected varies widely among schools and among fields. Talk to your friends and the junior faculty to help calibrate your negotiations.

As always, try to get the results of your discussion in writing. Schools vary considerably in the formality of their offers. Some schools will present you with a formal contract; others will send only an informal letter from the department chairperson.

THINKING ABOUT CHANGING POSITIONS

At the opposite end of academic employment is the question of moving from one school to another. Movement has always been common in academia and current trends in the market and in university tenure policies suggest that professors may become even more mobile. It is a fortunate group who landed the job of choice directly out of graduate school and have remained contentedly fulfilled ever since. It is far more common for academics to take a zigzag course toward the position that suits them best.

Your ability to obtain a position successfully certainly rises during graduate and postdoctoral studies. Some peak on the day of their dissertation defense and never fulfill the hopes of their advisers. A very high proportion of doctoral dissertations in all fields are never published. Only a few scholars continue to rise in stature until they are sought to fill endowed chairs at the most prestigious institutions. Most of us will fall in that vast middle group of promising young scholars who go on to timely promotion to full professors and then slowly burn out or go into real estate. The problem is to guess when you will peak as an academic commodity. I advise students to determine as soon as possible the kind of scholarly life they wish to lead and then to work hard to achieve it. Dedication to teaching and dedication to research are often in conflict, and it is important to realize your own goals as early as possible. When you obtain your first position, it is necessary to think about how you fit into a department and how you see your career developing. The first year or two of a position are intellectually, psychologically, and physically exhausting. Life may be lonely, too. The graduate student's social life may be very different from the life of a single assistant professor in a department where everyone else is over thirty and has two kids and a house. But everything gets easier. In the second or third year you will have a good chance of moving up. Your doctoral research should be published or in press; you should have a new direction to your research independent of that of your old adviser; and, most important perhaps, you should have a realistic view of academic life and your own evaluation of the relative importance of teaching and research.

It is far easier to move up as an assistant professor than as a tenured professor. A change of positions as an associate or full professor may require paying the price of chairing a department for a few years. The decision to apply for another position has to be considered carefully. When to tell your present employer is a difficult decision. If your motivations are obvious, such as a change from a small college to a research university, or vice versa, there is little problem. But a move that appears to be a lateral one may antagonize the very people you have to live with. It is probably better to be frank up front than risk an awkward situation later. Using job offers to extort salary increases and more research space is an old tradition in academia, but it can be a dangerous game. In my opinion it is an unnecessary game; your needs will be met if you do well and can demonstrate that your case is valid. The time and energy involved in empty interviews will detract from your research and teaching productivity, and you certainly risk antagonizing your current colleagues. Academics are inveterate gossips; you may be able to play a few rounds of this game, but the offers will soon start to taper off. Remember also that a threat to resign unless an outside offer is met may be accepted.

What if you don't get tenure? The school owes you a full explanation of how the decision was made and why it was negative. You owe yourself a careful consideration of your performance and your aspirations. Do you want to try again at the same kind of school? Do you want to shift type of department? Or is now a good time to get out of academia? It is relatively easy to move from a prestigious university with a reputation for not granting tenure to another research university with a different policy. It is probably hard to move from a college position with an emphasis on teaching to a research-oriented university. It may be best to find a research position, probably on soft money, for a couple of years to help establish, or rejuvenate, your research credentials.

CONCLUSION

This essay may seem a bit commercial and crass. Is this the way a community of scholars should treat each other? Am I doing things for the right reason? Colleges and universities are increasingly run by hard-nosed administrators. They may come from academic backgrounds, but most of them have been faced with a decade of declining enrollments, declining government subsidies, rising costs, and a surplus of eager applicants for every position they offer. You have to apply some tactics of your own in order to obtain the freedom to set your own directions and standards. The best preparation for professorhood is rapid intellectual growth and productive scholarship. The best way to present yourself at an interview is as a dedicated scholar with fresh ideas and a willingness to work hard. The best way to negotiate in response to an offer is to consider your own needs as a scholar, teacher, and person. The best way to get tenure is to maintain the proper balance between those three. Once you have made it, your students will ask you how you did it. If they ask why you did it, the answer is far easier.

12.

THE JOB MARKET

An Overview

SUDHIR SHETTY

Perhaps the greatest remaining mystery for the newly minted Ph.D. is the actual working of the job market. The description that follows is based entirely upon my experience of seeking a position in economics, but while the institutional details no doubt vary across disciplines, many of the general aspects noted below apply to the academic job market in other fields as well. My purpose, then, is to provide a look at this market from the perspective of the seller — the prospective Ph.D. The need for such a summary is inherent in my thesis: that success in the job market depends largely on preparation and awareness.

Although my emphasis is on the process of looking for a job within academia, there are sectors other than higher education (academics) that offer job opportunities for Ph.D.'s in most fields. One of the first decisions you, as a job-seeker, must make, therefore, is whether to concentrate on only one of these areas or to look at both academic and nonacademic positions. My experience has convinced me that trying to appeal to two or more sets of employers, each of whom is looking for somewhat different qualities in their candidates, can present tricky problems in changing your hats to suit the occasion. If you prefer the simple life or are fairly sure where your future lies, it makes a lot of sense to concentrate on either the academic or nonacademic side of the market.

Almost all the initial interviewing for tenure-track positions in economics (and for the majority of the nonacademic positions) takes place in three hectic days at the annual American Economic Association meeting in late December. It is natural, then, to divide the present discussion into three parts, corresponding to the phases before, during, and after these meetings.

BEFORE THE MEETINGS

Prepare your vitae well before any application deadlines. Make it snappy — not much longer than a page. In particular do not exaggerate your qualifications or achievements, especially with regard to specialization and work in progress.

Write it so that it appeals to the particular constituency you have in mind. If you are applying to different kinds of positions you should have more than one version of your vitae so that the most appropriate one can be sent out for each position.

In the semester before you plan to go on the market, you need to complete work on at least one paper that is worthy of being mailed out along with your applications and of being presented at job seminars. Usually, the paper represents the parts of your dissertation that have been written up for publication. It should follow the format of a journal article (even if somewhat lengthier), and particularly close attention should be paid to the introduction, conclusion, and the abstract since these are usually the only parts that potential interviewers have a chance to read. If you have not made sufficient progress on your dissertation so as to be able to write a good paper from it, then postpone going on the market.

Circulate a draft of your job market paper(s) to departmental faculty members in your field and especially to your adviser. This not only attracts constructive comments that will help you in rewriting the paper but also exposes you and your work to others in the department who might prove useful in either calling or receiving calls about positions in the field. Circulating papers in advance will also ensure that when you ask your faculty for recommendations they can speak directly and knowledgeably about the work you are doing rather than generally or vaguely about what a fine person you are.

By the middle of October start generating a first list of schools (or nonacademic jobs) to which you are interested in applying. In doing this, consult your department's job book and various issues of *Job Openings for Economists* (or the corresponding publication in your field). The latter is particularly important for academic jobs and might also include some listings for nonacademic positions.

In formulating this initial list, keep in mind the segment of the market you are aiming at: you should consider such things as the quality of schools, the types of positions, primary and secondary fields, and regional preferences. Use these questions as a basis for discussions with your adviser. Tell him or her what kinds of jobs you are particularly interested in. Talk to him about the positions on your list and others that he may know about. Find out at which schools your adviser has an inside connection or other links. Remember that the easiest way to get an interview with a school is for an adviser or faculty member to call a contact on the department's recruitment committee concerning your application. The most important consideration in deciding on this list of schools is position. Don't aim too high or too low. That decision is largely a judgment call, and the best guide for helping you make the right decision is a frank and honest adviser.

Consider the placement record of past Ph.D.'s from your department in estimating the appropriate quality range. Saturate this range with applications, but also apply to a few "insurance" schools (ranked lower) and some potential "miracles" (ranked higher). Apply to all schools within the range that you consider safe, irrespective of whether they have actually advertised any positions (unless, of course, you are sure that the school is not hiring). This is worthwhile strategy because job advertisements frequently appear later than you might anticipate.

By the end of October, you should have a tentative final list of schools or non-academic positions to which you will be applying. It is also time to polish up the paper and vitae. The next step is to coordinate the mailings of your applications. Mailings should be completed before Thanksgiving—mid-November is best. Any delays beyond the end of November seriously jeopardize your chances of arranging interviews. Remember also that it is almost impossible to schedule interviews once you are at the annual meetings.

Apart from your vitae, the packet mailed to each school on your list contains the letters of reference. You have to ensure that all these materials get to whoever is coordinating the mailings so that you can meet your deadlines. This is hardest to ensure for the letters of reference. Therefore you should start reminding your referees about their obligations well before your deadline and continue doing so until these letters have been written.

For the top schools or jobs on your list and others that specifically require it, send a copy of your paper either with these materials or in a separate mailing after the applications have been sent. If you send the paper separately, explain in a very brief cover letter that this material is supplementary and that your other application materials should already have been received.

If your mailings were on schedule, replies from the schools should start trickling in by early to mid-December. Schools vary, however, in promptness: some departments wait as long as the week before the annual meetings to schedule interviews. Do not panic, therefore, if your calls are a little late in coming. If there are any schools in which you are especially interested and from which you have not heard by mid-December, get your adviser or another faculty member to check with someone in that department. You should do this only as a last resort and only if the department in question is among your very top choices.

Be organized in scheduling interviews. Each lasts between fifteen and thirty minutes, although some can be as long as forty-five minutes. Ask how long the interviews will last and be sure to find out the hotel and room in which each will be held. Find out what alternative times the school can offer you. Try to space interviews evenly between and within days. Even five interviews in one day are exhausting; six or more are dangerous. Because most interviews (at least for academic jobs) are held in the same hotels as sessions of the annual meeting, look at the architectural layout of the hotels (these are usually found in the program of the convention) so that you can schedule interviews without having to spring between thirty-four floors. While scheduling the interviews, try to find out who will be interviewing (if this information is available). If possible, schedule important interviews on days two and three of the meetings; mornings and early afternoons are also preferable so that you are neither jaded nor quivering. Most of the time, however, the better schools on your list will leave you little choice on these matters.

Plan on spending almost all of the last three to four weeks before the meeting preparing for the interviews. Preparation with respect to the following is particularly critical:

1. *A five- to ten-minute "spiel" on your dissertation.* This will be your response to the most common opening line at the interview—"tell us about your dissertation." Concentrate on defining the questions that are posed in your work, their importance and novelty, the link with existing work, and how your contribution adds to knowledge or fills in gaps. You might also want to mention how you got interested in the topic. Be specific about at least a couple of results and note how far along you are in the research and the actual writing. Expect some dumb questions and a few nasty ones. This preparation is by far the most important part of each interview, so spend a lot of time working on it. Practice your summary on friends and colleagues, especially those outside your major specialty (so they can tell whether you "make sense" to the general interviewer).

2. *Your research interests.* This is another common question, particularly in interviews with research-oriented departments. You should have at least a couple of ideas ready. Even if these are not cut and dried, they should be conceived well enough to present to the interviewers an image of a serious and eager researcher who is prepared to set out independent of a graduate school mentor.

3. *Courses you can teach.* You must be prepared to be specific here, not only in terms of the courses but also their content, the texts you would use, your general preference for large or small classes, and so forth. Not all interviewers will ask you for such details, but one or two definitely will.

4. *Important ideas in your major field.* This question is asked only by some of the better interviewers and is a test of whether you have kept abreast of developments in the field outside of your thesis topic.

5. *Your questions about the department.* Always be prepared to ask a few of these, even if they sound trite. They indicate interest on your part, and they may elicit important information to help make your final decision whether to accept a job. The usual questions concern the interests of the faculty, the nature of the undergraduate and graduate programs, the normal teaching load, computer facilities, summer support, and so on. Do not ask about salary or the physical environment of the school. You will learn about these on a visit if you are invited to make one.

6. *Special factors.* If you are interested mainly in teaching schools or specific kinds of nonacademic jobs such as government agencies or consultancy organizations, be prepared to explain the basis for that interest. If you can give good reasons, your commitment will be established.

THE MEETINGS

When you are on the job market, the meetings themselves are a sideshow. You will barely have the time and energy to get through your interviews. Most interviews are held in hotel rooms reserved for this purpose by the various schools and organizations. Since hotel switchboards do not give out room numbers of guests, you will have to get this information directly from interviewers. Therefore, when you schedule the interviews, always ask for the name in which the department will reserve its room.

During the meetings, the advantage of staying at one of the hotels that hosts sessions is the proximity of most of your interviews. The obvious problem is the cost relative to staying in cheaper hotels or with friends. In choosing your hotel, do not underestimate the convenience of being close to the action, and be sure that you make reservations early if you decide to stay at one of the main convention hotels.

The types of questions asked at the interviews are usually some subset of those mentioned above. Although the emphasis varies among interviews, your dissertation will almost always have pride of place in the questioning. Since the questions are so repetitive, you will often be saying the same things over and over, but sound fascinated with your work, react to questions enthusiastically, and do not get fazed by the responses or eccentricities of the interviewers. Apart from being tiring, it is also tiresome to go through this process more than five or six times each day of the meetings. This is another good reason for not scheduling too many interviews, especially if the schools do not interest you. The number of interviewers varies, but it is usually two or three. Most are friendly or at least amiable. Dispositions, however, also vary with time of day and quality of the department (the later in the day and the higher ranked the school, the more obnoxious the interviewers are likely to be).

Get to your interviews on time. Being punctual is not usually a problem, provided not too many of your interviews are scheduled back to back. Dress so that you convey a professional image: attempt to look presentable and well groomed, which does not mean that you need to wear a five-hundred-dollar suit! Do not give the impression of being overly chummy with the interviewer, but be sure to shake hands before and after the interview. Most important, try to relax. While this is usually easier said than done, draw comfort from the fact that most of your interviewers probably have not read your paper or any other work in your field. Therefore, if you have prepared well, it is very unlikely that you will face a question that you are unable to answer satisfactorily.

Keep your answers short and make your points without technical detail. Try to avoid responses that appear glib or cavalier. Be sure to stress the relevance of your dissertation research, and if one or more of your interviewers has worked in the same area, note the relation of your research to his or her work. If you are interviewing at a teaching school, mention the importance you attach to teaching and the course material you intend to develop. Throughout these interviews and in preparing for them, remember that your ultimate objective is to portray yourself as bright, articulate, and congenial and to convince your interviewers that you will make a fine colleague.

AFTER THE MEETINGS

As with scheduling interviews, schools vary in the time it takes them to decide on which candidates to invite for campus visits. As a rule, higher-ranked departments tend to make these decisions earlier but this varies also with the length of the Christmas vacations taken by members of the recruitment committee. If you plan to be out of town during the semester recess, leave a number where you can be contacted with the secretary in the department. Some early birds may call back as soon as ten days after the meetings.

After you receive a couple of callbacks, if you have not heard from some of the schools that interviewed you and in which you are still interested, call and tell them as modestly as possible that you are in demand. This helps them make up their minds more quickly. If you are invited to a school in a given region (for example, California) and had interviews at the meeting with neighboring schools, call and tell them you will be in the area. If these schools were hesitant to pay the entire cost of your trip, such an offer often induces them to invite you to visit them as well.

If your interviews went exceptionally well, you may be flooded with calls from schools. Because each visit takes much energy, you may want to be choosy after a couple of visits. It is perfectly acceptable (even, perhaps, ethical) to turn down campus visits if you are not seriously interested in the school and think it likely that you will have offers elsewhere. Remember that the novelty of free rides vanishes quickly when a seminar awaits you at the end of each one. When you are contacted about the campus visit, you will also probably be informed about transportation from the airport and of the other arrangements for your visit. If such information is not volunteered, save yourself problems during the visit by asking for it at this stage.

In making your travel plans, it would be wise to make reservations via an on-line travel service such as Expedia or Orbitz. You will find that the whole process requires substantial resources since you will be expected to incur most of the travel expenses up front and will be reimbursed weeks or sometimes even months after your campus visit. The best preparation is to ask the department about reimbursement procedures.

Each campus visit is filled with a day of interviews and your seminar. The day usually begins at breakfast with a member of the department and ends only after dinner with a group of faculty. Each visit is exhausting, and you have to be prepared physically and mentally.

Apart from the sixty- to ninety-minute seminar in which you will be expected to present some of your work, the day will be filled with thirty- to forty-five-minute interviews with individual faculty members. These interviews with faculty are more informal than the interview at the meetings. The questions you will be asked during these can vary from technical ones concerning your current or future research to more mundane ones about your graduate program or faculty advisers.

Your objectives during these interviews should be twofold. First, to present yourself in the best possible light, particularly as being stimulating and well informed. Second, you should get information about the department and the school so that you can judge how well you might fit in if you are offered a position. Remember that most schools are selling themselves to you just as much as you are trying to impress them. They will be only too willing to talk to you about themselves. Relevant questions that you might ask include the research interests of faculty, the importance of teaching, relations between junior and senior faculty, research funding and summer support. You will definitely meet with the department chair and at least a couple of assistant professors—all of whom are good sources of information about the department.

The seminar is the most important part of the visit. Because your success usually hinges on your performance, work hard on preparing your presentation right after the meetings so that you are ready when the campus visits begin. Work especially on the introduction and conclusion. Give a practice seminar to friends or colleagues before you "take the show on the road." As you give seminars at different schools, pick up hints on substance and style and incorporate suggestions into your presentation at the next stop.

Don't count on being given time to prepare your talk right before every seminar. In your presentation, make your introduction and conclusion sufficiently general in tone and content so that you appeal to most of your audience rather than solely to those in your specific area. Try to keep calm even when some of the questioning turns pointed or critical. This will be easier if you can separate yourself from your work enough so as not to consider professional criticism a personal attack (obviously harder in practice than it sounds). It should help your nerves to remember that you know more about the material you are presenting than anyone else does and that you are the one in control during the seminar.

The key to your campus visit is to relax and enjoy as much of it as you can. This is not easy since you will be the focus of attention, but concentrate on being alert, personable, and bright, and above all, don't worry about your competition.

It is excruciating to wait for offers after you conclude a set of campus visits. Even a day seems forever at this stage, but it often takes quite a while for schools to make final decisions. So you have to keep visiting other schools until something comes through. But remember that all you really need from all these visits is one acceptable offer! Once you have an offer, you can either accept it or use it to pressure the other schools that you have visited into making a decision (if you think that you might prefer their offers).

Finally, it will all be over the day you sign on the dotted line, politely turn down any other offers you might have had, and celebrate your good fortune at not having to join the reserve army of the unemployed. After the partying is over, it will begin to sink in that the hardest part still lies ahead. You have to get back to the unfinished dissertation that has been almost forgotten in all the excitement but that still lies between you and life after graduate school. After the ups and down of the job market experience though, even the dissertation may seem more appealing.

13.

OFF-TRACK VETTING

JOHN G. CROSS AND EDIE N. GOLDENBERG

Academic positions off the tenure track have long been considered consolation prizes — jobs to take when nothing is available on the tenure track and jobs to occupy only as long as nothing better opens up. In this essay we take issue with that view. With support from the Andrew Mellon Foundation, we have been studying the forces that drive institutional decisions to hire faculty on or off the tenure track at a dozen of the nation's premiere research universities. Based upon that experience, we have learned that times are changing. Some non-tenure-track teaching positions are worth serious consideration by doctoral students who want to define themselves first and foremost as undergraduate teachers in their professional careers.

This discussion has four parts:

1. We begin by describing the traditional view of non-tenure-track academic employment, a view that is overwhelmingly negative in terms of the quality of working life for individuals, the functioning of the university, and the health of the tenure system.

2. Then we turn to a more positive view drawn from our study findings. Without claiming to cover entirely the diverse world of higher education, we describe some of the desirable non-tenure-track opportunities at elite research universities today for Ph.D.'s who prefer to place their commitments to undergraduate education ahead of cutting edge research.

3. We offer some advice to individual job seekers on how to vet these opportunities — what to look for as you consider a non-tenure-track opening and how to gather reliable information.

4. Finally, we close with some observations on the implications of the changing world of academic employment.

THE TRADITIONAL VIEW: TEACHING AS A CONSOLATION PRIZE

Many of those newly leaving graduate schools with Ph.D. in hand are interested in and excited by the prospect of teaching at the college level. Unfortunately, the attractions of teaching are often compromised by the widespread perception among mentors and peers that the only "respectable" positions in higher education place primary emphasis on research. Job recommendations by advisers focus on the top elite research universities, or, failing that, on strong research universities that encourage faculty to achieve a goal of outstanding research and scholarship. This strategy ignores the fact that the number of tenure-track positions in research institutions falls far short of the number of new Ph.D.'s who graduate every year, and it disadvantages those whose interests incline more toward teaching. There is no question that effective teaching always requires long-term intellectual growth and participation in one's discipline, but it is not true that a successful career in academia must always place research activity ahead of pedagogy.

This dilemma is heightened by the fact that those whose primary commitments are in teaching often find themselves in instructional positions that lack the prestige and security enjoyed by research-focused faculty. This lesser status may be reinforced by a graduate student's own advisers, who, more often than not, regard teaching-focused careers as low on the academic ladder. Occasionally, one hears from graduate students who hide their inclination toward teaching for fear that their own advisers will lose respect for them or even disown them.

Standard descriptions of lecturer roles are very unflattering: "contingent workers" who are poorly paid, insecure, unappreciated, part-time, itinerant, and lacking benefits.[1] Unfortunately, that characterization can be accurate. In many institutions around the country, including some community colleges, large public institutions, comprehensives, and private colleges and universities, Ph.D.'s who choose to take on non-tenure-track teaching jobs can have a difficult time earning a living wage in their chosen professions.

The burden of lower status can be compounded if the higher education employers themselves behave as though pedagogically focused positions are not central to their mission — in spite of the fact that colleges and universities are essentially teaching institutions. If employers hire non-tenure-track employees only because they must and not because they want to, no one should be surprised to find an environment for such hires that is less than ideal. Selection of a teaching-focused career off the tenure track may expose one to a set of academic opportunities that not only lack tenure but also lack job security, a living wage, decent benefits, intellectual respect, time and resources for intellectual development, and even the resources — such as a private office or a computer — needed to provide excellent teaching.

An important difference between the situations of tenure-track and non-tenure-track faculty has to do with their influence over their teaching assignments. Tenured members of the faculty have far more control over their own teaching roles than do untenured faculty. Unwillingness to accept a particular teaching assignment — commonplace these days among tenured faculty — would compromise the position of any untenured faculty member — including an assistant professor on the tenure track — and would almost certainly end the employment of a part-time faculty member.

The traditional view sees non-tenure-track jobs as exploitative and attributes the growth in the numbers of such positions to budgetary stringency rather than to any sensibly directed hiring plan. A corollary is that the faculty employed in non-tenure-track positions must be frustrated and unhappy in their work life since they really aspire to tenured positions at their institutions. Given the growth in union organizing activity among lecturers and adjuncts on many campuses, there is evidently some truth to these claims. The traditional view further asserts that the use of faculty off the tenure track produces a two-class system that erodes colleagueship on campus and the institution of tenure nationwide.

TIMES ARE CHANGING: TEACHING AS A CAREER CHOICE

Full-Time Non-Tenure-Track Teaching   Many faculty members find teaching-intensive roles fulfilling and intensely rewarding. They do not regret for a moment the time spent in the classroom rather than the laboratory. In the past, new Ph.D.'s seeking a teaching-focused career applied to liberal arts colleges rather than research-oriented universities. Today, it may be easier to pursue a teaching-focused role as an academic off the tenure track at a prestigious research institution than it is at a prestigious liberal arts college. The status of pedagogically oriented faculty is gradually increasing at research-intensive universities, as administrators are coming to appreciate their educational contributions and are responding with improved status, greater job security, and higher salaries. Ironically, the scholarly expectations at the most prestigious liberal arts colleges have increased over time, even in the face of very demanding pedagogical roles, and faculty there feel substantial pressure with regard to research and publication. The best of these colleges adhere to the practice of employing teacher-scholars, while the best universities have moved toward a model under which faculty take on more specialized roles.

Based upon our campus visits, we believe the conventional description of a non-tenure-track career is inappropriately generalized and too pessimistic for some situations; opportunities do exist with decent pay and benefits, security and appreciation. We have learned of recent moves to professionalize the non-tenure-track positions at a number of distinguished research universities, and we can now recommend those positions to some of our own Ph.D.'s. Professionalization of the non-tenure-track is a fairly recent phenomenon at most research universities and might even be considered a process happening in real time. The trend appears to be moving in the direction of making these positions more desirable for job applicants who choose to focus on their educational role. We find this an interesting and important development that has been largely overlooked.

Perhaps the best-known arrangement originated at Duke University, which initiated its "professor of practice" (POP) appointment system more than a decade ago. Administrators at Duke created these positions in order to end a system of rolling one-year appointments that offered little security and low pay. Today, an assistant professor of practice at Duke initially receives a three-year contract. As the faculty member moves up the promotion ladder to associate or full professor of practice, the contract term may increase to five, seven, or even ten years. Some of these faculty, like their tenured colleagues, are hired after national searches; others become POPs as a consequence of opportunities that arise, such as a dual-career negotiation, a decision by an assistant professor to switch off of the tenure track, or a Ph.D. who wants to be affiliated with an intellectually exciting institution and is willing to do so in a teaching role. Professors of practice have full benefits except for sabbaticals; they receive promotion increases; and they are considered part of the "regular" faculty. They can compete for "dean's leaves," which serve the same function as sabbatical leaves, although the number of these available each term is limited. POPs receive the same college tuition support/rebates for their children as do other Duke employees. Appointments to the POP system fill regular faculty slots; therefore, departments debate the desirability of these appointments and the tradeoffs implicit in choosing a POP rather than another tenure-track hire. A decision to hire a professor of practice reflects the value of the position for the department. These faculty often serve as advisers as well as directors of undergraduate studies in their departments, and two professors of practice currently serve as chairs of Duke academic departments. The system has become regularized; professors of practice today constitute 20 percent of the arts and sciences faculty at Duke.

Consistent with the increased emphasis on pedagogy, teaching expectations are rigorous for non-tenure-track faculty. Research expectations are much smaller than they are for tenure-track faculty, but teaching loads may be five or six courses per year. Salary levels vary widely, with some at levels similar to tenure-track or tenured faculty and others falling behind. However, we did not hear of cases at Duke of the low salaries that border on exploitation at some other large universities.

Although they are more recent in origin and are often less fully developed than the system at Duke, similar arrangements are becoming possible at several other distinguished research institutions. For example:

— Northwestern University has a promotion system for lecturers in arts and sciences, first to senior lecturer and then to college lecturer. Many are on three- or five-year contracts. In the Kellogg School of Engineering, non-tenure-track faculty members have "rolling" contracts that extend for five years from the current date of employment. Lecturers generally teach six courses per year, and everyone who teaches at least half time receives health and retirement benefits.

— The University of Michigan employs full-time lecturers on three-year contracts with health and retirement benefits. Michigan's lecturers recently unionized and now negotiate for salary and security. Systems of performance evaluation for lecturers are required and are under development.

— The University of California at Berkeley also has a unionized non-tenure-track category that is now called "non-Senate faculty" rather than "lecturer." In a memorandum of understanding, Berkeley administrators detail the salary scale as well as the minimum teaching activities required to qualify for benefits for non-Senate faculty. At their sixth year, the non-Senate faculty members undergo special reviews; if approved, they have an added degree of job security, receive continuing renewals, are reviewed every three years by the campus budget committee, and have access to an established appeals process. There are also a smaller number of positions at Berkeley called "lecturers with security of employment" that are not part of the union and are classified as Senate faculty.

Research-intensive universities hire full-time non-tenure-track faculty for many reasons. One is to fill in gaps in the curriculum that tenure-track faculty cannot or will not fill. Having hired tenure-track faculty for the sake of their potential contribution to the frontiers of research as well as for their ability to teach in these same areas, administrators are sometimes loathe to ask or require these faculty to teach courses in areas that are not vital research subjects. As it happens, there are a number of courses in any liberal arts curriculum that reside at the foundation of a student's education but that may not currently be subjects for significant research activity. These cover such subjects as basic calculus, introductory (and often advanced) language instruction, English composition, actuarial science, and the introductory courses in statistics and economics. These subjects are often assigned to non-tenure-track faculty in recognition of large enrollments, the need to offer effective instruction in these fundamental areas, and the fact that research opportunities in these areas are so limited as to make effective recruitment of research-active tenure track faculty to teach these courses very difficult.

These foundational courses are usually taken in the first two years of an undergraduate's career, and thus teaching assignments given to non-tenure-track faculty are overwhelmingly found in the "lower division" of a college curriculum. Moreover, even our most selective colleges and universities find that they have admitted a few students who are unprepared for college level work in one discipline or another, requiring either special courses or tutorial work to correct the deficiencies. It is very common for these teaching responsibilities to be given to non-tenure-track faculty.

All this is not intended to denigrate the significance of these teaching roles—indeed, many people find the opportunity to bring about tangible change in the intellectual awareness and capacity of younger college students to be extremely rewarding. Moreover, from the perspective of the college or university, these contributions are immensely valuable. In our own interviews, we have found that successful teachers in these areas are highly valued as colleagues and contributors to the overall institutional mission. There is no foundation for the widespread suspicion that capricious termination of non-tenure-track faculty in these roles is just around the corner.

Part-Time Non-Tenure-Track Teaching   General interest in part-time positions appears to be growing nationally. The opportunity to work under less stress, with greater opportunity to pursue independent goals or more rewarding home situations, can appeal even to graduates who have just received their Ph.D.'s.

For years, part-time non-tenure-track teaching positions have been commonplace and desirable in certain disciplines. Faculty in performance, the visual arts, or creative writing frequently have little interest in full-time teaching positions. For them, part-time teaching offers periodic opportunity for intellectual renewal and challenge at the same time that it leaves time for pursuit of their primary creative mission. Obviously, it also offers some degree of financial security in notoriously uncertain occupations. Nowadays, these individuals are being joined by others with established careers in engineering, business, and a variety of other professions who welcome an opportunity to work with students on a part-time (and occasionally full-time) basis. As programs in architecture, theater, film, and creative writing have grown, distinguished artists are more and more frequently welcomed as part-time members of the teaching faculty.

Institutions of higher education vary widely in the extent to which they are willing to support part-time employees. Multi-year commitments are rare, and a part-time appointment will almost certainly be the first to evaporate in the face of a decline of student interest or financial exigency. Moreover, colleges and universities vary in their willingness to offer benefit packages to part-time employees. Most of the universities that we have studied provide medical and retirement plans to any employee with an appointment fraction of 80 percent or more, and many offer benefits to 50 percent employees. This is far from a universal practice, however, and many comprehensive colleges, community colleges, and small private colleges do not offer benefits to any employee with an appointment below 100 percent. Apart from the obvious economic disadvantage, teaching positions at these institutions can still be rewarding. It is well to bear in mind, however, that inclusion in a benefits program is a status variable that can symbolize an institution's respect for, and commitment to, its teaching faculty. Positions that lack benefits are often not positions on which one can build a successful long-term career.

VETTING OFF-TRACK OPPORTUNITIES: HOW TO DECIDE?

An unfortunate aspect of the "traditional view" of non-tenure-track faculty as second-class citizens is that many new Ph.D.'s graduate with the belief that a research-oriented tenure-track position is the *only* viable career choice. When such a position does not materialize (which is statistically inevitable for many), these graduates often accept non-tenure-track positions as though they were merely interim positions, while they wait for "something better." This attitude leads them to place fewer demands on employers than they would if the positions were regarded as first steps in a career. This is a mistake, partly because for many, a tenure-track position in a major institution is unlikely, and partly because it generates self-confirming hypotheses. If no one is selective about accepting a position, employers will be given little incentive to improve the conditions that they offer. For Ph.D.'s who enter careers that are focused on undergraduate education, non-tenure-track positions, whether part-time or full-time, can be respectable and respected within the institution. The conditions of employment that have evolved and are still evolving set something of a standard of comparison that can be used to evaluate other opportunities. We have identified a few core issues that merit review by anyone considering a non-tenure-track opportunity:

1. Look for an institution with promotional opportunities that offer salaries that increase in real terms as non-tenure-track faculty advance through the academic ranks. An important indicator that a college or university takes teaching

roles seriously is that salary advancement occurs for teaching-oriented faculty. Indeed, in well-established systems, the salaries of some teaching-intensive faculty approach those of similarly ranked faculty on the tenure track. This is not surprising: as a general rule, merit-based systems can generate a very broad distribution of salaries of tenure-track faculty. In research-intensive institutions, some tenure-track faculty may have very high salaries, but less research-active faculty receive salaries that have not grown and that ultimately can fall below the salaries of non-tenure-track faculty.

If salaries are public, as they are at most public institutions, then look them up and see how they have changed for various types of appointments over time. At private institutions, salaries are rarely public and a job candidate will have to talk with a few individuals in non-tenure-track positions about their salary experiences over time.

2. Look at opportunities for continued employment. A number of research universities still have formal policies that limit the possible length of appointment of non-tenure-track faculty, either by limiting the absolute number of years or by limiting the number of permissible appointment renewals. Jobs with such limits may be just fine for someone who seeks temporary employment, but not for those interested in a career. It is almost impossible to build a successful teaching career in an environment in which termination is inevitable after a few years of participation.

An attractive situation should offer appointment terms of more than one year with adequate notice for termination and no stringent rule that limits the employment, in advance, to a set number of years. There may an initial probationary period of one year, but the rules should be clear for advancing beyond probation to a longer term contract.

Over time, rules that limit the length of permissible appointments are being dropped, but vestiges remain. In some cases, practices vary from school to school within the same university. Professional schools value the skills that practitioners bring, whether architects or dentists or doctors or lawyers, and appear to be more open to welcoming "clinical" or non-tenure-track faculty to their midst on a long-term basis. Arts and sciences colleges are only recently reassessing their reliance on and treatment of non-tenured faculty.

To assess a particular situation, you are advised to ask administrators about these rules, ask to see them in writing and then talk with a few non-tenure-track individuals to learn how the rules have been applied in practice. The bottom line is this: if, because of a university's policies, eventual termination is inevitable, start looking *immediately* for an alternative situation. Do not permit the convenience of a short-term appointment to lead eventually to an employment crisis.

3. Understand the system of performance reviews and the expectations for

performance. A regular (and productive) system of performance reviews is a must. All institutions of higher education engage in careful performance reviews of their tenure-track faculty. Obvious examples are the typical third-year reviews of new assistant professors and the very thorough tenure reviews that usually come in the sixth year. Less obvious are the annual performance reviews of tenured faculty that motivate individual salary changes.

Performance reviews of non-tenure-track faculty may occur every year or, more typically, every three to five years. The point is that a well-designed and serious system of reviews is an important indicator of the value that an institution places on teaching and is therefore an important indicator of the value that the institution will place on you and your commitment to good teaching. Find out what counts in terms of your education contribution and what counts for renewal and promotion. For example, is there any expectation of national visibility in educational circles? Can you count on something in addition to student evaluations and enrollment numbers as measures of your effectiveness if you plan to redesign courses or demand more from your students?

4. Although it may seem obvious, you should be acknowledged to be a colleague among the "regular" faculty. We occasionally encounter an institution that refuses to consider non-tenure-track instructors to be members of its "faculty." Acceptance of a position at such an institution virtually guarantees that, irrespective of performance, permanent second-class status is inevitable. This consideration is not meant to imply that every benefit available to tenured or tenure-track faculty must also be available to those off the tenure track, but most benefits will be available to all and there will be a very careful justification for differences. To avoid surprises, you should understand in advance whether you would become a member of the faculty senate and what your voting rights would be in your department, college, and university.

5. Negotiate up front for things that matter. For example, paid leave for research does not come automatically to non-tenure-track faculty. Funds for travel to conferences and to support professional development should not be assumed. Even if a non-tenure-track faculty member is asked to teach a training course for graduate teaching assistants, that same faculty member may not be part of the graduate faculty or eligible to teach any other graduate course or sit on a dissertation committee. Computer upgrades may not be automatic. Try to figure out in advance what matters to you and seek assurances in writing or write a letter of understanding to the responsible appointing authority yourself.

CONCLUSION

The number of non-tenure-track positions has been growing over time far faster than the number of tenure-track positions.[2] There are many reasons for this differential growth, and there is not room to dwell on them here. It is enough to acknowledge that it has been a fact of academic life for several years and shows every sign of continuing. This growth is widely condemned in professional magazines and the popular press, but without much effect. It is possible that we are witnessing a gradual but fundamental structural change in the organization of higher education, and that the frequent public criticisms of non-tenure-track positions as "second class" at the individual level and "points of erosion of the overall system of tenure" at the macro-level amount to little more than rear-guard objections to inevitable social change.

What is important to consider for a new Ph.D. with a strong interest in undergraduate teaching is that the environment of higher education has become fiercely competitive—for research active faculty, for students, and, indeed, for effective teaching. A reputation for outstanding teaching is becoming increasingly important in that competition, and hence pedagogically oriented instructors are becoming recognized at some institutions as essential to the core college or university mission. This is not to say that we expect a national competition for non-tenure-track lecturers to evolve on the same scale that we see for research-active faculty or top-rated students, but given the trends that we observe at a number of the nation's most prestigious research universities, we do expect institutions of higher education to be pressed more and more to conform to competitive personnel practices. The opportunities for non-tenure-track employment are growing and the conditions of employment at selected institutions are improving. To attract and retain outstanding non-tenure-track faculty, more and more institutions will need to improve the conditions of non-tenure-track employment.

We recognize that our systems of academic employment are changing in ways that have consequences for individuals seeking employment and for universities seeking talent. Our focus in this essay is directed toward individuals who consciously select teaching-intensive careers. There are certainly recent Ph.D.'s who have committed themselves to research careers but who have not found suitable employment; for them, a part-time teaching position or even a full-time teaching position off the tenure track will not be satisfactory. A casual review of the literature might give the impression that *all* academic jobs off the tenure track are part-time positions filled with frustrated research-oriented faculty, and that our transportation networks are clogged with "freeway faculty," who, not finding a full-time job to their liking, have assembled multiple part-time positions at several institutions in order to cadge together one full-time job. Unfortunately, the existing literature relies on surveys that do not reveal the *reasons* that faculty have accepted non-tenure-track appointments. The image of hordes of academics desperately accepting multiple poorly paid part-time positions as their only source of employment is certainly overdrawn, but we have no data sufficient to clarify the extent of this phenomenon.

With these provisos in mind, we can now encourage our best graduate students who want to emphasize their educational roles over their research roles in a stimulating academic setting to consider non-tenure-track options at selected distinguished research institutions, as well as at liberal arts colleges. Having learned more about the working conditions and job satisfaction in such roles at a dozen elite universities, we now believe it is possible to vet these opportunities and choose one that matches a student's employment objectives. For one devoted to a life as an educator who prefers to avoid the scholarly pressures of tenure, we encourage careful exploration of these opportunities.

NOTES

We gratefully acknowledge the generous support of the Andrew W. Mellon Foundation and the able research assistance of Keith Rainwater and Kharis Templeman.
1. Robert B. Townsend, "Changing Relationships, Changing Values in the American Classroom," in Ernst Benjamin, ed., *Exploring the Role of Contingent Instructional Staff in Undergraduate Learning*, no. 123 (Jossey-Bass: San Francisco, 2003), 23–32.
2. Ernst Benjamin, "Editor's Notes," in Benjamin, ed., *Exploring the Role of Contingent Instructional Staff*, 5.

14

THE TENURE SYSTEM

MATTHEW W. FINKIN

Most of the new Ph.D.'s who obtain positions as full-time assistant professors at one of the two thousand or so four-year colleges and universities in this country will serve under a system of faculty appointment and retention characterized by a relatively lengthy period of probationary service at the close of which the probationer is either given a terminal appointment or accorded academic tenure. Though the tenure system has always had its critics and is being eroded today by indirection, it continues to be a major feature of the academic enterprise. It is important, therefore, that the new assistant professor understand the history, the nature, and the purpose of the system.

Any such examination has to begin with the 1940 *Statement of Principle on Academic Freedom and Tenure* and the role of the American Association of University Professors (AAUP). The 1940 *Statement* was drafted jointly by the AAUP and the Association of American Colleges and is currently endorsed by over a hundred and eighty educational organizations and disciplinary societies. It has become generally accepted as the norm governing four-year colleges and universities. The 1940 *Statement* provides at the outset:

> Tenure is a means to certain ends; specifically: (1) freedom of teaching and research and of extramural activities, and (2) a sufficient degree of economic security to make the profession attractive to men and women of ability. Freedom and economic security, hence, tenure, are indispensable to the success of an institution in fulfilling its obligations to its students and to society.

The latter draws attention to the connection between freedom, economic security, and societal welfare, and it should be self-evident. The former refers to "academic freedom" and it is not self-explanatory. Whence a word on it, below. But this synopsis leaves one aspect unstated: it states how tenure serves society and the academic profession, but it does not state how tenure serves the institution. That will be treated a little later on.

The AAUP is a membership organization founded in 1915 to advance the standards, ideals, and welfare of the academic profession. It immediately assumed the role of defining and advancing the concept of academic freedom and the system of academic tenure in these institutions. It did this first in its founding document, the 1915 *Declaration of Principles on Academic Freedom and Tenure*, and in a series of investigations by specially appointed ad hoc committees of inquiry into contested cases implicating these standards. (The investigatory and reporting function became a major feature of the AAUP's academic freedom and tenure portfolio and has continued from 1915 to the present.) A decade later, the AAUP joined in a *Conference Statement* produced under the auspices of the American Council on Education; and, a decade after that, it commenced negotiations with the Association of American Colleges (AAC) on a successor document, which became the joint 1940 *Statement*. (The AAC, the leading organization of four-year liberal arts institutions, was later renamed the Association of American Colleges and Universities.) The joint drafting organizations agreed that the AAUP would serve the function of applying the 1940 *Statement* in discrete situations. The tasks of refining the meaning of the 1940 *Statement* (the "legislative" function) and of applying it in contested cases (the "judicial" function) were placed in the hands of the Association's Committee A on Academic Freedom and Tenure (which has sat continuously since 1915) and of the Association's professional staff attached to it. A word on these functions is necessary.

The judicial function. Any faculty member, irrespective of Association membership, who believes his or her academic rights to have been violated may approach the Committee A professional staff for advice and assistance. If Association action is sought thereafter the matter is regarded as a "complaint" in the AAUP's lexicon. (So, too, any college or university administrator who believes he or she would benefit from the Association's experience may seek advice.) If the faculty member's complaint appears to be of significance under the 1940 *Statement*, the staff member will approach the relevant officer of administration and attempt to effect a resolution satisfactory under Association-supported standards. This approach alters the status of the matter from a "complaint" to a "case" in the AAUP's lexicon. (The meditative work of the professional staff consumes a large amount, perhaps a plurality, of Committee A staff work.) Disputes that prove intractable of resolution and which are especially serious under Association-supported standards are subject to the investigation-report process via an ad hoc committee of inquiry, first undertaken in 1915, and made subject of possible institutional censure by the Association, which publishes a list of censured administrations.

TABLE 14.1 All Complaints and Cases Handled by the Washington Office of the AAUP

	Total
2000	1,051
2001	967
2002	998
2003	1,051
2004	1,121

Source: AAUP, Annual Reports of Committee A, 2000–2004.

To convey a sense of the AAUP as a national clearinghouse for issues of academic freedom and tenure, the "judicial business" of the Association for the recent five-year period, 2000–2004, is set out in table 14.1.

The legislative function. The 1940 *Statement* characteristically speaks in general terms. What these mean in particular and recurring situations often calls for further refinement. Some of these refinements are supplied in additional jointly formulated documents, e.g., the joint AAUP-AAC 1958 *Statement on Procedural Standards in Faculty Dismissal Proceedings*, and some in unilaterally issued documents such as the *Statement on Procedural Standards in the Renewal or Nonrenewal of Faculty Appointments* adopted in 1989. A complete compendium is available on the Association's Web site: www.aaup.org.

ACADEMIC FREEDOM

The American claim to academic freedom, though of Germanic origin, drew breath in the struggle of the academic profession to emerge from clerical and lay control at the turn of the twentieth century,[1] particularly in the claims of professors of economics and of the social sciences to teach, investigate, and publish conclusions at odds with the prevailing orthodoxies regnant on the governing boards of their employing institutions or occupying the chairs of their presidencies. The claim would draw continuing sustenance in subsequent controversies — over political affiliation and expression in the 1940s and 1950s, over the Vietnam War in the 1960s and 1970s, over "political correctness" and the "culture wars" in the 1980s and 1990s, and in renascent nationalism and ultraconservatism (whose critique is sometimes couched as in defense of academic freedom qua political heterodoxy in faculty selection) in the first decade of the twenty-first century.

The claim of academic freedom (and so tenure) was advanced at a time when higher education was dominated by private institutions, many under denominational control, and when the free-speech rights guaranteed against state infringement by the First Amendment did not extend to speech by public employees. Today, higher education is dominated by the public sector—at least in the number of students enrolled and of faculty employed; and, since a 1968 Supreme Court decision, public employees, including the faculties of public universities, do enjoy the protection of the First Amendment. But constitutional free speech is not coterminous with academic freedom: It applies only to the public sector; and it subjects the speaker to a judicial balancing test that weighs the speech against its potential for bringing "disharmony" to the workplace.

In contrast to a public employee's privilege to engage in political discourse, academic freedom rests squarely on the professor's special disciplinary competence. The professor's claim of freedom to express, test, and extend knowledge rests upon professional training, the development of specialized skills, and the mastery of a discipline. The claim is that one is exercising a professional prerogative not shared by the citizenry at large. In consequence, the academic is held to a standard of professional care. A university groundskeeper may publish a book arguing to the merits of astrology, but a professor of astronomy might do so at his peril.

The point is not the seemingly paradoxical one that as a matter of "free speech" a groundskeeper may write a bad book but a professor may not, but that academic freedom is at once more narrowly circumscribed and, within its confines, more protective than is a public employee's exercise of political speech. Within the realm of professional utterance, so long as the professor has adhered to the canons of responsible scholarship—has not falsified evidence, knowingly misrepresented the evidence, or acted in wanton disregard of the evidence—he or she is not to be placed at risk because of the controversial nature of what he or she has to say. So long as the professor has adhered to a professional standard of care, disciplinary discourse is not to be weighed against any consideration of collegial disharmony, hierarchical accountability, or extramural displeasure.

Academic freedom in teaching is less absolute, but not much. The freedom to select curricular materials may be constrained by a departmental prerogative to require a common syllabus and even a common text for multisectioned courses. The professor may be required adequately to cover the announced offering before addressing collateral, if seemingly more interesting, material. And the persistent interjection of controversial (or any other) matter not germane to the offering would not be protected. But, subject to a professional obligation to state opposing views fairly (analogous to the requirement in research that the evidence not be distorted) and to treat with respect students who disagree, the

teacher is free to espouse controversial views that are germane to the subject —
and passionately. Contrary to some contemporary critics, freedom of teaching
is not limited by any obligation of "balance" or "objectivity"; the freedom is
accorded equally to committed partisanship as to dispassionate dissection.

The professor is not only a researcher and teacher but, in a sense, a citizen of
an academic community. Faculty members are expected to serve on a variety of
committees and other agencies of academic government that recommend institutional policy or effectively make decisions under them; faculty play a host
of adjudicative and advisory roles. Accordingly, the AAUP long understood the
performance of these professional duties to be within the compass of academic
freedom. A professor's appointment cannot be terminated because of displeasure with the views he or she advances on the content of the curriculum, admissions standards, grading practices, and the like. By extension, the professor
is free to criticize institutional policies and practices with which she disagrees.

That extension, however, is not without recognized limits. As in the civil setting, the protection of speech on intramural affairs would not extend to the
malicious utterance of knowing falsehoods tending to destroy another's professional reputation, nor, on a very different level, would it extend to conduct
(including speech) that is destructive of a department's or institution's very
ability to function — the persistent proffering of pointless motions and objections during the conduct of faculty business with no purpose but to prevent the
business being carried out could claim no shelter.

The last aspect of academic freedom requires comment, for the claim has
been advanced even as to a professor's political speech and activity as a citizen.
The 1940 *Statement*, promulgated almost thirty years before public employees
were held to enjoy the protection of the First Amendment, subsumed the professor's speech as a citizen under the rubric of academic freedom. That sub-
sumption has been criticized because it would seem to assume that the professor is to be held to a professional standard of care,[2] a higher standard than that
accorded our groundskeeper. The error in connecting the two has been compounded, some argue, by the 1940 *Statement*'s admonition that the professor's
"special position in the community imposes special obligations" — that as the
public may judge the professor by his utterance, he or she should "at all times
be accurate, should exercise appropriate restraint, should show respect for the
opinions of others."

These admonitions, however, have not been understood by the AAUP as establishing rules of conduct. A failure to exercise "appropriate restraint" may,
under certain circumstances, be a basis to inquire into a professor's fitness for
office — total indifference to the facts in political speech may raise a question of
whether the scholar is equally indifferent in his professional work — but it can-

not be a basis for dismissal. Suffice it to say, the drafters of the 1940 *Statement*, writing at a time when professors were not free political actors, sought to shelter that activity from institutional restraint or censorship. Perhaps it might be well to think of this portion of the *Statement* as addressing an *academic's* freedom rather than an *academic* freedom.

Two additional points to this overview of academic freedom bear upon its relationship to tenure: First, the courts cannot be trusted to vindicate academic values, and, second, even if they could, that vindication would arrive only after the professor had been dismissed and pursued years of pretrial discovery, litigation, and, possibly, appeal. What is needed, in order to protect the exercise of academic freedom, is the insulation of the individual from that risk: whence tenure. As William Van Alstyne put it:

> The function of tenure is not only to encourage the development of specialized learning and professional expertise by providing a reasonable assurance against the dispiriting risk of summary termination; it is to maximize the freedom of the professional scholar and teacher to benefit society through the innovation and dissemination of perspectives and discoveries aided by his investigations, without fear that he must accommodate his honest perspectives to the conventional wisdom. The point is as old as Galileo and, indeed, as new as Arthur Jensen.[3]

This function of tenure has been challenged as "absolutizing" academic freedom: "[T]enure can never protect or guarantee academic freedom," John Silber opined. "Academic freedom is protected and guaranteed by the *courage* of individual professors, and by individual administrators who protect individual members of the faculty, and by students. If they express their freedom responsibly, they will not expect immunity from criticism or public disapproval; they will recognize these risks as one of the essential conditions of responsibility."[4] That argument was dispatched over forty years ago by the economist Fritz Machlup:

> Great scholars, great discoverers, great inventors, great teachers, great philosophers may be timid men, or they may not care enough to face vilification, or they may be too "realistic" to invite trouble. A society that wishes to avail itself of the fruits of their intellectual enterprise must give them as much immunity as possible. Assuming as a fact that scholars may be timid or too "realistic," society has developed the institution of academic freedom in order to reduce the penalties on unpopular unorthodoxy or on unfashionable orthodoxy and to encourage scholars to say whatever they feel that they have to say.[5]

TENURE

Irrespective of individual disciplines, all new academics are one in their hope to achieve tenure. They are also probably one in their misconceptions about what tenure really means. I shall try, therefore, to clear the doubts somewhat by dealing first with what tenure is and then with what it is not. A good general explanation of tenure has been supplied, again, by Van Alstyne:

> The conferral of tenure means that the institution, after utilizing a probationary period of as long as six years in which it has had ample opportunity to determine the professional competence and responsibility of its appointees, has rendered a favorable judgment establishing a rebuttable presumption of the individual's professional excellence. As the lengthy term of probationary service will have provided the institution with sufficient experience to determine whether the faculty member is worthy of a presumption of professional fitness, it has not seemed unreasonable to shift to the individual the benefit of doubt when the institution thereafter extends his service beyond the period of probation and, correspondingly, to shift to the institution the obligation fairly to show why, if at all, that faculty member should nonetheless be fired. The presumption of the tenured faculty member's professional excellence thus remains rebuttable, exactly to the extent that when it can be shown that the individual possessing tenure has nonetheless fallen short or has otherwise misconducted himself as determined according to full academic due process, the presumption is lost and the individual is subject to dismissal.[6]

Academic due process requires a trial-like hearing before a faculty body with the burden of proof resting upon the administration. Ordinarily, the faculty's power is only to make a recommendation to the institution's governing board, but the findings of the faculty are — or should be — entitled considerable weight. The faculty is more familiar with professional standards and is in a better position to pass upon questions of mitigation and level of sanction than is a lay governing board.

The ground upon which a tenured appointment may be terminated is "adequate cause," usually meaning some significant dereliction or misconduct but including professional incompetence as well: physical or mental incapacity and the existence of a bona fide financial exigency are additional bases for the termination of tenured appointments. The latter has been a major source of controversy as public higher education has endured periodic budgetary shocks. It suffices to say that the AAUP understands the 1940 *Statement* to allow an institution-wide financial crisis or an educational decision to eliminate a school, department, or program as grounds to terminate tenured (and nontenured) appointments but would not view as permissible the asserted need merely to reallocate resources — to terminate tenured faculty in unpopular departments in order to free up resources for expansion elsewhere. To the faculty members and college presidents who drafted the 1940 *Statement*, against the immediate experience of the Great Depression, tenure was not to be sacrificed on an altar of evanescent shifts in state budgets, alumni giving, or student interest. Were tenure to be so limited, faculty members would labor under the constant risk of summary termination at an administration's discretion to allocate funds. No decent administration should wish to claim such power, but, regrettably, several have made just that claim and taken just that action.

Now to what tenure is not. Tenure is assuredly not a guarantee of "lifetime employment," that is, a sinecure: it does *not* assure future rewards in rank or salary; it is *not* insurance against any and all forms of disapprobation, collegial or administrative; it does *not* insulate the tenured from any and all forms of subsequent evaluation. Tenure protects the professor's right, in the larger search for truth, to proclaim all manner of foolishness, but it does not insulate him or her from being thought a fool for having so proclaimed.

PROBATION

Most commonly, the new appointee will receive a written offer or a written confirmation of appointment. Elaborate documents entitled a "contract" of employment tend to be rare. The notice or letter of appointment customarily indicates rank, salary, department, and duration, that is, of one or more years. It may or may not expressly incorporate the institution's rules or regulations, most often found in a compilation labeled the "Faculty Handbook" or the like, but it is generally assumed that these documents flesh out the institution's and the faculty member's obligations.

The 1940 *Statement* requires that all terms and conditions of employment should be stated in writing to the appointee prior to the commencement of the appointment, but apart from the minimally essential terms just noted, new faculty members may not actually get a copy of the institution's policies and rules until months later. Nevertheless, because the terse letter or notice obviously does not spell out all the terms, it is customary to assume that such documents fill in all the gaps — indeed, supply part of the institution's contractual obligations. Thus, the prospective appointee should ask to be provided with a copy of the institution's rules prior to acceptance in order to assure himself or herself of the nature of the institution's guarantees of academic freedom and due process. (The prospective appointee is also well advised to consult the AAUP's journal, *Academe*, to see if the institution is currently on the Association's list of Censured Administrations.)

The 1940 *Statement* provides that the probationary period not exceed seven years, including a year's notice of termination in the event the tenure decision is negative. In contrast to tenure, the burden rests upon the assistant professor to establish his or her professional excellence and the promise of future performance as measured by the institution's standards.

The latter question, of ascertaining just what those standards are, has been the source of many a disappointed expectation and formal grievance. The AAUP's *Statement on Procedural Standards in the Renewal of Faculty Appointments* recommends:

1. *Criteria and notice of standards.* The faculty member should be advised early on of the substantive and procedural standards generally employed in decisions affecting renewal and tenure. Any special standards adopted by his department or school should also be brought to his or her attention.

2. *Periodic review.* There should be provision for periodic review of the faculty member's situation during the probationary service.

3. *Opportunity to submit material.* The faculty member should be advised of the time when decisions affecting renewal and tenure are ordinarily made, and he or she should be given the opportunity to submit material that he or she believes will be helpful to an adequate consideration of her circumstances.

Professional evaluation is necessarily subjective and, given the breadth of the standards adopted at most institutions — scholarship, teaching, and institutional service — each of those evaluating the candidate may assign a different priority to each category and weigh them differently vis-à-vis the candidate. One indication the candidate may have of what the operational standards are may be derived from observing, within the cohort of preceding assistant professors, who was recommended and who rejected for tenure, but even this weather vane (wholly apart from inevitable considerations of friendship, discipleship, personality, and departmental politics) has to be looked to with caution: First, tenure standards can vary over time — economists might say, in response to the labor market — so the fact that Assistant Professor X (who would not secure a favorable recommendation today) was favorably recommended only a few years ago does not lock the department into X's record as the governing standard. Second, a negative decision may rest on grounds having nothing to do with the faculty member's promise of professional excellence. The institution may, for example, find it necessary to devote its scarce — or dwindling — resources to areas of teaching or research thought to be more promising, though adequate advance warning and counseling to that effect are surely contemplated by the AAUP guidelines and by fundamental fairness.

An affirmative department or school tenure recommendation is not self-enforcing. It may be subject, depending upon the institution's regulatory system, to additional faculty oversight and is invariably subject to additional administrative review. This review tests how well the department has done its job — how powerful a case for tenure has been made. A negative decision at the departmental, school, or institutional level is usually further reviewable by a hearing or grievance committee. This is discussed in Craufurd Goodwin's very helpful essay elsewhere in this volume.

THE FUTURE OF TENURE

The beginning of this essay noted that tenure is good for the profession and for society. But no system of employment relations (if it is looked at that way) would survive for a hundred years, through financial crises and extraordinary technological change, unless it were of benefit to employing institutions: What is "in it" for them? Until recently, one would have to say that the maintenance of the system was bolstered by the critical function the tenure system performs in maintaining faculty — and so institutional — quality. Because the decision is so serious, because the institution is potentially committing resources for decades, it has to be very certain, as certain as it can be, that the probationer's promise will be realized. And because anyone can really be better than his or her record would show at the time a decision is made, the individual candidate may suffer as a result of the rigor of the process. A system of periodically renewable appointments is a kinder, gentler system; but one is more likely over time to conduce toward mediocrity precisely because tough decisions can be deferred indefinitely.

At the time the first version of this essay was published, fifteen years ago, it discussed what were then emerging as two serious challenges to the tenure system: the imposition of systems of "post-tenure review"; and the growing use of non-tenure-track, especially part-time faculty. The former has not proven to be significantly erosive of the system; but the latter has. A word on each.

Post-tenure review. The demand for a system of seemingly rigorous periodic evaluation of tenured faculty stemmed largely from concerns expressed in the halls of some state legislatures, faced with competing claims on scant public funds, about whether public college and university faculty were doing their all or had been lulled into semi-somnolence by having tenure. The demand was abetted at the time by members of the staff of the American Council on Education who called for the imposition of such systems despite the dubiety about them among leading academic administrators. That is, the proposal proceeded on the assumption that there is such slothfulness (or worse) in tenured ranks that a system of periodic evaluation would be necessary to ferret it out, which assumption more than remained to be seen.

One problem with the proposal lay in the amorphousness of the end to which the evaluation would be put. In a termination for cause of a tenured professor the burden of proof rests upon the administration to show that the faculty member is unfit for office. In such a case, the "evidence" accumulated in the periodic reevaluation process (student testimony, reviews by external referees of published work, and the like) would presumably be relevant to the incumbent's fitness or competence, to be decided in a hearing, but the fact of a negative evaluation could not itself be "cause" to discharge. Were a system of post-tenure review devised to make a negative evaluation "cause" for dismissal, it would, in practical effect, substitute periodic evaluation for a dismissal hearing and would be indistinguishable from the abolition of tenure and the adoption in its stead of a system of periodic appointments.

A second problem with the proposal was administrative. Assuming that an arbitrary interval, say of five years, would be chosen and that the evaluations would be staggered accordingly, the consequence would be that four-fifths of the tenured faculty of a school or department would be evaluating one another every year for the entirety of their professional lives. In addition to sheer burdensomeness, the implications to collegial relations are obvious and should give pause.

However, despite occasional abuses in the administration of these systems, they have not become a serious threat to academic freedom or to tenure. Some are more or less earnest efforts at shuffling paper; some are geared toward re-mediating those few who, facing midcareer crises, may have legitimate call upon institutional assistance. None thus far — with the singular exception of Bennington College[7] — had resulted in an AAUP report.

Contingent academic labor. The essay of fifteen years ago noted another concern in the increasing institutional resort to the appointment of faculty off the tenure track, either in full-time capacities or as part-time and especially as contingent (or "just in time") and so disposable academic labor. These forms of employment were used to increase institutional flexibility and to reduce labor cost, especially in the use of part-timers paid significantly less per contact hour (to use a quasi-industrial measure) than tenure-track faculty and for whom the substantial additional cost of benefits need not be sustained. The prospect of increasing retirements by the cohort that took up academic positions in the 1960s, when the professoriate doubled in size, led students of the subject to predict the rejuvenation of the profession — a replenishment of the tenured ranks. But that optimistic prediction has been blunted by the growth of the contingent complement. Note the statistics in table 14.2.

TABLE 14.2 Employment Status of the Professoriate

	Total	Full-time	Part-time
1991	826,000	65%	35%
2001	1,113,000	56%	44%

Source: AAUP, *Chronicle of Higher Education Almanac 2004–05*, August 17, 2004, 28.

Even this snapshot is misleading, for of the full-time faculty in 2001, 19 percent were not on the tenure track. Even accounting for the fact that two-year colleges rely far more on part-time staffing than do four-year institutions, one cannot blink at the fact that the profession has undergone a significant change. What institutions may have gained in flexibility and cost reduction, however, has necessarily been at the expense of continuity and, one hazards to say, quality or, at least, a key quality control: A cohort of insecure and poorly paid jobbers, ever mindful (and needful) of future employability, cannot devote the time, the energy, to sustain scholarship that nurtures teaching as well as contributing to a body of learning. Institutional leaders, administrative as well as professorial, have pointed to these consequences and have called for a redress in the balance. The new academic entrant, fortunate to secure a tenure-track position and whose promise of professional excellence is rewarded with and encouraged by the award of tenure, may wish intramurally to add his or her voice on the issue: Academic freedom gives you the right to speak out. Tenure gives you the freedom to exercise that right.

NOTES

Useful publications on academic freedom and tenure include the following: "The Academy under Siege," *Sociological Perspectives* 41, no. 4 (1998), special issue; *The Case for Tenure*, ed. Matthew W. Finkin (Ithaca, N.Y.: Cornell University Press, 1996); *Freedom and Tenure in the Academy*, ed. William Van Alstyne (Durham, N.C.: Duke University Press, 1993); *The Future of Tenure*, Proceedings of the Twenty-Fifth Annual Conference, National Center for the Study of Collective Bargaining in Higher Education and the Professions (Pt. 2) (1997); *The Questions of Tenure*, ed. Richard Chait (Cambridge: Harvard University Press, 2002).

1. The leading historical study is still Richard Hofstadter and Walter Metzger, *The Development of Academic Freedom in the United States* (New York: Columbia University Press, 1955).

2. William Van Alstyne, "The Specific Theory of Academic Freedom and the General Issue of Civil Liberty," in *The Concept of Academic Freedom*, ed. Edmund L. Pincoffs (Austin: University of Texas Press, 1972), 59.

3. William Van Alstyne, "Tenure: A Summary, Explanation, and 'Defense,'" AAUP *Bulletin* 27 (1971): 330.

4. John Silber, "Poisoning the Wells of Academe," *Encounter* 43 (1974): 38–39.

5. Fritz Machlup, "Some Misconceptions Concerning Academic Freedom," reprinted in *Academic Freedom and Tenure*, ed. Louis Jouglin (Madison: University of Wisconsin Press, 1969), 191.

6. Van Alstyne, "Tenure," 329.

7. "Bennington College: A Supplementary Report on a Censured Administration," *Academe*, January-February 1998, 70–74.

15.

SOME TIPS ON GETTING TENURE

CRAUFURD D. GOODWIN

You will spend some portion of your first few years as a young professor wondering if you have made the right choices about your career and about the institution where you find yourself. Over the same period, your colleagues in that institution will be puzzling over whether they made the right choice about you. Normally, at the end of six years they will decide whether they should invite you to spend a lifetime in their midst. Because it is typically conducted in secret, and because it involves so much human drama, there is more myth and misunderstanding about how the tenure decision is made than any other campus activity. Yet if you understand clearly and face squarely what is happening to you the likelihood is greatly increased that the result will be what you want.

Three separate groups on campus will take part in your tenure decision, each with its own methods, goals, and occasionally inconsistent criteria: your own department; the entire institutional faculty, represented usually by an advisory committee on tenure; and the college or university administration. A frequent reaction of a candidate for tenure combines anger with cynicism directed at all three groups. Both elements in the reaction are misplaced. There is no reason to be angry at your employer and associates for making this decision extremely carefully. They are making a judgment involving a commitment of possibly forty years or more and an investment running into the millions of dollars. If they guess right, you will bring luster to the institution, inspiration to your students, and joy to your colleagues. If they guess wrong, you may condemn a subdiscipline within your institution to shame or irrelevance and discourage and deter generations of students. You may increase, through your sloth, the workload of your colleagues, while injecting disharmony into the community of scholars. Nor, in most cases, are there grounds for cynicism. Those who are making the judgments on which your life depends are strikingly like you — with similar background, training, and values. There is no reason to think either that these people are out to get you or that the methods by which they proceed are inexplicable. In what follows I try to illuminate how each of the three groups thinks through the problem of judging you and how they arrive at a conclusion.

YOUR DEPARTMENT

Your immediate colleagues will have several criteria by which to judge your suitability to become a permanent member of their department. They will be the first persons asked to make an evaluation of your case, and their preparation of your tenure file will influence profoundly the probability of a positive outcome. The precise manner in which tenure is decided varies among institutions but typically the department has the responsibility of gathering relevant materials from you (curriculum vitae, copies of publications, student evaluations, statement of research agenda, course syllabi, and other appropriate items). A review committee of several department members, often in or near your own subfield, and perhaps an outsider or two, will read your materials and solicit letters of appraisal from a list of peers suggested by you and by themselves. The review committee will discuss the case and prepare a recommendation to the department. The review will, in all probability, bring to bear the most highly focused examination of your accomplishments and promise. Remember, however, that "promise" was the main criterion for your original appointment; now, after five years, you must have something to show. The committee will almost certainly contain the senior professor in or closest to your own field. She or he will be asked to show how you rank with your peers, how your interests complement theirs, and how together as a team you cover the subdiscipline. Other committee members from the department are likely to address the wider perception of your effectiveness as a teacher of nonmajors, majors, and graduate students. They will also testify to your qualities as a colleague and as an intellectual stimulus beyond the narrow coterie of specialization in your area. If those close to you and those distant from you in the department differ over your suitability for tenure, it may tell as much about relations among them as it does about you. But in any event such a division may be a serious obstacle to your successful progress through the tenure review. If the recommendation of the review committee is negative, the chances of departmental concurrence are high, although not certain, and I will discuss below some ways by which you can "move on," gracefully and with least damage to your career. If the probationary period is the customary seven years, you will learn of the negative decision in the sixth year and have one full year in which to find another appointment.

If the review committee submits a positive recommendation the full department will have to decide whether to join in the favorable judgment. Their decision will be based on several considerations similar to but somewhat more general than those of the review committee. The department will ask several questions. First, will you, over a lifetime, add to the reputation of the department? Is your research highly regarded by the field? Is it having a visible impact? Are you likely to remain productive? Is your success with students soundly based or is it rooted in flashy performance and the camaraderie of youth, which will not last? Are people a decade from now going to say "Oh, you're at State University, don't you have Professor X"? Or will they say "Professor who?"

A second issue for the department is whether you are a good colleague. Do you take your share of the burdens of teaching, advising, committee work, and other essential chores? Are you tolerant of others? Do you interact effectively in personal and professional terms?

A question often asked by candidates is whether teaching is really taken into account. This, of course, varies with the department and the institution. But don't be taken in by campus cynicism. Even departments and universities most on the make, and reaching desperately for improvement in reputation, will not ignore teaching effectiveness altogether. All teaching institutions are necessarily judged from time to time for their teaching success by their peers, legislators, students, or others; none wishes to be thought of as irresponsible or incompetent. Hence, even though teaching strength is not likely to overwhelm research weakness in a department that takes pride in a national reputation, it may go part of the way; in departments where teaching openly takes precedence over research, of course, your skills in that respect count a great deal.

With these considerations in mind you should plan carefully from the beginning a strategy of how best to use your six years to demonstrate your indisputable worth to your department. You must conduct research that will yield appreciable results within this time frame; you must teach effectively; and you must behave as a responsible member of the academic community. You must demonstrate that your career is on a proper upward trajectory and that you know how to get somewhere that is worth going. Remember that this responsible behavior does not include misusing your scarcest and most precious resource—time—even if for the moment this might seem to answer a pressing need. For example, a young faculty member who volunteers for, or accepts readily, those extra sections of the freshman course or serves unstintingly on those innumerable committees is likely to encounter gratitude at the moment but a judgment of irresponsibility and unsuitability for a permanent appointment when the tenure decision is at hand.

So now you have passed over the department hurdle; the chairman writes an enthusiastic covering letter to the dean recommending your tenure and invites colleagues to include their endorsement. He then sends the entire file onward.

THE FACULTY

The dean or provost will probably submit your file immediately to a committee made up of faculty, or of faculty and administrators, for advice and recommendation. This committee's task is essentially to make certain that the department did a thorough and impartial appraisal of your candidacy — and especially to assure themselves that the reviewers were well chosen and balanced and that the proper weights were applied in reaching a conclusion. This faculty or institutionwide committee will pay particular attention to the possibility that personal considerations have distorted the decision either way. They are fully aware that departments can be much like a family, where close bonds and deep enmities cloud professional judgments. Moreover, prejudices of all kinds may have full rein in the intense relationships within a department. The committee's task is to protect both the institution and candidate; it should provide detachment and a level of objectivity comparable to that sought for in our larger society in the civil courts.

One function of the institutionwide review committee is to make certain that in considering your case the department is adhering to standards observed, or aspired to, by the entire college or university. For you, this injects just one more element of complexity into the process of which you should be aware. The institutionwide review is complicated particularly if the institution is attempting at the moment to improve itself and to identify sources of strength and weakness. On the one hand, you may have done all that has been traditionally required for tenure in your department only to find that the institutionwide standards have been moved up, perhaps without your having been clearly told. On the other hand, even though on the surface your case looks strong it may receive unusually close scrutiny at the institutionwide level if your department is perceived as weak. Especially during a time of institutional self-examination, your tenure case will cause your department to be judged as much as you. This may cause several things to happen. The department will be reluctant to send on your candidacy to the higher level unless it is exceptionally strong; it will also cause the department to become an unusually vociferous advocate of your case because it perceives correctly that it too is to some extent before the bar of colleagues. Even though when considering your case among themselves your department colleagues were suitably judicious, weighing carefully the pros and cons of your candidacy, now before the larger court of the university and with their own reputations at stake, they will become your attorneys, exaggerating your virtues and suppressing your vices.

Many faculty committees will attempt to answer two questions about a candidate. First, how does he or she rank among the appropriate age cohort of peers in the relevant subdiscipline? Referees may be asked to give a specific ranking among a set of names. Naturally it is interesting to the committee to see if peers of roughly equivalent institutions have yet gained tenure.

The second question asked is whether the candidate has established a successful scholarly career separate from graduate school mentors. Typically a new assistant professor will arrive at the first job with several articles or a book having come out of the doctoral dissertation. The hand of an adviser or an entire graduate school committee can usually be seen in these products. The next research "program" selected by the young scholar is crucial. Does it demonstrate independence and autonomy from the graduate school or is it further progress down the short road to diminishing returns? Was the candidate able to identify an interesting question and provide the answer without external guidance? Clearly these are not easy questions to answer, and they may never be answered unambiguously by the committee. Neither the hope nor the expectation is that a young academic will abandon immediately old friends, former teachers, or valued associations. But a young faculty member is required during the probationary period to demonstrate independent intellectual qualities that will assure a rich and productive scholarly career long after the graduate school connections have necessarily grown old and cold. This demonstration may come through significant single-authored articles, selection of novel research projects, and in various other ways appropriate for particular disciplines.

Another one of the many myths that surround the tenure process is that tenure committees just sit around and count pages of publications. In some limited sense this is true; they do look for substantial and sustained scholarly effort. But they are also extremely sensitive to quality, both good and bad. If a candidate is found just to have been grinding out potboilers and textbook material during the probationary period, or has published only in inferior journals or nonrefereed media, these activities will sometimes count in the negative even more than inactivity would have done. Moreover, if referees comment repeatedly on sloppiness, misuse of tools and data, and hasty and careless preparation even in the presence of substantial quantity, that alone can sound the death knell. If, on the contrary, merely a single article of a candidate, though slight in size, is described as brilliant, exceptionally insightful, constructively provocative, or likely to make others in the discipline sit up and take notice, this alone may carry the day positively. Sometimes, to confirm such judgments, a tenure committee will examine citation counts published in the various "citation indexes" available in most college libraries. Tenure committees, especially at institutions with a clear research focus, want to know "does a candidate, or a candidate's work, really matter?" The answer "yes" may come on the basis of as few as two or three important articles. A resounding "no" may come even in the presence of a dozen undistinguished articles or more and a book or two.

If you are told that your institution's tenure committee ignores teaching in its evaluations, can't tell quality if it is rubbed in their faces, and makes decisions either by logrolling or favoritism, remember that soon you may be in their place. If the committee has been well selected, it will contain senior colleagues who are respected for their fair-mindedness and for their scholarly distinction. The chances are that most of them will know you only slightly, if at all, before they see your file, and they will attempt to perform their task with justice to you and their institution.

THE ADMINISTRATION

If you have passed successfully over the two hurdles of your department and faculty advisory committee, you are probably home free. But not with absolute certainty. You must still pass the more or less serious scrutiny of the dean, the provost (or academic vice president), the president, and perhaps even the board of trustees. There are not many conditions under which any one of these parties is likely to reverse the earlier two judgments. But there are some of which you should be aware. First, if the decisions come on markedly split votes, the administrators will want to know why, and on the assumption that departments are likely to exaggerate the virtues of their candidates (for reasons discussed above), they may find themselves persuaded more by the arguments on the negative side than on the positive. Second, it is just possible that they may know something detrimental about you that the other two groups did not, and they will exercise their prerogative to block your tenure. Third, the administrators may come to the conclusion coincidentally with your tenure consideration that either your department, or the school of which it is a part, has become weak, lacking in vigor, and unable even to operate its own processes. In that event the administration may duplicate the inquiry into your suitability for tenure through additional phone calls, letters, and discussions. In these circumstances your tenure might be denied as a prelude to some larger remedial action toward the department or school. Finally, the administration has the authority to deny your tenure on grounds of financial exigency: they find suddenly that they cannot see ahead the means to guarantee your salary to retirement without imperiling earlier commitments to already tenured faculty. Obviously a responsible and farsighted administration should not allow a tenure consideration to begin

if financial exigency looms, but legislators do cut budgets without announcements, depressions strike, and other untoward financial events occur that just
might catch you and others in the tenure process.

The word that your tenure has indeed been approved or denied will come to
you in a letter from an administrator: provost, dean, or department chairperson. Some form of explanation will probably accompany the terse communication, more in the case of a negative than of a positive decision, but not much
in either case because none of the parties to the decision wishes to enter into a
protracted discussion with you about details. From beginning to end the process is likely to take six months to a year. This may turn out to be one of the
most anxious and stressful periods of life, for you and for your family. If the
final word is "yes," it will all seem worthwhile.

BUT WHAT SHOULD YOU DO IF IT'S "NO"?

If the dreaded conclusion of the process of evaluation for tenure is that your
employer decides you should go elsewhere, you have several courses of action.
Once more, just as when preparing to make your case for tenure, you should
plan your strategy carefully. You have at least three possible paths to follow.

First, you can appeal the negative tenure decision, initially to the administrative officer who made the final decision, and then up the line until ultimately
you reach the governing board (trustees or regents) of the institution and even
the civil courts. However, you should recognize two facts of life when you consider such an appeal. First, reversals of decisions do happen, but not often, and
they seldom occur when they are carried beyond the major administrative officer who communicated the decision to you. Second, appeals are not costless,
either in time, money, or the goodwill of persons upon whom you may have
to depend in seeking a new position. Your best hope for a successful appeal is
on grounds of due process. You may charge that the review committee wrote
systematically to your enemies but not to your friends, that they neglected a
recent manuscript that has just been accepted for publication in the discipline's
most prestigious journal, or some other claim at this level. It is least likely that
an appeal will be successful if it is simply an assertion of a different judgment
from that of the institution. You may point out "my friends and former professors all say I'm the most promising person of my generation. How could they
be wrong?" This is seldom persuasive. Above all, present any appeal in a careful,
well-modulated fashion. A hysterical harangue (which may be your instinctive
reaction) against the process and on your own behalf will almost certainly put
the last nail in your coffin.

Your second possible course is to request more time and a second tenure hearing at some later date. Your argument in this instance must be that some new facts in the case are imminent: a significant work is soon to appear that will change the whole complexion of your case; you are about to receive a great honor or prize; the excellent reviews of your book are just now being published. If you were given your first unsuccessful tenure review before the customary six years of probation, a second review may not present any technical problems for the administration, so long as several reviews are permitted at all. If the review took place at the usual time you will be required to sign a waiver of your right to tenure under the seven-year rule. From your own perspective you should calculate as carefully as you can whether a second review is likely to go better than the first. If not you are simply wasting a year or two of precious time. Be encouraged, however, by the thought that the university is unlikely to grant you a second review unless it concludes that there is a strong likelihood of a positive outcome.

Your third possible path is to accept the fact that tenure is not likely to come to you at this institution under any circumstances and make plans to move elsewhere. If you accept the outcome with grace and good humor the likelihood is increased that your colleagues will assist you in the search and will support your candidacy at another institution. You will normally have a full year to conduct the search, and you will do so with the hard-earned wisdom of your recent experience to guide you.

The depressing reality is, of course, that if you decide to remain in academic life, and if you are not able to gain a tenured appointment at your new location, the whole agonizing cycle will begin again.

CONCLUSIONS

A tenure review is not something that anyone but a masochist would endure voluntarily, but it is a rite of passage that must be accepted for the benefits that tenure does confer. Like so many other of life's experiences, it looks less formidable in retrospect than when in progress. And like mumps, you will probably have to go through it only once. But unlike mumps, its discomfort can be minimized if it is well understood and it is approached in the right spirit. It is hoped that these observations will set you in the right direction.

16.

ACADEMIC SALARIES AND BENEFITS

A. LEIGH DENEEF

No one enters academia, pursues a Ph.D., or becomes a college professor to make money. We have all heard some such platitude many times enroute to the degree. I even recall saying it myself to a father who many years ago voiced concern over the bleak financial future of my chosen profession. I'm sure there was some validity in my response then, but more likely than not the stock answer served to disguise the fact that I had absolutely no idea how well or how poorly college professors were paid and knew even less about such things as fringe benefits, retirement plans, or special tax issues I was about to confront.

This is not to say, of course, that my own professors never mentioned salaries: salaries, in general and in generally complaining terms, were a frequent topic of conversation, but not in any practical or useful sense. I finished graduate school relatively ignorant about what entry-level assistant professors in my field made across the country and about whether I would make substantially more or less than a peer in a different discipline, or than a colleague in another kind of school or in another area of the country. A few interviews and campus visits later, I had a rough idea about some direct and indirect fringe benefits, but no sense about whether any of these were negotiable or whether I was supposed to be asking questions about them. Now, many years later, I am still puzzled by the tax laws (which change far faster than I can keep up with) and still not always sure I am taking full advantage of the opportunities available to me.

As this last confession will suggest, I make no claims here to speak anything like the final word on academic salaries, benefits, or income taxes. What I can provide is a general survey of the financial side of an academic's life and a sense of a few of the issues that any new academic will want to consider.

ACADEMIC SALARIES

I will begin with another anecdote from my own past. In 1968, when I first entered the job market, the average salary offer I received was $11,000. Individual offers ranged from $9,000 to $15,000 (yes, in those halcyon days, Ph.D.'s in English did receive multiple job offers). With that kind of range, salary alone became an important consideration when it came to the final decision about which offer to accept. That I eventually took the lowest offer obviously meant it was not the most important consideration, but I now marvel that I did not know at the time where that offer stood in relation to the national mean. Had I had that information, or bothered to look it up in the summaries of the salary data collected annually by the AAUP and published in both *Academe* and the *Chronicle of Higher Education*, I might well have negotiated a bit further with my subsequent department and dean. Salaries, of course, are not always negotiable, especially for entry-level positions, but no school seeking the best candidates available can afford to deviate very much from the national or regional averages, and therefore some flexibility may exist for candidates who are alert enough to use information about national ranges effectively.

Current salaries for starting assistant professors are considerably higher today than they were in 1968. In my own university and department, they are some $37,000 a year higher! (Of course, the general costs of living are higher as well, so these numbers need always to be seen in relation to the global U.S. economy.) The historical trend of academic salaries, however, is not likely to be of much help to the budding academic, so it is better to focus on the current range. Among the factors most significantly affecting average salary levels are the kind of institution involved, its geographical region, and disciplinary competition from nonacademic employers. In fields that offer multiple career options, academic salaries are likely to be substantially higher than in disciplines with few employment options. A glance at table 16.1 will show that faculty in law, business, health sciences, computer science, and engineering command very different salaries at every level from those in most of the humanities or social sciences. One conclusion that might be drawn here is that salary negotiations should be more possible in those competitive employment areas and the new Ph.D. might tactfully and tentatively explore them.

As others in this handbook have noted, there is a wide variety of institutions in the national system of higher education today. Table 16.2 shows the average annual salary in 2005–06 for all ranks in institutions distinguished along two axes. Vertically, the categories of schools represented are: I = doctoral degree–granting institutions; IIA = comprehensive institutions; IIB = baccalaureate institutions; III = two-year institutions with academic ranks; and IV = institu-

TABLE 16.1 Average Faculty Salaries in Selected Fields at All Institutions, 2005–06

Discipline and Rank	Weighted Average
AGRICULTURE, AGRICULTURE OPERATIONS, AND RELATED SCIENCES	
Professor	82,974
Associate Professor	64,667
Assistant Professor	55,315
New Assistant Professor	56,288
Instructor	40,998
NATURAL RESOURCES AND CONSERVATION	
Professor	85,141
Associate Professor	64,326
Assistant Professor	53,200
New Assistant Professor	51,262
Instructor	41,482
ARCHITECTURE AND RELATED SERVICES	
Professor	85,441
Associate Professor	67,086
Assistant Professor	53,593
New Assistant Professor	54,101
Instructor	44,715
AREA, ETHNIC, CULTURAL, AND GENDER STUDIES	
Professor	90,973
Associate Professor	66,427
Assistant Professor	53,655
New Assistant Professor	51,099
Instructor	38,548
COMMUNICATION, JOURNALISM, AND RELATED PROGRAMS	
Professor	77,496
Associate Professor	60,411
Assistant Professor	49,515
New Assistant Professor	47,806
Instructor	38,806
COMMUNICATIONS TECHNOLOGIES/TECHNICIANS AND SUPPORT SERVICES	
Professor	79,178
Associate Professor	66,244
Assistant Professor	52,973
New Assistant Professor	46,959
Instructor	45,942
COMPUTER AND INFORMATION SCIENCES AND SUPPORT SERVICES	
Professor	98,705
Associate Professor	78,944

TABLE 16.1 Continued

Discipline and Rank	Weighted Average
Assistant Professor	69,178
New Assistant Professor	68,257
Instructor	46,672
EDUCATION	
Professor	78,179
Associate Professor	60,615
Assistant Professor	50,296
New Assistant Professor	49,333
Instructor	40,344
ENGINEERING	
Professor	107,961
Associate Professor	80,206
Assistant Professor	70,019
New Assistant Professor	68,707
Instructor	49,592
ENGINEERING TECHNOLOGIES/TECHNICIANS	
Professor	79,446
Associate Professor	65,687
Assistant Professor	56,114
New Assistant Professor	56,113
Instructor	43,452
FOREIGN LANGUAGES, LITERATURES, AND LINGUISTICS	
Professor	79,964
Associate Professor	60,068
Assistant Professor	48,900
New Assistant Professor	47,016
Instructor	37,111
FAMILY AND CONSUMER SCIENCES/HUMAN SCIENCES	
Professor	79,665
Associate Professor	62,437
Assistant Professor	51,055
New Assistant Professor	49,988
Instructor	38,486
LEGAL PROFESSIONS AND STUDIES	
Professor	136,634
Associate Professor	98,530
Assistant Professor	81,005
New Assistant Professor	79,437
Instructor	56,667

TABLE 16.1 Continued

Discipline and Rank	Weighted Average
ENGLISH LANGUAGE AND LITERATURE/LETTERS	
Professor	76,413
Associate Professor	57,921
Assistant Professor	47,249
New Assistant Professor	45,882
Instructor	34,712
LIBERAL ARTS AND SCIENCES, GENERAL STUDIES AND HUMANITIES	
Professor	74,228
Associate Professor	59,982
Assistant Professor	48,635
New Assistant Professor	47,094
Instructor	38,620
LIBRARY SCIENCE	
Professor	77,583
Associate Professor	65,296
Assistant Professor	47,972
New Assistant Professor	49,783
Instructor	41,059
BIOLOGICAL AND BIOMEDICAL SCIENCES	
Professor	90,040
Associate Professor	63,929
Assistant Professor	54,101
New Assistant Professor	51,883
Instructor	39,798
MATHEMATICS AND STATISTICS	
Professor	84,059
Associate Professor	61,647
Assistant Professor	51,547
New Assistant Professor	50,151
Instructor	37,761
MULTI/INTERDISCIPLINARY STUDIES	
Professor	83,214
Associate Professor	62,098
Assistant Professor	51,710
New Assistant Professor	45,928
Instructor	38,060
PARKS, RECREATION, LEISURE AND FITNESS STUDIES	
Professor	73,748
Associate Professor	59,905

TABLE 16.1 Continued

Discipline and Rank	Weighted Average
Assistant Professor	49,618
New Assistant Professor	49,597
Instructor	39,413
PHILOSOPHY AND RELIGIOUS STUDIES	
Professor	82,030
Associate Professor	59,429
Assistant Professor	48,162
New Assistant Professor	46,785
Instructor	37,906
THEOLOGY AND RELIGIOUS VOCATIONS	
Professor	68,214
Associate Professor	56,943
Assistant Professor	45,927
New Assistant Professor	44,731
Instructor	41,072
PHYSICAL SCIENCES	
Professor	89,187
Associate Professor	62,743
Assistant Professor	52,775
New Assistant Professor	51,354
Instructor	40,256
SCIENCE TECHNOLOGIES/TECHNICIANS	
Professor	68,888
Associate Professor	62,953
Assistant Professor	—
New Assistant Professor	—
Instructor	—
PSYCHOLOGY	
Professor	82,554
Associate Professor	60,840
Assistant Professor	50,315
New Assistant Professor	48,698
Instructor	39,546
SECURITY AND PROTECTIVE SERVICES	
Professor	77,614
Associate Professor	62,000
Assistant Professor	49,711
New Assistant Professor	47,237
Instructor	40,625

TABLE 16.1 Continued

Discipline and Rank	Weighted Average
PUBLIC ADMINISTRATION AND SOCIAL SERVICES PROFESSIONS	
Professor	84,902
Associate Professor	63,523
Assistant Professor	52,311
New Assistant Professor	52,389
Instructor	43,747
SOCIAL SCIENCES	
Professor	87,079
Associate Professor	63,842
Assistant Professor	52,998
New Assistant Professor	51,720
Instructor	39,634
VISUAL AND PERFORMING ARTS	
Professor	73,177
Associate Professor	57,843
Assistant Professor	47,043
New Assistant Professor	45,382
Instructor	39,102
NURSING	
Professor	77,583
Associate Professor	63,615
Assistant Professor	53,075
New Assistant Professor	51,716
Instructor	46,292
BUSINESS, MANAGEMENT, MARKETING, AND RELATED SUPPORT SERVICES	
Professor	102,702
Associate Professor	84,095
Assistant Professor	78,151
New Assistant Professor	80,252
Instructor	49,271
HISTORY GENERAL	
Professor	80,706
Associate Professor	59,470
Assistant Professor	47,994
New Assistant Professor	45,723
Instructor	38,030

Source: College and University Professional Association for Human Resources, *National Faculty Salary Survey, 2005–06*.

tions without academic ranks. Horizontally, the categories are public, private, and church-related institutions. Looking quickly down this table, one could conclude that academic salaries are generally highest at private, independent doctoral institutions. One might also be inclined to assume that private institutions always pay better than public ones, although this is clearly not the case with Category III schools. What is clear is that across all colleges and universities, the average salary for an assistant professor (here, by the way, not a *new* assistant professor) in 2005–06 was $56,298. To give some perspective on those figures (although be sure to remember inflation), a decade ago the average salary of an assistant professor was around $36,000.

Geographic distribution also affects salary levels. Table 16.3 presents another tabulation of average salary by region, institutional category, and academic rank. The ranges displayed here vary considerably, from as much as $157,442 per year in the full professor rank of Category I in New England schools to $87,524 per year in the assistant professor rank at the same schools. Some of the discrepancies, of course, are the result of differing cost-of-living adjustments, but not all. It would be to a prospective employee's advantage to check the statistics for all schools in which s/he is seriously interested in either *Academe* or the *Chronicle of Higher Education* (fuller figures appear in the former journal). Has a given school met, exceeded, or failed to meet its category or regional average? Are the higher ranks substantially better or worse in relation to national salary levels? The answers to these questions should give some sense of your financial future were you to receive tenure, stay at that institution, and progress through the ranks. Where choice of geographical region is not a personal priority on some other grounds, salary distinctions could prove a useful factor in deciding what offer to accept.

It may be startling to all academics to see that, as a group, academic women are still receiving salaries that are roughly 10 percent lower than men at all ranks and all institutions (see table 16.4). The 2005–06 averages at the assistant and associate professor levels suggest that while there may be some long-term equalizing of salaries between genders, the disparities across the various academic ranks and institutions are not terribly different from what they were a decade ago. Given the positive changes evident in other areas affecting the status of women within the academy, this continuing inequity is troubling to say the least.

The raw data on average salary levels, of course, does not tell the whole story of an academic income. For one thing, it is important to remember that these figures represent salary for generally nine calendar months (even if paid over twelve): many academics supplement their incomes by teaching summer school. For another, many academics, maybe most, generate supplementary

TABLE 16.2 Average Salary and Average Compensation Levels, by Category, Affiliation, and Academic Rank, 2005–06 (dollars)

Academic Rank	SALARY				COMPENSATION			
	All Combined	Public	Private-Independent	Church-Related	All Combined	Public	Private-Independent	Church-Related
CATEGORY I (Doctoral)								
Professor	108,404	101,620	131,292	113,740	135,843	127,535	164,370	140,478
Associate	73,562	70,952	84,419	77,409	94,508	91,126	108,673	99,309
Assistant	62,730	60,440	71,877	65,286	80,492	77,971	91,031	81,833
Instructor	42,269	40,670	46,510	53,684	55,617	53,941	60,194	67,377
Lecturer	48,507	46,793	55,278	47,423	62,915	60,695	71,662	61,616
No Rank	54,169	50,010	60,851	54,660	69,323	64,296	77,508	69,681
All Combined	80,657	76,361	97,434	83,157	102,443	97,192	123,160	104,845
CATEGORY IIA (Master's)								
Professor	80,322	78,884	88,800	78,379	101,567	99,554	113,207	99,375
Associate	63,422	62,700	67,148	62,208	81,650	80,559	87,008	80,186
Assistant	53,014	52,873	54,996	51,411	68,463	68,436	71,031	65,675
Instructor	40,284	39,422	44,150	41,602	52,345	51,505	56,881	52,927
Lecturer	43,573	43,327	45,515	45,632	56,750	56,494	58,777	58,982
No Rank	46,032	43,626	53,726	49,950	59,672	56,944	66,970	65,655
All Combined	62,218	61,248	67,468	61,248	79,715	78,454	86,774	78,293
CATEGORY IIB (Baccalaureate)								
Professor	77,127	73,406	87,779	66,547	98,994	93,728	112,550	85,826
Associate	60,073	59,913	64,846	55,402	77,686	77,832	83,906	71,393
Assistant	49,446	49,546	53,083	45,873	63,597	64,371	67,959	58,894
Instructor	40,112	39,925	43,333	38,488	51,461	51,966	54,921	49,060
Lecturer	44,536	43,278	51,635	37,897	57,329	55,297	67,945	47,840

No Rank	50,867	43,648	56,290	41,807	65,963	54,197	74,410	52,123
All Combined	59,949	56,902	67,660	54,003	77,158	73,447	86,975	69,484

CATEGORY III (Two-Year Colleges with Ranks)

Professor	66,099	66,011	75,591	n.d.	85,290	85,223	94,470	n.d.
Associate	53,463	53,405	56,220	n.d.	69,994	70,023	69,591	n.d.
Assistant	47,046	47,116	46,464	n.d.	62,928	63,166	57,474	n.d.
Instructor	40,127	40,266	37,254	n.d.	53,351	53,774	43,546	n.d.
Lecturer	44,943	44,983	43,091	n.d.	61,132	61,242	56,064	n.d.
No Rank	42,435	41,918	47,343	n.d.	58,131	57,394	63,310	n.d.
All Combined	52,649	52,719	51,890	n.d.	69,183	69,393	63,970	n.d.

CATEGORY IV (Two-Year Colleges without Ranks)

No Rank	50,341	50,382	n.d.	n.d.	62,958	63,028	n.d.	n.d.

ALL CATEGORIES COMBINED EXCEPT IV

Professor	94,738	91,367	111,817	82,804	119,449	115,112	141,166	104,823
Associate	67,187	66,288	73,297	63,087	86,561	85,358	94,659	81,171
Assistant	56,298	55,918	60,975	51,537	72,595	72,487	77,883	65,635
Instructor	40,952	40,113	44,541	42,378	53,568	52,945	57,070	53,702
Lecturer	46,489	45,275	53,583	44,758	60,446	58,915	69,609	57,746
No Rank	50,489	46,515	58,201	50,793	65,197	60,406	74,484	65,118
All Combined	70,333	68,440	81,452	63,371	89,879	87,569	103,795	80,876

Source: AAUP, *Academe*, March–April 2006, 37.

Note: The table is based on 1,473 (salary) and 1,462 (compensation) reporting institutions representing 1,977 and 1,959 campuses, respectively. n.d. = no data. There were too few church-related institutions in category III and too few private-independent and church-related institutions in category IV to generate valid separate statistics. These institutions are included in the All Combined column, however.

TABLE 16.3 Average Compensation, by Region, Category, and Academic Rank, 2005–06 (dollars)

Academic Rank	NORTHEAST		NORTH CENTRAL		SOUTH			WEST	
	New England[a]	Middle Atlantic[b]	East North Central[c]	West North Central[d]	East South Central[e]	West South Central[f]	South Atlantic[g]	Mountain[h]	Pacific[i]
CATEGORY I (Doctoral)									
Professor	157,442	151,655	133,104	124,951	117,249	122,429	132,529	114,334	146,571
Associate	104,804	105,558	94,001	89,000	86,153	86,761	93,799	84,715	99,084
Assistant	87,524	87,971	79,746	75,432	72,396	75,985	79,859	73,465	86,935
Instructor	61,386	58,996	54,900	54,923	48,649	49,662	57,958	54,256	59,928
Lecturer	73,059	66,453	59,631	55,662	51,935	59,022	57,525	60,438	74,769
No Rank	72,043	65,016	59,524	64,577	63,209	69,247	77,114	47,484	74,705
All Combined	119,587	113,516	100,492	95,830	88,681	90,742	99,619	89,718	114,914
CATEGORY IIA (Master's)									
Professor	111,076	112,579	98,730	92,242	90,907	91,551	96,617	93,282	107,803
Associate	86,891	90,400	79,966	75,150	73,996	74,346	77,515	77,033	87,047
Assistant	72,821	73,802	67,489	63,908	62,838	62,871	65,731	67,307	73,844
Instructor	59,221	57,702	51,267	51,879	50,198	48,106	52,180	52,269	60,273
Lecturer	62,565	61,713	52,694	45,687	46,986	46,846	51,249	50,235	68,869
No Rank	66,805	60,889	58,339	60,953	48,618	58,810	60,527	53,876	60,639
All Combined	87,935	88,538	77,102	74,040	71,017	70,185	75,127	72,482	88,607
CATEGORY IIB (Baccalaureate)									
Professor	122,152	111,021	91,745	87,353	78,961	81,124	90,861	84,765	111,930
Associate	95,413	85,502	73,874	70,212	66,685	67,364	72,822	68,704	85,147
Assistant	73,530	68,560	61,305	59,746	54,479	59,154	60,383	57,235	69,157
Instructor	56,150	55,899	51,521	49,947	45,820	49,159	48,845	44,409	60,775
Lecturer	69,200	62,352	51,454	49,421	45,875	50,507	51,680	36,957	67,652
No Rank	65,976	60,933	52,030	47,448	42,433	43,863	68,664	89,020	70,937
All Combined	96,965	83,681	73,871	69,707	64,180	64,721	71,734	66,836	87,856

CATEGORY III (Two-Year Colleges with Ranks)

Professor	87,126	97,807	88,208	81,621	67,617	74,859	83,926	75,625	89,315
Associate	67,763	81,181	71,710	70,710	58,925	60,094	68,878	69,662	78,276
Assistant	62,909	70,973	60,543	62,802	49,657	54,652	60,408	63,596	69,082
Instructor	58,826	57,671	50,366	53,383	44,679	46,975	53,390	53,176	60,695
Lecturer	58,795	66,820	54,513	53,150	n.d.	n.d.	53,226	56,192	55,925
No Rank	n.d.	49,038	n.d.	55,226	55,773	n.d.	58,720	66,546	63,310
All Combined	74,627	79,041	67,308	69,491	56,087	62,944	67,352	64,941	74,859

CATEGORY IV (Two-Year Colleges without Ranks)

No Rank	n.d.	n.d.	64,791	69,748	57,569	61,335	53,054	71,850	83,898

ALL CATEGORIES COMBINED EXCEPT IV

Professor	136,299	130,138	118,480	106,000	100,529	108,397	115,671	107,900	128,730
Associate	95,853	94,619	86,009	80,127	76,003	79,881	84,493	81,319	92,164
Assistant	78,760	76,983	72,207	67,651	64,466	68,465	70,952	69,671	78,962
Instructor	59,319	57,838	52,838	52,110	48,026	48,683	54,223	52,488	60,299
Lecturer	71,324	64,768	56,362	52,210	49,838	55,173	54,865	57,263	71,336
No Rank	68,902	63,936	58,929	53,945	54,838	61,810	70,172	58,400	66,117
All Combined	104,405	97,036	88,863	82,265	76,084	80,365	86,508	83,158	100,964

Source: AAUP, *Academe*, March–April 2006, 40.

Note: The table is based on 1,462 reporting institutions representing 1,959 campuses. n.d. = no data.

a. New England: Connecticut, Maine, Massachusetts, New Hampshire, Rhode Island, and Vermont.

b. Middle Atlantic: New Jersey, New York, and Pennsylvania.

c. East North Central: Illinois, Indiana, Michigan, Ohio, and Wisconsin.

d. West North Central: Iowa, Kansas, Minnesota, Missouri, Nebraska, North Dakota, and South Dakota.

e. East South Central: Alabama, Kentucky, Mississippi, and Tennessee.

f. West South Central: Arkansas, Louisiana, Oklahoma, and Texas.

g. South Atlantic: Delaware, District of Columbia, Florida, Georgia, Maryland, North Carolina, Puerto Rico, South Carolina, Virginia, and West Virginia.

h. Mountain: Arizona, Colorado, Idaho, Montana, Nevada, New Mexico, Utah, and Wyoming.

i. Pacific: Alaska, California, Guam, Hawaii, Oregon, and Washington.

TABLE 16.4 Average Salary for Men and Women Faculty, by Category, Affiliation, and Academic Rank, 2005–06 (dollars)

Academic Rank	MEN				WOMEN			
	All Combined	Public	Private-Independent	Church-Related	All Combined	Public	Private-Independent	Church-Related
CATEGORY I (Doctoral)								
Professor	110,343	103,441	133,483	116,281	100,318	93,980	121,929	104,945
Associate	75,547	72,839	86,652	79,515	70,076	67,652	80,288	73,992
Assistant	65,128	62,713	74,812	67,202	59,632	57,506	67,885	63,135
Instructor	43,557	41,803	46,916	55,260	41,357	39,916	46,149	52,234
Lecturer	51,555	49,445	59,138	51,856	45,863	44,529	51,582	44,352
No Rank	58,520	53,771	64,331	60,619	50,060	46,875	56,859	48,877
All Combined	87,130	82,387	105,113	89,608	68,132	64,845	81,071	72,241
CATEGORY IIA (Master's)								
Professor	81,446	79,801	90,346	79,926	77,464	76,601	84,564	74,294
Associate	64,634	63,772	68,675	63,627	61,716	61,189	64,963	60,256
Assistant	54,183	54,006	56,135	52,718	51,809	51,671	53,833	50,211
Instructor	40,728	39,890	44,401	41,822	40,000	39,126	43,967	41,471
Lecturer	44,856	44,512	47,332	47,826	42,573	42,409	43,743	44,118
No Rank	47,882	45,323	54,696	51,463	44,109	42,014	52,235	48,357
All Combined	65,759	64,652	71,296	64,991	57,383	56,627	61,921	56,322
CATEGORY IIB (Baccalaureate)								
Professor	78,202	74,780	88,948	67,521	74,543	70,366	84,999	64,064
Associate	60,022	60,804	65,126	54,602	60,145	58,592	64,482	56,520
Assistant	50,264	50,711	53,930	46,324	48,620	48,281	52,224	45,440
Instructor	40,519	40,716	44,039	38,333	39,827	39,355	42,839	38,592
Lecturer	45,192	44,055	52,409	39,014	43,948	42,450	51,088	37,074

No Rank	54,977	47,531	59,084	45,321	45,994	40,222	51,942	39,219
All Combined	62,619	59,627	70,861	55,947	56,286	53,259	63,150	51,366

CATEGORY III (Two-Year Colleges with Ranks)

Professor	67,749	67,645	79,293	n.d.	64,230	64,177	70,039	n.d.
Associate	54,576	54,456	59,353	n.d.	52,333	52,346	52,807	n.d.
Assistant	47,670	47,750	47,371	n.d.	46,483	46,541	45,875	n.d.
Instructor	40,545	40,643	39,474	n.d.	39,770	39,955	33,479	n.d.
Lecturer	44,837	44,778	53,177	n.d.	45,036	45,166	41,257	n.d.
No Rank	43,610	43,542	44,080	n.d.	41,553	40,773	51,694	n.d.
All Combined	54,152	54,209	54,693	n.d.	51,177	51,272	48,901	n.d.

CATEGORY IV (Two-Year Colleges without Ranks)

No Rank	51,072	51,140	n.d.	n.d.	49,670	49,689	n.d.	n.d.

ALL CATEGORIES COMBINED EXCEPT IV

Professor	97,642	97,161	114,989	85,012	85,747	82,744	101,340	76,646
Associate	68,990	68,178	75,351	63,994	64,436	63,373	70,142	61,779
Assistant	58,296	57,869	63,401	52,781	54,052	53,666	58,222	50,324
Instructor	41,692	40,844	45,017	43,107	40,431	39,609	44,155	41,873
Lecturer	48,776	47,230	56,962	47,594	44,573	43,650	50,455	42,771
No Rank	53,757	49,127	60,705	55,173	47,240	44,221	54,928	46,661
All Combined	76,027	73,950	88,193	67,477	61,337	59,755	69,928	57,558

Source: AAUP, *Academe*, March–April 2006, 38.

Note: The table is based on 1,473 reporting institutions representing 1,977 campuses. n.d. = no data. There were too few church-related institutions in category III and too few private-independent and church-related institutions in category IV to generate valid separate statistics. These institutions are included in the All Combined column, however.

incomes through various kinds of consulting efforts. The real point is that the academy allows its members to be as entrepreneurial as they wish: you can spend three months during the summer staying at home and tending your garden (assuming you've done the requisite research and publication during the academic year) or you can spend that summer making significantly more money. Many new academics, trying to raise a family or buy a first home, will find the opportunity to add to their salaries by summer teaching a real benefit.

As an example of the kind of entrepreneurial opportunities the academy sometimes offers, take the case of a colleague of mine at a neighboring institution. As an assistant professor of technical writing at a branch campus of the state university, my friend's nine-month salary ten years ago was about $30,000. To support his family and to purchase his first home, he had taught summer school for twelve consecutive years (for an additional $4,000 for two months each summer) and developed a variety of external consulting programs for businesses to teach their employees the fundamentals of technical writing. This work was usually consigned to the summer months, but its financial rewards were considerable. From a minimum of $2,000–$3,000 in supplementary annual income, the consulting practice grew to nearly $30,000 a year. Obviously at this point, my friend faced a genuine crisis, for business and industry were paying almost the same amount for two to three months of consulting that his university was paying for nine months of teaching.

Not all academics, of course, will have or want this kind of consultancy option, but the more important point is that a variety of opportunities exist for college and university professors to make extra-academic use of their academic skills. During your years as a graduate student, this feature of academic life may not have been visible to you, but a brief look around your university might quickly reveal the English professor who is routinely called as an expert witness in free speech trials, the economics professor who serves as consultant to a number of private insurance companies, the biochemistry professor who has started his own molecular cancer laboratory outside the institutional confines. And your choices are not limited to ones using your academic skills. My own colleagues earn additional income, particularly during the summer, by part-time real estate sales, preparation of income tax returns, weekend carpentry and masonry, landscape gardening, and, in my own case, teaching adult classes in bird-watching and photography. I must emphasize, however, that there should be one cardinal rule governing all such supplemental options: whether financially necessary or merely desirable, they should not be pursued at the expense, either in time or energy, of your academic responsibilities or in violation of institutional employment policies. It would hardly make sense to jeopardize your primary income by over-committing to a secondary one.

One other aspect of the salary levels for new academics deserves mention and will lead to my next section on fringe benefits. The issue I have in mind is simply the fact that new assistant professors are unlikely to have the financial resources to attend a number of professional conferences or organizations unless their ways are paid by their departments. In most institutions today, the funding available for conference travel is extremely limited. The consequence is that junior faculty, who generally have more to gain from attending professional conferences than established scholars, may have considerably less opportunity to do so. How much opportunity will depend both on the support a given department or institution is able to provide—thus making that support something you should inquire about during on-campus job interviews—and on the amount of money you are able yourself to set aside for such expenses.

FRINGE BENEFITS

Although both the specific dollar levels and the particular kinds of fringe benefits vary widely, the majority of academic institutions provide at least nine standard benefits: some, like (1) workman's compensation, (2) Social Security, and (3) medicare contributions are mandated by current law; optional benefits include (4) some form of faculty retirement plan, (5) medical, and (6) life insurance plans, (7) disability, (8) unemployment insurance, and (9) tuition benefits for employee dependents.

Fringe benefits are often overlooked when figuring the total compensation received, but the figures are significant, as a second look at tables 16.2 and 16.3 reveal. In every institutional category, the average assistant professor salary is supplemented by more than $16,000 in additional benefits (table 16.5); full professor salaries are supplemented by almost double that amount. This means, of course, that the institutional investment in you is considerably higher than a mere accumulation of direct salary payments: on average, an additional amount equal to 27 percent of your salary is paid directly to these plans by the college or university. Of more timely concern to the new academic, however, is how fringe benefits provide both immediate services and long-range investments that an entry-level faculty member probably could not otherwise afford.

The most obvious instances of immediate benefits are medical and life insurance plans, although it is equally obvious that at this present moment, when Congress and the country are still actively debating the future of the health care system in America, there is little that can be said definitively about medical insurance, academic or otherwise. About the only assertion one could safely make, I think, is that whatever system is ultimately adopted to control the rampant increases in medical costs, group insurance plans will remain, as now, con-

TABLE 16.5 Average Institutional Cost of Benefits per Faculty Member and Average Cost for Faculty Members Receiving Specific Benefits, in Dollars and as a Percent of Average Salary, by Institutional Affiliation and Itemized Benefits, 2005–06 (all ranks)

Itemized Benefits	All Combined	Public	Private-Independent	Church-Related	All Combined	Public	Private-Independent	Church-Related
	IN DOLLARS				AS A PERCENT OF SALARY			
AVERAGE PER FACULTY MEMBER								
Retirement	6,898	7,008	7,590	5,131	9.8	10.2	9.3	8.1
Medical Insurance	4,816	4,767	5,267	4,394	6.8	7.0	6.5	6.9
Dental Insurance	223	232	224	164	0.3	0.3	0.3	0.3
Medical and Dental Combined	1,228	1,471	586	787	1.7	2.1	0.7	1.2
Disability	185	154	269	240	0.3	0.2	0.3	0.4
Tuition	551	156	1,534	1,367	0.8	0.2	1.9	2.2
Social Security	4,409	4,159	5,357	4,409	6.3	6.1	6.6	7.0
Unemployment	138	120	192	159	0.2	0.2	0.2	0.3
Group Life	147	126	213	170	0.2	0.2	0.3	0.3
Workers' Compensation	375	331	504	431	0.5	0.5	0.6	0.7
Benefits in Kind	216	153	433	252	0.3	0.2	0.5	0.4
All Combined	19,186	18,677	22,170	17,504	27.3	27.3	27.2	27.6

AVERAGE FOR FACULTY MEMBERS RECEIVING SPECIFIC BENEFITS

Retirement	7,118	7,114	8,120	5,540	10.1	10.4	10.0	8.7
Medical Insurance	6,270	6,303	6,426	5,808	8.9	9.2	7.9	9.2
Dental Insurance	511	541	467	405	0.7	0.8	0.6	0.6
Medical and Dental Combined	7,306	7,433	6,657	6,788	10.4	10.9	8.2	10.7
Disability	299	302	321	261	0.4	0.4	0.4	0.4
Tuition	5,878	2,029	10,263	12,720	8.4	3.0	12.6	20.1
Social Security	4,628	4,417	5,442	4,549	6.6	6.5	6.7	7.2
Unemployment	191	161	274	262	0.3	0.2	0.3	0.4
Group Life	189	179	224	179	0.3	0.3	0.3	0.3
Workers' Compensation	467	436	557	481	0.7	0.6	0.7	0.8
Benefits in Kind	1,447	1,239	1,785	1,599	2.1	1.8	2.2	2.5
All Combined	19,194	18,676	22,251	17,466	27.3	27.3	27.3	27.6

Source: AAUP, *Academe*, March–April 2006, 44.

Note: The institution or state contribution to the retirement plan(s) is included regardless of the vesting provision. Tuition includes both waivers and remissions. Medical and Dental Combined is limited to institutions that could not separate the two expenditures; it is not a sum of the other two categories. Benefits in Kind most often include moving expenses, housing, cafeteria plans, or benefits with cash options. Averages for All Combined are based on total expenditures, not the sum of individual benefit averages. The table is based on 1,462 reporting institutions representing 1,959 campuses.

siderably less expensive than individual plans. At this moment, for example, in the fall of 2005, the cost of a reasonably comprehensive Blue Cross-Blue Shield family plan covering basic hospital and major medical expenses is roughly one third less through university group coverage than it would be for a typical private purchaser.

Whatever the results of the current national health care debate, you should be prepared for two things shortly after arriving on your new campus. One will be a mandatory physical examination prior to enrolling in any health or life insurance plan, and the other will be a visit to your institution's benefits office to select the appropriate plan(s) for you. The options should be fully explained to you: the immediate financial choice will involve how much you need to contribute (if any) and how much the university contributes (if any) to each plan. More important differences in medical plans will involve what conditions are covered and at what rates, levels of deductibles, and whether or not you will be free to select your own doctors and hospitals. Some of these distinctions may not seem important initially, but they could become major as you move from individual to family coverage or coverage involving children. Another important consideration is whether additional insurance — such as dental insurance — is available under existing or supplemental university plans. With life insurance, it is likely that your options will be relatively simple: either some form of institutional group plan of decreasing term insurance or variable amounts of straight life insurance requiring potentially greater contributions from you. Initially, the decreasing term group insurance will seem the most economical course for a less than bountiful monthly paycheck; eventually, however, some faculty may wish to supplement group life with other forms of straight life insurance.

The two benefits that vary most among institutions are retirement plans and tuition benefit plans. Retirement plans may be limited to the institution or part of a statewide or nationwide system, and it is extremely important that you understand the advantages and options of each. Some common questions to be asked are: Is the personal plan "funded" or "defined"? What is the institutional contribution over and above whatever amount you defer from your own annual salary to the plan? What has been the record in recent years of investment return on the plan or the annual yield for retirees? Are optional investment opportunities available to you? Is the retirement plan portable should you decide at some point to leave the institution for another one? What survivor benefits are incorporated into the plan in case you die? What are the minimum and maximum amounts you may contribute to the plan, and does the university offer multiple plans? What is the maximum amount of pre-tax salary you can defer for this purpose?

Perhaps the most widespread personal plan in academia today is the Teacher's Insurance and Annuity Association (TIAA) and the College Retirement Equities Fund (CREF). Under this plan a typical arrangement might look something like this. You contribute directly out of your annual salary an amount equal to, but not limited to, 5–7 percent of that salary. The college or university may contribute an equal percent of that portion of your salary subject to Social Security tax and some greater percent of any salary in excess of the Social Security limit. Although this last figure is not likely to affect an entry-level position, it may be important as your salary rises commensurate with your academic rank.

Should this plan be available at your institution, you will still have to decide what portion of your contributions you wish to direct into the TIAA plan and what portion into CREF. The difference, on the simplest level, is that TIAA is based on the bond market whereas CREF is a mutual fund containing stocks. A common choice, at least initially, is to put one-half of the retirement contribution into one plan, one-half into the other. It is probably very difficult for a new academic to consider these options thoughtfully since the eventual outcomes are so far in the future. However, bear in mind that all investors must weigh the trade-off between risk and return. The longer one's investment horizon (i.e., the younger the faculty member is when beginning contributing to a retirement plan), the more aggressively one can invest (more stocks, less bonds) and expect to achieve a more desirable outcome. Your benefits office will be able to show you a projected level of income you might expect at various retirement ages, assuming your contributions continue (you may be shocked to discover these monthly projections are several times the level of your current salary in nominal dollars, but don't forget inflation), and what you can expect from Social Security. At present levels, for example, my own projected Social Security income would be under $2,000 a month if I retired at age 65 and 10 months, so obviously the amounts I have been contributing for over 30 years to my retirement plan will be extremely important in helping me fund the cost of living in retirement.

Although it is not very likely that a new assistant professor will want or need to take advantage of other supplemental retirement plans or long-term annuity programs available through the college or university, it is important that you speak periodically with your benefits office about the options available to you simply because your financial situation, like everything else, will change continually throughout your career. Moreover, contributions made early to such plans typically pay off dramatically at the end. Additionally, they can generate current tax savings.

Tuition benefits for dependents also vary greatly among schools, but at current and future levels this benefit may be one of the most important for the long-term financial security of your family. Does the institution, for example, offer tuition remission for any or all of your children? Does it limit that option to your own school or offer to pay an amount equivalent to its tuition for attendance at another school of your (or your child's) choice? If you are at a state university, are these amounts calculated on in-state or out-of-state tuition levels? Is this benefit subject to periodic review by the institution? Is the benefit subject, when used, to either state or federal tax? Since tuition benefits are applied across the university, you will probably not have any room to negotiate them. You do, however, have the chance to weigh the benefits of one school against another when initially considering job offers.

Given the difficulty of projecting future tuition levels, it is not easy to judge the real significance of such a benefit. But if one took even a conservative estimate—that an average annual tuition at a state university fifteen years from now would be at least $15,000—the annual cost to you for every child who attended college would be $60,000 just for tuition. With three children, your cost could be as high as $360,000 for all college expenses. (These figures would certainly be higher if your children were to attend private universities, where the present national average for tuition and fees is nearly $20,000 per year.) These, obviously, are enormous amounts to try to save over the initial years of your employment, especially when you will probably also be buying such things as new cars, a house, and other necessities. Any institutional contribution toward that potential debt is certainly worth careful consideration.

Other institutional benefits, such as laboratory and equipment start-up costs, moving expenses, housing, and other cash options, may be up-front monies negotiable with your college or university. In some fields, these benefits are an important component of any offer and should be discussed explicitly (preferably in writing). Not all institutions or departments offer such benefits, however, so you should negotiate for them as a component of a specific offer. Certainly you will want to know whether or not the institution will provide you with a computer and printer; whether it provides travel expenses to professional conferences and, if so, what the limits on such travel are; what electronic systems are available for routine faculty use and what secretarial or administrative support will be provided. Institutional benefits of this sort will not contribute, of course, to the money in your pocket, but they certainly can make a difference in the day-to-day life of a productive faculty member.

TAX ISSUES

Because the regulations governing state and federal income taxes are revised virtually every year, it is not possible in this section to be precise, and even generalizations must be hedged with an infinite number of exceptions and special circumstances. So long as you understand that these brief comments are at best introductory and need to be followed up by in-depth conversations with a good tax accountant, I will suggest a few of the general areas in which academics may confront special tax issues. One of these concerns the fringe benefits just discussed. Contributions to retirement plans, for example, may or may not be subject to income tax; you should explore the circumstances that apply in your case. Employer contributions up to a certain level, under current policy, are not taxable, regardless of which retirement plan is used. Employee contributions, however, are taxable unless they are paid directly by the employer under some form of a salary reduction agreement. That is, again under existing law, if you agree to, say, a 7 percent reduction in salary, the university will pay that amount, in addition to its own contribution, directly into your retirement plan and you will pay taxes only when the funds are actually withdrawn (but no later than age 70 1/2). You will also not be liable for taxes on any income these contributions accrue until such time as payments are received. You should be aware, however, that while salary reduction agreements currently provide for deferral of federal taxes, they may not affect state or local tax liabilities. Again, your benefits office should be able to explain what portion of your contributions would be subject to those taxes. You should also remember that in addition to your university retirement program, you may defer income tax on outside income you earn through establishment of a separate "Keogh" account.

Under the Tax Reform Act of 1986, there is a ceiling on individual contributions to retirement plans. This limit requires faculty to pay immediate taxes on any amount in excess of that limit. In effect, this limit restricts tax deferment options, especially the supplementary deferrals provided by IRAs and other implements. Although these restrictions are not likely to affect the choices of the new assistant professor, they will become important later and you should check with your benefits office annually to see what your own limit is.

Tuition remission plans for faculty dependents, prior to July 1985, were exempt from federal and state taxes. Beginning with that date, however, such benefits became subject to tax unless the institution made them available to all employees, not just to faculty. Even then, a portion of this benefit may be taxable upon use. Once more, you should explore this issue thoroughly with your benefits office.

Most of the other special tax options for college and university teachers involve deductions and unique tax exemptions that can change at any time. A few of the more common are: deductions for the cost of books, periodicals, supplies, and equipment you use in either your teaching or research; deductions for unrecovered expenses incurred while attending professional meetings or traveling to necessary laboratory or research facilities; tax exemptions for certain research grants you may receive; and deductions for use of a home office or laboratory. All of these are explained in the comprehensive *Tax Guide for College Teachers*, published annually by Academic Information Service, and which is your best home assistance for keeping abreast of any changes in federal and state income tax regulations. Let me summarize, though, a few issues related to each of the deductions/exemptions mentioned above.

Your own personal library, including the professional journals to which you subscribe, are deductible under two different plans: under the expensing option you can deduct the cost of the item in the year you purchase it up to a specified limit (currently $17,500); under the depreciation option, a specified percentage of the cost is deducted each year of the depreciation period, which is also specified by federal guidelines. To the new academic, this deduction will be extremely useful, for the capacity to purchase books and to subscribe to professional periodicals during the graduate school years was probably severely limited. Now, with a "real," if modest, income, that capacity will be increased substantially. Knowing that at least some if not all such expenses can be recovered, generally over a five-year period, will increase it even more and allow you to keep up with current research in your field.

The same principle applies to attending professional meetings and research travel to particular libraries or laboratories. Frequently your university will reimburse you for some of the expenses, either through direct departmental funds or through a university research council, but most schools have strict limits on the total amounts they will reimburse in any given year. If you do not restrict your own professional activity to that amount, you may retrieve at least a portion of the unrecovered expenses through this deduction. This benefit is especially important to those who need to travel overseas to conduct research, since the cost of such trips will almost invariably exceed the institution's reimbursement limits. However, there are very different conditions for deducting travel outside the United States than travel within, and you will need to check the *Tax Guide* carefully before planning any research or "business-with-pleasure" trip. In both of these instances, it should also be noted that the 1986 Tax Reform Act restricts employee business expenses to an amount *in excess of* 2 percent of your adjusted gross income. This means that a significant portion of such expenses are not recoverable at all, and this may be particularly true of your initial years in the university.

In an age when a home computer has become more of a professional necessity than a luxury, you should examine carefully the restrictions, as well as the usage and recordkeeping requirements, published by the IRS. The federal concern over this particular deduction seems to be founded on the difficulty of distinguishing business or professional use of computers from personal and leisure use. This means that the restrictions may be stringent, and you will have to keep verifiable records of use in order to validate any deduction. Recent case law seems to further restrict this expense by allowing only employer-required computers.

While you are applying for either university or nonuniversity research grants, you should pay cautious attention to whether or not such grants that are made directly to you (rather than to your institution) are tax exempt. Recent rulings by the IRS suggest that in cases of National Endowment for the Humanities and National Science Foundation grants, for example, exemption was dependent upon whether the original proposal stressed the *study* aspect of the research over the *result* aspect and whether the research tended to benefit the recipient of the grant rather than the grantor. As a general rule, grants that are exempt from Social Security payments are also exempt from income tax. Institutional monies received for research while you are on a sabbatical or during the summer are usually subject to income tax, but again see the *Tax Guide* for exceptions.

A majority of academics perform a considerable amount of their professional work at home and deductions for an office or laboratory in the home can result in substantial tax savings. In recent years, however, the IRS has severely tightened the rules governing when such a deduction can be claimed. For the new professor just beginning a career and probably buying a house for the first time, an alert eye to those rules could prove highly beneficial as long as current policies remain in place.

As already mentioned, I would strongly advise that every new academic study thoroughly the *Tax Guide for College Teachers* each year, but even this will not answer all your tax questions. At the relatively modest level of your present salary and probably the relatively few complications your finances will involve, it may well be to your advantage to consult a tax accountant for assistance in preparing both federal and state returns. The fees for such a service are very reasonable and themselves deductible, and if your older colleagues can direct you to an experienced specialist in academic tax issues, the savings to you could be considerable. After all, you will have worked hard for that initial salary and, given the limited resources of the first professional years, it would be nice to keep as much of it as possible.

CONCLUSION

I began this essay by observing how frequently my own colleagues speak disparagingly of their academic salaries. I conclude by wondering why. Many of these same colleagues have three months of vacation in the summer, have streamlined their effective time on campus to as little as two days per week (and then certainly not a full eight-to-five schedule), and routinely travel across both the country and the continents. They may imagine from time to time that their community neighbors working at IBM or American Airlines or wherever are making substantially more money and are generally more secure financially, but a moment's glance at national statistics concerning poverty rates and job layoffs ought to be enough to dispel such fantasies. The academic life is, as one of my more realistic colleagues says, "the best deal in the world." Since he is an economist, you can bet that his "deal" includes financial as well as emotional and intellectual well-being.

PART IV

TEACHING AND ADVISING

Like most new Ph.D.'s, you are well prepared and eager to begin independent research; your entire graduate career has been designed precisely to that end. What happens, then, when you suddenly discover that you are scheduled to teach four courses in the first semester of the new appointment? Sometime the four courses really are four: four different preparations, four different subjects and syllabi, two mass lectures, and two small seminars. The simple demand upon your time is unlike anything you have experienced in graduate school, and unless you served a year or so as a teaching assistant, the mere prospect of teaching may be fraught with terror. Of course, we all decided upon this profession because on some level we wanted to teach. But now the realities of that decision can seem overwhelming.

As the following essays suggest, successful teaching is never easy and does not, as it were, come naturally. It requires serious dedication, careful preparation, tremendous energy, flexibility, and sensitivity. Some of these requirements can be negotiated by advanced planning and a few tricks learned from experienced colleagues; some are dependent upon more individual characteristics, on your own senses of commitment and care. In either case, advice can help to smooth the transition from student to teacher, as well as that from teacher to adviser and counselor.

In the first two essays of this part, two exceptionally distinguished teachers attempt to explain the principles that have made them so successful in their very different styles. Norman L. Christensen offers advice on teaching large lecture courses; Anne Firor Scott on the challenges of small group discussions. The second half of the part confronts additional factors that continuously impinge upon actual classroom experience and therefore complicate the demands upon those who dare to take up the challenge to "profess." A. Leigh DeNeef and

Elizabeth Studley Nathans explain the complex and various functions of faculty members as mentors and advisers. Patrick M. Murphy discusses some of the technologies currently available to classroom teachers. Each of these essays is directed toward additional demands upon every teacher's time and effort. But each makes the more important point that all successful teaching depends upon your continued awareness of and sensitivity to the varied constituency that you have chosen to serve.

17

THE NUTS AND BOLTS OF RUNNING A LECTURE COURSE

NORMAN L. CHRISTENSEN

It could be argued that the lecture became an anachronism with the invention of the printing press. Although most of what is covered in undergraduate courses, especially courses at the introductory level, can be found in textbooks, we persist in this archaic tradition. This persistence might owe to our unwillingness to part with the past or our need to bolster our egos by publicly parading our knowledge in front of admiring students. However, I believe that the survival of the lecture format can be attributed to at least three more laudable factors.

1. *Pedagogical effectiveness.* I suspect (though I might not be able to conjure up data to support my suspicion) that ideas and facts presented orally and visually and reinforced by writing (that is, note taking) are more likely to find their way into our long-term memories than ideas and facts encountered in reading alone. Certainly, the lecture format offers opportunities for demonstration and illustration not available in a text.

2. *Interaction.* Lectures offer the opportunity for feedback and exchange between teacher and student. I suppose this most often takes the form of questions and clarification, but it can (and should) also facilitate challenge and debate. Compared to communication by textbook, it is much more difficult for either teacher or student to become isolated.

3. *Synthesis.* A lecture course is, regardless of topic and for better or worse, an individual creation of personal synthesis. Lecturers distill from a broad field those ideas they feel are most relevant or important. At its worst this synthesis may give a distorted or narrow view, but at its best it can bring together apparently disjointed ideas leading to insight at a higher level.

Much of what follows in this brief summary of dos and don'ts in preparing and running a large lecture course is simply common sense. Furthermore, aside from problems of scale (that is, course administration, grading large numbers of exams, and so on), I am not convinced that lecture hall teaching differs (or should differ) from teaching a small group. In fact, the most successful large lecture classes are those in which instructors are able to break down the barriers between the podium and the multitude, destroy student anonymity, and create the sense of a small seminar room. I should also warn the reader that I have drawn heavily in this exegesis on personal experience. What advice I give should be judged in the context of your own personal traits and aspirations; successful teaching is necessarily a very personal process.

COURSE ORGANIZATION

If there is an unforgivable sin in the eyes of students, it is lack of organization. This is true regardless of class format, but is particularly so in large lecture courses. Furthermore, attention must be given to organization at several levels, from the construction of the syllabus to the preparation of lectures.

If, indeed, one value of the large lecture is to abstract and synthesize information and ideas from a diverse field, then the first step in organizing a course is deciding exactly what will and will not be included. In some cases, such as introductory courses in a discipline, a certain portion of the curriculum will be almost mandatory. I cannot imagine an introductory biology course that did not cover cell division, DNA, or metabolism, or an introductory psychology course that did not touch on Freud, Jung, and Erickson. Nevertheless, successful lecture courses covering the same material may be remarkably different from one another. To use the example I know best, three courses taught at Duke by different instructors all go by the title of Biology 14. All three cover those elements deemed essential in such introductory courses (about 50 percent of the material), but they differ markedly in the content of the remainder of the course and in overall organization. My course places heavy emphasis on organism structure and function, and evolution. One of my colleagues emphasizes systematics and ecology, and much more time is spent in the third course on cell biology and physiology. The courses are equally well received, and there is no significant difference in performance in upper-level courses among alumni of the three courses. If you were to compare the syllabi from the three courses you might conclude that any organization of material is possible: one course begins with molecular and cellular biology and progresses eventually to global ecology; another begins with global ecology and ends with evolution and genetics. In each case, the content and organization of the course reflects the interests and priorities of the instructor, but each course has a clear sense of direction. Students know where they are headed and why.

No doubt every individual has a different technique for outlining a new course. You may find the following suggestions useful. Make a list of those topics you feel are essential, estimate the amount of time required to give them adequate coverage; then increase that by 50 percent. Arrange the items on this list with respect to an overall plan or rationale. This rationale should be stated explicitly at the beginning of the course. I once took an introductory course in genetics that amounted to forty isolated lectures. Each lecture was reasonably organized, but the course had no global organization. I must admit that, by not providing such organization, the instructor caused me to develop one for myself, but I discovered later that the wheel I invented had a number of flat spots.

Leave room in the schedule to fit in items of special interest to you. Students are usually annoyed by digressions into the backwaters of a discipline except when they feel they are being guided through the swamp by an expert. Such digressions provide students with a glimpse of how research is actually done by someone who is actually doing it.

Organizing lectures is necessarily a discipline-specific process. For the sort of material I cover, a three-step process seems to work best. I begin with a list of points, ideas, and facts that I feel should be covered on a particular topic. This list includes all the vocabulary I feel is essential. On some topics in my introductory biology course, all I know and all the students need to know are identical sets. However, on topics near to my heart, I constantly have to fight the urge to say it all. I have to remind myself that the goals of each lecture at the introductory level should be to stimulate interest in the topic and to provide sufficient vocabulary to pursue that interest. In the second step, I construct a rough outline that provides the overall rationale of the lecture. Finally, I prepare a detailed outline from which I will lecture.

The actual structure of lecture notes varies from individual to individual. Some people can stop at the second step. Many of my colleagues actually write their lectures word for word. I have relatively detailed notes arranged in a loose outline form. I have managed over the past several years to transfer all my lectures to Word documents and each year I print a new set that has been appropriately updated. I include in these notes illustrations I plan to use, as well as notes to myself regarding emphasis of particular points, items to be left out if time runs short, and instructions for the organization of material on the board.

LECTURING

Be suspicious of anyone who tells you exactly how you ought to lecture. If you consider all the lecture courses you have had, I am sure you will agree that there was no particular style associated with success or failure. There are, however, three common denominators to successful lecturing.

1. Know your stuff, but be willing to admit when you do not. This may be a minor problem when teaching a specialized course in your own subdiscipline, but it becomes a major challenge in an introductory course. During the semester of the introductory biology course, I lecture on topics ranging from ecology and evolution (my own areas of expertise) to cardiac physiology and biochemistry. It is not difficult to find fifty minutes worth of verbiage on the kidney, for example, but my confidence in presenting that material (and therefore the quality of my presentation) is bolstered by the fact that I spend considerable time anticipating questions and reading on this topic. I make it clear to students at the outset that I am not an expert in most of the lecture topics. Students will forgive (indeed, they are often encouraged by) a certain amount of professorial ignorance, particularly if it is coupled with a willingness on the part of the professor to pursue an answer. However, routine lack of understanding of material and inability to anticipate rather obvious questions that will arise from particular lectures are considered by most students to represent professorial sloth.

2. Know exactly how you are going to say what you are going to say. I have a colleague who maintains that if you have to use notes to lecture on a particular topic, you are not intellectually fit to speak on that topic. I do not mind adding that he is a notoriously poor lecturer. After twelve years of lecturing on the kidney, I can almost recite the notes in my sleep. Nevertheless, I would never appear before two hundred students without my notes in front of me. Although I confess that I use them only casually, they provide the structure for a coherent presentation. They are also a marvelous security blanket. Indeed, the lectures in which I rely on notes most are those in my own subject areas. Without the discipline of notes, I am quite likely to launch off into some ethereal digression on these subjects. In smaller lecture courses a certain level of disorientation is sometimes forgiven for the sake of a "less structured atmosphere." Success in a large lecture hall setting demands polish. I found it necessary during my first years of lecturing to large classes actually to give the lecture a couple of times to an empty room. I still do this with new lectures covering unfamiliar territory. This not only improves the quality of your presentation but gives you an accurate idea of how much time a lecture will take.

3. Be yourself. The most successful lecture courses are those that, while organized and polished, engage the students personally or create a small class atmosphere. A polished and organized lecture can be delivered in a relaxed and conversational manner not all that different from the way you might explain the same material to a small group over lunch. You should make every effort to let your enthusiasm for the topic come through (if you have none, do what you

can to conjure some up). If you approach a lecture as something that is preventing you from getting something else done (and it frequently is), students will approach the material you present in the same manner.

Humor, if it is natural and appropriate, is an excellent way to engage students. In my first outing in introductory biology, I felt led to write jokes into my notes and attempted to be funny in every lecture. I was demolished by one honest student's evaluation that read "if I had wanted a comedian I would have hired one." As I have relaxed, I have found ample opportunity for ad lib humor (frequently centered on my own foibles) that reinforces a particular point or, more often, simply breaks down the isolation of standing alone at a podium before two hundred quiet faces.

I will also pass along a few technical ideas that I have found helpful in large lecture courses. It is often useful to supplement lectures with illustrations or charts using slides or an overhead projection or, in today's smarter classrooms, PowerPoint projection or Webcasting. When I first tried this, students found it aided understanding on the one hand but often made note taking difficult on the other. I began to provide copies of these graphs and illustrations on handouts and included a fairly detailed outline of the lecture as well. Over the years this practice has evolved into a bound course guide that includes a detailed syllabus, a statement of philosophy and policy, copies of the previous year's exams, and handouts for each lecture. In fact, for one particularly difficult lecture on meiosis and genetics, I include a verbatim copy of my notes. Not only has this guide proved helpful to students but I find it allows me to cover more material in each lecture.

Another technical matter that is often given little thought is the use of the blackboard or whiteboard. Another student evaluation following my first lecture course suggested that I should learn to use that board. It is very annoying when a lecturer writes everything (or worse, random snitches of everything) on the board. Even more frustrating is the individual who seems to scribble messages on the board that only he or she can decipher. I have found it useful to plan exactly what I will write on the board, and how I will arrange it. I also had to learn to leave things up sufficiently long to allow them to be copied.

Taking questions during lectures can contribute a great deal to student involvement, but, if not controlled, can be distracting and lead to unnecessary digressions. I encourage questions during lectures and indeed solicit them when I am going over what I know to be difficult material. However, I encourage students with questions that go well beyond the scope of the material to see me individually. I also know that there are certain topics that will not be understood by even the majority of students without some thought outside of class.

Students usually feel a bit relieved when told that it is all right to not understand at this moment and encouraged to consider the problem on their own.

EVALUATION AND GRADING

I now and then consider that teaching would be the ideal profession were it not for the need to construct, administer, and grade exams. I am skeptical of the notion that any instrument I develop can, in fifty minutes, completely and fairly evaluate a student's understanding of what I have covered in a span ten times that long. I dislike the processes of exam writing and grading. Most of all, I resent the attitude that our evaluation-oriented educational system encourages the idea among students that the grade is *the* final product of a course.

One could lay blame upon our A–F grading system, but I have seen little evidence that alternative systems are much better. During the 1960s and 1970s a number of colleges experimented with gradeless transcripts. Students were evaluated by letters compiled throughout their tenures. Not only were such letters difficult and time consuming to prepare; they were equally difficult and time consuming to read and interpret. The experiment deteriorated when professors began ending their letters with the phrase "if we were using a conventional grading scale, this student would receive a. . . ."

Having said all that, I firmly believe that evaluations (flawed as they may be) are a necessary part of the educational process. They not only give us a comparative measure of student performance but they also provide the best measure I know of the effectiveness of our teaching. Their success is entirely dependent upon the thought and care that go into their preparation and execution.

Students should be informed at the outset exactly how they are to be evaluated. Will the course be graded by strict percentage guidelines or by some sort of curve? What proportion of the final grade will be determined by midterm and final exams, papers, and labs? Do you plan to drop a low quiz or exam? I suggest that this information have a prominent place in the course syllabus. Once stated, you should view this as a contractual agreement to be violated only by mutual consent. Have a clearly stated policy regarding late assignments and missed exams. For example, missed classes and assignments should be excused only by clearance from an academic dean. This arrangement puts the burden on the student to show just cause for missing a course event and leaves the decision in the hands of individuals most able to judge whether a particular excuse is legitimate.

In large courses, it is necessary to schedule the dates of the exams at the outset. Students will adjust their schedules to such dates if they have them well in advance. Trying to get a large class to agree at midterm on an exam date is a simple recipe for chaos.

In most large courses grades are heavily determined by exams. Regardless of its format, an exam measures two things: how well the student knows the material and how well the examiner and examinee communicate with one another. Ideally, the variance in exam scores resulting from communication problems should be small.

Constructing exams presents a real dilemma. Objective-style tests (multiple-choice, true-false, completion, and so on) are the simplest and fastest to grade. Answers are either correct or not and grading can often be done by machine. While I do not use such exams, I believe they can be very effective instruments in many disciplines when properly constructed. It is possible, for example, to write multiple-choice questions that require thought and synthesis. Nevertheless, such exams are incredibly difficult to write and are subject to abuse. Every now and then I get it in my head to write an objective exam for the general biology course. It takes me a minimum of an hour to write each multiple-choice question and, therefore, several days of hard work to construct the exam. Even with careful editing, I seem always to find serious glitches in one to several questions after the exam has been given. Furthermore, I have more difficulties with academic dishonesty on this style of exam than any other. Essay exams are generally easier to construct, but much more difficult to grade. I do feel it is easier with such questions to test a student's understanding of concepts and ability to synthesize material. As with objective exams, it is important that essay questions be carefully edited so that what is being asked for is absolutely clear. When I first started using such exams, I had a tendency to write wordy, "interesting" questions. I soon discovered that, in the turmoil of an exam, such questions were often confusing and subject to misinterpretation.

In large courses, unless exams are machine graded, multiple graders are almost a necessity. This can lead to a certain amount of unevenness in grading across the class. The problem can be minimized if each question is graded for the entire class by a single person. Graders should read a significant number of exams before grading to calibrate themselves and to be sure that the expectations of the key are reasonable. They should be as explicit as possible regarding lost points. A copy of the exam key, with indications of how credit was assigned on each question, should be posted. I feel (though not all my colleagues agree) that students should have some recourse if they feel they lost points unfairly. My students are allowed to submit their exams for regrade within a specified time period following receipt of the exam. A written justification for regrade is also required. Each grader then responds by making appropriate changes or providing a detailed explanation for points lost. I should add that on a couple of occasions I have caught students altering their exams before submitting them for regrade. This problem was solved by photocopying the exams before returning them to the students (the cost of such photocopying is included in the fee for their course guides).

Large courses present many opportunities for academic dishonesty. While I am not convinced that the problem is as large as the popular press would lead one to believe, I do feel it is the responsibility of an instructor to be cognizant of the problem and to make certain that opportunities for cheating are minimal. The first time I was confronted with a cheating problem, I was informed by an angry (signed) note from a student. Her anger was directed not only at the cheaters but also at my naïveté. I have found it best to meet this problem head-on. I devote a section of my course guide to defining what I believe to be academic dishonesty and to describing the "wages of sin." I have discovered from experience that it is essential to be explicit about what is and is not cheating. Clearly, copying an exam and plagiarism are cheating. But is it cheating when students turn in nearly identical laboratory exercises after being encouraged to cooperate? In all cases of academic dishonesty the student is entitled to due process. At most universities this means referral to a judicial board. Such hearings can be very time consuming and intimidating for both student and instructor, and it is very tempting to try to handle the matter internally. This not only leads to unfair or uneven treatment but also leaves the instructor open to potential future litigation.

CLASS RAPPORT AND INSTRUCTOR ACCESSIBILITY

I am convinced that successful lecture hall teaching depends upon breaking down barriers between the lecturer and the students. I have also discovered that some barriers will always remain and, indeed, probably should. I arrived at Duke with a disdain for titles and hierarchy characteristic of a student of the sixties. Furthermore, I had the phenotype of an eighteen-year-old, and therefore I had great difficulty convincing various offices on campus that I was a professor; indeed, I was not all that convinced myself. I was very concerned with student interaction and tried hard to "be one of the kids." Student reaction was quite mixed. Some students liked that sort of familiarity, but many felt it bordered on patronizing. Several students commented in evaluations that they were not paying tuition to be taught by "one of the kids." Because of the simple fact that the lecturer is also sitting in judgment with regard to grades, there are necessarily going to be barriers. I also quickly discovered that I did not have time to be constantly available. Indeed, with a large class I found it necessary to set rather strict limits on accessibility. Students understand, in general, that young faculty have many competing demands, and they are quite willing to take advantage of office hours or appointments. If you have additional course staff, such as teaching assistants, do not hesitate to delegate some of this work. Occasional review sessions will allow you to deal with the most frequently asked questions and will greatly diminish demands for individual conferences.

18.

WHY I TEACH BY DISCUSSION

ANNE FIROR SCOTT

Teaching and learning are among the most complex activities in which human beings engage, and neither is fully understood. Why can a boy who cannot remember the dates of the War of 1812 tell you who was up to bat in the ninth inning of the 1929 Red Sox–Yankees game? Why is a teacher who seems to whisper in the classroom, who never looks up and whose tone of voice seldom changes, remembered by her students for years after as the high point of the college experience? These are the kinds of mysteries that make us humble.

What I am about to write, therefore, represents one person's experience of nearly thirty years teaching undergraduates, and a good many forays into teaching adults. My pedagogical theory developed as I tried to understand what I could see (or thought I could see) happening in the classroom. It is offered here in the hope of stimulating new teachers to think hard about what they are doing.

Real learning changes the way people think. It occurs when the learner is actively engaged in discovery—discovery of "facts," of what other people have thought, of the way in which knowledge in a particular field is created, or of the existence of unanswered questions.

It follows that an important part of a teacher's responsibility is to plan classroom experiences that promote that sense of discovery. One is not engaged in pouring knowledge into an empty vessel; one is trying to activate an intelligence to begin learning on its own. My purpose in any course is less to communicate a body of knowledge than to help students learn how that knowledge came to be and how it can be used to think through problems and organize concepts. There are many ways to do this, and they differ from one subject to another. My examples and anecdotes grow out of the experience of teaching history, but I think some variation of these methods could be developed for virtually every field of knowledge.

What follows can only be a bare outline, to be filled in with experience. Its purpose is to encourage the beginning teacher to experiment.

Let us suppose that the new teacher is assigned a course about which she knows at least something and knows, further, how to learn more. In preparing to teach the course the first question must be, What do I want to accomplish? What do I hope my students will know how to do at the end that they do not know now? At this stage be as idealistic as you like; you will fall short no matter what, but it is better to fall short of a lofty goal than to achieve a puny one.

Having established your goal, try to put it in straightforward words so that you can offer it to the class at the beginning. "This is what I hope we shall achieve this semester—I would also like to find out what *your* goals are." Since some will have no goal whatever, beyond filling a requirement or taking a course that meets at a convenient hour, this challenge gets you off to the right start. From the beginning eschew passivity; *assume* students are anxious to learn.

How do you design a syllabus for a course based on active learning? Choose reading assignments and research projects that introduce students to the basic knowledge that you consider essential. This means reading must be carefully chosen and small writing and research projects (which keep the students fully involved) must be planned so that they are not overwhelming and so that they promote an incremental growth in competence. They should gradually become more demanding as the semester goes along.

The syllabus should be clear and complete. Each day's responsibility should be spelled out, along with a few questions to guide the student's reading. "Upon what evidence does the author build his argument? Is that evidence convincing to you? Come to class prepared to discuss two or three concrete examples." If the students know these questions will be discussed in class, they will usually read carefully.

A class of this kind requires attendance. I point out on the first day that this class will produce very little that can be gotten by reading someone else's notes, that attendance is therefore expected, and that anyone who is unavoidably absent will be expected to turn in an essay on the day's assignment. Under this rule, cutting is infrequent.

To prepare for the actual class meeting, the instructor needs a list of logically articulated questions that will elicit the principal ideas covered in the day's reading. In practice, however, it is well to allow room for the unexpected. Sometimes the discussion takes off after the first question, and then the class develops its own direction and may develop ideas quite new to the instructor. On bad days (say the Monday after Homecoming) a fair bit of extempore lecturing may be the only way to move ahead. But, by and large, when there has been adequate preparation on the part of both student and teacher, most of the day's work can be carried along with discussion.

The nature of the instructor's questions is crucial. They should only occasionally be answerable with information. Mostly they should ask students to think and to bring to bear what they have read, and their own knowledge of the world, on the issue at hand. "Have you had even a brief experience in your life that helps you understand what it was like to be a slave? A master?" "What was Lincoln trying to accomplish in his First Inaugural? Why is the Second Inaugural so different?" "What would you need to know if you wanted to understand the real motivation for the founding of Hull House?" "What do the Mexican War, the Spanish-American War, and the First World War have in common?" And so on.

If we come down to the nuts and bolts: how does one begin? With a provocative, if possible an unexpected, question that wakes up the drowsy and challenges the alert. How does one bring everybody in? By assigning specific questions ahead of time, it is possible to bring along the shy students whose inclination is to sit still and listen. For example: "John, would you find out before next time what happened to the cost of living during the depression of 1893?" How does one handle the loquacious who never know when to stop? First, by not always calling on the first person who raises a hand; second, by being prepared to say "Ah—let's stop there and ask what other people think."

People ask me over and over: How do you keep the discussion on track? This is where your own outline is critical. In the midst of a lively discussion of a minor issue it is often necessary to say, "This is all very interesting but before we leave today we simply must address . . ." And thus bring everybody back to the main issues.

It is helpful to summarize frequently. After you feel enough has been said on a particular question, you might say, "Now, let me see, I gather that most of you think . . . and a few of you also think . . . and assuming for the moment that you are all right, the next question would be . . ."

I like to begin sometimes with a summary of where we have come so far in the course, with some reference to the way our ideas are changing and developing as we go along.

Skeptics often ask me, "What do you do when there is dead silence?" There are many ways to deal with an absence of response—some spontaneous. "Is this rush week or what is wrong with you folks?" Or rephrase the question. Make sure it has no simple answer. Sometimes it is possible just to wait, looking expectant. One of the most successful discussion leaders I ever knew used to walk into class and sit down and simply look around in a friendly way. It wouldn't be long before someone would pipe up—and the class would be off to a lively session.

The point on which I differ with many colleagues, and about which we argue a good deal, is that of what is called "coverage." Discussion, they argue, is fine for making people think, but it takes so much time that one is in danger of not "covering" the subject at hand. My view is that what is called coverage is usually a matter of memorizing a body of material that the instructor, or the consensus of people in the field, has determined to be important. All the psychological evidence I have seen suggests that this kind of learning is lost in a few weeks or months and is almost all gone within a year. So, of what use is it to the developing mind?

My own view is that the kind of learning that I call active, if it succeeds, changes the student from a spectator into a participant, one who is capable of learning whatever, out of the vast body of what we call knowledge, she needs to know for a particular purpose. There is no space here to go into the history of educational thought since Plato, but I am convinced, from all I can read, that the truly great teachers have always tried to teach students how to teach themselves.

There are various practical cautions:

1. Try to find out what students already know, since part of your task will be relating what they don't yet know to what they do.

2. Learn names fast. There are a number of techniques for doing this, but the sooner you can do so, the better the discussion will go.

3. Be willing to admit error. "After listening to you, I can see that I missed the point." Then it is easier for *them* to admit error.

4. Be willing to experiment, and if one question doesn't work leave it quickly and try another. Over the years you will develop a kind of sixth sense about what will work even though students change and each class is different.

5. Keep on learning yourself all the time. This is the *only* way to communicate what we call the joy of learning. Remember that the adage — what you do speaks so loud I can't hear what you say — is a vital principle in teaching.

6. Try to help your students feel more and more competent as time goes on. Never, no matter what the provocation, make fun of a student or belittle his or her effort. The most confused statement can be rephrased in a way that makes a little sense — and if the student thinks "aha, that is what I meant," maybe the next effort won't be quite so confused.

7. Be accessible out of class, which means not just that you are present and accounted for at your stated office hours but that your *mind* is accessible to what your students have to say.

8. Keep thinking about the educational process, what it ought to accomplish, how one can make it work better. The kind of teaching I have here described does not grow tiresome since it is always changing and developing. And since the teacher is not bored, students are not either.

A course taught in this mode requires different kinds of examinations and different standards of evaluation from a traditional lecture course. Examinations must be designed with the goals of the course in mind: they must set problems that students can tackle, using the information and tools they have learned daily in the classroom. Such examinations are more difficult to construct, but the reward is that they are also much more interesting to read, since each one is different.

One could write endlessly on this subject but — in keeping with its philosophy — I would much rather lead a discussion than write a didactic essay. However, perhaps enough has been said to stir the reader to experiment, and experience suggests that once you try it you'll never go back to straight lecturing!

19

NEW FACULTY MEMBERS AND ADVISING

ELIZABETH STUDLEY NATHANS

Time-consuming, demanding, anxiety-provoking, expected, and exceptionally rewarding if often unrewarded: such is advising. As a newly minted Ph.D., or in some institutions even as an ABD instructor, you will advise. You will advise whether or not your department assigns you formal counseling responsibilities, whether or not you are commandeered for a "general" or underclass advising program, whether or not you want to advise. If you teach, you will advise. Your advisees will undoubtedly survive their encounters with you, whether you advise well or badly. How can you survive yours with them — and both contribute to your students' development and enjoy the advising experience?

DEPARTMENTAL (MAJOR) ADVISING

Some advising, the easiest when you are new to the faculty, will be that done within your own department. Your department (through the chair, the director of undergraduate studies, or perhaps even a department secretary) will present you a list of majors, probably several more or less complete folders containing transcripts, scribbled notes from your predecessors, and other miscellaneous items. In large departments, individual faculty members may advise as many as thirty or more students; more often, you will carry ten to fifteen advisees. Declared majors all, some of your advisees will be sophomores; probably most will be juniors or seniors. In your first year on the faculty, most may know far more about the institution, your colleagues, and your department than do you.

What do major advisees expect of you, and how do you deliver? The basic desiderata are easy to enumerate. You must know your college's requirements for graduation, and you must know your department's own major requirements. If you do not know them, you cannot advise effectively — and in extreme cases, you may even share legal liability for your deficiencies. As an undergraduate and as a graduate student, you doubtless avoided slogging through the murky prose of the institutional bulletin. You can avoid it no longer.

Nor can you avoid the handouts that your department will surely bestow upon you: advertisements for this course and that seminar, special notes about what will "count" for which requirement and what will not, endless errata sheets that correct the errors in the supposedly infallible bulletin. Your temptation to trash all such scraps of information will be strong. Resist temptation — and devise a filing system. Your advisees won't automatically understand or remember the requirements, and your colleagues will expect you to tout their courses and seminars. A minimal investment of time to file bits of paper as they accumulate can save you precious minutes when your appointment schedule becomes crowded and information needs to be at your fingertips.

Let's assume that your department does advising well: that it has given you a list of students (perhaps even with pictures and local addresses), relatively complete transcripts, and all the information you need to be a "good adviser." You are told that advisees know your name and that each advisee will see you "at least once" each semester, to talk over progress and academic plans. Fresh, enthusiastic, and eager to impress, you look forward to meeting "your" students. You post your office hours on your door, perhaps even list them with the department secretary. You are careful to add extended hours during the registrar's designated course selection period each term. And you wait. No "real" work gets done during office hours: it would scarcely pay to write when you might be interrupted at any moment, and even serious reading of more than book reviews is problematic. So you wait some more — and few or no students come.

This, indeed, is the frustration particularly of upper-class advising. Students profess to want good advising, and in several schools, student governments have literally begged the undergraduate administration to leave in force requirements that students meet with advisers at least once each semester. But relatively few of your advisees will seek you out until (or unless) compelled to acquire your signature on their registration forms. And then many will appear (some without appointments), completed course cards in hand: "Would you please sign this." For such encounters, all your careful preparation, the hours of making sense out of requirements, of planning how to justify your recommendations, seem wasted. The students seem not to want advice — and they certainly resist investing the time to receive at your hands the best you can offer them.

And yet, if you recall your own undergraduate days, you probably sense that they need advice. Not, perhaps, about what courses to take next semester; of those choices, they may be quite certain. But more important advice, of the sort they cannot get from their peers or from institutional publications. What should they do during the summer? Should they go to graduate school? What will it be like? How can they cope with the inevitable "down" times? Should they take a semester (or a year, or more) off? What courses outside the major should they consider taking—and why? What, in short, should they know about both the present and the future that they cannot readily learn through the student grapevine?

These are precisely the things that you—even (and perhaps especially) as a young faculty member—are well equipped to help them decide. The trick is to involve them, to get them to want what you have to give.

You will find the devices that work best for you. Some advisers invite their advisees to lunch (one-on-one) each semester. Departments often have funds to cover such entertainment, and if they don't, students are generally happy to pay for their own food. Others invite groups of advisees to their homes for informal suppers. Again, departments will often pay, and some colleges even provide meals or snacks catered by the campus food service. Other advisers send a note to their advisees each term (sometimes, different notes for juniors and seniors). Here, the department secretary, the computer, and e-mail can combine to produce something better than a photocopied form letter, even one on which the adviser has added a handwritten PS mentioning some item he or she has noticed in the record that might initiate a discussion.

Whatever devices you choose, the temptation to be a friend to your advisees will be strong. The age differences may be minimal, and you will be fresh from the teaching assistant mode of easy first-name informality. Informality is fine; collegiality based on common interests is encouraged. Genuine friendship between equals, however, is probably out of the question. Advisers occasionally must do things students find difficult to accept in friends: they must reject choices; they must interject a note of reality into what may be a student's overly optimistic plans; ultimately, they must produce realistic and balanced letters of evaluation and recommendation. One can be informal and still maintain a certain distance and the ability to make judgments when the occasion demands; one can be friendly and open and welcoming without again becoming a student. It will take time to find your own right approach and niche. Being aware of the ramifications of the adviser's role, however—and being aware that undergraduates often welcome an adult who will tell them honestly where they stand—may help.

Whatever the requirements of your institution, whatever its advising procedures, and whatever the records and future plans of your advisees, the students majoring in your discipline will want and expect of you certain types of information. As you prepare for one of the first administrative tasks you will undertake as a faculty member, be certain that from reading your department's own materials, from conversations with experienced colleagues, from (if necessary) research in the library and contacts with colleagues in other campus offices, you can discuss the topics listed below authoritatively and can provide guidance to the student who wants more detailed information. Be sure, too, that you know what services and support your department's director of undergraduate studies or similar officer will provide your advisees and you. Attend any meetings convened by your department for its majors—partly because senior faculty will expect attendance of you and students will welcome it as a sign of interest and commitment, but mostly because you can glean valuable information. Read your institution's teacher-course evaluation booklet, if only so that you will know the student grapevine wisdom on the courses and colleagues you will be discussing with advisees. Do not ally yourself with the legions of advisers who are always underprepared. Even if you use only a fraction of your information in working with students, you will benefit from learning more about your institution and its resources. Consider the following:

— Departmental and institutional degree requirements

— Special requirements (languages? statistics? and so on)

— Graduate and professional school requirements/procedures

— Nonacademic job markets for graduates

— Summer internship/job possibilities

— Special programs (study abroad, research programs, and so on)

If you can handle these topics comfortably, you will be prepared, as a new departmental adviser, to go beyond your role of providing competent technical advice and ready to do that which your students in the end will prize more than any specific assistance you offer. You will be prepared—however busy you are, however rarely you may see many of your advisees—to make majoring in your department a personal experience for each of your students. For you will, in the course of acquiring the technical expertise, also begin to acquire the judgment to apply it to individual circumstances.

ADVISING OF NONDECLARED STUDENTS

Occasionally you may be asked to advise nondeclared (usually freshman or sophomore) students. Many selective colleges and universities avoid requiring this task of new faculty members, preferring to wait a year or so until new professors are acclimated to the institution and know its curricula, practices, and personnel. If as a first-year faculty member you are asked to perform this service, discreet enquiries are appropriate among other junior colleagues or (if you are lucky enough to have one) of a trusted senior mentor in the department. Is such service customary for first-year faculty at your institution? If it is, you are certainly willing to serve; you want only to ensure that you acquire quickly the information you will need to do a commendable job for the department and for your students.

If you are assigned nondeclared or general education students in your first faculty year, your advising tasks will be vastly more difficult and more demanding than those you will assume in the department. You will have to know the whole curriculum; you may even need a nodding acquaintance with other schools and colleges in your university, if your institution is a comprehensive one that permits students to transfer among undergraduate programs during their first two years of enrollment. You will need to know at least the rudiments of your institution's policies on such matters as housing, Greek rush, financial aid, and the like, for nondeclared students will expect you to be the source of all such knowledge, not merely that which pertains to your academic discipline. And you will need a comprehensive storehouse of referral information: to whom should you send the former would-be English major who awoke this morning certain that her future lies in electrical engineering? What do you do with a tearful freshman, cut from his single-shot rush choice, who can't take his chemistry test because he's "too upset"?

Most comprehensive state-supported institutions and many of the selective private colleges and universities recognize the enormity of the nonmajor advising task, and they genuinely try to support those who work with undeclared or nonmajor students. Support for advisers will generally take one of several forms. Advisers may work within a central facility where they have access to deans, to more experienced senior colleagues, and to some all-knowing individual called variously an advising coordinator, advising director, or some such, who schedules appointments, keeps track of students' records, and is available on a moment's notice to answer questions and provide referral guidance. Often, in such a system, advisers leave their offices and go to a central location for their appointments with students. This can seem an inconvenience, to be sure, but it is a boon to inexperienced advisers who are not left on their own, isolated in their departmental offices, to deal with matters beyond the depth of their experience or knowledge in the institution. Centralized systems generally provide other forms of support, as well: comprehensive advising handbooks, often organized around the "questions most asked" by freshmen and sophomores; training workshops and meetings to update advisers on specific topics before and during the academic year. Handbooks can be cumbersome to read from cover to cover, but the best are indexed, and most advisers ultimately find them useful. Workshops are undeniably tedious in the heat of late summer or the slush of winter, but again they can alert inexperienced advisers not only to facts they need to know but also to approaches, to tricks of the trade that can save time for both faculty and students.

In decentralized systems, advisers to freshmen and sophomores generally work out of their departmental offices, often with some sort of handbook as a guide, but otherwise on their own to deal with any and all questions as they arise. To the uncaring and cavalier, such an arrangement may be welcome: it demands little of the adviser and imposes few restrictions. To the conscientious, it can be terrifying; what to do about the question the adviser can't answer? Whom to call? To whom to refer? The new adviser would do well in such circumstances to call on a more experienced colleague, either within the department or in the office of the dean. However decentralized their advising systems, all colleges and universities employ vast numbers of deans, assistant deans, and assistants to the dean. Such persons are paid to know the rules—and the best also know how and when to circumvent them. Most would rather field a question—any question—from an adviser than pick up the pieces of disaster later. Often, the campus telephone directory or staff director will make clear to which office questions should be directed, and new faculty members can profitably spend some time familiarizing themselves with their institution's roster of counseling services and personnel. Lacking a handbook or other guide that suggests where to go or whom to call, the adviser can direct questions to the person who appears to rank lowest in the hierarchy—in arts and sciences, for instance, an assistant dean or an assistant to the dean. If the individual taking the call is not the appropriate person to field the particular query, no harm is done: the call will be referred by a secretary to a more appropriate member of the staff.

Whatever the system in which the adviser labors, he or she will find that nonmajor advising demands special skills. It demands, first, tolerance. Nondeclared students are, sometimes on successive days, absolutely certain that they will become Nobel laureates in medicine and that they will win next year's Pulitzer Prize for literature. They are, in turn, arrogant and overconfident and paralyzed with self-doubts. Eager, compliant, and seemingly grateful for your suggestions at one conference, they may return a week later to berate you for your supposed incompetence, your lack of interest, your inability to help them. Or, worse yet, they may report your alleged shortcomings to their parents—who won't bother with you, having long since learned that going straight to the president gets prompt attention. (There are ways to survive even this eventuality; see the hints below.)

In any event, your nonmajor advisees will need from you, first and foremost, interest. They will forgive your lack of expertise; they can learn to accept "I don't know," if it's accompanied by "Let's find out." They may break appointments with you, but they will not forgive your breaking appointments with them. Most likely, you are the first faculty member with whom they have spoken face-to-face. Whatever you think of yourself, you are to them an awesome and exalted figure — idealized, in some ways, beyond any reasonable standards. Often, they generalize their impressions of the faculty as a whole from their specific impressions of you. You will develop the expertise to answer your advisees' technical questions over the course of your career. The interest, and the willingness to communicate that interest, must be there from the start.

THE CLASSROOM TEACHER AS ADVISER

Much of your advising will be done not as formally designated adviser to either major or nonmajor students specifically assigned to you but in the context of classroom teaching and the conferences and casual conversations you have with students in your courses. Your own preferences will dictate how open to such informal contacts you should be: for most junior faculty members, it takes time to strike a balance between appearing overly accessible and protecting the time that is essential to complete research and writing that will be necessary to your survival in the institution.

The size of your classes will dictate to some extent how well you know your students. If you are lecturing to a group of two hundred, you will likely know only the few individuals bold enough to seek you out — unless you are unusually good at associating names with faces or determined to resort to such relatively outmoded and unpopular devices as a seating chart. Even if you occasionally teach sections normally presided over by your own teaching assistants, you will not have the frequent contact with small groups of students that invites individual conferences or close relationships.

If you teach smaller sections, however, and if you are comfortable enough in the classroom to convey a sense of informality (not, note, incompatible with being perceived as tough or demanding) and interest, you will likely be approached by individual students, either before or after class or during office hours.

Generally, the initial approach will be limited to the course material: the student will profess not to have understood a certain point in the reading or to be encountering difficulty with a particular experiment or with a paper topic. First, of course, you deal with the concern the student presents, and your interest in the subject matter and the student's concern to master it give you common ground for a productive conversation. Whether to go beyond — whether to in-quire, for instance, if the student who has yet to submit a paper when it was due in your class is having similar difficulties in other courses — is more problematic. Young instructors often shy away from posing such questions, fearful, perhaps, of learning more than they want to know or cope with. Some, almost brazen in their disinterest, announce flatly that they don't care whether the student is having difficulty, that conversations must be restricted to the work at hand, and that any problems the student has should be taken up with someone else, some-where else. For the latter group of instructors, the problem of advising students outside the classroom is generally short-lived: one edition of the institution's teacher-course evaluation booklet suffices to spread the word, and the faculty members in question will likely be troubled little by students in future years.

When confronted with student concerns that go beyond the scope of a single course, what can the classroom instructor appropriately do? First, and prob-ably most important, recognize the limitations of his or her perspective. The professor sees the student in only one course: if a student hints at a concern or problem that goes beyond the scope of a class, that problem probably also transcends anything with which an individual instructor should be expected to deal. The instructor can play a crucial role by explaining to the student that, while he or she can help within the context of the particular class, the problem is one that deserves the attention of someone with broader expertise than the instructor possesses. This is the time for a call to a dean, and for encouragement to the student to seek the help that even the most cumbersome and insensitive bureaucracies can offer in such situations. And it is the time for follow-up, both to assure the student of continuing interest and to ensure that appropriate at-tention is being paid to the student's problem.

The instructor who spots a problem not reported to him or her by a stu-dent faces a more difficult dilemma. The playground ethic remains strong even among Ph.D.'s, and the temptation not to tell on the student will be overwhelm-ing. Often, young instructors will confront the student, hoping to deal with problems themselves. Most commonly: "Bill, you haven't turned in the last four papers in the course. You know that the syllabus announces a penalty for late papers, but if you have a really good reason for not turning them in, we can talk about it." This approach invites the student to devise an appropriately heart-rending story — and virtually forces the instructor to waive the penalty. Naively, the instructor accepts the student's assurances that it will never happen again — only to go around the same circle once more, when the next paper falls due. Or an instructor may notice that a student misses class regularly or, attending, dozes brazenly, often in the front row. Again, the temptation to do nothing is strong: students are, after all, responsible for their own attendance at most colleges and universities, and if confronted by their negligence, most will simply excuse themselves as having been ill or having had a lot of tests this month. Not wanting to doubt the student's word by demanding the written, official excuse for which most colleges make provision, the faculty member is trapped: either accept the story and forgive the transgression or brand the student a liar.

Again, more experienced colleagues and particularly the college deans can and should be asked for help. The deans keep comprehensive records on students in all but the largest universities: if anyone knows whether a student is genuinely encountering difficulty, they will. They will also know, in many cases, whether a particular student seems to become ill before every scheduled test, whether there has been a consistent problem with late submission of work, whether there have been in the student's past a remarkable number of inept instructors who have failed to recognize the student's talents and have (in the student's eyes and those of his or her parents) evaluated work unfairly. The dean's office is both resource and protection for the instructor in such circumstances, and it can even reassure the inexperienced of their own expertise and sanity. The dean's records may suggest, simply, that the problem student is lazy or distracted. Or they may reveal genuine difficulties: learning disabilities, underdeveloped skills in reading or quantitative reasoning, lack of adequate secondary school preparation in certain fields. Occasionally the record points to marginal intellectual abilities and to Herculean efforts by the student in question to meet parental or societal expectations that may be beyond the student's reach. In any event, the dean's staff will have a breadth of perspective and experience that you, as a relatively new instructor, will lack. They can be of inestimable help to you in your efforts to aid the student in your class. And your care and concern in reporting apparent problems will in turn assist the deans in their task of identifying students in difficulty and directing those students to appropriate sources of aid.

THOSE AWKWARD SITUATIONS

Inevitably, there will arise those awkward situations when the best preparation, all your efforts to anticipate your responses, and everything you've read and learned won't be much help. A few of the more common:

Cheating. No one ever prepares for his or her first cheating case, and most of us have probably been "burned" several times, because we neither suspect cheating as often as we might nor feel comfortable confronting it when it occurs. If you encounter cheating, it will generally take one of two forms: the plagiarized (or, perhaps, the borrowed or stolen) paper or lab report, or the cribbed or copied exam. Most often, instructors suspect cheating when they receive a

paper markedly better — and more intellectually sophisticated — than its predecessors; occasionally, another student will drop a broad hint that the instructor
should "check on" student behavior on a recent exam or the integrity of submitted papers. Some prudent instructors in grading objective or short-answer
submissions photocopy papers before returning them; a relatively modern but
all-too-common form of cheating is the submission of a paper for regrading,
with original answers altered on the basis of in-class discussion of the test or
perhaps a posted exam key. In any event, if you confront the cheater, he or
she will either profess innocence and outrage (and you will feel off guard and
threatened) or dissolve in tears of remorse and protestations that the incident
will never again be repeated.

In neither case are you in a position to judge the events objectively or to assess
the appropriate penalty. Every institution has judicial and counseling procedures for students accused of academic offenses. The faculty member who fails
to use the proper procedures in cases of suspected cheating subverts the system that upholds the integrity of the whole community. And he or she may
be subject to charges of violating the student's due process rights by assessing
a penalty within the course that the student finds unreasonable or damaging
and subsequently elects to challenge. In all cases of suspected cheating, photocopy everything; tell the student that you are holding the grade on the work in
question; and report the matter to your institution's designated administrator.
The faculty handbook provided at most institutions will guide you through the
procedure; if in doubt, consult your departmental chair or the office of your
institution's academic dean.

The poison pen letter. Almost every faculty member, sooner or later, is the
object of a spiteful letter to the president, the chancellor, or the dean from a dis-
gruntled student or parent. Often, the information in the letter is secondhand;
often, the student will excuse his or her own poor performance by complaining
to the parents that the adviser recommended the "wrong" courses or the professor "didn't tell us" what would be on the test or was "unfair" in assessing the
student's work. The parents then write to the administrator, presenting the student's side of the tale as gospel and demanding anything and everything from
tuition refunds to the faculty member's decapitation. Such letters can be devastating to inexperienced instructors; most often, the charges are unfair and the
complaints unfounded, but administrators, who are far removed from the daily
round of classroom teaching and advising, take them seriously and forward
them to deans or to departmental chairs for response. Your temptation when
confronted by your first such complaint — whether from a student or a parent —
will be to panic. The student pays tuition; you are a hired hand. Who will believe your story? Relax! Your best defense is a good offense: routine, accurate

recordkeeping that indicates what advice was given, and why, or in your classes, when papers were due, when they were submitted, and how they were evaluated; a comprehensive syllabus that indicates what is required in your course and when; and notes, written immediately after the fact, about any classroom or advising encounter with a student that your instincts tell you may be problematic (a controversy over a grade, a student's protest that you failed to accept a class excuse, an undergraduate's insistence that you lost a paper you are convinced the student failed to submit, an accusation that you "didn't tell" a student about a particular requirement). Contemporary notes will be vastly more convincing than those written weeks or months after the fact; they require little of your time, but they will prove immensely useful in the one situation in a hundred that proves problematic for you. And they will endear you to the department chair or dean who must draft a diplomatic but firm response to the parents, the provost, or the president.

Relationships. Almost all faculty members now understand clearly that social relationships with enrolled students are inappropriate. Virtually every college and university now has explicit guidelines, designed to support appropriate professional behavior and interactions and to address situations in which behavior violates professional standards. As a new faculty member, you should review institutional guidelines carefully and, if necessary, discuss them with senior colleagues or with your department chair.

Most times, you will not see as much of your students as you might wish. Except when exams are approaching or papers are falling due, days may go by without student visitors to your regular office hours, and you may in fact worry that students are not seeking you out for the help and guidance you are ready to provide. At some point, however, you may see too much of the student who seeks a personal relationship with you and who seems to need and to demand a major share of your attention. Quite likely, you won't initially recognize the situation for what it is. Flattered by the student's seeming interest in your course or discipline and by the way he or she hangs on every word in advising sessions or in the classroom, grateful, perhaps, for the visits that relieve the tedium of office hours, you will notice too late that the student turns up wherever you do; that the visits become longer and the occasion for them less clear; that, perhaps social invitations even become explicit. Phone calls at home are commonplace; late evening visits aren't unheard of (nor are irate spouses). Sometimes, the student who acquires the crush is physically unattractive and socially inept; idealized from afar, you become the friend he or she has never had. Perhaps more often, however, the student is highly intelligent, serious about intellectual endeavors, deeply involved with you as a potential role model — and socially too immature to fit readily into the college social scene. Either way, even the slightest attention from you will become a precious commodity, and your every glance and word endowed with a significance (described, often, to room-mates and corridor-mates) you never intended. In one instance of this sort, a faculty member found himself pursued to Europe during his sabbatical by an especially ardent young woman who delayed arranging her own study abroad until she knew where he would be working and living. Fortunately, his wife is both balanced and understanding.

What to do? First, the obvious things. Minimize opportunities for the student to speak with you alone and avoid absolutely situations where you meet behind closed doors! Confide in a trusted senior colleague and in your mate: the former can offer protection within the department if rumors ultimately start to fly, and the latter can fend off phone calls and late-evening visits and at the same time establish to the student the fact of his or her presence. Encourage the student to take courses with others next term when the student wants to do advanced work — or, heaven forbid, independent study! — with you. And, if all else fails, confront the student, gently but firmly: "I'm flattered that you enjoy my course and that you find conversations with me interesting and helpful. But I must spend time this spring finishing an article for publication, so I'm going to have to cut back the time I have available to any one student. And I'm sure you'll understand that my time at home is so limited that I won't be able to take calls there from students any longer." Such comments get the message across, without demeaning or embarrassing a student who is likely to be quite vulnerable — and without damaging a classroom or advising relationship that must, after all, last at least until the end of the current semester.

Your department, your dean, your institution, will reward you for the research you do and the articles, papers, and books you contribute to the store of your profession's knowledge. Inevitably, however, your greatest satisfactions as an academic will often come from your interactions with students. The days will be long, the tangible rewards few, and the frustrations of student interactions many.

But for virtually everyone who embarks upon an academic career, there was, somewhere at some time, one individual who — with a word of advice, a chance comment, a bit of encouragement — made a difference. Degree in hand, faculty status (however temporary or precarious) conferred, you will be the one now who, probably at the time and under circumstances you least expect, will make that difference for one of your students. That, in the end, is what advising comes down to — that and caring enough about your students to do the job well.

20

SOME THOUGHTS ON FACULTY MENTORING

(WITH A FOCUS ON GRADUATE STUDENTS)

A. LEIGH DENEEF

Each year, for the past decade or so, I have led, with a colleague from a neighboring institution, an orientation workshop for new graduate students, "Issues Related to Faculty Mentoring." We are always surprised that this workshop attracts more students than we expect or sometimes even have room for, but, of course, we shouldn't be surprised at all. The relationship between a graduate student and a faculty mentor is the very core of graduate education in this country and even incoming students know this and worry about it. I'm sure you did too, for the fact is that lots of things can go wrong between mentor and mentee, and when they do the student is almost always the one who suffers. Well, now the shoe is on the other foot: as a new academic, you are in the powerful position of the would-be mentor. How do you begin to think about this responsibility? What are the pitfalls that you have to avoid? What can you take away from your own experiences to help you be a better mentor? Are there any general tips on how to become a successful faculty mentor? Why should you even be concerned about mentoring at this point in your career?

I am going to treat these questions particularly as they pertain to mentoring graduate students, although mentoring occurs at every level of higher education, including the mentoring of junior faculty members, a point to which I will return momentarily. I focus on graduate students in part in order to complement Elizabeth Nathans's informative essay in this volume on undergraduate advising, in part because many of you who are joining institutions that have masters or doctoral programs will be anxious to serve as a graduate mentor. Let me begin, then, with the last question above: why should you even be thinking about mentoring now? You are a "new" academic and therefore, to some extent at least, still finding your own way in the academy and, more than likely, in a new institution. The best guides through the academy are not generally the last ones to enter, and you should think carefully about how much you can realistically take on at the start of your career. This question is especially important since, whether you are at a research university or a liberal arts college, you will certainly be expected to advise and mentor undergraduate students. With graduate students, you have more of a choice.

Maybe you said to yourself at some point in your graduate training, "I'm going to be a better mentor to my students than my adviser was to me." This is a laudable goal, I think, but achieving it will take a significant amount of work, part of which consists of distinguishing between those two terms you've just lumped together: "mentor" and "adviser." But even if you can already make that distinction, you need to step back at this stage and ask where mentoring figures, or whether it even should figure, in your own goals as a budding academic. How much time are you willing to spend on mentoring students? Are you prepared to sacrifice energy you could otherwise direct toward writing or research, or preparing more fully for that new class you are going to teach this semester? A good mentor never says, of course, "What's in this for me?," but it is important that you don't set out to be a faculty mentor for wrong or purely idealistic reasons. You have to be realistic about what you can and cannot do at this point in your career. You need to protect your time and make sure that you put most of your energies into those areas that are required for tenure and promotion. This is not to say that being a good mentor need detract from other responsibilities; it is only to urge that you be pragmatic about how much you can afford to do right now. That being said, what is "in it" for you? What might being a good mentor do for you or for your new career?

Chances are very good that it won't bring you financial reward or a leg up in the tenure process (although some schools are now trying to find ways to acknowledge mentoring as an important part of one's teaching and service obligations; several have even initiated "best mentoring" awards along the lines of "best teaching" awards that have been in existence for some time). The National Academy of Sciences gives a number of useful suggestions about why you might want to become a good mentor, the first of which is simply the human desire to share knowledge and experience. Okay, perhaps that's still rather idealistic. More pragmatic reasons are (a) to experience the satisfaction and pride that derive from helping your students develop, succeed, and become friends and colleagues; (b) to develop the ability to recruit the best students, who can, in turn, help you produce better research, better articles, and secure more grants; (c) to keep yourself sharp professionally by always having junior colleagues who can challenge your ideas and keep you aware of the shifting disciplinary and interdisciplinary boundaries; (d) to strengthen your own professional contacts by helping students develop their networks of academic and nonacademic colleagues; and (e) to initiate a legacy of good mentoring that will reach generations of future students long after you retire. Even the most idealistic of these motives can be observed very tangibly: go to your institution's hooding ceremony or Ph.D. commencement program and watch the proud interactions between the new Ph.D.'s and their mentors. This is not a moment that can be faked, and the genuine respect that you will witness here is a measure of how personally rewarding good mentoring can be.

So you've decided that you want to be a good mentor. How should you go about it? First, take some time to try to define what a mentor really is—as distinct, let us say, from an adviser or a dissertation director, or the lab PI (many faculty think these are synonyms, but they are not). A mentor may, of course, serve all or any of these roles, but mentors are also faculty who give students emotional and moral support; who provide specific, timely, and honest feedback on students' academic work and their research; who serve as "masters" of a discipline to whom students are "apprenticed" to learn the epistemological and ethical norms of the profession; who give students information about and aid in obtaining career opportunities; who model the life and values of the academy. What is perhaps most interesting about this list of mentoring roles is simply its breadth. Can you really serve all of these roles at the same time for all or even any of your students? It is unlikely. Maybe you can be a career sponsor for one student and a tutor for another, a role model for a third and an academic adviser for a fourth. Maybe you can serve several functions for a few students, but you cannot be all things to all students.

This, I think, is the first important lesson about mentoring, one you perhaps have already learned in graduate school. The best mentoring relationships are multiple. You cannot be the Über-Mentor for all or any of your students, so you need to find ways to create for them "a community of mentors" who can share the responsibility of socializing them into or within a particular discipline. That process starts, quite literally, at home—in the academic department or program. Sharing mentoring responsibilities with your colleagues—including other, more advanced, graduate students in addition to other faculty—begins the socializing work and creates a handy network of budding professional relationships.

How else might we characterize an effective mentor? First and foremost, as suggested above, to be a good mentor you have to be genuinely interested in helping students become competent scholars, teachers, or scientists. Your goals, in short, as a mentor, are to optimize their educational experiences, socialize them within a particular discipline, help them become independent and passionate thinkers and scholars of that discipline, and help them find suitable employment after their formal education is completed.

Let me emphasize that word "passion": one of the most important things you have to offer your students—at any level—is passion for your subject. Perhaps that's what socializing someone into a discipline is really all about: making them feel passionate about the kind of work the discipline demands, the kinds of questions it seeks to answer, the kinds of knowledge it tries to build. If you can succeed in bringing that passion to your students, you will be well on your way to becoming an excellent mentor.

All of the mentoring objectives noted above are lofty goals, but they begin pretty simply: take your students seriously and recognize that each is an individual with unique capacities and needs. Effective mentoring, in short, is not a generalizable list of do's and don't's: it is a one-on-one personal and professional relationship. So you have to listen carefully to what your students tell you about their own educational or career goals, and see if what you think about their capacities accords with those goals. Remember that your job as a mentor is not to clone yourself but to promote the student. By far the complaint I hear most often from students is that their advisers/mentors have no knowledge of or interest in their intellectual or professional expectations: all the "mentors" seem to want is someone to help them get their own research done. That is not the mark of a true mentor; it is not even the mark of a good boss. Respecting the individuality of your students is the first step to earning their respect as well. Promoting them, you may occasionally need to be frank about their capabilities and what career options are likely for them. If their own expectations are completely unrealistic, you have an obligation to show them why. It is, of course, far easier to be always positive and promoting than to be critical and cautionary, but if you establish a level of clear mutual respect and understanding with your students, it will make being honest and forthright with them a whole lot easier.

Effective mentors not only take their students seriously but they work hard to help them develop their own self-esteem. There are many ways this can be done: recognizing student contributions in weekly lab meetings; developing collaborative research projects with your students and publishing co-authored articles on the results; taking them to professional conferences; offering team-teaching or even guest-lecture opportunities; hosting "journal clubs" involving both students and faculty. The point here is that by treating your students as junior colleagues, you empower them professionally and intellectually; you generate the mutual respect upon which all good mentoring relations are founded. In helping students develop self-esteem, of course, you are also helping them become independent scholars and researchers.

Bringing students into your discipline is not a simple or straightforward task. Many faculty have probably never tried to articulate exactly what their discipline is in anything other than obvious or simplified terms. Many do not know, for example, that most professional organizations do have specific statements of disciplinary missions and explicit codes of behavior for the discipline. But even were this not the case, part of your job as a mentor is to make explicit those implicit habits of thought and behavior that govern the community of scholars that make up the discipline. In an age when interdisciplinarity and multidisciplinarity are becoming increasingly prominent and expected, the whole context of disciplinary norms becomes very complicated. Can, for example, a student of literature begin using quantitative social science methodologies without fully understanding their disciplinary backgrounds and their ethical dimensions? Perhaps this complexity is one reason why institutions are much more committed than ever before to training—for faculty and for students—in the ethical conduct of research. This too is clearly a responsibility of any serious mentor: you must not only model ethical modes of research and publication but you must be open and explicit with your students about why the entire academic community depends upon its ability to trust the academic integrity of all its teachers and students, its scholars and its researchers.

I said above that you have to be frank and direct with students, but the other side of this coin is that students are then free to be frank with you. The most satisfying exchanges you can have with your mentee is when s/he feels free to challenge your ideas, even to disagree with you, and be able to back up that disagreement with a strong counterargument. In a sense, this is what mentoring graduate students—rather than, say, undergraduates—is all about because the graduate student has sufficient disciplinary knowledge to represent completely novel perspectives. The intellectual challenge and stimulation of a good mentee is both the result and reward of successful mentoring. But students, like all of us, also have fears that are sometimes difficult to share: fears about financial security, about self-esteem, about not being able to satisfy you or their other professors, about their future in the academy or in any other professional route, doubts that they really have what it takes to succeed. One of your roles as an effective mentor is to be alert to and try to address these anxieties as best you can. Share your own worries at comparable points of your career. Encourage your students to talk among themselves or to other faculty mentors about their concerns. This would be another way to develop the community of mentoring that I mentioned earlier.

Sharing students with other mentors is also an effective way to avoid some of the pitfalls that crop up in mentoring relationships. One is simply becoming too protective of "your" students. Students are quick to catch on when this happens in a classroom or a lab and it creates, whether you are conscious of it or not, an environment that is isolationist and competitive rather than collaborative and mutually respectful. Such divisive feelings can begin very innocently, with a passing remark about how the American Lit wing of an English department has it "easier" since it doesn't need to learn Anglo-Saxon, Latin, or perhaps any other foreign language to do its work. This is an especially insidious trap in the academy today, where sub-sub-specialties are the cutting edge and broader, integrative knowledge is often viewed as either outmoded or of lesser quality. A good mentor, in my view at least, is one who can instill in students a fascination with and hunger for all aspects of the discipline, not just the corner occupying her own thoughts and research.

There are, of course, even more dangerous traps in the mentoring relationship, especially at the graduate level where the age differential is often minimal between faculty members and students. Failure to maintain an appropriate neutral and professional distance, for example, leads, at best, to discomfort and misunderstanding, at worst to the kinds of affairs that are not only immoral but institutionally prohibited. The mentor/student relationship is, even on the best of terms, an axis of power; although institutions themselves often have little authority to stop consensual relationships, you should not be blind to the fact that no faculty/student relations can be truly "consensual" if one participant holds power over the other. I want to emphasize that the consequences for this kind of breach of professional ethics are multiple: they affect not only the particular individuals involved, both you and the student, but the entire academic community, especially your own department. It does not take long for a professor who has violated these standards with one student to discover that fewer and fewer students really want to risk working with him (and, let's be frank here, it usually is "him").

A third pitfall in the mentoring relationship is investing too much in your students. At some level, this may be a version of wanting to clone yourself, but I'm thinking of those situations in which you know you have a brilliant student who can accomplish whatever he wishes, but who, for some reason, has chosen not to pursue the kind of life you have envisioned for him. It is very easy for this kind of disappointment to become registered, with your student, as disapproval: if she does not become what you expected, she has somehow failed. Often, among graduate students, this disapproval rarely derives from something that is said, but it is certainly felt. I cannot count how many graduate students over the years have told me "if I don't get a job in a top-ten research school, my adviser will think I'm a failure and his investment in me has been wasted." Either the mentors of these students were not truly interested in them as individuals or something went terribly wrong with the communications between them. Mutual respect, careful listening, and frequent interchange can mitigate against this kind of misunderstanding.

I have spoken so far about your role as a faculty mentor, but, as a new academic, it is also important for you to receive good mentoring. In fact, one of the hallmarks of a strong academic institution and department is their commitment to careful mentoring of junior faculty. If you are still considering whether or not to accept a position you have been offered, this might be a subject worth inquiring about a little more deeply. Can the chair or the dean explain what the system is for faculty mentoring? How successful has the department been in recent years in bringing its junior appointments to tenure and promotion?

The same principles obtain here as for student mentoring: you should not settle for the advice and support of a single senior colleague. This can often lead to unforeseen political consequences, such as having to take sides on particular issues because not to do so would be seen as a "betrayal" of your mentor. You should instead talk with as many of your colleagues as you can, across as broad a range of senior and junior faculty. Like the graduate student we have been talking about, you too need socializing into the new department and the new college or university. What can the senior faculty tell you about the realities of the tenure process, about publication and teaching expectations, even about mentoring expectations? What have junior colleagues been told? Do they feel they have sufficient knowledge about what is expected of them? Most importantly, remember that just because you are now a new faculty member does not mean you don't need nurturing and competent mentoring. As other essays in this volume attest, new faculty face complicated choices all the time: what is the relative weight of articles in relation to books in tenure and promotion considerations, in what kinds of journals or with what kinds of presses; what committee assignments are you free to decline; how much do teacher-course evaluations and other instructional assessments count in departmental contract renewals, and so forth. It is important to get as many perspectives as you can on these matters, for they may well determine your future. A community of mentors is the best mechanism for doing that. In fact, as you negotiate your way among this community of faculty mentors, you will certainly increase your understanding of the complexities of the entire mentoring process. This, then, is another way to improve your own mentoring of undergraduate and graduate students by recognizing the similarities between your needs and theirs.

21.

CONSIDERING THE IMPACT OF

TECHNOLOGY IN TEACHING AND LEARNING

PATRICK M. MURPHY

There is nothing new about using technology in the classroom. Whether by means of chalk or an overhead projector, teachers have long sought the best way to present materials to their students. What *is* relatively new is the field of "instructional technology"; it is only in the last decade or so that intense interest in this area has generated conferences, publications, and positions dedicated to the application of technology in teaching. This proliferation is the result in part to the increased pace in the rate of technological advancement, as well as increasing complexity and sophistication in the technologies employed. Perhaps a more important reason for this attention is a renewed interest in the art of teaching, and a sense that we could be doing some things better.

Some academic prophets have predicted that universities as we know them will cease to be fifty years from now, suggesting distance and just-in-time learning will obviate current classrooms. Others are much more modest in their prognostications. What seems clear, wherever the truth of the matter lies, is that advances in technology will continue to offer new tools to enhance teaching and learning and will change the way educators do business. Students now communicate in fundamentally different ways (such as adding multimedia to text or using instant messaging), and are expected to use a different set of communication skills when they go on to their chosen professions; community colleges and public institutions see distance and hybrid courses as additional sources of income, or at least as a way of more efficiently sharing common resources among instructors; and so on. If you are curious as to how your teaching may be transformed, it is likely that you can simply look to how technology is transforming research in your field.

With these changes, it is possible that you will have to use such technology in conjunction with your teaching. Perhaps you will teach a distance education course, where remote students are connected only by the Internet. Maybe you will teach a large introductory course, and the chair of your department will decide that the only efficient and timely way to get students' grades back is to have them take the test online and let the computer grade it.

It may also be the case that you will have no such restrictions, and that you can opt to use no technology at all in the classroom. There is absolutely nothing wrong with deciding not to use instructional technology in your class . . . unless it really could aid you and you are just being too stubborn to adopt it. Some instructors will use electronic tools heavily in their classes, while others will shun anything of the sort.

One mathematics professor at the university where I work laments the transcription that students must do while copying the formulae he writes on the board. He would prefer his students to be thinking about the "big picture" and the theoretical import of the things he is writing, but instead he feels they are engaged as "scribes" and are more focused on meticulously recapturing what he is writing. So he employs an electronic whiteboard that records his board work, transferring his formulae to a file that students can later download. This saves the students the trouble of copying them and frees them to concentrate on the theoretical aspects of the course during class.

Another professor, who teaches chemistry, dismisses such ideas. He uses old-fashioned chalk on an old-fashioned chalkboard and prefers that his students copy down the chemical equations he writes on the board. He believes the repetition of the material necessary to record it helps students later remember it, and he sees value in the students thinking about the equations as they are transcribing them. The method worked just fine for him, and he thinks it will work just fine for the newer generation of graduate students.

So who is right? I suspect they both are, but then again, I do not usually feel comfortable dictating to teachers how best to teach their classes. I think the best answer is that your solution will vary depending on any number of factors: the material you teach, the students you are targeting, the amount of time you have available, your teaching style, resources available, incentives, and the like.

For that reason, much of what follows is meant to get you thinking about the role of technology in your teaching, and not as a checklist of things you need do, nor a prescription for better teaching. I would ask you to ask yourself: "Why should I use this?" That question, of course, applies to anything in the classroom, and not just technology. Like all good teaching practices, effective use of technology in the classroom is best done after careful thought and matching of tools with your pedagogical goals. Think of this as a survey of possibilities, some of which may suit your teaching needs, others of which surely will not.

POSSIBLE AREAS OF TECHNOLOGICAL IMPACT

To start you thinking about places where technology can positively affect your teaching, I present some common areas of success below. I suggest to faculty members that they think of an area of weakness in the courses they teach and then examine some of the approaches below to see if they might be able to augment their traditional teaching with a new tool.

I long recognized an area of such weakness in my own teaching. I taught an introductory linguistics course in graduate school. Part of this survey course involved talking about the sounds of the world's languages, and I would spend a few lectures explaining what a voiced pharyngeal fricative was and which languages employed it in their phonological inventories. Now, I did not expect every student to embrace this topic — and in writing this, I have to admit that my description does not sound terribly interesting — but I got the sense that this part of the course could be a lot better. The students never seemed overly engaged with this topic, and I knew that even though I was biased, language is very interesting and such "exotic" sounds should be doubly so. I thought about it for a while and decided that having me — a West Virginia hillbilly and native speaker of English only — approximating these sounds devoid of all context was not a compelling way to present the material. I located a collection of such speech sounds in digital format and brought my laptop into the classroom, where now I could supplement my lecture with the speech of actual native speakers: not in a clunky way but smoothly and efficiently, requiring only a mouse click to play whichever speech sample I wanted, and not fiddling with cassette or DVD players. Making them available online afforded my students constant access to these normally alien materials. Student engagement picked up, and test scores indicated that student mastery of these materials increased as well.

Course Administration Made Easier   Consider first that technology can simply make your life easier in your role as course administrator. Just as calculators and computer software make the tedious work of balancing your checkbook just a little more tolerable, important but unglamorous work like keeping track of grades or collecting papers may be eased by using course management software. This software, such as Blackboard, webCT, and others, may feature grade books where you can store your students' grades electronically. Should you lose your grade book — as I did for the longest five days of my graduate tenure — knowing that your students' grades are on a school server which is regularly backed up can be reassuring, to say the least. That you may be able to specify grades that students can check online can also benefit your students and alleviate the traditional flood of questions about what marks students made on their last paper.

One of the most obvious areas of technological impact is in our communication: e-mail and cell phones keep us in constant contact with the world around us. Considering how important it is to get information to students, this is likely another area where technology can aid you in your role as course administrator. Posting announcements on a course Web page, or keeping students apprised of developments via e-mail, keeps everyone on the same page, whether it is about an upcoming exam, a canceled class, or that documentary on TV you meant to tell them about.

Assessments of various kinds can also be done online now, and students can get feedback right away. If you have a large lecture course, or are teaching at a distance, having your students take an exam online—which is automatically graded and entered in your grade book—may be appealing, or even the only feasible option for grading student work. Such assessments have their own pitfalls: computers grade literally, and inflexibly, and if cheating during exams is a universal problem, the ability for students to cheat with the full range of Internet technologies at their disposal only compounds it. Your school's instructional technology support staff can advise you on confronting such problems and help you devise effective assessments.

Even if you are not interested in having your students take exams online, there remain a number of compelling reasons to consider employing electronic assessments. First, many assessment packages are designed to allow for student surveys, whether anonymous or otherwise. Instead of collecting notecards or having students raise hands, it may be more efficient to have them take an online survey so their answers are quickly and straightforwardly available to you. You may have access to a classroom with a personal response system (PRS). With a PRS, you can poll students about their understanding of the material, and they submit their answers via a handheld device, giving you instant feedback and allowing you to adjust your teaching appropriately.

Pre-assessment may also be a good way to think about such tools. Even if you are handing out traditional pencil-and-paper exams to be taken in class, consider what advantages might be offered to a student who has seen something similar from you before. If I offer a sample midterm via an online assessment tool, I might use its instant feedback capabilities to give my students a "practice test." The student taking the test might then see what kinds of questions I ask, what sorts of materials I think are important, and what their mastery of that material is like. Even the technical limitations might be of use: whereas the computer might return an "incorrect" response for a misspelled fill-in-the-blank question, hopefully that will start the student thinking: "Well, at least I knew the right name. Surely, my instructor would count that correct. Or would she? Maybe I had better ask her." In short, the student is thinking about the exam before the exam, and that is useful.

Communication and Collaboration   Again, communication is one of the more transparent areas of technological impact in educational settings. We communicate with students regularly as instructors. Technology provides new tools for communication. That these new tools should make their way into instruction is natural.

There are two categories of communication tools: *synchronous*, or real-time, tools, and *asynchronous*, or time-delayed, tools.

Synchronous tools include chat clients, video conferencing, and virtual classrooms, among others. Chat clients may be built into course management software, but that instant messaging program you use to talk to your sister does the same thing: they allow you to see what the person on the other end is typing, with minimal delay. Video conferencing allows you to hear and/or see the participants, while virtual classrooms are most often chat clients with "virtual whiteboards" which allow participants to draw or otherwise present visual information. In many ways, these tools simply stand in for face-to-face discussion or phone conversations. However, synchronous tools can enrich those discussions which are not face-to-face; whiteboards can allow instructors to present visual materials to a student at a distance while still communicating in real time via text or voice chat. While not for everyone, many instructors offer "virtual office hours" utilizing such tools, making themselves available to students during evening hours at home that better fit a student's schedule. Of course, this may not be for everyone, and instructors must be wary of overcommitting themselves.

Communication tools allow more speedy interactions outside the classroom, and for many instructors, that is a boon. This is particularly true of asynchronous communication tools like e-mail, blogs, and discussion boards. But beyond quicker communication, or more communication, such tools provide *different* communication, and at times that may mean *better* communication. Consider that discussion boards and e-mail may provide *threaded* responses, in which participants can more easily follow the flow of a discussion, and that there is a written record of who said what, and the possible positive impact of the use of such tools becomes transparent. Consider also that students who say little in class might eagerly stay up until three o'clock in the morning participating in chat rooms. Reaching more students through these tools not only solicits more comprehensive participation but also potentially democratizes the class-room, establishing equal opportunity among your students.

Consider some other potential benefits for instructors of the modest discussion board. By monitoring this discussion, the instructor can get a sense of the level of class understanding of a given topic, or what the big issues are for them. Instructors are assured that students spend greater time on task on central ideas. The discussion board also extends the discussion beyond the classroom and allows the discussion to go on before and after class. The technology of online discussion forums facilitates additional classroom interaction, thereby increasing opportunity for instruction.

The possibility of increased communication is one of the results of using these tools. It may be easy to assume an "us and them" mentality as an instructor and forget that one's students likely do not know each other or communicate outside of class. Similarly, one may be teaching a distance course where it is impossible for students to meet in person. For these reasons, giving students more ways to communicate with each other outside of class is important. E-mail, online chats, and discussion boards afford a straightforward solution to such concerns. The same tools can also give your students greater access to you as an instructor, if you are amenable. While you should always let your students know what are reasonable ways and times to contact you, the Internet can afford easy access to you outside the classroom.

Individuals from outside a course can also participate virtually in the course thanks to such communication tools. Perhaps you have a colleague in another geographic location whose area of expertise coincides with your course's next topic. Without the ease of modern communication, the only way for your class to benefit from their expertise might have been to fly your colleague in for a guest lecture, or having him or her participate in a garbled conversation with your students via speakerphone. With the ubiquitousness and ease of Internet communication, your colleague might now agree instead to take part in an online chat, or to play a part in one of your discussion forums for a week. That this expert may be from industry and not even part of academia, or all the way across the world, need not be as large a concern if his or her participation is virtual.

The accessibility of Internet resources also can provide educational opportunities for collaboration. Collaborative learning increases involvement, and discussion and debate promote deeper understanding. Class projects have long been used to test student mastery of materials: we want our students to do research, discern good sources of information from bad, synthesize and distill this information, and then turn around and present it back to the class as a whole. Sharing such information with the class is useful, but consider the possible impact of presenting this information to the world. The Internet affords a means by which to share such research globally, and what was once "just a course Web site" can, over time, metamorphose into an online resource for everyone interested in a particular topic. Students frequently report that they derive great satisfaction from contributing to projects with such influence and permanence.

Increasing Interactivity   Educators have long recognized the merit of providing different modes of learning. Students learn in different ways, and we hear a lot about "visual learners" who best pick up things they see and "kinesthetic learners" who best master materials after trying it for themselves. Presenting materials in one way only may then do a disservice to the learners who would benefit from another presentation style. Of course, presenting materials in different ways in the classroom can be difficult. Students are unlikely to appreciate having the same material presented to them three different times in class, even if you are maximizing your coverage of learning styles by doing so. You are not going to have the time to present materials in class in multiple ways without sacrificing time you could use to present something else.

Still, those personal response systems I mentioned before, or really any of a number of similar tools, allow students to engage the instructor more fully, and change the lecture into an interactive exercise. Students can indicate what they did not understand and describe the need for further elaboration, whether they cannot or will not give voice to their questions.

And outside of class this potential for increased interactivity is perhaps more apparent. If materials are available to students online in a variety of formats, then you can allow them to investigate course materials which best correspond to their own learning preference. Since online materials can include text, video, and audio resources, tailoring these course materials to different learning styles is at once feasible and attractive.

Additionally, online tools allow for instructional activities that require student input, thus keeping the student engaged. Just as lectures should be broken up with discussion, questions, or activities that make the student interact with the material, online materials can necessitate the same interaction. Optimally, we would like students to be driving the learning process; student mastery is going to correspond directly with their level of interest and engagement with the topic they are studying. Give students control over pacing and presentation of the materials, and you let them take charge of the learning process.

Finally, if students need more work on particular topics, online activities can give them valuable practice, which they may repeat as needed. Similarly, working with remedial exercises may assist students who enter your course without some prerequisite knowledge without slowing down the rest of the class.

Ease of Access   Perhaps the most obvious area of impact of instructional technology outside the classroom is the possibility of instant feedback and anytime, anywhere access. Prior to online resources, a student could only reasonably expect access to course materials through textbooks and notes, unless she contacted the instructor or teaching assistants. With course Web sites and online communities, the student can now access whatever course materials are present at whatever time is convenient for them. Moreover, the student does not have to wait for feedback if tools like online assessments are used, again increasing interactivity.

SOME EXAMPLES

While discussing application of technology in teaching in the abstract is well and good, actual examples from the disciplines may better help faculty members gauge what is possible and useful for their courses beyond posting syllabi and sending e-mail. There are a multitude of resources online which can serve as tactile, real-world examples, and the instructional technology staff at your school can further advise you after hearing about your pedagogical goals and needs. Although these staff members are often loathe to prescribe to faculty members "what they should be doing" in their classes, instructors may be interested in comparing their efforts to others in their field, and instructional technology staff can assist in considering your options.

The examples below are based on actual course Web sites. Hopefully, one can extrapolate how the teaching problem facing the humanities instructor is really the same as one faced by many natural sciences instructors, and thus how the same technological approach might benefit both.

Humanities: Music Theory. Students in this course can read texts explaining key concepts of the course, accessing the materials at a time and pace most convenient for them. Given the importance of audio in the subject material, the instructor augments the texts with sound clips that demonstrate these concepts. To afford students the opportunity to gauge their mastery of the material, practice quizzes follow each relevant section, complete with further audio clips. For example, students are asked to identify a musical key; this is done alternately through graphic presentation of a musical staff or by listening to a music clip. After examining the staff or listening to the clip and making a selection, students get instant feedback, letting them know whether they correctly identified the key and reminding them how to correctly do so.

Social Sciences: Sociology. As part of the requirements for this course, students must identify a religious movement, research it, and report back to the class on it. While this is a standard type of assignment, students are also required to work in teams that collaborate on materials online, and then they add to the course Web site the reports that they generate. Visitors to the site can then benefit from the students' research, which is now more than "just another course assignment" and instead a contribution to a long-term, growing project.

Natural Sciences: Chemistry. Given the large numbers of formulae for students to take in during lectures, the instructor decides to use an electronic whiteboard to record her board work; the recorded notes are distributed through the course Web site to minimize scribing errors. The large size of this introductory course creates problems for timely return of grades, so students take online exams that can be graded by the course management software. Lab procedures are filmed and stored on the course Web site for students to watch before the lab, while a virtual workbench allows students to practice identifying reagents using a simulation in a Web browser. The end result is that students are better prepared for, and more comfortable with, required labs.

Core Requirements: Writing. To facilitate collection and return of papers, students submit their work electronically through a digital drop box which is part of an online course management system, or simply by e-mailing them to the instructor. The instructor can comment on papers electronically by using commenting tools, or tools for tracking changes, in a word processor like Microsoft® Word®, or by using the appropriate tools in Adobe® Acrobat®. Having avoided squeezing illegible handwriting into the narrow margins of a printed copy, the instructor returns the paper electronically, so no paper has changed hands. Discussion boards allow students to post their papers for peer review, with comment threads providing a natural means to talk about the work online.

SOME POTENTIAL PITFALLS

There are many exciting things going on with instructional technology, but even should a technological solution to one of your pedagogical problems present itself, there are also a number of reasons why you might ultimately decide against adopting one. For example:

— Many technological solutions are inexpensive, but others are not, so cost may be an issue. Find out whether a given solution is free, affordable, or prohibitive in cost, and then decide whether or not the cost is justified.

— While technology can be a huge timesaver, some technological tools will require a significant startup cost in terms of time. This may be because you or your students will have to spend time learning a new tool, or may result from some sort of conversion process; e.g., while having your thousands of slides in digital format may be a huge boon to your course, someone has to spend the time to convert them into that format in the first place. This burden will ease with time, because you can build up collections of resources that you can reuse for later courses, but until then, it will take *more* time, not less, to use digital resources. Find out what sort of time commitment a given solution will require, and whether or not you can expect any help in actualizing a project. Your time is valuable; also consider whether your time investment is worth it or not.

—Nontechnological considerations may have a huge impact on your use of instructional technology. Consider time constraints again, but leave out the technology. Is your institution a research-oriented one? Are you being pushed to spend more time on research, and less on your teaching? Does your institution have the resources to support your project? The push and pull of these sorts of factors should be considered in your planning.

—Copyright can also play a role here. Copyright laws are Byzantine enough, but the addition of electronic considerations into the mix can make use of some materials problematic at best. For instance, fair use and the TEACH Act (Technology, Education and Copyright Harmonization Act) might give you the right to use material from a DVD or CD-ROM in your classroom, but if you have to circumvent copy protection to get the DVD into a format suitable for viewing on the World Wide Web, you are likely in violation of the DMCA (Digital Millennium Copyright Act). By the time this handbook is published, the rules may have changed again, and as with all things legal, until someone argues something successfully one way or the other in court, no one really knows for sure what the law says. Find out where you might run afoul of copyright issues before using other people's materials.

—There are also a host of potential pedagogical pitfalls as well. Consider, for instance, that while your discussion boards afford you a means to prolong the class conversation you had yesterday, you might want to give some thought to how to stop the conversation lest it go on too long, or at the expense of other points of interest. Consider also the implications if you are getting three hundred posts a day to this discussion forum and you cannot keep up with them all.

For those areas that pique your interest, the next step is to speak to someone about the feasibility of employing them in your classroom.

FINDING HELP ON CAMPUS AND ELSEWHERE

New instructors should consult with others knowledgeable in such areas as to what is not only possible in instructional technology but also feasible and consonant with their instructional goals and style. Many people have given these considerations a great deal of thought, in many different fields of endeavor. Exploit their expertise, and the time others have invested.

Unfortunately, telling new instructors where to go to get help is problematic at best. Campuses differ wildly in their levels of support, types of support (time, money, equipment) and in the organization of this support. What follows is a partial taxonomy of typical campus resources that may be of use when considering instructional technology resources.

— If you are fortunate, your campus may have an organization specifically dedicated to the exploration and support of technology in teaching. These are usually "centers for instructional technology" and their staffs typically specialize in precisely the issues I have outlined above. They are glad to listen to your particular teaching needs and to help you identify appropriate technological solutions.

— Many campuses will also have "centers for teaching and learning" which concern themselves with pedagogical issues more generally, but which may nevertheless be useful in thinking about technology specifically. In fact, you will find such organizations useful regardless, since they can give beneficial advice on all areas of your teaching, not just those involving technology.

— Schools and departments may have their own IT staff, and here, "IT" indicates *information* technology rather than *instructional* technology. These staff may be less concerned with technology in teaching specifically since they are likely charged with everything from aiding professors with programs they use in their research to keeping the e-mail server running. While they may have less time to think about pedagogical issues, and less experience doing so, such staff can still be useful for consultations if you explain your teaching needs to them. They may even be more useful than members of other organizations in that these IT staff tend to spend more time thinking about your discipline-specific needs than do members of more general organizations.

— More general IT organizations are probably the rule, rather than the exception. There is likely an overarching IT organization at your school, and they may provide useful information as you think through the issues above. Still, while school or departmental IT staff may not have much time to focus on pedagogical issues, this is probably even more true of the staff of general IT organizations, which will not have the benefit of even being familiar with your discipline-specific problems.

— You are almost certainly not alone on campus when it comes to wanting to employ technology in your classroom, so it is probable that other instructors are trying to do similar things. Investigate and participate in faculty organizations and you can connect with like-minded individuals who may be able to offer not only advice but perhaps actual pedagogical resources which you can use.

— Whether or not you cannot locate organizations on campus to support you in your endeavors, there are a multitude of online resources you can avail yourself of. You can find online organizations and publications dedicated to instructional technology, many of which can point you to further resources. A little searching can also point you directly to course Web sites full of materials you can recycle for use in your own courses; you will doubtless find many instructors eager to share their materials with you. Best of all, if you participate in a mailing list or bulletin board of like-minded educators, you will have gained not only invaluable contacts but a better idea of how you can use the same tools with your students.

The bottom line is that you should ask around. While it may be easier to find useful instructional technology resources on some campuses than others, someone likely knows who you should speak to, and it is far better to get help with these resources than to attempt to go it alone. Once you get help getting started using these technologies, you will find that beyond the hype, there are extremely positive results to be had.

PART V

FUNDING ACADEMIC RESEARCH

For a new assistant professor whose credentials are yet to be proved and whose research skills are yet to be tested, research funding can be difficult to obtain. In the humanities, small grants from a college or university research council may suffice, at least for a while; in the natural and social sciences or in technical and professional areas, such grants will not go very far. Indeed, in these disciplines the amount of external funding obtained is one form of professional validation and may be every bit as important in the eventual tenure decision as your publications. Applying for government or foundation grants may consume large portions of your academic time and give rise to untold worries and fears. But where external funding is a necessity, not merely an academic luxury, it is essential that you enter the competition boldly and optimistically. Yet this is not easily done. In the essays that follow, four specialists on funding sources and procedures try to clarify the grant-making process and offer suggestions that may help to ensure your success. As they stress, a research proposal that is truly worthy will probably be funded, but not, perhaps, without considerable effort, preparation, persistence, and patience.

Nonprofit foundations and corporations have distinct missions and different patterns of grant giving. Beth A. Eastlick and Zachary B. Robbins discuss these differences and offer some strategic advice about applying to either set of institutions for research support. Judith Argon explains the five basic mechanisms through which the federal government funds academic research. She also provides a thorough, step-by-step roadmap, from developing a clear and convincing proposal to filing appropriate progress reports should that proposal receive support from NIH, NEH, NSF, or any of the other major federal agencies. Fred E. Crossland, focusing more narrowly on private foundations, suggests strategies for finding the grant that seems best suited to your project and for writing a proposal that is likely to be successful.

22

CORPORATE RELATIONS AND FOUNDATION FUNDRAISING

BETH A. EASTLICK AND ZACHARY B. ROBBINS

In many disciplinary fields, fundraising is an expected part of a faculty member's academic responsibility. Much of the funding of academic research comes, directly or indirectly, from various local, state and federal programs. But a significant proportion comes as well from corporations and foundations. This is a world that may not be as familiar to you as the NIH, NEH, or NSF. The overview that follows may help you become better acquainted with alternative funding opportunities.

Since the establishment of many large foundations at the beginning of the last century and the concurrent rise of corporate philanthropy in the United States, universities have been seeking — and receiving — funds from these two sectors. From the 1950s into the 1970s, higher education received a steady, fairly predictable stream of funding from corporations and foundations, while each sector developed its own mores and styles of philanthropy, which will be discussed below. In the 1980s and 1990s, the boom in the economy and the Internet-driven surge in the stock market led to an extraordinary increase in personal wealth, an economy-driven increase in corporate philanthropy, as well as a staggering increase in the number and size of family foundations and donor-advised funds. While corporate philanthropy has steadily increased in real terms since the late 1980s, there has been a dramatic decline in corporate giving as a percentage of corporate profits (50 percent).[1] This, along with the puncturing of the technology balloon in the late 1990s, the sharp correction in the stock market post-9/11, and the globalization of corporate giving, has significantly increased competition for a limited pool of U.S. philanthropic gifts by corporations. On the other hand, foundation giving has been fairly resilient, both because so many donors created their family foundations prior to the recession and because most large foundations either diversified or were managed conservatively.[2] Another factor that moderated the impact of fluctuations in income for foundations is that nearly all foundations make grants based on a three-year rolling average (in order to smooth out their investment hills and valleys).

FOUNDATION FUNDRAISING

Foundation Climate   After 2001, many foundations began to reassess their grant making in light of lower expected income or drastically reduced assets, and at the same time the United States saw a rash of nonprofit mismanagement scandals. While not as dramatic as those in corporate America, the impact of these developments on foundations has been to alter business-as-usual in several ways: many foundations are reevaluating program areas, reconsidering internal processes for deciding which grants to fund, formalizing reporting requirements, and demanding more rigorous evaluations from grantees. In the process of this reform, many foundations have tightened their guidelines and refocused or narrowed their giving (sometimes away from higher education). They increasingly ask the following questions: how does this grant help us to meet our goals; is this the best investment in this grantmaking area; and does it provide the best "bang for the buck" available? The results of these changes are that while there are more foundations than there ever have been in the history of the United States, they are more tightly focused on their priorities, and they have higher expectations of their grantees when they give their money.

How to Get Started?   Since foundations, by IRS definition, are nonprofit, *mission-driven* entities and they seek to make a difference in society (whether at the grassroots level or via policy change), the best possible scenario is for an academic project or program to help achieve the foundation's own goals. One way to think about foundations is that most are seeking to address a specific set of unmet needs and your proposed project should be presented as the best method by which they may attain this end. Therefore, while a project may seem extraordinary in concept to you, the applicant, in order to be funded, it must also fulfill the needs of the funder.

What Should You Do before Identifying a Funder?   A faculty member should have a very clear understanding of what is planned: What do you want to get done? Why? How long will it take? Who will do it? How much will it cost? A short written description will help you think through the plan and to identify the resources needed.

What Kind of Funder Should You Approach?　It depends! Foundations, corporations, and individuals all support different things. Generally speaking, foundations fund a wide range of projects and programs. Corporations fund efforts that provide tangible returns. Individuals contribute to programs and operating funds, to endowment and bricks and mortar. Of course, there are always exceptions, so even if you have identified a funder you want to approach, the next step should be to seek out more information and good advice. Visit the funder's Web site and carefully review its grantmaking philosophy. Look for deadlines, application guidelines, and recent grant descriptions. You should begin to be able to answer the question of whether your project fits well with this particular funder's areas of interest. If it is not a close fit, applying anyway will not increase your chances of being funded and may very well annoy the funder.

Who Can Help?　Often the best resource for more information and assistance may be found within your own university's infrastructure — an award office (sometimes split into pre-award and post-award), or in a corporate and/or foundation office within the college or university's development or external affairs area. Often, these offices offer a wide array of support services. The kinds of assistance available will vary depending on how much money you are seeking, how much support you have for your project from the administration (is it an institutional priority?), and how your particular project fits with a particular foundation's mission. With the advent of the Internet, an enormous amount of information is readily available to anyone with Internet access and a little time. The Foundation Center is a good place to start when looking for private funders (http://fdncenter.org/). Talking with senior colleagues and administrators may help you to narrow your search to a group of funders, or to identify a specific funder to review. Keeping your departmental chair apprised of your fundraising plans provides both an opportunity to tap that individual's personal experience and also allows you to measure the institutional support you will have for your project. Many funders require letters of support or financial commitments from your university, and these are best sought early in the process. For a more nuanced understanding of a potential funder, actual experience is best. A brief straightforward conversation with your university's fundraisers should clarify what assistance you can expect from them and what procedures you should follow. Your college or university may have a priority-driven agenda with selected funders. Your university fundraisers will help you negotiate institutional policies and politics or submission sequencing concerns. Many universities now see fundraising as a faculty member's responsibility and offer training in grantwriting for new faculty and graduate students.

While each foundation will have its own operating procedures, many foundation program officers now prefer to have a conversation early in the process — both to fend off proposals that have no chance of being funded (wasting the time and energy of both applicant and grantmaking staff), and to provide an opportunity for advice and assistance in shaping the particular request. While the board of trustees of the foundation usually makes final funding decisions, foundation staff actively seek out the best projects to meet the foundation's own goals, and it is in their best interest to present well-thought-out, well-written, feasible, and focused proposals. Review available information before calling so that you may ask substantive questions. If asked, many program officers will answer specific questions from applicants, review proposal and budget drafts, or help with the increasingly required evaluation segment of a project. Grant seekers sometimes fail to listen carefully to program officers and the result may be a rejected application.

Preparing the Proposal   Carefully review any guidelines provided by the funder, consider who your audience will be (it may range from an expert panel to a group of educated generalists or business people), then write clearly and with the assumption that at least some portion of your proposal will be read by nonexperts. If you have already presented the project for internal review, you may need to reconceptualize it for an external funder with the understanding that the arguments you need for internal approval are not necessarily the same arguments that will successfully persuade an outside funder to make a grant. If you have questions that are not answered on the funder's Web site or by your colleagues, call the program officer to ask them and be sure to listen carefully to the response. If you are given no specific guidelines, most proposals should include an executive summary, background of the institution and project, a discussion of why the project should be pursued (taking into account its value to society, to academe or your department, to some set of constituents, and to the mission of the funder), methodology, a description of what will take place and who will carry out the work, a set of expectations and how they will be evaluated, a timeline, and a budget. Review any internal university procedures to find out how far in advance of a funder's deadline you will need to seek institutional approval and signatures.

Timing and Negotiation with the Funder   Foundations have nearly as many variations in their grantmaking cycles as there are foundations. In deciding to approach a funder, after you have ascertained a good fit with your project, you will want learn more about that particular funder's decision-making timeline. Some funders have a single review cycle each year, others have quarterly or ongoing review processes. Some proposals are reviewed at several stages and applicants may be required to revise and resubmit the proposal or to answer lengthy questions. Some funders allow program officers to approve small grants at their own discretion and some require full board approval for any grant. The time period for the project should take into consideration the length of the funder's review process and the timing of receipt of funds if a grant is awarded.

A foundation may request changes in a proposal or budget. The funder is seeking to meet its mission through your project, and they may have a slightly different perspective on the objective and strategy. A spirit of collaboration may result in modifications that better suit the funder yet do not detract from your larger vision of the project's impact. Be open to some adjustment but then consider carefully if the changes have so altered your project that it no longer meets your needs as a scholar. It is better to withdraw a proposal than to accept a grant and not be able to fulfill its requirements, potentially damaging not only your own relationship with the funder but the larger university's relationship.

What Needs to Be Done after Receiving a Grant?   Your institution's fundraising staff will guide you through your institution's red tape, but the typical post-grant list includes the following: a formal thank-you letter, review and acknowledgment of the terms of the award letter, accurate accounting and activity records, and timely reports. Keep your funder apprised of any significant changes in your project. After a grant is made, the funder has a large stake in the project's success and most program officers will assist you in reaching that goal. It is best to inform the funder of bad news rather than have it discovered some other way; and a positive way to approach a bad situation is to suggest a plan for correcting the problem. In the long run, good stewardship of one grant received is the best next step in a second approach to that funder. And it will also increase your reputation as a scholar and researcher with other funders as well.

What if Your Proposal Is Rejected?   Resist the temptation to write an angry letter. Most funders receive many more applications than they can accept; the acceptance rate of unsolicited proposals for a major foundation like Ford Foundation may be as low as 5 percent. The closer the fit between project and foundation mission, the better the chance the project has of being funded, but there may be other reasons for rejection. Many program officers are willing to provide advice after a proposal is rejected, so a call or letter to thank them for considering the proposal, with an inquiry as to how it might be improved, may result in helpful information for a resubmission or for revision for submission to another funder. It is always useful to maintain a good institutional relationship with any funder, because there will be other Requests for Proposals (RFP) down the road. Finally, don't be discouraged. Faculty who are very successful in obtaining external funding do not receive every grant they seek, and building a good track record at a low dollar level may well lead to greater success in the future.

CORPORATE RELATIONS

Corporate Climate   Increasingly corporations have moved away from unimaginative check-writing philanthropy, to a targeted, strategic, and global model.[3] Unlike foundations, which are required by law to give money away, corporations exist in order to make money for their owners and stockholders. Therefore corporate contributions may increasingly be characterized as strategic investments, often with the intent of generating some return or impact that will eventually improve a company's profits. Corporate gifts are increasingly targeted toward a small group of key "partner" colleges and universities in order to develop broad and strong strategic alliances that promise numerous points of potential value: strengthening their public image, recruitment of top students, and development of key research relationships. But companies are able also to bring a wide variety of resources to their partnerships that are not available through other sources. For example, universities benefit from special deep discounts and donations of products and services, internships and employment opportunities for graduates, and a vast array of potential collaborations including executive guest lecturers and joint research projects. Corporations frequently make their most important contributions through channels not connected with their corporate foundations (from marketing, recruiting, or research budgets), and these strategic investments often lead to later funding from their corporate foundations. As corporate investments become increasingly strategic, programs that demonstrate a clear potential return (generally those in business schools, engineering, and the sciences) may expect to reap larger proportions of corporate funding.

How to Get Started   Do some research and make sure that you are targeting the right companies. While company foundations generally follow the same patterns as other charitable foundations (described above), the gifts from corporate foundations are usually associated with advancing the firms' bottom lines. Even if there is no measurable connection to profits or sales, corporate gifts often target a particular social/recruiting issue (e.g., improving science education, or increasing the pool of qualified minorities in a particular field), or they may facilitate placement of the company name and logo (marketing/brand recognition) strategically in front of students, faculty, or attendees at conferences or athletic events. Therefore, it is critical to know the specific interests of a potential corporate partner before making a request.

How to Build Strong Partnerships   In order to get the most out of corporate relationships, faculty should view them as partnerships. In practice this means attempting to design realistic, win-win projects that provide clear benefits to both partners. Faculty will want to work with appropriate corporate staff in seeking these relationships. Some of the most common points of value and leverage that should be considered when approaching a funder include:

— Highly placed alumni, or internal champions

— Supplier, service provider, and vending relationships

— Internships and recruiting relationships

— Intellectual Property (ip)-licensing and commercialization of technology

— Access to seminars, lectures, university libraries

— Collaborative and/or contract research

— Faculty, researcher, executive-in-residence exchanges

— Subcontracts and matching support on federal grants

— Conferences, just-in-time, and custom education

— Executive education, health, and services

— Sponsorships and uses of marketing funds for athletic events, exhibits, conferences, etc.)

— Philanthropic support of specific programs and projects (e.g., scholarships, professorships, centers, buildings, etc.)

What You Should Know before Approaching a Corporation   Recently, international pressure to improve "corporate citizenship" has forced traditional corporate giving programs to spread their donations globally.[4] This has had the effect of increasing competition among U.S. nonprofits for a reduced percentage of total corporate spending. In addition, company executives are more frequently being asked by their boards and stockholders to justify their giving decisions. These two related trends have resulted in many companies dramatically increasing their percentage of "gifts-in-kind" (60 percent of corporate gifts were products and services in 2004) as opposed to outright gifts of cash,[5] because for tax purposes, gifts of products or services are valued based on the market and not on what they cost the company, allowing the corporation a larger write-off. Gifts-in-kind also have the benefit of leveraging those things that the company does best and most efficiently. Therefore, before approaching a potential corporate partner you should always ask, "How can we best leverage the various potential points of interest, core competencies, and strengths on both sides of this relationship, to maximize our mutual benefit?"

How Should You Identify and Develop Relationships?   Before approaching potential corporate partners, faculty should consult with their campus corporate relations, tech-transfer, career center, and/or development staff. Often these people are excellent resources and can help identify promising opportunities and contacts. Also, they can assist you in developing effective strategies for approaching potential corporate partners and help you negotiate university guidelines and policies regarding corporate affiliate or partnership programs, recruiting and internships, conflicts of interest, faculty consulting, sponsored or collaborative research, intellectual property, copyright, gift-naming thresholds, and sponsorships.

Do not underestimate the influence of well-placed and appreciative alumni, friends, and former colleagues in developing useful corporate partnerships. These relationships are often the key to significant corporate donations. On the other hand, even without these advantages, many corporate relationships evolve directly out of mutual interest and complementary abilities. In fact, often corporations enlist university faculty members as consultants when their particular expertise is valuable. The bottom line is that if your particular activities or research are clearly of interest to large industries, then the odds are better that you will find a valuable corporate partner. In 2005, the hottest areas of growth were in markets related to the health and defense industries; these also accounted for many of the most valuable university corporate partnerships. On the other hand, outreach programs to K-12 schools and programs involving underrepresented groups also saw increasing corporate support. So the best advice is probably to coordinate your efforts with your campus's advancement and other corporate relationship offices to ensure that you are targeting the right companies and using appropriate points of contact.

The expectation that faculty will obtain external funds to support their academic research and projects is becoming the norm in many disciplines beyond the hard sciences. Therefore support structures to assist faculty are being put in place in many institutions of higher learning. Like learning how to teach well or mastering a difficult methodology within your discipline, fundraising is a skill that may be learned through a combination of advice, training, and personal experience.

NOTES

1. Michael Porter and Mark Kramer, "The Competitive Advantage of Corporate Philanthropy," *Harvard Business Review*, December 2002.

2. One obvious exception would be the Henry R. Luce Foundation, which was heavily invested in AOL/Time Warner stock and saw a decline of nearly $500 million in its assets when that stock dropped dramatically in 2001.

3. James Austin, *The Collaboration Challenge: How Nonprofits and Businesses Succeed through Strategic Alliances* (Cambridge: Harvard Business School, 2000).

4. See the United Nations Global Compact (www.unglobalcompact.org).

5. The Conference Board, *The 2004 Corporate Contributions Report*.

23.

SECURING FUNDING FROM FEDERAL SOURCES

JUDITH K. ARGON

Despite the doubling of the NIH budget during the five-year period from 1997 to 2002, the impact of the events of September 11, 2001, the unprecedented federal deficit, and underinvestment in the National Science Foundation, the Department of Energy, and the basic research arms of the Department of Defense have created similar, if not worse, conditions for funding than when this essay was originally written in 1994.

INTRODUCTION

Since the late 1940s, the federal government's dollars and the brainpower of the nation's colleges and universities have joined to advance basic and applied research. This has been a most productive partnership, serving the needs of the nation as well as promoting the expansion of higher education. Unfortunately, like many long-term relationships, this one is showing signs of strain. The concerns for national security, growing public mistrust of the academic community, a burgeoning federal deficit, and increasing numbers of faculty competing for constant or shrinking federal dollars are taking their toll on this partnership. In contrast to the 1960s and 1970s, when 40 to 50 percent of grant applications to the NIH, for example, were funded, or the late 1990s and early years of the twenty-first century when success rates were in excess of 30 percent, today fewer than one in four applications receives an award.[1] Moreover, with the end of the Cold War, some agencies, such as the departments of Defense (DOD) and Energy (DOE), moved away from their traditional strengths, focusing instead on funding research that will "enhance economic competitiveness." Even the National Science Foundation (NSF) and the National Institutes of Health (NIH) increasingly supported "strategic" projects that seem more immediately relevant to the nation's economic competitiveness than the traditional investigator-initiated basic research. The events of September 11, 2001, and the resulting emphasis on national security, the threat of bioterrorism, and military readiness have narrowed the focus and funding levels further.

There's no doubt that budget realities, international economic competitiveness, and political pressures are redefining the university-government relationship. Indeed, although a report issued in 1994, *Science in the National Interest*,[2] reaffirmed the importance of fundamental research to future technological innovation and to improvements in the quality of life, it also asked each federal agency to "delineate its fundamental research and education missions with respect to national goals" and emphasized the link between basic research, applied research, and technology.[3]

To compete successfully in this difficult environment, a faculty member should approach the search for funds as a serious and, unfortunately, somewhat time-consuming endeavor. It takes time to devise an appropriate project and to describe it in a clear and compelling way. Learning how to navigate through the maze of federal agencies and their varied and diverse programs is equally challenging. The following is a map of sorts for new faculty, describing the principles of federal funding and grantsmanship that will, I hope, allow you to compete successfully for your first federal research dollars. The number of federal programs and agencies, the vastness and complexity of the federal bureaucracy, and the relative independence of individual federal agencies can be confusing and intimidating to anyone, but particularly to you as new faculty. In addition to describing sources of information and types of award mechanisms and delineating federal agencies and proposal content, this essay will also suggest strategies for junior faculty that may make the search for funding more successful and less distressing.

DEFINING THE PROJECT: FUNDING FOR
WHAT AND WHAT KIND OF FUNDING

The first step in a successful search for funding is to define the project carefully and articulately. Different projects have vastly differing budgetary and programmatic needs; defining the parameters of the project will help direct and identify appropriate funding sources, as well as determine the appropriate funding mechanisms. While one research project may require the stability and scope of a multiyear grant or contract, another may be accomplished through fellowship or travel-only monies. Similarly, while research on general topics such as mental health economics might be best supported by a grant mechanism, research in a more targeted area, such as mortality and morbidity in hemodialysis patients or an animal model for chronic Lyme disease, might be supported through a cooperative agreement or contract.

The federal government has five primary funding mechanisms, divided into two categories. Fellowships, grants, and cooperative agreements are categorized as Financial Assistance Programs; contracts and consulting agreements are Procurement Programs. Each mechanism has its own expectations and requirements.

Assistance programs: These programs are designed to support meritorious programs and projects. Thus, the majority of investigator-initiated proposals are either fellowships, grants, or cooperative agreements. The availability of funds under Financial Assistance Programs is announced by the agencies directly, either through Program Announcements and Requests for Proposals (RFP) published by the agency, or through the *Federal Register*.

Fellowship: A fellowship provides financial support to individuals within the context of their career development. Fellowships generally establish a direct and legally binding relationship between the funding agency and the fellowship recipient. Proposals for most fellowships are submitted directly by the researcher, who receives the funds directly from the agency. In some instances, the fellowship application, such as those for NIH Kirschtein Awards, require institutional approval and/or the fellowship may be awarded to the researcher's institution. The NEH Summer Stipend is an interesting hybrid—while the submission of the application requires institutional approval, the fellowship is awarded directly to the recipient. While some fellowships are for periods of one year or less, some training fellowships may be for longer periods of time. Generally, fellowship funds are given at pre-established levels for living expenses (stipend, health insurance, tuition, and perhaps travel) during the fellowship period.

Grant: A grant is a financial assistance mechanism that provides funds to carry out an approved program of activities. The grant mechanism is used when the idea for the project is investigator initiated and "whenever the awarding agency anticipates no substantial programmatic involvement . . . during performance of" the activities.[4] Grants are awarded to the institution, which bears the legal responsibility for the project and its administration. Grants vary in duration, usually for periods of one to five years. Grant budgets may contain funds for all reasonable costs of the project, including staff, graduate assistants, travel, supplies, equipment, and other necessary items.

Cooperative agreement: A cooperative agreement is similar to a grant and is governed by the same federal regulations but is "used in lieu of a grant when substantial Federal programmatic involvement is anticipated."[5] Cooperative agreements provide a mechanism for the sponsor and the researcher to spell out, from the outset, terms of the award that are specific to the particular project to be funded. These terms are mutual: they indicate responsibilities of both the sponsor and the researcher. In addition, the terms may be conditional. For example, a term of an award may be that the agency provide a specific funding amount or a particular piece of equipment by a certain date before the researcher is responsible for carrying out the project. The use of program-specific terms and conditions through the cooperative agreement is one way to ensure the success of projects that are programmatically complex or that may involve more than one sponsoring agency.

Procurement programs: Contracts and consultant agreements are "procurement" or "acquisition" vehicles whereby the federal government has identified a particular need, solicited proposals, and determined which proposal has the best likelihood to fulfill those goals. Since the issuing agency wishes to advance knowledge in a particular area with an interest in solving a specific need, performance is monitored closely.

Contracts: Opportunities for federal contracting are published in the *Commerce Business Daily* and in agency specific publications, such as the NIH *Guide for Grants and Contracts*. Each RFP will contain very specific programmatic and technical requirements, as well as evaluation criteria. Contracts are awarded to the institution and are administered under the *Federal Acquisition Regulations* (FAR) and the relevant agency supplements to the FAR. Therefore, contracts carry substantially different, and usually more onerous, administrative and reporting requirements. Institutional officials will review the contract terms carefully to ensure that there are none that unduly limit academic prerogatives in areas such as publication, data retention and use, and involvement of foreign nationals in the research. An institution may be unable to accept a contract if issues such as these cannot be negotiated successfully with the sponsoring agency.

Consulting agreements: Similar to consulting agreements with private organizations, these are mechanisms to provide the federal government with the precise expertise it needs to accomplish a task at hand. In a consulting agreement the government essentially hires the services of an individual for a specific task. Like most fellowships, consulting agreements are between the individual researcher and the hiring agency, but unlike fellowships, grants, cooperative agreements, and contracts, consulting agreements generally vest title to data and intellectual property with the federal government.

SEEKING HELP AND INFORMATION

There are many avenues for determining appropriate sources of funding for a particular project. You can rely on the advice of senior colleagues—many will be willing to provide you with the name of their program officer; some will offer to act as an intermediary; and others may suggest preparing a collaborative proposal. Another source of information may be professional journals or the newsletters of professional organizations. In addition, most universities and colleges have offices that can provide comprehensive, individualized, and service-oriented help in determining the most appropriate funding sources. These offices have many different titles—Office of Research Support, Research Services, Grants and Contracts, Research and Projects Administration—but their mission is similar: to maintain a library of funding information, to work with faculty, postdoctoral fellows, and students to identify funding opportunities, and to provide guidance in proposal writing and grantsmanship. In addition to maintaining a vast selection of program announcements and funding guides, these offices will review the *Commerce Business Daily* and *Federal Register* for opportunities and have access to computerized databases of funding information, including those of NSF, NIH and other federal agencies. Moreover, professional staff are familiar with many of the funding sources and can steer you toward the most promising. They also have contacts in the federal agencies, can solicit information on your behalf, or can provide basic background information to help you navigate through the enormous federal bureaucracy.

A FEDERAL PRIMER

Before applying for funds from a federal agency, it is important to understand some of the basic features of the federal government and its funding of university-based research, conferences, curriculum enhancements, and other programmatic activities. Almost all federal agencies have funds to support extramural activity by nonfederal entities, including universities and colleges. The nature of the funds and the types of activities supported can differ widely, however, depending upon the agency. Some of the federal agencies (NIH, DOD, USDA, NASA, DOE, EPA) are considered "mission agencies." Each was established to fulfill a very specific role and the research or educational programs supported by each agency must advance that mission. As a result, solicitations from these agencies tend to be much more specific and tied to particular areas of research. The Department of Agriculture, for example, supports basic agricultural research through its Cooperative State Research Service; the annual solicitation, however, is exceedingly specific in its interests and lists topics such as Plant Responses to the Environment, Improving Human Nutrition for Optimal Health, Enhancing Animal Reproductive Efficiency, and Plant Growth and Development. Proposals in areas not covered by these priorities will not be considered. In these situations, the importance of the area has already been determined by the agency and the proposer's task is to convince the program official and reviewer of the novelty and compelling nature of the methodology, proposed approach and experiments, and likelihood of success.

Other agencies, chief among them NSF, National Endowment for the Humanities, and National Endowment for the Arts, are "non-mission agencies." Their goal is to support the best research and projects in broadly defined disciplines — science, social science, and engineering for NSF, the humanities for NEH, and the arts for NEA. Solicitations from these agencies tend to be more open-ended, requesting proposals in a general and broadly defined field and inviting the investigator to determine an interesting issue within the broad discipline. For example, NEH has a yearly deadline for "Scholarly Editions" but leaves it to the investigator to decide what project to undertake, define its parameters, and convince the program official and reviewers of the importance of the topic. Similarly, while NSF is divided into directorates, divisions, and programs of disciplinary specificity, most program announcements broadly solicit proposals within a subspecialty or speciality area. For example, the Cognitive Neuroscience Program, which resides in Social, Behavioral, and Economic Sciences Directorate, supports "proposals aimed at advancing a rigorous understanding of how the human brain supports thought, perception, affect, action, social processes, and other aspects of cognition and behavior."[6]

As mentioned above, a paradigm shift in federal funding has been taking place over the last ten years. NSF, for one, underwent significant changes in its funding programs in the mid-1990s. Political pressures, the economy, and shifting priorities pushed the agency toward increasing strategic, or more narrowly defined, research. For example, within the Human Capital Initiative of the Social, Behavioral, and Economic Sciences Directorate, six areas were identified for particular development: employing a productive workforce; educating for the future; fostering successful families; building strong neighborhoods, reducing disadvantage in a diverse society; and overcoming poverty and deprivation. In addition, NSF targeted five areas for foundationwide emphasis: biotechnology; environment and global change; manufacturing research and education; advanced materials and processing; and high performance computing and communications. NSF has continued to evolve, to limit programmatic expansion, and to concentrate resources in strategic areas. Similarly, the National Institutes of Health's *Roadmap Initiative* is designed to identify the most compelling opportunities in three main areas: new pathways to discovery, research teams of the future, and re-engineering the clinical research enterprise.[7] Funding for these initiatives is taken annually from the budgets of each of the NIH's institutes, and individual projects within these areas are announced in the NIH *Guide for Grants and Contracts.*

The emphasis at NSF and NIH on balancing strategic research and basic, investigator-initiated research is closely paralleled within certain offices of DOD and DOE. Although a mission agency with very specific research targets, DOD supports four divisions with more open agendas: the Office of Naval Research (ONR), the Army Research Office (ARO), the Air Force Office of Scientific Research (AFOSR), and the Advanced Research Projects Administration (ARPA, formerly DARPA). Each of these offices issues Broad Agency Announcements (BAA) and a Guide to Programs, which describe the basic thrusts or areas of interest. As described on its Web site,[8] the Air Force Office of Scientific Research, for example, has four major areas of research — aerospace and materials sciences, physics and electronics, chemistry and life sciences, and mathematics and geosciences. These extremely broad areas are further subdivided into fields such as structural mechanics, mechanisms of materials, and particulate mechanics. The descriptions, which include the names, addresses, and telephone and fax numbers of the program officers, clearly indicate the precise areas of interest and priority in which AFOSR would like to receive proposals. The Office of Energy Research in the Department of Energy operates in a similar manner.

SPECIALIZED FUNDING OPPORTUNITIES FOR JUNIOR FACULTY

Don't be discouraged if you have yet to write your first successful grant application. Federal agencies recognize that inexperienced faculty may be at a serious disadvantage competing with senior colleagues for the same pot of money. Thus, NIH, NSF, and others have established special programs, sometimes with separate dollars, designed for those who have not yet held awards or who do not have the track record or previous results necessary to be fully competitive. Other similar programs exist for individuals from underrepresented minorities, or for those returning to research after hiatuses. Although the details will undoubtedly change, the following programs are illustrative of these targeted opportunities.

NIH Small Grant (R03) Mechanism: Most NIH Institutes accept applications for small research projects that can be carried out with limited resources in two years or less and with $50,000 per year. Although not directed preferentially toward new investigators, the size and scope of R03 applications make it an excellent vehicle for initiating a new project, developing the data needed for a

larger research grant, and demonstrating a track record of competitiveness at
NIH.

NIH Exploratory/Developmental Grant (R21) Mechanism: As with the R03, the
R21 does not target new faculty preferentially but does provide a vehicle for proposing new, exploratory, and developmental research projects for which less
preliminary data is available. Limited to two years of support, these award offer
up to $275,000 in direct costs over the two-year period.

NIH Career Development Awards: More commonly known as K-awards, these
recognize that some new faculty need additional time to develop a fully independent research program or may need time to develop skills in new or emerging areas. With more than ten Career Award types,[9] these awards provide support and "protected time" (75 percent effort over three, four, or five years) for
an intensive, supervised career development experience in the biomedical, behavioral, or clinical sciences.

NSF CAREER Awards: Initiated in FY 1995, CAREER Awards replaced NSF's
Young Investigator Program, the ENG/CISE Research Initiation Award Program,
and the Research Initiation Award component of the Minority Research Initiation Program. CAREER supports junior faculty in the development of academic
careers that include both research and teaching.

Presidential Early Career Awards for Scientists and Engineers (PECASE): Each
year, eleven agencies select the most meritorious new awardees to compete for
the added distinction of a PECASE designation. The PECASE program recog-
nizes outstanding scientists and engineers who, early in their careers, show exceptional potential for leadership at the frontiers of knowledge. This Presidential Award is the highest honor bestowed by the United States Government on
scientists and engineers beginning their independent careers.

NEH Summer Stipend: Institutions are invited annually to nominate up to
three faculty to receive $4,000 stipends for at least two full months of summer
research. Projects involving extensive travel may ask for an additional $750.

ONR Young Investigator Program: This program makes fourteen awards of
$75,000 per year for three years to faculty within five years of receipt of the Ph.D.
who have research interests consistent with the Navy's. A program of matching
funds can increase the amount of the award.

PREPARING THE PROPOSAL

Without a doubt, the two most essential aspects of a successful proposal are a
powerful new idea or project and a clear, convincing, and compelling presentation. Program officers may not read beyond the second paragraph of a poorly

written proposal and will reject a well-written proposal that lacks substance, creativity, originality, and significance. No amount of grantsmanship can substitute for an excellent research idea, but because many excellent proposals are rejected each year, the following tips may help make your proposal stand out from other competitive ones.

Preliminary Steps   There are essential steps in the preparation of every successful proposal. First, carefully review the entire solicitation or program announcement not only to ensure (yet again) a programmatic "fit" but also to learn about the administrative requirements. Then, telephone the program officer. A program officer can supplement the information contained in the solicitation and provide presubmission advice and comments about the general approach taken in the proposal. He or she can also provide insight into the review process and evaluation criteria. Moreover, a program officer can help ensure that your proposal is submitted for review under the most appropriate program or study section. In some agencies, program officials may agree to read and comment on a draft or prospectus. When at all possible, don't submit "cold." Talk to a program officer first.

Although most program announcements ask for complete proposal packages, others require a two-step process. Sometimes this means submitting a nonbinding letter of intent. The agency can then anticipate just how many proposals it will have to review. In other instances, pre-proposals or "white papers" are requested so the agency can screen out less competitive applications. After a quick, usually in-house review, program officers will invite the most competitive and most responsive applicants to prepare full proposals. Often the program officer will have some reviewer comments to share with you that can strengthen your final proposal. If they don't, ask.

Considerations   Before you begin to write your proposal, find out how it is going to be reviewed. If the program solicitation does not provide sufficient information, feel free to discuss this with the program officer. Some agencies, such as the NIH, have prepared materials about the review process for the asking. Understanding the review process is important. Knowing who will review the proposal allows you to write to the appropriate audience. If, for example, your proposal will be reviewed by a panel of specialists or even subspecialists, you can write a highly technical proposal and know that the reviewers will understand it. On the other hand, if your proposal will be considered by a group of nonspecialists, as is often the case for proposals to the NEH, your proposal must be clear and compelling to the educated nonspecialist, free of technical jargon, and with its significance highlighted and set within the broadest disciplinary context.

It is also helpful to understand the process and timeframe for proposal review. Many federal agencies use some form of peer review, especially for fellowship, grant, and cooperative agreements. The precise nature of the peer review, however, differs both by agency and by program within agencies. Divisions within NSF, for example, adopt one of a variety of review mechanisms: some programs solicit review by mail from three to five experts, leaving the final decision to the program officers; others employ a review panel; and still other programs may use a combination of these approaches. A complete NSF review process can last from six to nine months. At NIH, the review process can take up to ten months and generally involves a scientific review by one of many standing NIH Scientific Review Groups, commonly known as "Study Sections," and review and approval by the NIH National Advisory Councils. NIH has recently begun experimenting with changes to its traditional reviews to streamline and quicken this process.

Reviewer comments on unsuccessful proposals should be seen as valuable tools for revision and resubmission. Some agencies, such as NEH and the Department of Education, typically send only general comments describing types of mistakes or shortcomings in the proposal. Telephone the program officer for more specific information. In contrast, NIH and NSF respond with detailed information. NSF will usually send copies of the reviewers' verbatim critiques, while NIH sends a comprehensive *Summary Statement*, often referred to as a "pink sheet." Although sometimes brutal, the criticism can and should be used constructively and can form the basis for a revised proposal.

PROPOSAL WRITING

The heart of a proposal is the statement of work—alternately called program narrative, project description, or research plan. Most solicitations contain explicit specifications about what should be included in this section and how long it should be. Regardless of the specific format, however, your narrative should include the following basic elements:

Introduction: Usually limited to one or two paragraphs, this section does not function as the abstract or project summary (which are designed to stand alone) but as a coherent and interesting preview to the project description. Some agencies, such as NIH, invite a separate introduction only in the case of a resubmission. The introduction may also function as a forum to respond to the criticisms of a previous pink sheet.

Background/Need: This section can be used to describe the background of your project, the state of the field, and the recent evolution of the field. It should also critically evaluate existing knowledge and identify the need or gap that your project is expected to fulfill. You might also use this section to explain how you are qualified to conduct the project and how your interests and expertise have evolved in this particular area or direction. Finally, you should indicate the importance of the project by relating the specific project goals to broad long-term disciplinary interests.

Goals and Objectives: This section functions like the Specific Aims section of an NIH proposal. In it, you describe the basic hypothesis you want to test or the project you are undertaking, the broad, long-term objectives, and the anticipated results, outcomes, or accomplishments of your project. This section, together with the abstract, takes on particular importance when the review is divided between primary reviewers, who will read the entire proposal, and secondary reviewers, who will focus on the abstract and the specific aims or goals and objectives.

Program Narrative: In this section — the heart of the proposal — you describe your proposed project in detail, including research design, methodologies, and procedures, and also indicate the anticipated outcome of your project: a report, algorithm, book. For programmatic, curricular, or conference proposals, this section describes the proposed courses, project, or conference, including detailed information like weekly syllabi, conference schedule with proposed speakers, and numbers of participants, sites, and activities.

Significance: Although significance of the project and its potential impact are often clear to the proposer, they are equally often less clear to the reviewer. The importance of the field, the project, and its expected outcome should be clearly articulated.

Qualifications and Resources: Here's where you discuss your qualifications and the qualifications of your team as well as the special resources — facilities and equipment — you have at your disposal. In part, this serves to explain how your research or project will be accomplished and why you can accomplish your goals. In proposals for curriculum or other types of projects, this section can be used to convince the reviewers that your particular university is the right place to conduct this project. For example, the appropriate groundwork is already in place, and your faculty, chair, dean, and others are already committed to this type of project.

Administration: Although this section is unnecessary in a research proposal, it is essential in a programmatic or curricular one. Here is where you explain who's responsible for what, who reports to whom, and the general administrative structure.

Your completed proposal should read smoothly, with elegant transitions from paragraph to paragraph and section to section. If well written and appropriately ordered, a proposal can captivate the reader with its order, logic, and importance. Avoid common mistakes by observing the following:

—Ensure that your proposal has a clearly articulated hypothesis or needs statement and that the validity of the hypothesis or the importance of the project is absolutely clear to the reader.

—Ensure that your proposal is interesting and compelling.

—Keep your proposal focused and its scope reasonably narrow.

—Avoid reliance on an anchor experiment whose success is key to all subsequent experiments and without which the entire proposal is unfeasible.

—Describe how the project fits into the field and how it will advance it.

—Recognize that this is your opportunity to "say it all." Make sure that your proposal articulates clearly everything that you want the reviewers to know about you and about the proposed project. Do not assume that the reviewers will know anything that is not in the proposal. What is written in the proposal is what the reviewers will discuss. Do not assume that the program officer, with whom you may have spoken at length, will offer any additional particulars during the review discussion. Do not expect anyone to compensate for a missing experiment, understated significance, or unstated qualifications.

A final hint: ask a faculty colleague or your mentor to review your proposal. Seek out individuals who are familiar with not only the work you are proposing but also with the needs, expectations, and requirements of the funding agency. Ask for, and expect, honest, if brutal, criticism. If your colleague or mentor reacts negatively to an aspect of your proposal, imagine how a reviewer might respond.

BUDGETS AND OTHER (ADMINISTRATIVE) FORMS

A completed proposal packet includes much more than just the project description. Additional elements vary widely, of course, among the different agencies so it is important to read the solicitation carefully. The most common elements include:

Cover Sheet: Many agencies, including NSF, NIH, and NEH, have developed unique and individual cover sheets. Others use a governmentwide form, Standard Form 424, while still others allow the investigator to develop his/her own packaging. Under a push toward greater uniformity and electronic grants administration, the federal agencies are moving toward electronic submission of proposals through a common interface, grants.gov, and the use of common application forms. Major elements of unique or standard cover sheets include information on the PI and co-PI, title of project, solicitation number or program name, amount requested, information on institutional administrators responsible for managing awards, and signatures of the PI and co-PI and the authorized institutional signatory. Often, as in the case of NSF and NIH, the signature certifies not only approval of the proposal but also the institution's compliance with federal regulations.

Project Summary or Abstract: This section functions as a succinct and self-contained summary of the proposed work. Agencies differ as to the desired tone and level of the summary. For some, a fairly technical or scientific description is appropriate, while others want a version directed to a lay audience. Unlike proposals, which are protected under the Freedom of Information Act, proposal summaries are considered public documents and may be released by the agency, some of which submit all abstracts (and technical progress reports) to the National Technical Information Service (NTIS) and, in the case of DOD, the Defense Technical Information Center (DTIC). It is important, therefore, to ensure that no proprietary intellectual property is included in the public abstract.

Curriculum Vitae: A proposal packet should include the CV of everyone who will assume major responsibility for the project. Minimally, this means the PI and co-investigators, if any. To reduce the amount of paper, many agencies request abbreviated CVs, often called "biosketches," of limited and specified length, often two pages.

Budget and Budget Justification: Again, many agencies have developed specific budget forms, while others use Federal Form SF424 or allow the PI to develop his/her own. A well-developed and well-justified budget is essential and the budget must reflect the statement of work. A proposal involving the use of specialized computer resources, interlibrary loan, or animals that fails to ask for computer costs, library loan costs, or daily animal charges will seem sloppy and inconsistent to reviewers.

Costs are broken down between direct and indirect costs. Direct costs are those that can be specifically identified with a particular project and are easily tracked and accounted for. These include salaries and wages for project personnel, materials and equipment, travel associated with the project (including both travel directly related to the research for field work or collaboration and travel to conferences to present the results of the project), long distance telephone charges, computer charges, animal costs, publication charges, and so forth.

Indirect costs are those incurred for common or joint objectives and that therefore cannot be identified specifically with a particular project. They include costs for maintenance and operations for buildings (including heat, electricity, gas, water, maintenance, and repairs); the costs of libraries; the cost of local telephone service; departmental administration and university administration, such as accounting, sponsored projects, grants and contracts management, personnel, purchasing, plant accounting, and the like. Universities and colleges have formal indirect cost rates which are negotiated and approved by one of the federal agencies, DHHS, ONR, or DOE.

According to federal guidelines in the Office of Management and Budget Circular A-21, only certain types of costs are appropriate and allowable costs for a budget. For example, in no instance are alcoholic beverages an allowable cost. Moreover, if a cost is included in the cost pools that make up the institution's indirect cost rate, the same cost may not appear as a direct cost. Therefore, costs for local telephone service or clerical help may not be included as a direct cost unless the nature of the project makes unusual demands on these resources. While all budgets should be realistic, budgets for grants can be less precise than those for contracts. Recognizing this, NIH has moved toward the use of modular budgets in which PIs request up to eight increments of $25,000 per year and which require justification and detail on selected budget elements only. In contrast, contracts, particularly large ones, are often subject to pre-award audits that require justifying each and every cost. While estimating travel at a round figure may be a sensible approach on a grant, travel costs for a contract should be calculated using government per diem rates and air ticket rates. Similarly, equipment costs should derive from a quote or from a catalog.

When preparing a budget, check with your department and institutional offices to determine basic considerations and parameters. What, for example, is the anticipated support for a graduate student in your department? Are faculty expected to request a percentage of their academic year salary? What are the user fees for shared equipment or facilities? In addition, each school has fringe benefit and indirect costs rates, formally negotiated with the federal government, that must be applied properly to the budget for grants, cooperative agreements, and contracts. Fellowship funds that are paid directly to you by the agency do not carry fringe benefits or indirect costs; those that are administered by the institution might.

Certifications and Representations, Assurances and Checklists: Federal law requires that an institution certify that it is in compliance with an array of federal regulations before an award can be made. In some instances, certifications are required at the proposal submission stage; in other cases, pre-award certification is sufficient. Customary certifications involve compliance with regulations on drug-free workplace; debarment and suspension; loan delinquency; misconduct in science; equal employment opportunity; lobbying; and civil rights, including age, sex, and handicapped discrimination. In contrast, since few certifications apply to individuals, fellowship applications will impose only those on loan delinquency (which includes federally financed student loans) and debarment and suspension certifications.

SUBMITTING THE PROPOSAL

While it is imperative to follow agency instructions about proposal submission, it is also necessary to learn and follow the internal requirements of your institution. As mentioned above, because grant, cooperative agreement, contract, and many fellowship funds are awarded to the institution rather than to the individual directly, the institution must endorse or sign the proposal. Each institution has mechanisms for internal review and approval of proposals. Institutional requirements are usually supplemented by those of the school and department. Ask your department chair, business manager, or grants administrator to explain the steps and necessary sign-offs.

If your research involves the use of human or animal subjects, DNA, certain chemicals, or hazardous materials, additional reviews of the project by the relevant university committee will be required. In the cases of research involving humans or animals, review and approval of the research protocol must generally be completed before an award can be made; some agencies may require approval before the proposal can be submitted or reviewed. Other approvals, such as one for the use of radioactive isotopes, are handled solely by the institution. Again, your department will have information on your institution's human subjects committee (Institutional Review Board), animal care and use committee, or environmental and radiation safety committee. If not, you can either call your institution's grants office or refer to the campus telephone directory.

MODIFYING THE BUDGET AND WORKPLAN

The review process is generally a lengthy one, taking from six to ten months on average. This can be a most difficult time, and if you feel anxious, you should feel free to contact your program officer to find out at what stage your proposal is and how it is faring. Program officers are usually very open about the progress of a proposal through the system; they will tell you when the review committee is meeting, when a decision will be made, and will often suggest a follow-up call at a specific time.

If your proposal is successful, it is likely that the agency will request some modifications, in most instances a revision to the budget. Sometimes, budgets are cut across the board and no special action is required by the researcher. At other times, the study section or review committee will specifically cut out certain budget items that they feel are unnecessary or insufficiently justified. Finally, the program officer may offer a "bottom line" and ask the researcher to prepare a revised budget. Usually researchers are delighted to find that funding is forthcoming, even if the amount is less, and in some instances far less, than was requested. Despite the euphoria which accompanies a promise of funding, you should seriously consider whether your work, as proposed, can effectively be accomplished with the reduced funds. It is appropriate and acceptable to alter a statement of work when submitting a revised budget. Under a cooperative agreement or contract, this is even more essential because work under these funding mechanisms is more closely monitored, and failure to meet programmatic milestones, especially for budgetary reasons, may jeopardize future funding. Use your best judgment to ensure that the budget, barring any unforeseen complications, is sufficient to accomplish the tasks proposed.

RECEIPT OF AWARD

Once the budget and statement of work have been set, the agency will issue an award notification. In the case of some fellowships, notification will be sent directly to the researcher; for other types of awards both the investigator and the grants office will receive copies or an electronic notification. Some awards are unilateral, do not require any indication of acceptance, and are effective either upon receipt or on a date indicated on the award letter (e.g., project start-date); others are bilateral and are not considered legal, binding, and "fully executed" until all parties at the agency and university have endorsed the agreement. Cooperative agreements and contracts are more often bilateral, while grants are often unilateral. In this case, the institution signals its acceptance of the award and its terms by expending the federal funds.

The Principal Investigator should review the award carefully to verify basic information such as start-date, project period, and budget and should become familiar with the terms and conditions which govern the award. With the help of the institution's grant office, any discrepancy should be resolved immediately.

TERMS AND CONDITIONS

As a first-time award recipient, you should review the award regulations and seek out assistance on both the institutional and department/school level in interpreting them. This is especially important in instances where the award

letter does not include the terms and conditions explicitly but only by reference. Meet with the institutional grants officer, who can explain institutional
policy and procedures as well as interpret any unfamiliar terms and conditions.
In addition, try to discover what services the department or school may already routinely provide. For example, many departments provide accounting
services or maintain a database of reporting requirements and will inform the
award recipient that budget categories require realignment or that a programmatic report is due in a month or two.

It is important to remember that, except in the case of fellowships or consulting agreements, awards are made to the institution on behalf of the project, and
the legal relationship is between the institution and the government. Therefore,
any modification to an award — programmatic, budgetary, or otherwise — must
be approved by the institution before the federal agency will consider the request. (Often, departmental or school approval is also required, but that is an
internal requirement and not a legal one.) For the same reason, title to equipment purchased with award funds legally resides in the institution.

The same is true of intellectual property rights — title to inventions is vested
in the institution, which assumes the responsibility to pursue patent protection and to market the invention. Copyright also resides in the institution, but
many institutions have adopted policies which in turn vest copyright in the author. A thorough discussion with the institutional grants and contracts officer
can review these and other issues. He or she can provide not only guidance on
the federal regulations but also information on the university's policies.

PROGRESS REPORTS

While regulations may vary somewhat from agency to agency, all impose regular financial and programmatic reporting requirements. Financial reporting
will be handled on a routine basis by the post-award accounting or sponsored
projects accounting office, but the responsibility for programmatic reporting is
the PI's alone. Some awards, primarily contracts and cooperative agreements,
require periodic reporting during the year, while others, primarily grants, request an annual progress report and require its submission before second- and
subsequent-year funding can be made available.

CONCLUSION

The competition for federal funding is likely to escalate, especially as funding to universities and colleges by federal agencies continues to be viewed as
vulnerable by those in Congress. Meanwhile, pressure from within the insti-

tution to secure outside funding for research, curriculum, and outreach programs is likely to continue as the costs of education and research continue to increase. Likewise, individuals will continue to feel pressures to receive funding and publish research results as publication records and grantsmanship are used as evaluation criteria in promotion and tenure cases.

There are, unfortunately, no simple solutions and no magic bullets to ensure successful federal grantsmanship. Even a solid, well-written, and well-presented proposal that matches the needs of the agency to which it is submitted is no guarantee of success. Keep in mind that a rejected proposal is not a dead proposal. Rework and resubmit. Most proposals are not funded the first time around. Once funded, successful completion of the proposed project and prudent stewardship of the funds is essential, although neither will ensure a successful competitive renewal. My hope is that combining your innovative and creative ideas with the information and suggestions contained here will result in a highly competitive proposal and provide the funding you need to meet your research and teaching goals.

NOTES

1. B. Rensberger, "Era of Transition: Successful Science, Troubled Scientists," *Journal of NIH Research* 6 (August 1994): 29.
2. Washington: Office of Science and Technology, August 1994.
3. Ibid., 19.
4. PHS Grants/Policy Statement (Rockville, Md.: Public Health Service, 1990), 2-2.
5. Ibid., 2-1.
6. See http://www.nsf.gov/funding/.
7. See http://nihroadmap.nih.gov/.
8. See http://www.grants.gov/. Then search for science and technology grants and from there access the AFOSR home page.
9. Search for "career development" at http://nihroadmap.nih.gov/.

24.

NEW ACADEMICS AND THE QUEST FOR PRIVATE FUNDS

FRED E. CROSSLAND

One of the more difficult problems facing first-time faculty members is finding financial support for research. Academic promotion, tenure, and enhanced professional reputation ordinarily are based on the quality and quantity of published scholarship, so support for research is critical. Since it is virtually impossible for young assistant professors to finance their own projects, they will have to turn elsewhere for funds. Three of the most common sources include:

1. *The institution where you are employed.* A relatively modest sum may be available for faculty research projects, but there is likely to be keen competition for these funds, and staff newcomers may be at a disadvantage.

2. *Public sources.* Scores of federal agencies underwrite research requiring the expertise of virtually all academic disciplines in one way or another. State governments — and to a much lesser degree, local governments — also occasionally subsidize specialized research by higher education faculty.

3. *Private sources.* Possibilities include the following:

a. *Individuals.* This is rather unusual, but not unheard of.

b. *Corporations.* Ordinarily they are interested in research directly related to their products or services.

c. *Special-purpose, nonprofit agencies.* Often bearing the title of "foundation," these include medical research entities, religious organizations, charitable societies, trade associations, and lobbying groups. Almost all have sharply focused program interests.

d. *Broad-based philanthropies or foundations conducting regular, ongoing grant programs.* For the most part, the discussion in this essay will be limited to funders of this type.

COPING WITH DIVERSITY

It is important to note the tremendous diversity that characterizes both higher education and private philanthropy in the United States. For each generalization about them there are uncounted exceptions, so in your quest for funds you must be sensitive to the differences and be flexible.

There are roughly 3,900 degree-granting colleges and universities employing about 900,000 faculty members in the United States. These institutions are public and private, large and small, serve distinctive purposes, attract markedly different student bodies and staff, and hence do not present the same research opportunities and do not have the same expectations regarding faculty research. More than 1,500 of these institutions are public two-year community colleges; typically, they are service- and career-oriented, with strong local identification. Another 800 are private, four-year, liberal arts colleges; emphasis here tends to be on teaching and individualized service to students. Perhaps 100 or so higher education institutions may properly be designated as major research universities; these include both public and private schools offering graduate and professional programs, with faculty expected to conduct sophisticated and original research in appropriate disciplines.

Faculty members from all these types of colleges and universities very likely will be seeking some sort of external support for some sort of project or activity from some sort of private funder. So you can be sure of three things: first, that the field of applicants will be both large and diverse; second, that requests will far exceed available resources; and third, that grant rejections will far exceed approvals.

American philanthropy is at least as diverse—in its forms, purposes, and procedures—as American higher education. One form is the private foundation. In 2005 there were more than 68,000 of them operating in the United States, and their total grant awards come to $33.6 billion. Although the combined value of their assets exceeds $510 billion, the holdings of individual organizations run from less than $10,000 to more than $29 billion at the Gates Foundation.

Only about 22,000—almost a third of the 68,000 grantmakers—actually have assets exceeding $1 million and award more than $100,000 annually. The overwhelming majority are quite small, essentially family-run philanthropies with sharply limited program interests that operate rather informally without professional staff. Others are, in effect, the philanthropic arms of corporations; they vary considerably in size, purpose, and independence from their corporate parents. In fact, relatively few foundations—regardless of their size, stated purpose, or financial origins — are truly free and independent of control by the individual, family, or corporation that established them.

Parenthetically, you also should be aware that the designation "foundation," used to describe organizations with charitable purposes, is also used by groups that are actually grant-seekers rather than grantmakers. Such fund-raising organizations are not included in the twenty-two thousand figure noted above.

All grantmakers find it necessary to restrict their program interests. Many have self-imposed geographical limitations. Others may support only certain religious groups, research relating to a particular disease, projects dealing with specific social or economic problems, or members of certain groups in society. Only a handful of the largest grantmakers could appropriately be called "general purpose foundations," but even they can't cover all possible fields of interest.

Almost certainly there are no more than fifty private foundations that have assets of more than $100 million, annually award $5 million or more in grants, have reasonably broad objectives, operate on the national scene, have full-time professional staffs, and evince interest in higher education activities. Even among these few large private foundations, most grant dollars are awarded to colleges and universities for general institutional support, endowment, facilities and equipment, or student assistance rather than to individual faculty research projects.

Moreover, even among the very few large philanthropies willing to consider seriously requests of the latter type, several limitations are often applied. For example, foundations usually emphasize "practical" research likely to lead to early, demonstrable results. Most of the large, professionally staffed philanthropies do not perceive themselves to be "charities" doling out dollars to the worthy or needy but organizations "investing" in ideas, projects, and people that hold promise of finding solutions to specific problems.

Among the larger and better-known foundations meeting many of the criteria set forth in the preceding paragraphs are the following: Carnegie, Danforth, Exxon, Ford, Hewlett, Robert Wood Johnson, Kellogg, Kresge, Lilly, MacArthur, Mellon, Pew, Rockefeller, and Sloan. Some are relative newcomers to the philanthropic scene; some have demonstrated interest only in specialized areas or problems of higher education; some were active in the national arena thirty or forty years ago and subsequently became more local in orientation; some are relatively passive bankrollers, while others clearly are activists; some could appropriately be labeled liberal and others clearly are conservative.

As a group, these few large organizations continue to exert considerable influence on both the philanthropic community and higher education, and it would be wise for you, as a new faculty member, to learn more about them. It is not likely, however, that you personally will have direct contact with these foundations during your early years in academe; initially, you probably will be seeking support from smaller, local, less well-known potential funders.

To find out about these, large and small, there are certain resources to which you can turn. The most important and useful is the Foundation Center, located at 79 Fifth Avenue, New York, New York 10003. Established and supported by foundations and corporate grantmakers, it is the primary source of public information about private foundations. Through its Web site (http://fdncenter.org) the Foundation Center provides a range of services, courses, and tutorials on seeking foundation support. For graduated costs, you can also subscribe to Foundation Directory Online for different levels of access to the center's massive database.

There is also a Council on Foundations, but it resembles a trade association for grantmakers and does not purport to be a public information agency. Rather, it seeks to advance professionalism within its ranks, to encourage better management of foundations and their resources, and to keep an eye on federal and state legislation likely to have bearing on philanthropic activities.

Given the diversity and complexity of the funders' landscape, no wonder most new academics are intimidated and despair of ever mastering the so-called art of grantsmanship. In fact, many resources will be available to you, but you will be trying to find a productive match between your interests, talents, and concerns and those of a potential funder. This is not easy to achieve, but several simple and practical steps can be taken to increase the likelihood of finding that ideal match. The suggestions offered below should be helpful as you make your first moves into the foundation community.

TAKING THOSE IMPORTANT PRELIMINARY STEPS

The essential starting point is this: be confident that you really do have something to offer—a *new* idea, a *different* approach, a *distinctive* solution to a *significant* problem, the *time, talent,* and *energy* to get the job done, and the *qualifications* (if a fellowship competition). This is no time for either false modesty or an overly inflated ego. Be realistic, and always remember that you must have something to offer that is truly worthy of support.

To be sure you meet this essential first criterion, check with others in your discipline, in your professional associations, in neighboring institutions. Know what they are doing. Know what else has been tried, has succeeded, has failed. Read your journals and keep up to date. Don't reinvent the wheel. Don't automatically dismiss the possibility of collaborating with others in developing and carrying out your project. Since it is still early in your career, consider playing the role of junior investigator in a joint proposal. It may provide exactly the sort of experience and visibility you need.

It is extremely important for you to check with colleagues in your own academic department and with administrators in your institution before you start seeking outside funds. There will probably be established procedures that you are expected to follow, and certain clearances may be required. Check them out, for they vary considerably from one campus to another. Also remember that it is unwise to spring surprises on your department chair or senior faculty colleagues. At some crucial time, you may need them for references, advice, or assistance.

Even at this early stage, it is useful to put your ideas on paper. Preparation of a draft proposal (with a fair amount of detail, a projected time frame, and an estimated budget) will help clarify in your own mind what you hope to achieve and how you would go about it. This draft will probably be for your eyes only, but it would not be amiss to test it out with colleagues who have your full respect and confidence. Weigh their advice judiciously and remember that as successful grant-seekers themselves they may be an invaluable source of promising leads.

DECIDING WHERE TO APPLY

Now it is time to take an initial survey of possible private funding sources. First, sit down with the key people in your institution's development office. Their advice and help may be crucial. After all, the overwhelming majority of grants are made to *institutions*, not individual faculty members. Universities receive the funds, account for them, and accept responsibility for funded activities. In deciding where to apply, and in all subsequent steps in the funding quest, it is important for you to go through institutional channels. The foundation field initially will appear discouragingly large, but almost certainly there are only a very few realistic possibilities for your specific project or proposal. Your institution's library undoubtedly has reference books and directories with pertinent information, and they should be consulted. In several locations in the United States there are centers where data about foundations are kept on file. A visit is best, but you can get some help by mail or telephone. Your local research development office probably has copies of recent annual reports, lists of program priorities and interests, and grant application guidelines issued by several of the larger foundations. With advice from the local fund-raising staff and others, try to reduce the field of potential funders to no more than a half dozen of the most promising.

In this winnowing process, by no means limit your consideration to the well-known, big-name, national, or wealthiest philanthropies. The important thing to remember is that you are trying to find a match. If by some chance your research project happens to have a local or regional focus, you will probably be much better off seeking support from a local or regional foundation, even if it happens to have only modest resources. Generally speaking, if you are a young faculty member with limited foundation contacts and if your proposal clearly falls within its range of program interests, it may be easier for you to get the attention of a smaller funding agency. In any event and regardless of where you apply, you certainly will be better off if your proposal does not attempt to be global but focuses on something carefully defined and limited, and hence more likely to be accomplished. With that limited definition and focus in mind, look for foundations—large or small, near or far, specialized or general purpose, corporate or otherwise—with a similar program focus.

Once you have reduced the field, it is time to review your draft proposal in light of the programs and procedures of the funders you have identified. Consult the professionals in your development office or office of research support. Consider modifying your draft, taking into account specific funder interests. Perhaps one foundation would be interested in only a part of your proposal; perhaps another with somewhat different concerns would be responsive to a different aspect of your project. Don't hesitate to adapt to donor priorities so long as you keep clearly in mind, and do not distort, your own basic objectives. Getting the grant is not an end in itself; it is merely the means for achieving your project.

Look further into the foundations you have identified and feel comfortable and confident in dealing with. If you know someone on the staff of a potential funder on your list, place a telephone call asking for advice on next steps. This would not be out of order, but don't ask for or expect a definitive judgment about funding prospects for your draft proposal; that question would be premature and possibly counterproductive.

If you know someone who recently received a grant from one of the foundations you have identified, you might call that person for advice on how to proceed. Do not be disappointed if the help you receive is minimal. Remember that competition for grants is keen and many who have been successful may be reluctant to share their secrets. But don't be afraid to ask.

If the printed materials you have reviewed about a particular foundation do not appear to be adequate or are out of date, write a brief letter on institutional stationery requesting more current information—new guidelines for grant applications, a list of program interests, the latest annual report. At this juncture there is no point in providing any details about the project or proposal you may have in mind or are developing. The nature of the response you receive may give you some clues about your prospects. The likelihood is, however, that you will receive very general information, much of it couched in the vaguest of terms and seemingly designed to discourage potential applicants. Be realistic, but don't be put off too easily.

Now you should begin to prepare a final draft (or drafts) of your proposal, basing it on the information and advice you have received from several sources. Depending on circumstances and the advice of your local funding experts, it may be decided that your proposal should be submitted to more than one foundation. You may do that simultaneously, or perhaps serially if at first you don't succeed. In any event, do not send photocopies of a single proposal to all potential funders. Certain elements of it should be included in every version of your proposal, but it is wise to prepare an individually tailored document for each foundation you plan to approach.

MAKING APPLICATION FOR A GRANT

Now you should be ready to approach a foundation directly with a specific grant request. Check first with your local research development office. Do you visit, write, or telephone? It depends. Foundations are often quite explicit on such matters, and it is best to follow their advice. Much depends, of course, on the specific nature and policy of the funders you hope to contact. Most of the smaller ones (for example, family foundations, modest community foundations, and the like) are little more than mail drops, have no full-time professional staff, and meet only infrequently (usually with outside consultants and advisers) to review requests and make decisions. Many of the corporate foundations operate along similar lines. Often there simply is no one to visit and no one to talk to on the telephone. You have no option but to resort to the mails.

The large, well-known, professionally staffed philanthropies usually present different possibilities for a new faculty member hoping to make initial personal contacts. By no means, however, should a grant hopeful appear at a foundation office without a scheduled appointment. Sometimes foundation staff members will agree to a meeting set for a predetermined day and time, but in almost all instances a personal visit by a petitioner to make a grant request will prove to be of little value.

A telephone inquiry—assuming it deals with substance and is not merely a request for an appointment—also is not likely to provide any satisfaction for the applicant. Almost certainly, the young faculty member's first contact with private funders will be through the mails.

Unlike most public funding programs that have prescribed (and often long, complicated, and detailed) application forms, virtually all private foundations suggest that you initiate your request by sending them a one-page letter setting forth briefly and informally what you hope to do and why. In this fashion the potential funder can quickly screen out the bulk of unsolicited inquiries.

If the one-pager does happen to generate foundation curiosity, the petitioner will be asked to provide more information, perhaps to submit a formal proposal along certain specified lines, or may even be asked to visit or be visited. Positive initial responses, however, are rare, and disappointed grant-seekers almost always—and too often with good reason—are certain their one-pagers were never carefully read or seriously considered.

What goes into that first piece of mail to a foundation? If a one-pager is asked for, that is what should be sent. But in most cases it would be quite acceptable to enclose with it a copy of your proposal (it would be wise at this stage to mark it "draft"), tailored to that foundation's programs and priorities.

The one-page covering letter obviously must be brief and should present a summary of the proposal, highlighting (1) the problem you hope to address, (2) what you propose to do, (3) why you are qualified to do it, (4) how long it will take you, (5) how your effort could be evaluated after the fact, (6) how much the total effort will cost, and (7) how much support you are seeking. It is difficult to compose such a letter within this space constraint. You would be well advised to check very carefully for grammatical and factual accuracy, write very lean prose, avoid hyperbole, keep adverbs and adjectives to a minimum, and resist all temptations to butter up the addressee or the foundation. An effective letter, in this instance, is one that commands the respect of the reader and arouses sufficient interest to persuade the recipient actually to read the draft proposal you enclosed with it.

Institutional policy at your college or university, as well as the specific nature and scope of your project, will have a significant bearing on the content and style of your one-page letter and on the form and substance of your proposal. For example, the letter may have to be signed by the institution's president, some other senior academic administrator, or perhaps a representative of your local research development office. In any event, you will have to provide the basic information to be included in the letter, and probably you will be asked to draft it.

If your proposed project requires the use of institutional facilities or personnel, there may be certain direct charges or overhead considerations that will have to be included in your budget. Again this point must be emphasized: as a faculty member—and especially as a new and junior member of the staff—you must touch base with the appropriate people at your institution *before* knocking on foundation doors. Almost always, if a grant indeed is awarded in support of your project, it will be to your college or university, not to you personally.

Furthermore, your requests to specific potential funders quite properly must be set in institutional perspective. It is almost always counterproductive when several unrelated proposals from a single college or university descend simultaneously on a foundation, especially a smaller one, thus forcing the latter to ascertain what may or may not be considered important by that school. Coordination of fund-raising efforts is essential. Your campus should have established its own priorities, and you will be expected to accommodate yourself to them.

PROCESS, PATIENCE, AND PROSPECTS

No two foundations operate exactly the same way. Some will acknowledge receipt of your proposal immediately but say nothing of substance. Others will send you a rejection form letter by return mail. From still others you may hear nothing at all. If your proposal does strike a responsive chord, however faint, you may be asked to provide more information, clarify a point or two, defend your research design, or consider certain modifications. Such responses are encouraging, of course, but they are no guarantee of a positive final decision.

Since each foundation conducts its own business in its own way, you should anticipate great differences in decision-making procedures. As a general rule, your proposal will go through several screening steps (assuming it is not simply turned down out of hand); the number will depend upon the size and bureaucratic style of the particular foundation. If the proposal survives the winnowing process—which unfortunately may take several months and many reworkings of your draft—ultimately it will require approval by the foundation's governing board. This process cannot be hurried. Board meetings are infrequent and scheduled far in advance. If you push for an early and probably premature decision, it almost always will be "no." Even junior foundation staff members usually can reject a proposal; only the board (or in some cases the president) can say "yes."

If your proposal receives serious consideration, you can expect to engage in some negotiations with the potential funder. Rarely are projects funded exactly as originally submitted. Discussions may involve almost any aspect of your proposal. If you are dealing with experienced professionals at the funding agency, their advice and counsel may be very helpful. In any event, you would be well advised to be attentive, flexible, reasonable, and articulate in stating your positions, without compromising the essential elements of your proposal.

Unfortunately, the odds are that your requests for foundation support will be rejected. This should not be taken personally. The supply of philanthropic dollars always is exceeded by the demands of petitioners. Most likely, your turndown will come very early in the screening process, and most likely no significant substantive reason for the rejection will be given. You will find this frustrating, but you should resist the temptation to engage the foundation in debate. It is an argument you cannot win. It would be wiser to send a polite acknowledgment thanking the foundation and its staff for its consideration of your proposal. If you believe that no satisfactory reason has been given for the rejection, you might ask for additional information to enable you to do better next time. But don't be too optimistic about receiving a response; most foundation staff members are busy and don't encourage pen pals.

If you are among the fortunate few who do receive foundation support, there are several considerations to keep in mind. *This is important*: Read carefully all the terms and conditions of the grant letter. Perhaps interim and final narrative and financial reports are required. Check with the appropriate officials at your institution about the financial administration of the grant and reporting responsibilities and procedures. In many respects, a grant resembles a contract; you have certain obligations, and failure to carry them out will jeopardize any future proposals you may hope to submit.

Finally, here are three points to ponder. First, notwithstanding several observations made above, seeking a grant from private sources is neither a game nor a contest. It is a serious endeavor, to be sure, but grantor and grantee should not adopt adversarial postures. Ideally, they both must recognize that they are (or should be) partners seeking to achieve a common goal. If the process degenerates into a battle of wits, there likely will be no winners.

Second, there may well be a widespread sentiment in academic circles that foundations are insensitive, unresponsive, and given to making unwise and capricious decisions. These sentiments, although based largely on personal disappointments, may not be entirely incorrect. But the fact remains that private philanthropy has been and probably will continue to be a powerful and salutary force in American society generally, and in higher education particularly. You should not be blinded to the larger goals and accomplishments of foundations simply because you were not successful in gaining their support last time around. Of course, foundation personnel are not infallible, but they are not necessarily rascals either.

And third, do not be easily discouraged. As you embark on an academic career, there will be much to learn, important personal and professional contacts to be made, and ever-expanding opportunities to contribute to your discipline and to increased public understanding of it and its potentials. In your early years as a faculty member, patience will be both a virtue and a necessity. And in your quest for foundation dollars, the first grant very likely will be the most difficult to secure. It never will be easy, but then few things of lasting value merit that designation. May you have good fortune in your quest. And more importantly, may you deserve good fortune.

PART VI

PUBLISHING RESEARCH

So you've gotten the coveted academic position, secured a foundation grant, and completed your research; another hurdle now appears, the mysterious and foreboding prospect of publishing your results. As many of the contributors to this volume emphasize, the publication of research is at the very core of academic existence. The aged exhortation to publish or perish is cited on more than one occasion. To this extent, of course, our authors may be reflecting, albeit subconsciously, their own careers in primarily research-oriented institutions. Certainly the pressures to publish vary widely across the academic landscape, but just as certainly the fundamental stages and procedures of publishing are reasonably standard across disciplines. The four essays that follow attempt to chart those stages and define the procedures.

Although each of the essays addresses a particular aspect of publishing, from articles to books, from matters of style to questions of content, from traditional print media to newer electronic ones, all agree that the quality of scholarship, not its quantity, is the most important desideratum. And while each author has spoken to the obvious relations between publishing and making it through an impending tenure decision, all again agree that worthy scholarship that is well received by the profession at large and contributes significantly to the knowledge or thinking of a particular field is an end in itself. One might say, in fact, that it is *the* end of academic life, for the effective communication of the results of research brings scholar, student, professional peers, and lay community into intelligent and fruitful dialogue. In so doing, publication of any sort could be seen as the fulfillment of the academic mission.

Of course, not any sort of publishing is what you wish to do. Whether consciously or unconsciously, your reading in professional journals and books has already influenced your own scholarly aspirations. But how, other than being the best scholar-author you can be, do you set about fulfilling those aspirations? The suggestions that follow — how to select an appropriate journal or press, how to prepare and send off a manuscript, how to endure the sometimes lengthy review process — are designed to help alleviate some of the normal anxieties and to present a clearer picture of how publication really works.

Our authors provide unique perspectives on the field of publication as a whole. Louis J. Budd speaks here largely from his experience as editor of a distinguished humanities journal. Boyd R. Strain writes mainly from the perspective of an author, in particular a distinguished scientist. Cathy N. Davidson and Ken Wissoker offer an overview of the process by which a manuscript becomes an actual book and a general sense of the different kinds of publishers available. Deborah Jakubs and Paul Conway write from the vantage of administrators of a major research library, who are primarily concerned with how research gets disseminated, however its results are "published," to the academic public at large. In their essay, in particular, we see something of the opportunities and challenges that you will certainly face in the near future as online systems and international electronic networks change forever the nature of academic research.

25

ON WRITING SCHOLARLY ARTICLES

LOUIS J. BUDD

I will cheerfully admit to a squinting view because I am mostly going to discuss pitfalls, but the writing up of original research or new insights into a text or fundamental theory does bring deep satisfactions, and I intend finally to sound not only helpful but upbeat. I certainly intend to encourage beginners, if only for the sake of their professional self-development, which should include humility. Too many recently appointed instructors who grade undergraduate term papers tyrannically have never run the gauntlet of their peers, have in fact not subjected their own work to criticism since they finished graduate studies.

I also admit to a hope that nobody will follow my advice blindly. In dealing with editors and, through them, with usually anonymous but very human referees, authors should trust their own reasoned sense of how they would behave from the other side of the transaction. Too many beginners listen gullibly to somebody who, elated by an acceptance (maybe a scratch single or even a bunt), is hot to explain the trick of hitting a home run every time at bat. The accomplished scholars who have offered advice on how to get an article published don't bother with the tactics of outwitting editors. They know that a veteran editor, like a weathered traffic cop or a ticket-taker at the Super Bowl, has already seen most dodges many times.

PREPARING A MANUSCRIPT

Although my details and examples draw on the field of literature, I believe that my advice applies more generally, for the humanities anyway. Experienced critics and scholars from many fields will agree on basic principles about content and style. First, and perhaps surprisingly, they will say: submit one article at a time. A common mistake is to add a loosely related but revealingly detachable section to an already substantial manuscript (which perhaps compresses a Ph.D. dissertation). Likewise, too many manuscripts include tangential mini-essays disguised as footnotes and endnotes. As a mechanical but generally sound rule: if a comment longer than two or three (brief!) sentences does not rate promotion to the main text, it is probably dispensable. In any case, most readers will pay little attention to long notes unless to decide that the article looks too heavy for mental transport. A corollary rule is to avoid inflating notes with information that is just marginally relevant but is "new," that is, supplies a lost fact or obscure linkage that happened to resurface along the research way. A scholarly article is not a personal essay (which is still harder to do success-fully) or a bet-you-didn't-know kind of chat.

Another overdone feature of the notes is the phrase—literal or implied— that announces "on the other hand," and even "on the other, other hand," sug-gesting a scholarly octopus. I don't mean to grow supercilious. Sometimes the notes poll a mob of quarreling predecessors because the author wants to ac-knowledge all debts or, more anxiously, to avoid any hint of plagiarism. But I'm simpleminded enough to believe that anyone at the undergraduate level or above who is trying to operate honestly will refer here and there to the main sources being used and so has nothing to fear. I also believe that plagiarists know exactly what they are up to, no matter how skillfully they play the part of shocked innocence later. And I am content to believe that plagiarism, once published, is always spotted, that the diligent, bleary-eyed scholars who cover out-of-the-way journals will remember where they had already seen some pas-sage. As for deliberately twisting or even just bending the documentary sources to make a believable case, the *Chronicle of Higher Education* regularly features reports on how the academy deals with this cardinal offense.

The converse of the principles of relevance and unity is to have enough genu-inely fresh and up-to-date material for the article. The starting Ph.D. is usually assigned a substantial load of students (and, these days, feels lucky to get it). By the time an article gets into the mail, four or six years (surprisingly) may have elapsed since the last careful search of the bibliographies for a dissertation. Referees comment regularly on a lost block of years in the citations. My point here is not to spread nervousness about getting "scooped." That very seldom happens, in fact. But other scholars and critics are, happily for them, working away and, happily for us, do keep adding insights and facts useful for our own immediate project.

As for enough fresh material, some of the submissions to every journal are dangerously inflated, ready to explode. No doubt, as rumor has it, a harried committee on tenure may be tempted to measure by quantity rather than bril-liance. In the humanities, a new idea takes much explaining and defending, and

I don't know of any major scholar-critic whose reputation grew out of a one-line equation. But that fact doesn't translate logically or practically into the law that the longer, the better. Most journals give a section over to notes, and that's respectable housing too, more impressive than a note that tries to last as long as a sonata by sounding all imaginable variations or by claiming cosmic reverberations for a down-home fact. But, to follow my own precept here, I now drop this point.

Two narrower matters also concern content rather than form. First, although wit and eloquence ordinarily give pleasure, titles of articles should be not only as short as functionally possible but so descriptive as to make sure that the reader starts out right. Incidently, punning, ironic, allusive, or otherwise elusive titles can get an essay lost in bibliographies that are coming to depend on key-words for sorting more items than any employee or committee of volunteers can scan closely. Second, and increasingly important as long-range editing projects reach their multivolume goal, a would-be scholar must use the most dependable text for primary sources. Citing *The Scarlet Letter* from an anthology or a cheap paperback rather than the centenary edition shakes the faith of better-informed readers in a scholar's alertness. Or, to argue positively, finding and using the most authoritative text "expresses a simple preference for quality."[1]

Forty or fifty years ago, perhaps as a way of striving toward the prestige of the sciences, it was still common to counsel scholars in the humanities to aim for a no-frills, objective style. The classic statement, itself enlivened by irony, came from a distinguished researcher and editor:

> We ought, I think, at the start to realize that no reader whom we are likely to have will be nearly as much interested in our views or discoveries as we ourselves are. Most of them will be people who are a little tired, a little bored, and who read us rather out of a sense of duty and a wish to keep up with what is being done than because they have any real interest in the subject; in return for our reader's complaisance it is our duty as well as our interest to put what we have to say before him with as little trouble to him as possible. It is our duty because we ought to be kind to our fellow creature; it is to our interest because if the view that we wish to put before him is clearly and competently expressed, so that he understands without trouble what we are trying to say, he will be gratified at the smooth working of his own intelligence and will inevitably think better of our theory and of its author than if he had had to puzzle himself over what we mean and then in the end doubt whether he had really understood us, so raising in himself an uneasy doubt whether his brains are quite what they used to be![2]

This statement proceeds to a set of commandments (no. 7: "Do not try to be humorous") that are still useful to consider although, in practice, editorial boards will grumble about a conspicuous lack of color or verve. The basic wisdom here may be double: authors have to depend on their own judgment, taste, and goals while expecting the usual human variability of response from readers as well as an editor, the immediate lion in the path.

Beyond generalities and tips on niceties of detail, nobody can explain how to compose a publishable article, although a senior scholar-critic came close several years ago, after warning that "there is no formula."[3] Most cogent of all is his rule that beginners "assume too little and tell too much" and his advice that rather than worry that somebody may have scooped them, they should think in terms of joining a "dialogue" about their subject. My own gloss on that latter point warns against quickness to scold someone known only as a signature to published work. The young scholar may eventually meet that victim with embarrassment and, in some instances, with a blocked chance for interplay. The wisdom of diplomacy aside, none of us should cry up our own originality by running down predecessors. Indeed, we should blow the annunciatory trumpet lightly, if at all. The experts, our key audience, know what's already in print, and the other readers will infer that the fact of publication certifies some degree of firstness. As a related misstep, beginners are too quick to conduct a census of the relevant bibliography in the opening paragraph or first note. The expert audience knows all that, and the cogency and balance of any article should quietly testify throughout to mastery of the recorded scholarship.

Two other tangential issues on content. First, the "most consistent reaction" of editorial boards is to call for "substantial cuts."[4] This call is not made automatically and should not be anticipated by the tactic of submitting forty pages while expecting to come down to twenty-five. Editing a journal uses a more direct approach than selling used cars, and we all need to stay aware that wordiness and overkill are standard mistakes. Second, my decades (I'm sorry to be able to say) of scanning journals in my field lead to advice against invoking the latest innovators of theory; the pollster would discount their eminence for the recency effect. An idea is sound not because a sage said so but because our minds accept it. Though we want to give credit where due, our readers will sense the difference between integrity and the urge to flaunt some name; especially glaring are those notes that conduct a minicourse in trendy wisdom. The guru-worshipping article will sound outdated sooner even than young scholars will hear a new instructor addressing them as "sir" or "ma'am."

The job-seeking ABD may wonder if a term paper is publishable right off. While real-life cases answer "Yes," one accomplished veteran, putting himself on the schedule of the seminar he was directing, found that he could not create a mailable article from scratch. Besides the pressure of time, it is most unlikely that a paper shaped for a seminar of one's peers or just its ayatollah will suit the editors as well as the format of some journal or — far more fundamental — will have squarely matched the gestalt of standards, tone, and niceties currently favored by the subprofession involved. Another veteran warns both young and old: "Resist the desire" to mail out an article "right away. After a week or two much which looked like very oak may well turn out to be slash pine instead."[5] To be sure, the job market pushes even ABDs into print, but if they recognize the underlying dilemma, they may decide more shrewdly: the home department often prefers speed and quantity, while out in the profession and for the long run, quality counts much more. In any case, no pressure for speed can excuse a submission that carries half-erased, term-paper stigmata such as the professor's red pencilings.

The fresh-minted Ph.D. may have to decide whether to aim for a book from the dissertation or to mine a few chapters. Again, the answer will differ from campus to campus. Where quick results are needed, it's not likely that a single article can condense a dissertation yet hold to an acceptable length, which very definitely includes the notes. It's plain improbable that any single chapter as once written will make a successful article; it will have to be reworked to look and sound freestanding. Then, like a revamped term paper or, indeed, any manuscript, it needs a critique from a tough-minded, candid friend. The editorial board can get still tougher, though not because the author is a beginner. In spite of rumors of cronyism, referees and editors can come down hardest on their peers who "ought to know better by now."

SUBMITTING THE ARTICLE

After the pressures and anxieties of getting an article ready, the author should stay keyed up for the decision of where to submit it. In the field of literature the MLA *Directory of Periodicals* can help you choose among scores of possibilities; for example, some journals refuse to consider a note-length item whereas others especially welcome it. Here and elsewhere, common sense should make detailed advice superfluous. Choosing a journal that the author reads regularly should prevent an obvious misplacement.[6] Just leafing through several issues of a journal will reveal, for instance, that the *Sewanee Review* will "seldom publish analyses of single works (and never of short stories and poems)." *American Studies* warns that many manuscripts are rejected "not because of their quality but because they are too narrow for use: their authors seem unfamiliar with our editorial policies and the nature of our readers' interests." On the immediate level, someone who's been too busy getting through graduate school to feel surefooted among a forest of journals should consult an older colleague about the best matchup. In the longer run, of course, the would-be author has to keep up with the relevant journals and books to nurture a realistic sense of what is publishable and where.

To come back to the rumors of cronyism, I state flatly: it's worthwhile for anybody to try the most prestigious journals. As calm analysis shows, they publish many first-time authors. Money, furthermore, is not a problem; no journal in the humanities exacts a fee for submission or "page charges" for printing. (On the other hand, very few journals pay at all and none pay handsomely for either articles or book reviews; anybody needing immediate income will earn more by selling encyclopedias door to door.) In choosing the level to try, however, the author has to judge realistically whether the manuscript itself is major or minor, whether—to adapt Herman Melville—it deals with a whale or a flea. But what if the subject is so major that some desirable journal has lately carried two or three articles related to it? *American Studies* takes the trouble to assert: "Articles are accepted or rejected because of our perception of their worth, and not because we have run too few or too many on given subjects." To put the matter positively, some editors believe that their subscribers like a cluster of articles, particularly on a major subject.

About twenty years ago the younger cohort began pressing for anonymous submission. A few journals do now carefully hide the names of authors from the referees, but nobody has yet proved that such a policy raises the rate of acceptances for any group who consider themselves outsiders. Although *PMLA* had its first "all-female" issue in October 1984, its male editor doubted that anonymous submission made even part of the reason for that. Blind referencing (no slyness intended) has the possible virtue of letting the young or otherwise supposedly excluded feel less suspicious. Still, in considering where to submit an article, I would not use this policy as a criterion.

To put another increasingly live matter as negatively as possible, nobody should even contemplate making a double (or multiple!) submission. After growling that "we strongly resent" it, *American Studies* threatens that "our policy when we identify" it is to "notify the [would-be] contributor's academic dean or chairman," who will, I predict, side grimly with the editor. Of the double-dealers who pretend surprise that anybody could object, I merely ask that they inform all editors concerned. A problem more cheerful and even amusing to those who look up from the bottom rung is whether it's wise to appear in the same journal a second or third time. As a yuppie might ask, should we diversify our portfolios? If that journal has at least average standing, I would seize the day. In the long run the quality of the article counts much more than its former companions.

Although I am focusing on articles, the tenure-track scholar will wonder about their payoff relative to a book. Coffee-break wisdom used to make six (or whatever) "solid" articles equal to a solo in hardcovers, but I seldom hear any such formula lately. Now the grimmest sages warn, "Go only for a book!" That's dismaying to those who don't believe they have as yet developed a line of thought that deserves and will find such a berth. But only the very attractive departments can insist on so high a price for tenure.

A specialized anxiety asks, "How much does an edited book count?" Even a showily decisive umpire would have to answer, "That depends." Depends on the variety of editing and on the person counting. Mere compilation rates close to zero, while sophisticated handling of texts that pose intricate problems will impress anybody except the loftiest metatheorists (who could respond that a few textual enthusiasts deride analysis and speculation as ersatz whipped cream). In big-league calculation the ordinary textbook counts low and may even arouse scorn hiding envy of royalties. Getting back to articles, papers read at conferences may count much less with more dignity. However, if published later their tenure points will vary directly with the quality of the symposium and its publisher or the journal that prints it. As for the relative prestige of journals, there is probably measurable agreement among the members of any specialty.[7] But I grow uneasy as questions keep arising: "How's the Dow Jones on coauthors? on coeditors?" In such dogged calculating the figures can add up to a humanly wrong answer. I am idealistic enough to predict that young Ph.D.'s will find the most satisfaction — and material success, quite possibly — by following their own personal and professional common sense.

For nitty-gritty details, the ideal is professionalism without bells and whistles. Because any would-be contributor to an established journal is bucking the odds, having all zippers secure can help in borderline decisions. For example, since editors do retire eventually or just choose another incarnation, an author should check the latest masthead before addressing a cover letter. The target journal will state or show what system of documentation it follows although most editors waive such criteria until acceptance is likely.[8] While neatness is desirable, editors understand that revisions to achieve precision will slip errors past the tiring author who has almost memorized the text. Sending a neat, clean copy tends to reassure all concerned and pleases the copy editor when the transaction gets that far. Word processor texts have graduated to full respectability and rate as the natural format among those who have played with computers since kindergarten. Whatever the technology of the printout (or disk), I can't imagine the day when editors won't want everything double-spaced. Everything, even the block quotations? Yes, everything! While as dazzled as anybody by electronic agility, editors also want the manuscript printed on one side of the sheet only. The savings will come in their bill for over-the-counter drugs.

Shifting to don'ts for emphasis, I repeat that an author merely wastes time by playing games with an experienced editor who long ago saw, for example, the trick of hiding length with margins so narrow that the copy editor will have to sit sideways to use them. Authors should not devise a table or diagram without realizing that it means added expense—higher than they're likely to estimate—for any journal. They are probably wiser to draw the diagram verbally or to tell readers where to find a painting already reproduced elsewhere. But I don't mean to make authors approach the editor on their knees. Publish or perish applies to a journal too, and it depends on volunteered articles. Furthermore, editors are just as upward-striving as the most ambitious author and will tolerate many annoyances in order to produce a better issue. Nevertheless, editing a journal entails borderline choices, just like shopping for tomatoes or selecting a patient for an artificial heart. In a few cases the editor has to decide irritably, at midnight, whether some article is worth all the niggling labor needed to tidy it up.

Editors, I must confess, tend to grin wryly over many a letter of inquiry. Too often it betrays that the writer has not bothered to read the journal or even the inside cover. Sometimes it tries for an advance commitment, which no editor of a refereed journal would dare to make; the only immediately definite answer can be "No." An offer of a rough draft is only slightly more welcome than a letter bomb. Offers of a sprawling manuscript that the editor would be free to trim are welcome only if signed by either Thomas or Tom Wolfe. An admirably scrupulous author may wonder if a seminar paper must confess that it was lately waxed and buffed into an article. I see no obligation or hope of benefit for doing that.

Editors, I confess further, laugh out loud at a few covering letters for the manuscript. Since one veteran flatly warns that the letter can do more harm than good, the safest tactic is to keep it short and of course mildly sweet. Editors do understand why an author might expect them to want a brief autobiography, a list of medals, or even a cv, but their minds fasten on the self-contained manuscript. Its author can raise distracting hackles by quoting Professor Goodheart's praises, by pressing for a quick answer (through being jumped to the head of the queue), by threatening double-submission (if the wait for response grows "excessive"), or by puffing the article as the chapter of a soon to materialize book. Ironically, journals with a high rate of rejection judge that they serve the profession best by not squandering their pages on an article scheduled soon for hard covers.

Three do's for a covering letter, the first to the author's benefit alone. It should explicitly ask for any criticism the editor can find time to transmit. Having felt the sting of rejection themselves, editors tend to filter out the harsher commentary from the referees, and to transmit all of it only when urged. I'm not preaching masochism, but in order to revise effectively the author needs the frankest critiques. A second positive feature for a covering letter is to show, where necessary, alertness to problems of quoting restricted materials. Although the author will have to accept the legal responsibility in writing, journals balk at any chance of getting drawn into litigation over copyright. Therefore, authors must remember to honor those forms that a repository of manuscripts presents for signature at the door. The tenured cohort will line up against a colleague who breaks such a vow because the research library is their temple. Third, a covering letter should fit the particular addressee rather than revealing that it perhaps serves for a variety of journals.

WAITING FOR A RESPONSE

There's a relief when the article flies off in the mail along with, ominously, a stamped, self-addressed envelope. But after a well-run journal acknowledges safe arrival, the next problem sprouts: how to behave while the jury is out. Usually its verdict will take at least three months. After six months a simple inquiry, undisguised as a concern for the editor's happiness, is forgivable, although, ordinarily, some referee is the bottleneck. Phone calls can be annoying unless the editor happens to live inside the filing cabinet and has everything within reach. However long the delay, editors seldom bawl out a referee, who is by definition a busy scholar, and they cannot withhold a salary adjusted at zero.

But all sides deserve empathy. The author suffers with no assured date of relief and perhaps with a decision on tenure grinding toward its deadline. What about trying to withdraw the article and resubmit it elsewhere? I say "trying" because it is probably out in the pipeline and the editor can't recover it quickly. Another dilemma: to withdraw is to waste months of waiting, perhaps just a week short of a verdict. With most journals the sufferer will do best simply to meditate upon the relativity of emotional time. Or the action-oriented mind should draft another article. But what if the author tinkers meanwhile with the one creeping through the mail and discovers major flaws or just improvements? Should these be rushed off to the editor? Theoretically, perhaps. In practice, however, the ongoing round may as well finish up. The editor will feel delight, not chagrin, at learning that an article just accepted will upgrade itself. In the gloomy case, the author should feel that the particular journal has devoted as much effort as one article has a right to ask. In other words, if rejected the rebuilt manuscript should go elsewhere without an appeal.

RESPONDING TO THE RESPONSE

To take the darker but more likely result, a familiar envelope comes back eventually. Then, as Hyman Rodman asks, "What shall I do if my excellent article is (foolishly, mistakenly) rejected?" First, I remind myself that the odds were against me. Second, I remember that eminent scholars have confessed to having tried two or three or more journals before an acceptance. Editors presume that now and then an article has rebounded from another journal, and they have had many chances to marvel at conflicting judgments, even as they may believe the real blunders occur elsewhere. Because they trust the collective judgment of their own referees, they don't try to discover the previous travels of a manuscript. On the other hand, the author, who has no obligation to describe those travels, can consider it courteous rather than shrewd to remove any signs of a world tour, if only by running off the first page to match the next journal's format for titles and the name of a contributor.

The author who believes in an article (and therefore feels ethical in burdening unpaid referees) will keep resubmitting it elsewhere with deliberated speed until the criticism grows convincing. A cleverly sardonic letter of protest will change not a rendered verdict but the writer's reputation with the addressee. Anybody who asked to hear any and all criticism has implicitly promised to take it without a whimper. Likewise, demanding to know the identity of the mistaken referees is pointless. If the editor did not include that fact routinely, it's because referees have been promised or have requested anonymity to avoid a time-consuming and mostly futile debate. Another unwritten principle bars resubmitting even a basically improved article to the same journal. The absence of a specific invitation is in fact a genteel version of "Don't call us; we'll call you." Nevertheless, editors remain sincerely open to a different submission from any author who has behaved with at least minimal courtesy. I repeat: editors want good articles to accept. At their desk they don't see any humor in the gag: "Who won the beauty contest? Nobody."

So the author reenters the process of choosing a target, quicker this time perhaps. But not too quick! First, those causes for rejection must be considered — not supinely adopted, yet pondered, pondered. But perhaps not even that quick! One veteran challenges the author to achieve the discipline of rereading the article before taking in the letter of rejection.[9] Less heroically, I warn against assuming that the editor's report covered all the flaws. Now that time has distanced the article mentally, the author should struggle to judge it impersonally. If the criticisms still look wrong, then a qualified colleague could break the tie. But the votes must be counted honestly, not by a beginner who daydreams about proving to be the scholars' Billy Arnold or Francis Coppola. And the voters must be honest — not a Willie Loman desperate to be well liked nor a tweedy Boss Tweed.

Although that manila envelope eventually returns, sometimes it carries an acceptance. If it only breathes come-hitherness, how often did all the judges award a ten during the 1992 Olympics? A bill of revisions is an omen of eventual acceptance, especially if the author takes them up reflectively — not conforming humbly but not turning pigheaded either. Four more *don'ts*. First, a gullible author should not listen to the dopester's wisdom that suggestions for changes are just wordplay because editors want to flaunt their authority and will accept whatever comes back. Second, a weary author should not sag into simply correcting the article to mollify a superteacher. As I said, editors are delighted to let an article rise to greater excellence than they asked for. Third, the anxious author must not hurry just because the journal might fold or the editor might have a change of mind or scholarship might go out of fashion. So far only the first disaster has happened, rarely. Fourth, the triumphant author must not skimp when the call for rechecking of fact and style brings back the superbly crafted article too. Surprisingly many authors turn careless after the precision and effort needed to get that far. Errors have inevitably crept in between taking notes and polishing a typescript, and, fairly or not, readers will blame even the flagrant typos more on the author than on the editor.

Not all journals now incur the expenses of sending out a set of proofs. Authors lucky enough to get it should assume that it will contain typographical errors to be hunted down. They must prepare to hunt stoically also because some phrasings will cry out for improvement. But a subsidized journal cannot run up its bills to indulge the writer who didn't take the rechecking stage seriously. Any tinkerings with the proofs cost money. I'll always remember the request for very late changes if they "are not too much trouble for the printer." It visualizes an editor strolling to a ramshackle shop where an old-timer ("Doc" or "Pop") wearing a green eyeshade picks type out of a case and makes changes free of charge while chatting laconically. To steal from Mark Twain, I wish the world could be that young again. Changing "just one word" in a plate done through a computer may cost still more than casting and inserting a slug of linotype: an expert has to instruct a very expensive machine how to search its circuits while the savings promised by technology keep slipping away like a balanced federal budget. More generally it is helpful to remember that every journal has to stay within its income-plus-subsidy.

BREAKING INTO PRINT

But we do achieve some of our dreams. A copy of the glorious issue will turn up followed months later by offprints, either free of charge or else at cost. If at cost, how many to buy? or how many to photocopy? The answer could dodge behind another, embarrassing question: How many friends do you have? I have never managed to send out many more than thirty offprints to friends and fellow specialists. The proud author who waits for requests will save handsomely on postage.

Having joined the side of editors and publishing scholars, the author may even start thinking in terms of solidarity. In positive terms that includes urging overly modest colleagues or students to aim for the pleasures of breaking into print. However, true solidarity also forbids encouraging the unready as a way of building a local image for kindness. Every journal gets submissions that don't rate so high as amateurish. Whoever encouraged them should pray that the covering letter did not identify him or her. Only the rarest undergraduate paper deserves to travel beyond the campus. A teacher can lavish enough praise, greedy as we all are for it, without causing work and expense for a subsidized journal. Another path toward solidarity with the profession leads to giving a frank and prompt critique if a colleague asks — and seems able to accept it.

BOOK REVIEWING

My biggest surprise as managing editor of a quarterly has been the flow of offers to review books. Do journals welcome an unsolicited review? Categorically, no. Besides, because they receive their copies early, they have already lined up a reviewer. Is it worthwhile applying for a specific review? Though the answer should again be "no," editors are always looking for qualified recruits and may gamble on having allowed press agentry or having seconded a vendetta. Before applying, check to see whether the journal designates an editor especially for book reviews; also, consider that the few journals that give all their space to reviewing are more likely to need volunteers. More specifically, is it worthwhile to submit a curriculum vitae or a statement on areas of strength? That can often bring results. But — the most important question by far — is it worthwhile for an untenured academic to do any reviewing at all? That answer depends on the home department, which can range from beaming proudly at any sign of print to deducting points for popping small corn. Finally, doing a review just to get a free copy of a book really means working far below the minimum wage.

The scholar who publishes several good articles will probably be offered more than enough reviewing. Even when moved solely by altruism, anybody who accepts a book should meet the deadline, if simply out of pity for the author, who hasn't been so impatient since childhood over how slowly time can pass. The reviewer should also honor the limit on words set by editors, who agonize over the deserving books that the journal can't make room for and who will bristle at excuses that the assigned length was unfair to the author, the subject, the large field, or — most deplorably of all — the reviewer.[10] While editors dislike having all the reviews wallow in kindness, they realize that usually more effort pours into a book than a gaggle of articles. Therefore, they welcome only the severity that is clearly deserved, and they know that the acrid reviewer will suffer through keeping poised to stroll the other way while scanning nametags at a convention.

THINKING POSITIVELY ABOUT EDITORS

I hope that nobody will avoid or else snub editors. There's no benefit in feeling resentful toward them. As publishing scholars they have learned that rejections hurt and that revising can feel like swimming in army boots. Editors who enjoy sadism soon get run out of the office. Those who last will commit errors of kindness, inconsistencies, oversights, and stupid mistakes, all of which are inevitably pointed out because they are so public. Editors have to apologize for any bloopers they helped to cause while silently digging out perhaps worse and certainly more frequent errors. They have to console themselves privately that they also helped an author add effectiveness as well as missed sources.

A former adviser on scholarly publication to the American Council of Learned Societies has philosophized:

> Scholarly editors seem not infrequently to be harassed by the very people who should be their pride and joy, the apples of their editorial eyes — their contributors. And this is strange, because, much as the editor needs his contributors, the more do the contributors need him.
>
> For this reason, the maintenance of an editor in good health and humor is not only a worthy but a very practicable pursuit. He is a man who gives up to this work a good deal because he has probably long neglected his own research because of it; who is often unpaid or underpaid for his editorial services; who is assisted, if assisted at all, by colleagues half a country away; who is continually forced to argue with his treasurer or his university press or provost over his printing bills; and who on top of all this quite rarely receives manuscripts in really top condition, written with the style of his journal in mind, in good English, clear, clean and succinct.[11]

Obviously Professor Silver wrote these lines in an age when editors were invariably male, but his hopes are to fan not sympathy but empathy, to humanize editors in the mind of the author, who should see them as allies and who should recognize that they will respond to candid sincerity. They are particularly eager to hear what the profession is thinking and saying about their journal.

To finish where I began, I apologize for any dampening effect. Still, I don't intend to persuade the cynics to enlist. If they are not moved to publish for idealistic reasons, in good part anyway, then they won't write much that's worthwhile. Rather, I mean to assure the willing beginner that in spite of the pains there's much pleasure in conducting research and then promoting it into print. Hang gliding may carry sharper thrills, but scholarship can anchor a lifetime.

ADDENDUM: HINDSIGHT ON SITE

Rereading this essay written fifteen years ago, I am startled by the futuristic advice that "word processor texts have graduated to full respectability." Actually, dominant practice was already verging on requests, then requirements for a disk rather than hard or print copy. Now, most lately, editors of encyclopedias and collections want e-mail attachments. So I obviously do not qualify as a prophet about the electronic era, and friends would hurt themselves laughing at me as a guide to how high-tech publishing will keep changing.

My bit of benighted advice does not, I hope, make my whole essay seem as quaint as a black and white, knob-controlled television set. The last fifteen years have not convinced me that basic human responses have changed and that common-sense intuiting of how editors and referees of journals will react no longer works. Those same years, however, have convinced me that the pleasures and inner rewards of publishing scholarly or critical articles are as strong as ever, that the old idea is still valid: to write an article that is sound and interesting and that will last.

NOTES

1. Terence Martin, "Meditations on Writing an Article," *American Literature* 55 (March 1983): 74. Hershel Parker's *Flawed Texts and Verbal Icons: Literary Authority in American Fiction* (Evanston, Ill.: Northwestern University Press, 1984) recurringly makes this point among much more substantial reasons.

2. From "Form and Matter in the Publication of Research"; published first in *Review of English Studies* in 1940, it gained semiofficial status by being reprinted in *PMLA* 65 (April 1950), and then as part of a pamphlet from the Modern Language Association; it now is best available in John Philip Immroth, *Ronald Brunlees McKerrow: A Selection of His Essays* (Metuchen, N.J.: Scarecrow Press, 1974), 195–202.

3. Martin, "Meditations," 76. Barbara R. Reitt, "An Academic Author's Checklist," *Scholarly Publishing* 16 (October 1984): 65–72, gives an excellent practical and compact set of guidelines; she also recommends other sources of advice.

4. "Editor's Column," *PMLA* 99 (October 1984).

5. Henry M. Silver, "Putting It on Paper," *PMLA* 65 (April 1950): 14.

6. This and other pointers appear in Hyman Rodman, "Some Practical Advice for Journal Contributors," *Scholarly Publishing* 9 (April 1978): 235–41.

7. In *College English*, April 1980, Michael West rated journals mostly in the field of British and American literature; the December 1980 issue carried a storm of responses.

8. In the field of literature and languages, many journals have adopted the latest MLA manual for style. But surely those journals keeping an older form will not insist on it before a first reading.

9. Murray E. Markland, "Taking Criticism—and Using It," *Scholarly Publishing* 14 (February 1983): 139–47.

10. I amplify this point in "Bootcamp for Book Reviewers," *American Literature* 54 (May 1982): 277–83. More generally useful is Roy S. Wolper, "On Academic Reviewing: Ten Common Errors," *Scholarly Publishing* 16 (April 1985): 269–75; Wolper contains references to other sources, furthermore.

11. Silver, "Putting It on Paper," 11.

26.

PUBLISHING IN SCIENCE

BOYD R. STRAIN

This essay addresses the problems experienced by young scientists in publishing the results of their work. Why publish and how does one go about it?

Several handbooks and manuals have been published on the subject. The most useful is *How to Write and Publish a Scientific Paper*. The sixth edition of this little book by Robert A. Day and Barbara Gastel appeared in 2006. It is up to date and contains sound advice from an experienced managing editor of a major scientific journal. The bibliography of this handbook lists several other publications that provide additional information on the issues presented below.

PURPOSE OF SCIENTIFIC PUBLISHING

The purpose of publishing scientific papers is to complete the task of doing research. A scientific experiment, no matter how spectacular the results, is not completed until those results are published. Knowledge gained by the scientific method but not passed on to society by scientific writing is of no more value and is no more reliable than the folk stories of prehistoric tribes.

WHY PUBLISH SCIENTIFIC PAPERS?

There are primary motivating forces that encourage scientists to complete their research efforts. One of these is the scientific establishment. In 1974 the official government policy of the Federal Council of Science and Technology stated: "The publication of research results is an essential part of the research process. This has been recognized in part through authorization to pay publication costs from federal research grant and contract funds." The scientific establishment demands that research results be published. The investigator who does not publish will not be retained within that establishment. The nonpublisher will be barred from normal vehicles of scientific interaction, that is, meetings, invited oral and letter symposia, and cooperative book-writing projects. The nonpublisher will not continue to receive external grant or contract funds awarded through the peer review process. The scientific establishment soon excludes those who fail to complete research by writing scientific papers.

A second force that encourages individuals to publish scientific papers is the simple fact that people like to be recognized. Individuals become known to the scientific community by publishing the results of their research. It is a great feeling to see your work in print; it is even more pleasing to have others contact you to discuss your research results after a paper has appeared in print. Thus, for some people, a personal sense of gratification is obtained from seeing their name and their research results and ideas in print.

In contemporary academia, there is a third reason for publishing. Investigators who do not believe it is necessary to publish to complete research, who neither expect nor desire personal attention, or who feel that their research is not yet ready to appear in print, frequently learn firsthand of the dictum *publish or perish.*

Universities and research institutions expect employees to do research and to carry it through to publication. Basically the employers believe that research unpublished is research not completed. Investigators are expected to organize their research so that it can be completed in units with some reasonable time scale. The average number of research papers your chair expects you to publish per year varies with discipline and with institution. The "wise" young professor at a major research university, however, will strive to have six to nine senior-authored titles by the end of the third year of his or her initial appointment.

THE FORM OF SCIENTIFIC PAPERS

Writers of papers to be published in scientific journals do not have the freedom to arrange their papers in unique ways. By three hundred years of tradition, enforced by the need to communicate precisely and concisely, scientific writing has become rigidly stylized. Every scientific paper will have a title, an author with address, an abstract, an introduction, a section on methods and materials, a section on results, a discussion of those results, and a list of references cited in the paper. Lengthy papers may have additional sections or appendixes, but these too must fall within traditional guidelines. Very short research papers may be published without all of these section headings, but the information must be arranged in the above order. Some scientific journals have adopted modifications of this order, and the final authority to determine the actual form to be published is the editor-in-chief of the publication. Therefore an author may partially control the form of the paper by selecting a journal that uses an acceptable style. Rarely, however, can an author diverge from the traditional style of a given periodical and rarely do journals differ significantly from the historical norm.

HOW TO WRITE SCIENTIFIC PAPERS

Since the objective of publishing a scientific paper is to complete a given study by communicating the new discoveries, a paper should be direct, concise, and uncluttered with extraneous information. If a paper reports new and original results, it will be necessary to completely introduce the subject, state the objective, clearly describe the methods and materials used, and state the results in sufficient detail to allow others to judge the adequacy of the discussion and the accuracy of the conclusions. A paper may be much shorter if it is reporting results of a study conducted to repeat or test a previously published observation.

All scientists develop their own procedures for the preparation of papers. Many people prefer to write the results section first, but I begin with the section on methods and materials. This serves to get the easiest part on paper and to get me focused. Then I write the section on results. The discussion flows naturally from writing the details of the results. Then the major conclusions can be stated in an itemized summary or in narrative form. Preparing the reference list is a purely technical operation and must follow the requirement of the journal to which the paper is to be submitted. This step should be postponed until the journal selection has been made. Experienced scientists may be able to select a journal style before preparing the first draft, but the beginner will need a draft in hand before advice can be sought on an appropriate journal.

After completing these sections, the author should write an introduction that specifically addresses the paper as it will go out for review. If you attempt to write the introduction first, you may have difficulty staying on track. If your project is complex, it will be difficult to know how to introduce the paper until the content sections are finished.

Now, you have only to write a concise abstract and finally to select an informative and specific title. Titles and abstracts are the most read sections of all scientific papers. Consequently, both should be prepared very carefully. A good title contains the fewest possible words that adequately describe the content of the paper. Its purpose is to inform readers that something was done in a specific research area. If the reader is interested in that area, he or she will take the time to read the abstract. A good abstract will inform the reader of the basic content of the paper and will enable the reader to decide if the paper should be studied in more detail.

HOW TO COMPLETE A PAPER AND TO PREPARE IT FOR SUBMISSION TO A SPECIFIC SCIENTIFIC JOURNAL

Once a paper has been completed, it should be circulated among your colleagues and students for help in revisions. All papers will benefit from revision, revision, and more revision. You need assistance in clarifying sentences, finding redundancies, and discovering missing critical information. Ask your reviewers to consider the paper as if they had received it for an anonymous review from a journal editor. Take their suggestions seriously and improve the manuscript as much as possible. Avoid spelling, grammatical, and typographical errors. If you have figures, draw them neatly and carefully to ensure that the manuscript looks professional. A reviewer with confidence in style will tend to have confidence in content.

It is now time to make the final decision on the journal to which the manuscript will be submitted. Several factors must be considered in making a journal selection. List the journals that have been publishing papers in your subject area. Scanning recent issues of *Current Contents* may help if you are not certain.

To determine if the editor of a given journal may be interested in your material, read the masthead statement in a current issue, review the table of contents of several recent issues, and read the Instructions to Authors usually provided inside the front or back cover of each issue. It is also appropriate to ask the editor if your material is suitable for the journal in question.

Of those journals that publish in your field, what is the average time from the date of first receipt by the editor to the date that the paper appears in print? Some scientific journals now have a two-year lag time, while the total elapsed time in others is less than six months. A young professor cannot afford to submit to a journal that takes a year or more to decide on publishability.

From those journals that you deem to be appropriate for your paper, select the journal that has the best prestige factor. Generally the highest prestige occurs in the journal of the major society in your discipline. Unfortunately, journals of the major societies are frequently the slowest in review and publishing. Another unfortunate fact is the high rejection rate of prestige journals. Some major journals must reject 60 percent or more of the manuscripts received for review. You will have to weigh prestige against lag time and the probability of acceptance to make your final selection.

Once you have determined the journal, obtain a copy of the Instructions to

Authors for that journal. Usually instructions are printed in at least one issue of each volume. Instructions may also be obtained by writing to the editor or by checking the journal's Web site for submission and other guidelines. Follow these instructions as closely as possible. Study papers similar to yours published in recent issues of the journal. Carefully prepare your paper following instructions on length and style, graphs, tables and illustrations, and citation style. As stated above, most prestige journals receive more good manuscripts than can be accepted. Reviewers and editors do not have time or patience for authors who do not follow instructions. Do not forget that your manuscript can be rejected for any reason. Do not give the editor the opportunity to reject your manuscript on the basis of style alone.

SUBMITTING THE MANUSCRIPT

Follow the instructions to the letter. Send the number of copies with all materials in the exact form and size required. If instructions call for all graphs to be submitted in three copies on glossy photographic paper in a size to be reduced 50 percent for printing, do just that! If the journal allows electronic submission, do that!

Provide a cover letter addressed to the editor or as instructed by the journal. Include the title of your paper and any information that you think the editor may need to manage the review. I recently advised a student to include in his paper a lengthy and detailed review of the assumptions required to utilize his methods but to tell the editor in the cover letter that the material could be deleted if the editor considered it to be unnecessary for the average reader of the journal. If you will be at a different address from the one given on the manuscript when the editor will have to communicate with you, give complete mailing, e-mail, and telephone information with appropriate dates in the cover letter.

RESPONSE TO THE REVIEW

A frequent response from scientific editors these days is that the material is appropriate for the journal but that the paper will have to be revised and shortened before it can be published. My advice is to make every change required and to return the corrected manuscript within two weeks. Delays in resubmitting the manuscript will increase the probability that the editor will send it back to the reviewers or even send it out to additional reviewers. It is sometimes possible to argue a point of disagreement on a required revision, but unless the change introduces an error, you should not pursue the issue. If you disagree with an editor's decisions on revisions to the point that you cannot change the manuscript as suggested, my advice is to reformat the paper as required by another journal and send it there. Unless you can conclusively prove your point, the editor will not change the decision. Remember, most top journals are rejecting good manuscripts on the subjective decisions of the editors. You seldom will win in a disagreement on style or emphasis.

If your paper is rejected, revise it to correct problems detected by the reviewers, clarify material where necessary, and prepare it for submission to another good journal. Even though science is supposedly an objective enterprise, decisions on approach and significance are subjective matters. Material that seems mundane and boring to one scientist may seem critically important and carefully done to another. You are an expert in your field, and your subjective opinions are as good and as justifiable as those of other experts. Rather than enter into a frustrating and sometimes lengthy dialogue with reviewers and editors, it is advisable to simply try another journal and keep going.

READING PROOF

After your manuscript has been accepted it will be sent to a compositor to be typeset. At some point you will receive page proofs or galley proofs with instructions on how to read and correct the proofs. You will also usually receive instructions to change only those items that are incorrect. Printers' errors in typesetting will be corrected and minor changes made by the author will be made at no charge to the author.

Significant changes required after the type has been set will only be made if the text is in error. If the error was on the manuscript sent to the printer, the author may be required to pay a charge for resetting the type.

Most printers send detailed instructions on how to mark the proofs. Follow these instructions as closely as possible. The *CBE Manual* (6th ed., 1994) has extensive instructions for editing proof copy. If specific instructions are not provided by the printer, find a style manual appropriate for your field and follow it to the best of your ability.

Many errors can creep into a manuscript in the typesetting process. You must read proofs with all the care that you can muster. My technique is to have a coauthor or other knowledgeable person read the manuscript to me while I follow along studying every word and symbol on the proof. Another technique is to compare the proof to the manuscript word for word. One of my colleagues swears that he gives the proofs to a graduate student along with the threat that the student will never graduate if that paper contains a printing error when it appears!

Remember, your published papers are the permanent record of your contributions to your discipline. A mistake that appears in print in a scientific paper will be there forever. You are the final authority for your published work, and the ultimate responsibility for its quality is yours. Reading, correcting, and approving proofs is your final opportunity to get it right.

Proofs should be corrected and returned to the printer by return mail. Some journals allow only forty-eight hours to correct and return proofs. If you cannot meet the designated time, write or call the person to whom proofs are to be returned and give the date that the proofs will be returned.

AUTHORSHIP OF SCIENTIFIC PAPERS

Multiple-authored papers have become commonplace in science. Modern research is often complex and may require two or more experts to design and conduct the experiments. Laboratory heads sometimes add their names to every paper originating in their laboratory. Professors frequently expect to join their students as coauthors because of their conceptual and financial inputs into the work. As a professor, you should explain your policies to each of your students.

In multiple-authored papers, the order of listing the authors should be determined and agreed upon at the beginning of each series of experiments leading to a publication. The first listed author should be the person who actually did most of the work and writing. Second or third authors should be listed in decreasing order of time and effort put into the study. The last named author is traditionally the laboratory director or the major professor who may have been instrumental in framing the overall research direction and capabilities of the group. Paid technicians normally should not be listed as authors unless they have made significant contribution to the conceptualization, interpretation, and writing of the research.

ACKNOWLEDGMENTS

You should acknowledge colleagues, associates, or students who loan equipment, collect material for the experiment, help integrate the results, or review the manuscript. Acknowledgments of financial support from grants or contracts are also appropriately made in scientific papers. Institutional service people (for example, technicians, typists, draftsmen) are paid to perform their services. Normally it is not necessary to acknowledge routine technical contributions to the preparation of research papers. Each journal has its own style for the inclusion of acknowledgments in the manuscript.

OTHER CONSIDERATIONS IN SCIENTIFIC PUBLISHING

Reviewing Manuscripts   Most journals utilize unpaid peer reviewers to read and comment on the publishability of scientific manuscripts. Reviewers are usually anonymous. As a beginning scientist you will occasionally be asked to review manuscripts. If you do a good job and do it quickly, your name will soon move into the "good reviewers" card file of several editors. Before you know it you will be receiving more manuscripts than you care to read. If you begin to receive more invitations to review than you can comfortably manage, decline them. Do not delay manuscripts because of lack of time to complete good reviews.

Conceptually, all manuscripts should be reviewed from a completely objective viewpoint. Practically, however, there are two primary approaches to the review of scientific manuscripts. One approach assumes that every paper is weak, contains errors, and should be rejected. Your responsibility as an anonymous reviewer is to find the problems and explain them to the editor so that the manuscript can be rejected. A second approach assumes that every manuscript reports good research, properly done, that should be published as quickly as possible. Your job is to identify the strengths of the paper and to make suggestions for improvement where possible. Only those manuscripts that cannot be salvaged by detailed revision are recommended for rejection.

The former class of reviewers exists in a subsection of the card file of editors entitled "hatchet reviewers." If the editor is predisposed to reject your manuscript for any reason, it will be sent to "hatchet reviewers." This is a primary reason for you to submit the most perfectly prepared manuscript possible. Carefully follow the Instructions to Authors for the particular journal to be used.

My advice is to be the second class of reviewer but not to accept manuscripts outside your area of expertise and not to accept more than you can comfortably handle. We all must do our part to keep the peer review process working in scientific publication. Do not go overboard with this community service, however. Your primary obligation as a young professor is to your own work. Help the system where you can, but remember your priorities and guard your time well to ensure that your own work gets done.

Book Reviews   Writing book reviews does not count in the credit column of your publish or perish ledger. A book review is not a scientific publication. If you are going to study a new book in detail for some other reason, summarizing your findings in a published book review may be a desirable by-product. But do not fall for the temptation to write book reviews in order to obtain free books. Your cost in hours spent to write a good review will certainly exceed the cost of the book itself. Buy the book and use the time for jogging.

Ethics in Publishing and Reviewing   An original scientific paper can be published only once in a scientific journal. If the same material is to be published in another journal it must be clearly marked and the original source cited. A copyright release must be obtained. Dual publication in primary research journals is unethical. Where it can be justified, it must be done with the full awareness of all editors, publishers, and coauthors involved. Most scientific journals carry a statement that informs the authors that submission of a paper to that journal implies that the information is original and that it is not being submitted for publication to any other scientific journal. Previously published information can be republished in scientific reviews, but here also complete citation must be given and copyright laws must be honored.

Scientific writers must exert every effort to cite prior publication of concepts or results. Individuals who may have contributed ideas to a given original study should be acknowledged in the paper. It is not always possible to remember all of the stimuli leading to a scientific breakthrough, however. We must always be aware that our understanding is cumulative and is built from all the experiences we have had. The individual components that lead to a new idea on your part may not all be remembered or identifiable. Don't forget they are there, however. Acknowledge or cite as many as possible.

Proprietary Information   As a peer reviewer of manuscripts and proposals you will become aware of data and concepts before they are published. The use of this information before it is printed or without the consent of the original author is unethical.

I hope these few remarks on publishing will be helpful to those scientists (and nonscientists) about to embark on their publishing careers. If they are, of course, I will be doubly rewarded: in the knowledge that I have provided for you and in the knowledge your own work will shortly provide for me.

27

ACADEMIC BOOK PUBLISHING

CATHY N. DAVIDSON AND KEN WISSOKER

In most humanities fields and many in the social sciences, the publication of a book with a reputable academic press is the key to jobs, advancement, merit raises, and professional status. As with anything with such life-altering power, the academic publishing process is often shrouded in mystery and fraught with anxiety. We hope to demystify that process by providing clear guidelines for selecting a press, submitting a manuscript for publication, seeing your manuscript through to its publication as a book, and then shepherding that book once it is out in the world.

WHAT IS ACADEMIC BOOK PUBLISHING?

Academic publishing is that slice of the large and varied publishing world that is dedicated to books geared to higher education. There are many kinds of academic publications: textbooks, short introductions, handbooks, reference guides, collections of essays, readers or anthologies of previously published materials, monographs, and broad synthetic works. Some of these publications are meant primarily for students, some for colleagues in a field or subfield, some for academics working across fields on a topic or area. Some works are aimed primarily at academics, others primarily at the general public; some assume the reader knows most of what the author knows, others assume the reader will be brought into the terrain for the first time.

Different kinds of books are associated with particular kinds of publishers. There are textbook publishers as well as publishers that specialize in scholarly editions for teaching. Some publishers aim to reach the broadest public and others specialize in a specific discipline. While most publishers stretch across at least some of these categories, they are also mostly organized to focus on the areas most central to their enterprise.

A textbook publisher hires college representatives, salespeople who will go door-to-door from school to school, urging professors to adopt their company's books rather than another publisher's. Such a textbook can be immensely successful without ever appearing on a bookstore's shelves outside the area set aside for course sales. By contrast, a trade publisher hires sales representatives who visit bookstores presenting the new books that are about to be published in the next few months. These books may or may not be adopted in a course, but, in most cases, course adoptions will not be crucial to their success. Their primary audience is the book-buying public.

This essay will concentrate on scholarly book publishing. Writing textbooks or reference works are their own subjects, and the reader will need to consult other guides.

SCHOLARLY BOOK PUBLISHERS

The bulk of this essay will focus on university press publishing but, before we turn our attention to that topic, we will look briefly at the other forms of scholarly book publishing. For scholarly writing, there are three main classes of publishers: trade publishers such as Random House or Norton; academic commercial publishers like Routledge or Blackwell; and university presses. The first question any scholar must ask is which type of press is best suited to your work and your goals. This is a complex question and there is no simple answer. However, once you have signed a contract with a press, your book will be published according to the implicit and explicit rules of that particular type of publishing. Before you make a decision about which kind of press to choose, you need to be realistic about how your book will be treated, what its sales might be, and how long it will be kept in print, for these matters all vary with the type of publisher.

TRADE PRESSES

Trade houses, now largely parts of bigger international conglomerates, are looking to make money from the books they publish. They are also looking for certain kinds of prestige, but at a very large scale. A book must have strong potential to reach a general audience—the so-called literate general public. That means that trade potential will vary with subject. The World War II historian will have more possibilities for a trade publication than will her counterpart studying the working class in Buenos Aires.

For trade publication, writing style is at a premium. These are books written for those who are not obligated to read them. They are not assignments; they are not part of the scholarly requirements of others in a specific field. Trade books need to be accessible to readers with no background on the subject, while not condescending to their readers. For trade books, the academic is assumed to be the expert on the subject. The publisher will not be obtaining peer reviews or checking to see if the theory is up-to-date or if the facts are straight. The publisher may, however, have the book rigorously evaluated by the house lawyer to make sure there is nothing that can be seen as potentially libelous about any living subjects mentioned in the book. (The dead have to fend for themselves.) With few exceptions, the way into a trade publisher is through an agent. Agents are the gatekeepers. They sort out what even gets presented to trade editors. But that makes it often difficult to obtain an agent. Agents make money by taking a percentage (generally 15 or 20 percent) of the proceeds of a book, so they have no reason to take on projects that they are not confident they will be able to sell at a high rate. There are many places that list agents, but referrals from colleagues that have them may be the most successful way of getting a hearing. Agents also have specialties, so locating one who handles your type of project is essential.

In the world of trade publishing, nonfiction books are usually sold by a prospectus. An interested agent will spend a good deal of time with you to help craft a proposal the agent feels is saleable. Such proposals form their own genre, and, in the course of shaping a prospectus, you may find that your project has taken on forms you hadn't considered or predicted. This is, once again, because an agent's charge is to find the saleable angle, not the angle that will make the biggest impact in the author's discipline. Methodological issues may need to disappear; while a gripping but minor part of the narrative is brought to the fore. If you don't like shaping your subject in this way, you should think twice about trade publishing.

Once an agent deems the proposal to be satisfactory, she will then pitch the book to all the editors she thinks will like it. The pitch may start with a lunch conversation or with mailing the proposal to likely editors. Hopefully there will be a few editors interested. Perhaps they will want to meet the author and, ideally, they will make a bid on the book. If not, the agent will go to a next set of possibilities. If a satisfactory bid on the book is made, the agent will negotiate the contract. It is not infrequent now for an author to be asked to hire a "book doctor" (also known as an "independent editor") who will work on the text for a fee paid by the author him- or herself. Some editors still line-edit their books, sometimes agents will offer editorial advice, but being asked to hire a professional book doctor—often a former editor or agent who has gone into business for herself—has become very common. None of this is hard or fixed. In the time that *The Academic's Handbook* has gone through its three editions, the publishing world has undergone drastic changes. Besides the consolidation of independent houses into larger international publishing conglomerates such as Bertelsmann, there has been a decrease in the amount of space for academic work at this level of trade publishing. Some of the largest publishers who used to publish scholarly books no longer do so and the number of trade publishers specializing in these high-end areas has decreased. Again, this varies a good deal by discipline and topic, but most would agree that the bottom line has become more and more important over this period, leaving less room for the serious book coming out of the academy.

At the same time that the possibilities of trade publishing have been restricted, the advantages of trade publishing have become more pronounced. Over this same period the number of independent bookstores has sharply decreased. While the chain bookstores that drove independents out of business picked up some of the slack for a while, the chains themselves are very bottom-line oriented and increasingly feature the titles that sell the best. To have a book included in a display in these stores often requires paying a fee, something trade publishers are in a better position to do than are scholarly presses. Over the last decade, book review sections in newspapers and magazines have shrunk, making it even less likely that your book will be reviewed. In these and other ways, there are more and more books trying to get attention in less and less space. Under such circumstances, a publisher with clout and resources can be a huge advantage, at least if you are trying to reach a general audience. That large publishers have these tools at their disposal doesn't mean they use them on every book. Not by a long shot. Someone estimated that at the big houses 95 percent of the resources go to 5 percent of the books, which are expected to bring in 95 percent of the revenue. It is not uncommon to hear academics, perhaps used to a more hands-on university press experience, or having big crossover dreams, complain that the trade press didn't take out ads or support their book in the ways they thought they could expect. Academics are often unrealistic about sales figures. Serious scholarly books published by commercial presses, even with the best advertising, may well sell less than ten thousand copies. The academic's fantasy of getting rich through trade publication is, in 90 percent of the cases, just that: a fantasy.

Still, there is no question that having the trade name on the spine, having a sales force dedicated to selling the publisher's books, and having coordinated and connected publicity is a big advantage. A particular book may do better as a big fish in a smaller pond at an academic publisher, but such examples—

and they are plentiful — are notable because they buck the trend. Typically, if a trade publisher pays a large advance for a book, the company will work as hard as is necessary to recoup that cost. Once the book has paid for itself, there is often a significant diminishing of attention to the book or its author. And, in the end, once the book is no longer selling, the book is likely to be shredded or remaindered. Trade publishers are not known for their sentimental attachment to keeping books in print after they've stopped paying their way.

UNIVERSITY PRESSES

University presses are justly known for their attention to scholarly content and for keeping books in print. But, of course, publishing with a university press comes with its own positives and negatives. University presses themselves vary greatly, from small presses that publish a handful of books a year to large ones that have multiple divisions and publish hundreds of books each year. Some may focus more on regional concerns, others are more heavily academic. Most publish some books aimed at nonacademic audiences, and most have at least part of their list devoted to scholarship. Within the scholarly part of the list even the largest presses have areas in which they specialize, and whole other fields that are barely represented.

With few exceptions, university press books will be peer reviewed. Though procedures vary greatly (as will be explained later in this essay), scholars in the field read a manuscript and it will also go before a press board composed of faculty of the hosting university that must give their imprimatur on behalf of the university before the book can be published.

While in some countries a university press will publish work primarily or solely from its own university, in the United States university presses almost always operate independently in choosing which titles to publish. It's rare for more than a small percentage of titles to originate at the press's home institution and these will generally be the result of a particular coincidence of interests rather than some preplanned program or obligation.

University presses can be expected to speak the language of scholarship. Acquisition editors at most presses have one or more areas of academic responsibility, depending on the size and structure of a particular press. While they do not necessarily have formal academic training in these areas, they attend scholarly meetings, track intellectual trends, and are responsible for guiding presses' presence in these disciplines. They solicit manuscripts and choose which books presses should publish and then help explain and situate the scholarship for other people at the press. Marketing departments at a university press will be familiar with many of the meetings, journals, and priorities in the fields in which the press publishes. However much they are also concerned about sales, the press as a whole will take pride in the recognition and awards that a book receives from its scholarly audience.

Approximately one hundred university presses publish the work of all the scholars from all the universities in the United States. Not every university has a press and almost all university presses lose money publishing academic books. They publish scholarly books because that is their mission. They exist to publish scholarship that would not be viable in an open market. Some presses make up their losses from scholarly publishing through subsidies from their own institutions. A few are fortunate to have endowments or publish certain kinds of books (varying from regional guides and histories for state presses to ESL texts and Bibles for Oxford or Cambridge) that are perennially strong sellers. Sometimes one part of the press cross-subsidizes another part. For example, a large journal-publishing operation might cross-subsidize the books division of the press. Still other presses run warehousing operations that make enough money to pay for scholarship. More and more, individual authors in the humanities and social sciences are being asked to help seek subsidies from foundations or their own institutions (in a manner analogous to the way scientists pay a per-page fee for articles published in refereed science journals). At this point in time, scholarly publishing will only succeed with one form of subsidy or another.

Every scholar must be concerned about the economics of scholarly publishing because, in a way different from and yet also analogous to trade publishers, trying to stay as close as possible to a "break even" point makes a difference in which scholarly books university presses publish. A press can be proud when a book wins the prize for best in its field—but if that book then only sells eight hundred copies, the press will have to publish another book, somewhere, that will make up the amount of money that book lost.

Most university presses have sales representatives who sell their books to bookstores, but only the very few largest presses have representatives who work for the press itself and only sell the books of one particular press. Most presses sell their books through consortiums or the use of independent sales groups that work on commission. This means your scholarly book is most likely to be in a bookstore in a college town or in urban areas. Nearly all the books will be available through the main book wholesalers (it's a very concentrated industry) and from online booksellers. But there is no denying that over the last decade the amount of bookstore space devoted to university press books has declined as a result of commercial pressures.

University presses will pitch their trade books—the books deemed to be of the most general interest—to reviewers. Although they compete over shrinking space, university press books are still reviewed in the major newspapers and magazines. Since university presses operate in the academic sphere, they generally give greater marketing emphasis to reaching the audiences for their books by advertising in academic journals, sending those journals review copies; by direct mail to all or part of a disciplinary organization or to those teaching a particular subject; and through displays at academic meetings.

COMMERCIAL ACADEMIC PUBLISHERS

Within the world of scholarly publishing, there is a good deal of variety. Commercial academic publishers combine aspects of the academic and trade publishers with additional characteristics of their own. They are commercial, often multinational, and frequently part of larger corporate entities that expect a substantial rate of return on their investment. Routledge and Blackwell are two examples. Commercial academic publishers may be more academically focused than a given university press or may have a balance of general interest titles and specialized ones. Some are oriented toward bookstores; others put most of their marketing energy into reaching scholars directly.

Peer review may or may not be a requirement. Since commercial academic publishers deal with scholars all the time, they are comfortable with peer reviews, but these may be more optional or less binding than at a university press. As with university presses, many scholarly presses specialize in a discipline or group of disciplines; the largest will cover at least as wide a range as the largest university presses.

If university presses can barely break even publishing scholarship, how can commercial academic publishers make a profit doing it? There are a number of answers to this question. Some commercial presses may see less need to publish monographs in a given area, putting more emphasis on general introductions or other works meant for teaching. Some publishers are able to use benefits of scale, in multinational reach, or in cutting costs in production. Many publishers are also journals publishers, or reference or textbook publishers, and other parts of the same larger corporation may be involved in distribution or other aspects of the publishing business. Commercial academic publishers may also devote less attention to the details of publishing your work than university presses (which can be artisan-like in attention to details or quality in editing, design, and production).

There are some books that one could imagine having a successful life at all three types of publishers. There are many more that could be published at either a university press or a commercial academic one. How does one choose which press is right for a given book? This requires a good deal of honesty with oneself about the book itself, a realistic understanding of who is going to read it, and one's reasons for publishing it. What will the reader be expected to know ahead of time? What questions will seem relevant and expected, what citations familiar, what will make the argument convincing? Is the book directed at a particular subdiscipline, or an interdisciplinary space, at those working through a particular question? Is the hope that the book will get the author tenure or promotion? Or to influence national policy? To get on television? To make as much money as possible?

It is difficult to sort through these hopes, plans, and motivations. Often the needs of different readerships guide the text from section to section or paragraph to paragraph, with parts meant to reassure colleagues sitting uneasily next to sentences addressed to an imagined wider audience. Academics will sometimes judge their own work as available to a general audience based on its topic, or because there are large sections that are written with narrative verve. When the work is published, reviewers in general-interest periodicals focus not on these sections but on academic arguments or language, citations, and references to other academic work. Since they expect the whole book to read like trade nonfiction, reviewers point out the parts least accessible and often use them to dismiss the work as "too academic."

You need to be honest about what you are writing and for whom. Beyond that, the best advice is to look at your own bookshelves. What has been published recently in your area, with the slant that you find appealing, and who published it? You will find certain kinds of books clustering at certain presses. If you see yourself in that company, then you should begin the process of trying to place your manuscript by writing to the editors at those presses.

APPROACHING A SCHOLARLY PUBLISHER

If you've decided your book is best suited to commercial academic press or a university press, what do you do next? At this juncture the advice is the same for both kinds of academic publishing: Check out the Web sites. Most presses will have directions for submitting proposals and a list of editors and their areas. After selecting presses that seem best suited to your work, you can contact the press to see if they are interested in you. You might start with a list of five or ten possibilities—this will vary with your field—and then choose to write to your top choice first, or to write to five or six viable ones at the same time, depending on how sure you are of where you would like the book to end up.

There are several common pieces of advice to bear in mind. In general it is better to write to someone in particular than to "Dear Editor" or "Dear Social Science Editor." It shows that you have done some homework. Few if any editors will want to see a whole manuscript at this initial query stage unless they have previously requested it. Similarly, most editors will not want to see a proposal sent by e-mail attachment, unless the author has been invited to send it in that manner. An initial e-mail inquiry about the editor's interest in seeing a prospectus or the suitability of the project for a press is generally welcome, though not at all necessary.

A standard proposal consists of a cover letter explaining the project, a chapter by chapter breakdown, a cv and a sample chapter or two of the text. The cover letter should emphasize the most important information first: the field of the author, the argument or contribution of the proposed book and how it will fit into the list of the particular press. It's useful to say something about the intended audience — "graduate students and faculty in political philosophy" — but not useful to extend that audience unrealistically "everyone interested in issues of race and justice." Remember that the editor will know much more about the market for books in the areas in which the press publishes than you do, so elaborate lists of courses or areas of interest will rarely show you in a good light. Similarly, a shorter cv is fine; the press will not need to know every course you have taught or every guest lecture you gave.

The letter should also explain how much of the manuscript is now ready for review and your timetable for completion of the full manuscript. If the manuscript is a revision of a dissertation, say so. Explain where you are in the process of revising and the scope of your revisions. If it is a new work, explain what parts are finished. If the editor is interested, she will want to see more. The proposal should be timed so that she can; if an editor writes back excited about the project and soliciting more material, you will want to be able to provide some, not say it will be ready in six months.

FROM DISSERTATION TO BOOK

If you are sending an editor a manuscript based on a dissertation, you should not only acknowledge its origins but you should also indicate the ways that the new book departs from the dissertation that spawned it. Almost no scholarly publishers in the United States will publish a dissertation as is, but many first books start their lives as dissertations. The reason that no one will publish them is not pride (or prejudice). It is because in very concrete ways a dissertation is a radically different genre of writing from the book that arises from the same dissertation.

Much has been written about the topic of revising a dissertation into a book. William Germano's *From Dissertation to Book* (University of Chicago Press,

2005) is the best and most comprehensive guide to how to transform a dissertation into a book. And "transform" is the operative word in most cases. The crucial difference between a dissertation and a book is that your committee members are paid to read your dissertation. You wrote it knowing who your readers would be. By the end of the dissertation, you may have made an argument but the purpose of the dissertation is to show you have mastered the field and added something of substance to it. Its purpose is not to argue a position and marshal evidence in a way that supports that argument.

Because no one has to read a book, it becomes the author's job to move the reader from the first sentence, paragraph, page, or chapter to the second. Rather than assuming the reader will be willing to slog through all the genuflections and summaries of other scholarly work before getting to the writer's own contribution, in writing a book, you have to present your argument from the start. It becomes the arc and measure of everything else you include in the book. Unlike a dissertation, which may include parts adapted from seminar papers or written so you can make a case that you deserve a job in a particular field (e.g., the chapter on Phillis Wheatley might qualify you for an early Americanist position), every part of a book needs to develop the argument and push it further along.

In short, revising a dissertation is not about salvaging as much of the original as possible. One or even several chapters may turn out to be journal articles and not be part of the final book at all. This may seem to be frivolous, but it isn't. Finding the best way to make the book's argument is more efficient in the long run than trying to salvage that dissertation—and leads, in the end, to a book manuscript more likely to be accepted for publication.

SUBMITTING YOUR MANUSCRIPT

Presses receive many more proposals than they can possibly publish. Presses often must turn down manuscripts that they could publish with pride, simply because there are more good possibilities than time or staff allows. Generally, the number of books a press publishes is roughly or even exactly budgeted well in advance. The books it chooses to publish have distinguished themselves in some way from many equally good possibilities.

For that reason, among others, it is worth trying to meet an editor before or at the same time as submitting a proposal. If one is choosing among presses, this is a good way of sorting out who understands the project. The editor can provide much helpful advice not only about how to submit the manuscript but on how to finish it, how long it should be, how it might be organized, and so forth. The editor often has a better grasp of what is the latest work coming out in a field than many scholars within the field simply by virtue of the stream of new manuscripts constantly coming across her desk.

If you are at or close to the stage of shopping your proposal, you can e-mail prospective editors to see if they will be attending an upcoming academic conference. In general, editors are more likely to attend national disciplinary conferences than local or regional ones, but that will vary with the press, editor, and field. An editor will only have a finite number of slots available to meet with people, and the schedule will include authors and potential authors at all stages of the process, so she may or may not have time to meet at a particular event. Some editors make a practice of being in their press's booth at the conference book exhibit and may encourage you to stop by. Others may offer to make an appointment to talk about your work. They may express interest in seeing a proposal but be too busy at the conference to meet you in person. They may let you know that the project is unlikely to be suitable for their press's list at that time. All of these are productive outcomes.

It is generally not a good idea, at least in most disciplines, to simply plan on walking through the book exhibit hoping to meet editors and talk about your proposal. Editors may or may not be in the booth. If they are there, it's a fine place to introduce yourself, but a poor place to do a standing full pitch for your book, unless asked. It's also not a good idea to pass out copies of your proposal, or to leave copies unsolicited for the editors at the press. Such proposals may or may not make it back to the press itself and rarely would be considered an actual submission requiring a response.

Once you have made contact with the editor, once you believe your manuscript is ready to be evaluated, you should ask the editor about the next steps. She may want to see a prospectus and a sample chapter or the entire manuscript. The sample requested may vary if this is a revised dissertation or a second or third book.

If you send a prospectus by mail, the response time will vary from editor to editor and press to press. You may hear back right away or it may take as long as several months. Different editors and presses will have different systems in place — and of course editors' efficiency and habits vary as much as anyone else's. Timing may or may not reflect the level or clarity of interest. Sometimes a quick response will mean an obvious yes or no for the editor; a slow response may mean the editor is traveling or simply backed up. It is fine to check in occasionally after the press has had the proposal for a month or so. One might check with the editorial assistant or contact the editor directly. If a press is your first choice, but other presses are expressing interest, it's usually a good idea to let the editor know.

THE REVIEW PROCESS

Typically, an editor reads the material you send and decides whether it suits the needs of the press and has good publishing prospects. The editor may read the whole proposal or just enough to make a decision. That verdict may reflect a judgment about the work itself, its academic interest and importance, or it may be based on the press's priorities — list-building or financial — at the moment. Even if a press has published a lot in an area, they may not be looking for more such books at a particular time. A decision that is based on the work might reflect the topic or the execution or a combination of both. It's rare to get as much frank feedback about the particulars as you would like, though on occasion a good relationship with an editor can help elicit some guidance.

Once an editor decides to pursue a project, scholarly peer review is the next step in the process. Here procedures begin to vary from press to press as well as with the stature of the author and the type of book involved. Most academic presses like to have two external reviewers. There are presses that might regularly use more and some that use one reader internal to the press and one external reviewer. Generally review will be a single-blind process — the readers will know your name, but you will not know theirs, though some presses allow reviewers the option of revealing their identity to the author. In most cases presses will exclude people at your own institution, or if this is a book developed from your dissertation, members of your dissertation committee or home department. Some editors will be open to suggestions for people who might be appropriate reviewers or will ask if there is anyone who should be avoided. It's fine to offer to provide such a list. It is not appropriate to try to insist on who the particular readers should be. Some presses will look for a combination of junior and senior readers; or ones presumed to be friendly and less-friendly to a particular approach; or someone who knows the theory or method and someone who specializes in the particular subfield; or, in the case of interdisciplinary work, one person from each of the intersecting fields.

With a commissioned book, or a proposal from a very senior person with a long track record in a field, a small amount of material may be all that is required for a review. A reader is presumed to have a lot of extratextual knowledge about the author's ability. In general, the less a reader might know, the more of the manuscript the press might want to send to readers. Since the readers give helpful advice, the more they see, the more useful their advice can be to first-time authors or to those new at the particular kind of project. Some presses would prefer to send out a whole dissertation with a cover letter about the revision, for example, rather than a revised chapter or two. Writing a single chapter can be like writing a journal article and may say little about the way the whole argument works.

Reviewers read manuscripts as a service to the profession and are doing this in addition to their other academic obligations. Thus the time the review process takes is always more unpredictable than presses or authors would like. Some readers read remarkably quickly while others drag on for far too long. You should ask up front how long the press expects the process to take, but also expect considerable variability.

Unlike submission of journal articles, there is no automatic proscription against submitting book manuscripts simultaneously to more than one press. Some presses will only look at some projects if they can look at them exclusively; other presses are willing to compete for a manuscript. If a press asks you if they can consider your manuscript exclusively, it's your choice. If you agree, you are bound by it. The press, of course, is not obligated at all, so if you have initial interest from several presses at an early stage, it would be wise to consult them before agreeing to give one exclusive rights of review. It is important to know that exclusivity never applies to initial inquiries, only to the review of the manuscript. While exclusivity appears to express enthusiasm, it also reflects that the press may feel it's not worth their time and effort to send out your book to reviewers if they can't be sure they will be able to sign the book up in the end.

If you decide to submit your book simultaneously to more than one press, it is both ethical and useful to let each of the presses know. They will want to know which presses they are competing against, which makes sense. If they want to publish your book, they will need to highlight their strengths against those of the other specific presses.

It is rarely advisable to have more than two or three presses reviewing a manuscript at the same time. The burden of work for the presses and the reviewers in your field grows with each additional press. If your manuscript has made it this far, chances are that if one press wants to go forward to contract, the others will as well. Eventually you will need to make a decision, which becomes harder as relationships deepen during the process. This is not a situation where you need a "safety school." Interestingly, senior scholars, who one might think could have more to gain in a competitive situation, submit simultaneously much less often than junior scholars. If you are a junior scholar with an editor you like who is enthusiastic about your project, you probably will have no need for additional suitors.

After reviews are in, the possible paths begin to vary even more. If the reviews are negative, or discouraging in some way to the press, that may be the end of the process at that press. At some presses, this endpoint may come at the moment of financial reckoning. They might send a manuscript out to see if it seems like a potential prize-winner, but, if it is judged to be merely very good, the press may decide that it's not a project they can afford. In most cases though, if the reviews are generally supportive—even if they make pages of suggestions—the author will be asked to write a response.

RESPONDING TO REVIEWERS

The author response is an unusual genre of writing, and quite different from the response you might offer to a critique of your work in any other forum. In fact, the art of reading and responding to reviews is one of the most important parts of a publishing career. And it isn't easy. Criticism is seldom easy to accept, especially when it comes on a project on which you've been spending many of your waking hours for three or five years. Learning to accept what you can from readers' reports and to read them with the awareness that someone spent a lot of time reading your manuscript (and for a token fee) is truly an art.

Instead of trying to defend your manuscript or arguing that your questioner is off-base, when you write your response, you need to assume the responsibility of making your manuscript work. Authors often will point to their excellent intentions and good motives. Those are not the issue. The point is how well you are *communicating* your ideas and your argument. The review process is the first official test of whether you are succeeding or failing. It can be compared to a Hollywood test screening. If the director expects the audience to be weeping at a certain scene and instead they are giggling, it's not helpful to curse the audience. The director has to go back and re-cut. The same is true of your manuscript. You control the text; you have to make it work. The response to reviews is an opportunity to say how you will do that.

Sometimes readers will offer contradictory solutions to the same problem. In other words, two readers will focus on the same part of the text but will provide different diagnoses and different prescriptions. Authors often, understandably, feel confused or angered by such contradictions. But what you should try to see is that something important is happening in this aspect of your book but it isn't quite working. Your readers are trying to find a solution but *you* are the author. What they are really saying is that, in one way or another, this is an argument that needs more work, more attention, more development. They may not have the right solution, but they are urging you to pay close attention to this part of your manuscript and to work to develop it successfully. Your editor will help you write your response and may provide you with some guidelines for what is the appropriate kind of response necessary to move to the next stage in the publishing process: a contract for your book.

OBTAINING A CONTRACT

Once you have responded adequately to your reviewers, procedures will be initiated within the press that will lead to a contract. These procedures vary and your editor will need to explain how the process will work in your case. Often presses have boards, which may be of two types. First, at commercial academic presses and most university presses, there are internal boards involving some combination of editors, sales or marketing people, the press director; sometimes managing editors, a press financial officer, and managers of design and production. At some presses the board might be all editors, at others it might include representatives of a number of departments; at some presses the director may have sole say, at others a wide consensus may be required.

The second kind of board is typically an advisory board composed of university faculty. Some state university presses include faculty and other representatives from the different campuses. These faculty boards "guard the imprint" and represent the academic oversight for the press's list.

Procedures at this stage may vary as well. At some presses, an internal board approves a project which then goes to a faculty board, whose approval is necessary for a contract. At others an internal board makes the decision on a contract and the faculty board gives its approval later on, when the revised version of the manuscript is deemed ready for production. Most faculty boards consider each manuscript separately; others approve wholesale the press's activity over a longer period. There are advantages and disadvantages to each of the systems. As an author, you should query your editor about the particular process at the press. Don't assume it will be exactly the same process that colleagues have gone through at a different press.

Once you are offered a contract, read it carefully. Some contracts issued in advance are also final contracts. Others will be replaced by final contracts. Some advance contracts don't commit the press to anything more than reviewing a later manuscript; some are binding unless something unusual happens. Again, the best advice is to ask your editor about the press's own conditions and procedures.

If you have questions about the contract, start by asking your editor. If there is some point about which you remain unsure, you might consult colleagues who have published at similar presses. Most contracts are conventional. Consulting friends or relatives who are agents and accustomed to the substantially different conventions of trade publishing, or lawyers used to poking holes in contracts, rarely turns out to be productive.

ROYALTIES AND ADVANCES

Earlier in this essay we noted that most scholarly publishing loses money. This is important to remember as you read your contract and get to the bottom line. Every contract has a royalty agreement but, for the vast majority of academic books, the actual amount of money earned from the book itself will be trivial, especially relative to the other indirect forms of remuneration (promotions, merit raises, competitive job offers) that result from academic publishing.

Most university and commercial academic presses will pay royalties on sales of the book. Usually these will be on "net receipts" — the amount of money the press receives from sales of the book. Trade publishers generally pay royalties on list price, regardless of the discount at which the book was actually sold. It would be a rare author who could move a press from its normal way of accounting, but if you are comparing arrangements with others, you should understand this difference.

It is fairly common when books are published simultaneously in library cloth and paperback editions for authors to forgo royalties on the library cloth edition (which rarely sells more than two or three hundred copies). Other than that, an author could expect to have some royalties on most sales, though there are some presses which offer no royalties on the first hardcover monograph sales. This is not the usual practice, however. If presses vary royalties from contract to contract, it usually reflects some combination of the perceived status of the author and the sales prospects for the particular book, together with any competitive considerations.

An advance is the payment of some of the expected earnings from royalties paid in advance of the publication and actual sale of the book. It is not a signing bonus, in the sense of additional money, but rather represents the faith of the press in the book's eventual sales. It is customary for advances to be paid in parts, such as half on signing and the remainder on final acceptance or publication. In cases where advances are offered — and this also varies from press to press and book to book — the amount can vary from a few hundred dollars to a few thousand. There are cases where university presses have paid advances in five figures rather than three or four, but they are comparatively rare.

If you have more than one press offering a contract, you should compare the royalties and advance between them, but you should also inquire about how the press plans to publish and position the book. Some things will be negotiable and some not. Presses will often match an offer from another press in some way to get a book. For instance, a press might slightly up an advance or royalties, or a press that would otherwise plan to publish clothbound editions only might agree to a simultaneous paperback. In the end you will need to decide where you want the book, since ultimately the offers are unlikely to differ by much. A five hundred dollar difference in the advance from one press, for example, may not counterbalance another press's reputation in your field, or differences in book design or marketing approach, or an offer to publish the book simultaneously in hardcover and in paper.

DEADLINES AND DELIVERY DATES

A contract signed in advance of the final manuscript will usually contain a date for turning in the revised and completed version. If you are asked to proffer such a date, be kind to yourself. Choose a date that gives you enough time for the many changes in location, institution, partner or family status—not to mention the complications of research and writing itself—that can intervene. Unless the publishing program changes radically while you revise, publishers are likely to understand if you need more time than expected (as long as you aren't churning out books for other publishers in the meantime). Stay in touch with your editor and apprise her or him of your progress, and if you need more time, ask.

This might be a good time to mention that the full process from contract to publication takes much longer than scholars imagine when they emerge from graduate school, mostly because the process of producing manuscript and seeing that manuscript through all the different stages of review and revision is a larger task than anticipated.

When you turn in the revised manuscript, procedures once again will vary by press. If the faculty board voted at the time of contract they may or may not need to approve the completed manuscript. At some presses it will be between author and editor to determine if the manuscript is ready for production. At others, the manuscript will go back out to reviewers for their judgment. Again, each of the systems has advantages and disadvantages; you will want to understand the procedures at your press.

FROM MANUSCRIPT TO BOOK

Once the manuscript is finally complete and goes into production, however, schedules are no longer flexible. Typically, it takes nine to twelve months for a university press manuscript to be transformed into a book. This will usually involve the press's professional copyediting, you reviewing the edits, manuscript clean-up back at the press, design of the interior, typesetting, proofreading, indexing, cover design, and finally printing and binding. As you have no doubt guessed by this point in the essay, the particulars will vary from press to press and the timing from book to book, depending on length or workloads, even at a single press. At many presses, a managing editor will oversee the copy-editing, which is done by freelancers. Elsewhere it is done in house by press staff. Many presses freelance design, while others are proud of their in-house designers. Some presses have stock interiors; others design them afresh each time. You may be solely responsible for proofreading or there may be a professional proofreader as well. Indexing is often, but not always, the responsibility of the author. You may be tempted to hire a grad student or a professional and should bear in mind the needs of the audience that will be reading your book, and what they will expect to find in the index. A professional indexer might be perfect for a narrative history but lost in a theoretical work featuring a variety of unfamiliar terms.

Commercial academic presses tend to be faster, sometimes by skipping, combining, or reducing stages. In all cases, though, there will be absolute deadlines, with tight turnaround times, at several stages in the production. You will be expected to meet these deadlines, even if it means changing your vacation dates or proofreading days after your child's birth.

Your book will be in a catalog, with an announced date, and the production process is geared to ensuring that what is promised in that catalog is available when the press says it will be. That date, by the way, is conventionally a publication date — for publicity — and is usually a month or two after physical books are available. This comes from the trade necessity of having books already in the bookstore when reviews appear. You, your editor, and the press's marketing department will all want the book out in time for important academic meetings. It becomes crucial to treat the schedule for returning copy-edited manuscripts or page proofs like a train schedule. You have to show up on time. Once the book is out, you will be certainly glad you did.

BECOMING AN AUTHOR

After your book is published, as with a basketball shot or a golf swing, the follow-through is critical to the success of the whole effort. The press will work hard, but there are many things that happen for a book primarily because of the attention, presence, and networks of the author. The moment of publication is not a time to disappear in postpartum abjection. You should make a special effort to show up at conferences or to arrange to give talks about the topic of your book. It's a crucial part of promoting the book and it is also part of your responsibilities as an author. Again, university press books lose money for the universities that own them. Doing your part to ensure that your book sells enough to pay for itself should be seen as a professional commitment —

and it is a commitment that will be as good for your career as it is for scholarly publishing more generally.

The best reason to stay engaged with your book even after it has appeared in print is because you've earned it. The whole process of writing a book and seeing it through publication is a long one. It is often frustrating, almost always solitary. Seeing your book actually read and appreciated by others, being part of an ongoing discussion of its ideas, and being able to watch its impact on the thinking of others is one of the joys of publishing. Otherwise, why not simply think one's thoughts? Why bother about a book if it isn't to communicate? Reaping the personal satisfactions of authorship, of communicating your ideas with the world you may not have known before you began writing, is an extremely positive part of the publishing process. But it is not the end of the process. Not at all. In fact, it may well be simply the beginning of your *next* book project.

28.

THE MODERN RESEARCH LIBRARY

DEBORAH L. JAKUBS AND PAUL L. CONWAY

It is undeniable that research libraries are undergoing dramatic change. The impact of new and rapidly evolving technologies on library collections and services, while not unanticipated, has brought about a transformation in both the kind of resources offered and the relationship of the institution to its users. The availability of new formats has also transformed teaching and research. It is common to read about "the changing nature of research libraries in the information age," and yet the library's traditional role has endured, albeit within an environment that is very much in flux. The modern library still fulfills its established role by providing materials for research, teaching, and study, but it does so in very different ways and has assumed important new functions as well.

INTRODUCTION

The modern library is a dynamic organization at the heart of the learning process in the university. Research libraries today spend a significant proportion of their collection funds on the intangible: access to electronic databases, on-line journals, digital books. New service models are in evidence, and librarians have come out from behind that forbidding reference desk to be increasingly active partners with faculty in the academic enterprise. Technology has made research and teaching easier in some ways, but much more difficult in others. With so much information available, it is more important than ever that students and faculty learn to discriminate, to pick and choose, to analyze, and to select carefully. Technology has decentralized many library functions, making it unnecessary to set foot in a library building, but the array of resources can be overwhelming and users of these resources still need guidance. Librarians are available to provide a general introduction to collections and services, an orientation to the literature of a particular field, or a specialized session on a specific topic.

These new roles for research libraries do not come without a price. Striking the balance between conducting traditional collection development, for example, and moving quickly into the digital era presents a true challenge to libraries. Supporting the needs of all disciplines—those that rely on print materials, or rare books, or film and video, or foreign language resources, as well as those whose literature is mostly or even completely online—all within a finite budget is one of the most significant tightrope acts that research libraries must perform these days. The array of databases and other digital resources available is dazzling, and these new (and not insignificant) costs must be factored into the larger equation of library funding.

What do these changes and challenges mean to you as a new faculty member? As a graduate student, you developed a special relationship to the library where you conducted your own research, in the institution where you wrote your dissertation, worked as a teaching assistant, designed your courses. That was most likely an intense relationship, based on your broad and deep knowledge of the library's book and journal collection in your specific field of research, perhaps the primary sources available to you in the special collections department, as well as your discovery of digital resources relevant to your own work. The odds are that you gave very little thought to how those materials got to the library, or how the librarians made decisions about resource allocation. As a faculty member, you may have the same relationship to the collections that you had previously, but you also have responsibilities with regard to the library. You will have the opportunity to learn more about the internal workings of the library, to serve as an advocate for the library on campus and beyond, to understand the budget process and the tensions when trade-offs are necessary. Library administrators will welcome your active participation in determining how the library can best meet your needs and those of your students and how to set priorities amid a climate of practically constant change. You will also be able to count on librarians to be resources for your teaching.

COLLECTIONS: THE FOUNDATION OF LIBRARIES

For the 120-plus libraries of the Association of Research Libraries (ARL; http://www.arl.org.), deep and broad historical collections, including rare books and primary resources, are central. These collections were developed over the years through various means: the efforts of librarians and faculty, and through gifts, exchanges, subscriptions, and approval plans. Subject-specialist librarians, basing their decisions on explicit or implicit collection policies, purchased those materials they considered to be of importance to the research and teaching of the university, in the process building especially strong collections in selected areas. Faculty returning from research trips abroad often donated to their library foreign books that would otherwise be unknown outside of the country in which they were published, or made contacts with organizations that contributed such materials. Some of the resulting collections are the richest and deepest in North America and reflect the intellectual interests of the faculty of a given institution at a particular time. Gifts of books and journals have also contributed to the creation of strong library collections, as have materials received on exchange from research institutes or universities around the world.

That was the print environment. With the shift to new electronic formats, and the integration of multimedia into teaching, the definition of "collection" has changed dramatically. The access offered by the Web, along with the proliferation of databases, e-journals, and e-books, has transformed the collection-development function (as well as service to users) in libraries.

"I never use the library anymore," quips one faculty member in the physical sciences. What he means is that he never sets foot in the library. But as he reads electronic journal articles at his desk, or checks facts in a database from his lab, he is, in fact, using "the library," since those resources are acquired — or rather access to them is contracted — by the library. For another professor in classics, the bound journal collection is her bread and butter and her carrel in the stacks is her lab. For a geologist, the digital map collection is critical to research, and he tailors his assignments so that students will develop a familiarity with it. A historian of South Asia depends on the British Parliamentary Papers for his work. Slave diaries in the special collections department form the focus of a colonial U.S. history class. A database containing the publications of non-governmental organizations (NGOs) offers information on the public health aspects of AIDS in Africa. A Web site that gathers and preserves the Web pages of Latin American political candidates serves as an important resource for students in a political science class. A collection of Chinese videos supports both a language class and a course on popular culture. The list goes on and on; suffice it to say that the array of formats has changed dramatically, and the sheer volume of information to which the library serves as a gateway has grown exponentially. Emphasis on interdisciplinary programs of research has also had an impact on the nature of library acquisitions.

Nowhere is this effect more apparent than in the area of electronic journals (e-journals). As new areas of inquiry develop, they spawn new journals. In a phenomenon known as "twigging," new journals take on more and more specific emphases as subfields emerge and scholars specialize. As if the rise in the number and diversity of journals were not enough of a new variable for libraries, the costs of e-journals have increased from exorbitant to outrageous, particularly in the "STM" (science, technology, medicine) fields. What is often not apparent to library users is the fact that the individual subscription rate is very considerably lower than the institutional rate. Libraries are, on average, charged a subscription fee that is ten times higher than what individual subscribers pay.[1] It is not unusual for subscriptions to scholarly STM journals to cost libraries $10,000–$20,000 per year.

THE SCHOLARLY COMMUNICATION CONUNDRUM

The library's collections budget, in the most basic terms, is divided into one-time costs (books, videos, etc., items that are paid for once) and ongoing or recurring costs (journals, databases, etc., items that have annual costs). As the number of journals increases, and their costs rise, and more electronic products enter the market, the portion of the budget that must be earmarked for ongoing payments grows. This reduces the pot of funding available to acquire books—an issue of serious concern particularly to university presses, which note the decline in library purchases of scholarly monographs. These are often the first books of junior faculty, and thus of critical importance for gaining tenure.

This example of the potential domino effect among scholars, libraries, and academic presses is but a part of the scholarly communication arena. A similar ironic interrelatedness can be seen in the research and publication continuum. Faculty generate new knowledge based on their research, which often relies on library resources. That new scholarship is then published in journals, which own the copyright, and which are then purchased by the library at very high prices. Concern about this situation has led to the Open Access movement, in which research is made freely available to the public and the costs of publication are borne not by libraries but by authors, often through grant funds.[2]

Libraries have not been passive observers. The Scholarly Publishing and Academic Resources Coalition (SPARC) was founded in 1997 to raise awareness among scholars of the scholarly publishing conundrum and call their attention to the high prices of STM journals. SPARC is an alliance of universities, research libraries, and other organizations, and was begun by the Association of Research Libraries as "a constructive response to market dysfunctions in the scholarly communication system . . . [which have] reduced dissemination of scholarship and crippled libraries."[3]

SPARC has helped incubate new lower-cost, directly competitive journals, some in partnership with scholarly societies and often with editorial boards that essentially have defected from a journal they deemed to be priced too high, to compete with the expensive ones. For example, *Labor* is a joint project of SPARC and the Labor and Working Class History Association, and the *Journal of Vegetation Science* is cosponsored by the International Association of Vegetation Science. SPARC also produces numerous other journals in a variety of disciplines that are low-cost and/or open-access publications, for example, the *New Journal of Physics; Theory and Practice of Logic Programming; Evolutionary Ecology;* and *Geometry and Topology.* It has been heartening for libraries to note the new activism among some faculty who, now that they are better informed about the dynamics of the scholarly publishing environment, have refused to serve on the editorial boards of journals published by conglomerates that are known to charge exorbitant and unreasonable prices for their journals, and have refused to serve as reviewers for such journals. Faculty are powerful players in this arena and are in the best position to change the system, as they work with librarians toward the common goal of improving access to scholarship. New faculty should become well informed about the pressures placed on libraries by the rising costs of access to journal literature and should work as advocates with librarians to seek solutions.

PARTNERS IN TEACHING

As a new faculty member, you will find librarians to be creative and willing partners in the process of educating your students. Beyond the more informal and spontaneous interactions between students and librarians at the reference desk, there are opportunities to engage library subject specialists for one-time class sessions to focus on research methods and the specific bibliography on a topic of study. Some libraries have more formal instruction programs focused on "information literacy." These sessions may or may not be required and will orient students to the library, its collections, and services. They will remind students of the proper care and handling of books. They will teach students how to evaluate Web sites for accuracy and to identify bias, how to value both print and electronic sources, how to make the most of the library's online resources, and how to incorporate, when appropriate, primary materials into their papers and presentations. This assistance with the discernment process, developing analytical and critical thinking skills in students as they carry out their academic work, is an important contribution of librarians to the learning process. In this way, they are valuable partners with faculty.

The modern academic library is technology-rich. Library information technology—in concert with a wide range of common computer desktop software—enables the use of digital information for research and learning, for individual and group productivity, and for the innovative creation, distribution, and preservation of new knowledge.[4]

The initial challenge that faculty face in applying library technology to their work is the simultaneous explosion of information available in digital form and the blurring of the line separating information that is "owned and operated" by the campus library from information that is available more widely through the Internet. Paul Gandel and his colleagues summarize the issues that face library users in an era of abundance: "The current and prospective era of information abundance will challenge many basic assumptions and practices about safeguarding, protecting, filtering, preserving, evaluating, purging, describing, cataloguing, and vetting information for the purposes of teaching, learning, and scholarship."[5] They identify four factors driving both the appearance and the reality of the information explosion: (1) the shift from an industrial to a knowledge economy, (2) the abundance of and speedy access to digital information, (3) information integration, and (4) education as a lifelong process. The emerging complex *knowledge economy* generates new information in digital form at an alarming rate. A recent study at the University of California, Berkeley, estimates that 93 percent of all new information is created in digital form. Accompanying the increase in the amount and nature of information is an equally dramatic decrease in the cost of storing digital content. *Abundance and speed*, when combined with the unified look and feel of Web browser technologies, have fostered the illusion of *information integration*, where everything you need is at your fingertips. The elegance of a Google search result set has the uncanny ability to obscure what we know to be true: much valuable research information is buried deeply in difficult-to-find databases or is not in digital form at all.

Newer-generation library systems may provide scholars with tools to personalize their interaction with the library catalog. Among the most common features of "MyLibrary" services, for example, are the ability to remember and recall search history and the ability to view materials charged to a given account or to renew books online, reminiscent of the services offered by Amazon.com. Increasingly, libraries are linking delivery and support services to catalog personalization tools, including interlibrary loan, eReserves, and on-demand copying.

Online access to library collections today is a conundrum. On one level, today's library access systems have similar features, are relatively easy to use, and are powerful in the hands of an advanced user. In other ways, library public access systems are maddeningly inconsistent in nagging little ways, especially in comparison to Internet search engines such as Google and Yahoo.

Ideally, a scholar would be able to capture and save to a personal workstation only that portion of a work that is relevant for the anticipated use. If all that is needed is a paragraph from a chapter of an electronic book, then it ought to be possible to "cut and paste" the paragraph, along with the relevant citation information, in a single step. If what is needed is an entire work or a substantial portion of that work, then comprehensive downloading, in a format useful for the scholar, should be equally seamless.

We know, however, that those who market digital resources have developed ingenious mechanisms for limiting both the selective and the comprehensive capture of content in useful formats. Many electronic books available through commercial and not-for-profit enterprises, for example, allow online reading and digital capture only on a page-by-page basis. Some digital resources are available in formats (e.g., PDF) that do not permit the use of "chunks" of text or embedded images. Restrictions on local capture of content are driven equally, it seems, by the reluctance of digital publishers to forgo any possible economic value of the intellectual property they own, and by the reluctance of authors to encourage the use of text and/or image out of context.

If text and references are available for download from commercial and not-for-profit providers, then it is increasingly simple to load this information into tools that will automatically format it based upon personal preferences. Tools such as ProCite and EndNote, for example, can accept the results of searches in a variety of abstracting and indexing services, formatting the citations (along with appropriate links back to the original source) according to a variety of bibliographic publication standards.

Traditionally the work of manipulating text and/or images to create new knowledge and analysis has been the domain of scholarship, conducted in the quiet of the faculty office or the hubbub of the campus computing lab, but libraries are now providing the space, the means, and the support for extended writing, for image management, and for multimedia production—by individual scholars as well as by groups of students working together. Library facilities are clearly reflecting these new roles and functions.

Libraries are also assuming new roles in facilitating the distribution of new knowledge and are increasingly enabling the publication or republication of faculty output through the development of digital repositories of faculty publications. Librarians are facilitating new forms of communication—represented in part by the emergence of weblogs (blogs) and collaborative Web authoring tools (wikis).

DIGITIZATION AND DIGITAL ASSET MANAGEMENT

Since the early 1990s, the digitization of scholarly resources has been a driving force in the transformation of library services and of the scholarly enterprise itself. Virtually every research library in North America has undertaken digitization projects over the past decade, although the scale, complexity, and long-term viability of these projects vary significantly. The results of most digitization projects usually are available through the library's Web site.

Libraries are challenged not only to build and maintain large scale digitization services but to take actions necessary to sustain their digital assets over the long term. The terms "digital archive," "institutional repository," and "digital asset management" are sometimes used interchangeably in the higher education community. Interest is now emerging on campuses in taking steps to ensure that digital preservation needs are met.[6]

Early digital archive efforts focused on making available via the Web electronic versions of theses and dissertations or pre-print articles in a few scientific fields. In the early years of the twenty-first century, institutional repositories have gained momentum internationally through the release of several free, open-source systems to build them, and after the publication of works defining the issues around developing them. In the past four or five years, attention to the technical and administrative underpinnings of institutional repositories has exploded, fueled in part by the release by the Massachusetts Institute of Technology of the DSpace software and by the growing recognition by faculty and librarians of the importance of managing digital content.

Hundreds of digital repositories now exist around the world and a handful of systems have emerged as the basis for most university repositories. These systems are:

— *DSpace*: Developed through a partnership between MIT Libraries and Hewlett Packard, this system is now used for more than seventy repositories. (See http://www.dspace.org/.)

— *Eprints*: Developed through funding by the U.S. National Science Foundation and the Joint Information Systems Committee in the UK, Eprints is now in use for more than 145 repositories. The Eprints system is the key system used by advocates of the Free Online Scholarship (open access) movement. (See http://www.eprints.org/.)

— *Fedora*: Developed through a partnership between the University of Virginia and Cornell, this system aims to be an all-purpose repository, managing and providing access not only to scholarly papers but also to large collections of digital images, data sets, and other types of digital media. Because of its broader scope this system is also significantly more complex than the others and is currently in use for only nineteen repositories. (See http://www.fedora.info/.)

— *Digital Commons*: This is the only commercial and proprietary system that is currently widely used for university digital repositories. It was originally developed by the Berkeley Electronic Press and is now marketed and supported by ProQuest/UMI. (See http://www.umi.com/umi/digitalcommons/.)

TECHNOLOGY IN THE EVOLVING IDEA OF LIBRARY SPACE

Information technologies, along with a newly energized focus on the teaching and learning enterprise, are driving fundamental changes in how library spaces are designed and used. The architect Geoffrey Freeman writes eloquently about continuity and change in the value of the campus library:

> No other building can so symbolically and physically represent the academic heart of an institution. If the library is to remain a dynamic life force, however, it must support the academic community in several new ways. Its space must flexibly accommodate evolving information technologies and their usage as well as become a "laboratory" for new ways of teaching and learning in a wired or wireless environment.[7]

Since the early years of the twenty-first century, librarians have experimented somewhat successfully with emerging communication technologies to facilitate and improve communication between patrons and librarian subject specialists. Tools such as "virtual reference" and "reference chat rooms" have expanded the reach of traditional reference services and increased the flexibility that patrons have in asking questions and getting answers outside of normal business operations.[8]

Libraries are increasingly adapting information technologies to leverage the social aspects of the learning environment. The technologist John Seely Brown was one of the first to comment on the transformative nature of the World Wide Web in the university context. In 2000 Brown wrote in his important article "Growing Up Digital" that "the Web helps establish a culture that honors the fluid boundaries between the production and consumption of knowledge."[9] Brown concluded by reflecting on the emerging trend that moves from using technology to support the individual to using technology to support relationships among individuals. Librarians are just now beginning to adapt their physical spaces to facilitate both greater social engagement among learners and the greater use of information technologies across the entire spectrum of the scholarly process. At present these new collaborative spaces are referred to as "Information Commons."[10]

The Information Commons is an evolving approach to campus library services that combines—in flexible physical spaces—rich content in digital and analog formats, ample information technology tools, and expert support services for students and faculty. Colleges and universities throughout North America increasingly are creating information commons because they present their communities with service models that can transcend the traditional boundaries between reference and technology support in libraries, on the one hand, and between library and campus technology operations, on the other. An information commons typically features flexible, well-equipped, and inviting spaces with ample room for individual and group study and presentation, deep subject expertise, and personalized advice on research methodologies and on the choice and application of technology tools for teaching and learning. Increasingly librarians are designing their spaces and revising their services in recognition of the library as an essential workplace for the scholarly enterprise.[11]

NEW ENGAGEMENTS AND CAMPUS COLLABORATIONS

The modern library is an organic organization, remaking itself as an essential partner in the learning enterprise. In her extended essay for the Council on Library and Information Resources (CLIR), Wendy Lougee describes this evolution in the roles that libraries play on campus, partly in response to new technologies and partly in anticipation of new opportunities for leadership that technology provides:

> [W]e see the library becoming more deeply engaged in the fundamental mission of the academic institution—i.e., the creation and dissemination of knowledge—in ways that represent the library's contributions more broadly and that intertwine the library with the other stakeholders in these activities. The library becomes a collaborator within the academy, yet retains its distinct identity.[12]

The University of Virginia's dean of arts and sciences, the distinguished historian Edward Ayers, endorses the principles articulated by Lougee and agrees that transformations in the deployment and use of technology and new digital content are critical components of new scholarship. Ayers, the creator of the innovative, Web-based teaching and research tool on the Civil War, *Valley of the Shadow*,[13] points to a larger challenge ahead: "Over the last decade, American higher education has created a doughnut IT infrastructure: all periphery and no center. We have invested in the machinery but not in the teachers and the scholars to make that machinery worthwhile in the classroom and in scholarship."[14]

CONCLUSION

Expanded partnerships between faculty and the library in a variety of arenas bring not just new intellectual challenges but broad benefits to scholarship and to research institutions. For example, as more faculty become familiar with and concerned about the alarming rise in the costs of STM journals and the resulting crisis in scholarly communication, they enter the fray as strong, articulate advocates for new publishing models and adequate funding for library collections. As librarians engage more actively in teaching — whether through formal library instruction programs or team-teaching with faculty — students and faculty alike acquire new skills in information retrieval and research methods. Technology in support of teaching and learning depends on new collaborative relationships. For a new faculty member, this is a time of change, challenge, and experimentation in research libraries. You will undoubtedly be part of the transformation that is well underway and will find willing partners in librarians.

NOTES

1. Deborah Jakubs, "The Irresistible Force Meets the Immovable Object: Or, How Libraries are Just Saying 'No' to Journal Publishers," *Duke University Libraries* 17, no. 2 (Winter 2004): 3, http://magazine.lib.duke.edu/issue 14/.

2. For more information on the Open Access movement, see http://www.plos.org/about/openaccess.html.

3. For more information on SPARC, see http://www.arl/sparc/about.index.html.

4. See *Beyond Productivity: Information Technology, Innovation, and Creativity*, ed. William J. Mitchell, Alan S. Inouye, and Marjory S. Blumenthal (Washington: National Academy Press, 2003), http://books.nap.edu/.

5. Paul B. Gandel, Richard N. Katz, and Susan E. Metros, "The 'Weariness of the Flesh': Reflections on the Life of the Mind in an Era of Abundance," *EDUCAUSE Review* (March–April 2004): 40–51, http://www.educause.edu/.

6. See Abby Smith, *Strategies for Building Digitized Collections* (Washington: Digital Library Federation, 2001), http://www.clir.org/; Donald J. Waters and John Garrett, *Preserving Digital Information: Report of the Task Force on Archiving of Digital Information* (Washington: Commission on Preservation and Access and Research Libraries Group, 1996), http://www.clir.org/.

7. Geoffrey T. Freeman, "The Library as Place: Changes in Learning Patterns, Collections, Technology, and Use," in *Library as Place: Rethinking Roles, Rethinking Space* (Washington: Council on Library and Information Resources, 2005), http://www.clir.org/.

8. See Bernard Frischer, "The Ultimate Internet Café: Reflections of a Practicing Digital Humanist about Designing a Future for the Research Library in the Digital Age," in *Library as Place: Rethinking Roles, Rethinking Space*, http://www.clir.org/.

9. John Seely Brown, "Growing Up Digital: How the Web Changes Work, Education, and the Ways People Learn." *Change* (March/April 2000): 11–20, http://www.johnseelybrown.com/.

10. Donald Beagle, "Conceptualizing an Information Commons," *Journal of Academic Librarianship* 25 (March 1999): 82–90.

11. See Scott Bennett, "Righting the Balance," in *Library as Place: Rethinking Roles, Rethinking Space*, http://www.clir.org/.

12. Wendy Pradt Lougee, *Diffuse Libraries: Emergent Roles for the Research Library in the Digital Age* (Washington: Council on Library and Information Resources, August 2002), http://www.clir.org/.

13. See http://valley.vcdh.virginia.edu/.

14. Edward L. Ayers and Charles M. Grisham, "Why IT Has Not Paid Off as We Hoped (Yet)," *EDUCAUSE Review* 38, no. 6 (November–December 2003): 51, http://www.educause.edu/.

PART VII

ACADEMIC COMMUNITIES AND ADMINISTRATIONS

It will no doubt seem odd that we have devoted a section of this volume to describing governance of the modern university. After all, most of our readers have already spent several years as students in such an institution and ought, therefore, to know what it is. And yet it is clear that most new Ph.D.'s have experienced only a small fraction of the university as such, and that even here, within a single program or department, they do not really understand how decisions are made or how business actually gets done. Perhaps, in short, the new academic has never thought of the university as a corporation, with all the problems of diversity, governance, and structural hierarchies that affect any business.

In the essays that follow, therefore, we give three different views of the system of higher education in America today. The first, offered by A. Kenneth Pye, may be called the macrocosmic view: what are the types of schools, kinds of administrative structures, duties of a president or provost, responsibilities of boards of trustees, and general problems of university governance? The second is a more microcosmic view: Joel Colton discusses what a department is and how it is run. For new academics, negotiating their way between the urgent daily demands of teaching and the equally urgent demands of research and publication, the structural politics of the university or college may not seem as pressing. But this is the community the new academic has chosen to call home, and it is essential, therefore, that he or she discover as quickly as possible the basic laws by which it operates. In any community, the well-being of the whole depends upon the wise and committed service of each individual, and the university is no exception to that rule.

In fact, it is precisely the importance of active faculty participation in a variety of academic communities that is the focus of Philip Stewart's final essay in this section. At whatever level you choose to participate, your citizenship in these communities offers you the chance to make a difference in the academy of the future. We hope you will seize that opportunity boldly, and that the following essays will start you on the path to productive and rewarding academic citizenship.

29

UNIVERSITY GOVERNANCE AND AUTONOMY

Who Decides What in the University

A. KENNETH PYE

A recurring issue in academic life is that of governance — who, trustees, administrators, faculty, students, or others, should decide or participate in the decisions on matters that arise in the conduct of university affairs. An equally important issue is that of autonomy — which matters directly affecting university life should be decided on campus and which should be decided elsewhere, by state boards, legislatures, courts, or other public or private persons or bodies.[1]

Young professors may understandably inquire why they should be concerned or involved with matters of governance or autonomy. Two reasons should be obvious. Participation in significant matters affecting a community is a component of good citizenship and faculty are citizens of an academic community. Effective participation requires knowledge of issues and processes by which they are resolved. A second reason is more self-serving. University communities are not composed solely of scholars. Faculty participation in governance is necessary to ensure that academic priorities receive appropriate status in university planning and that scarce resources are used most effectively. The purpose of this essay is to provide a general description of the processes and problems involved in governance and the impact upon the role of faculty in governance posed by recent threats to university autonomy.

GOVERNANCE

Patterns of university governance vary widely in higher education between liberal arts colleges and universities, research universities and universities whose primary mission is teaching, larger and smaller institutions, private and public institutions. There are significant differences among institutions that are similar in purpose, size, and primary source of support. Such diversity makes it difficult to generalize. This essay attempts to describe processes that are common in private and public research universities of the first rank. Many of the observations also apply to other institutions of higher learning.

Many young professors approach the mysteries of university governance with an institutional model that Robert Paul Wolff once described as "a sanctuary of scholarship":[2] a self-governing community in which experienced and apprentice scholars engage in a mutual search for truth with relatively little concern about factors other than admission of newcomers and quality of the scholarship being undertaken. Faculty make all important decisions because the mission of the intellectual community is research and teaching and these functions are performed by faculty. The faculty is not *a* constituency; it is *the* constituency.

This perception offers a generally accurate description of European universities before World War II, with the caveat that authority rested almost exclusively in the senior professoriate, but it does not describe European universities today nor American universities at any time in their history. The increased size and complexity of universities, impact of the "egalitarian ethic," democratization of all societal institutions, increased dependence upon funding from governments for medical and scientific research and financial support to students, and more intense regulation of all institutions in society for health, safety, equality, security, and other social objectives have combined to make the process of governance much more complex.

University governance today is a process in which trustees, administrators, faculty, students, and sometimes others share responsibility for making important decisions required for an institution to perform its missions of teaching, research, and public service. The crucial issues are who participates at what times in what decisions in what ways.[3]

BOARD OF TRUSTEES

The hallmark of the American governance process in private, and in many public, institutions has been the independent campus governed by laymen, usually called trustees or regents, who are neither state officials nor professional educators. Most early American colleges were private institutions, but even the early publicly controlled colleges had their own lay boards of trustees. The great thrust forward in public higher education occurred in the mid-nineteenth century when Congress, through the Morrill Act, stimulated development of land-grant universities aimed primarily at providing instruction in the mechanical and agricultural arts. These institutions were also conceived of primarily as autonomous units, more closely akin to publicly supported, chartered, independent private colleges than to a coherent integrated state system of higher education.⁴ Despite a recent trend toward consolidation in state systems, the single-campus lay board of trustees continues to be the most prevalent form of governance and almost the only form in the private sector.

Boards of trustees differ in size. Some have fewer than ten members; some more than fifty. Frequency of meetings also varies, although most, if not all, meet at least quarterly. Larger boards that commonly meet less frequently have executive committees that transact business during intervals between board meetings.

The source of board authority also differs. Some boards receive powers from state constitutions; others were created as corporate bodies and given certain powers by virtue of their incorporation. Some were created through special enactments of state legislatures. Most public universities derive their authority from state statutes or the state constitution. The legal source of authority in private colleges is sometimes ambiguous: some claim authority by charter; others through incorporation; many have had no reason to face the question.⁵

Boards are also selected in different ways: external election, external appointment, self-selection, or ex officio selection. Some public officials may be ex officio members of boards by statute. Most members of boards of trustees of public universities are appointed by state officials, usually by governors. Trustees are elected by the public in a few states. The most common method of choosing new trustees in private institutions is self-selection; members of an existing board elect their successors. Boards in some private institutions are selected by religious organizations or other groups that originally created the university, but a board may be de facto self-perpetuating because of willingness of a group to accept nominations proffered by an existing board. Alumni of an institution may elect some members.⁶

Composition of boards frequently reflects the history and purposes of an institution and current societal concepts of the need for representation of different segments of society. Approximately one-third of board members are from the business community.⁷ Women and minorities are still underrepresented in many universities.

A board of trustees is entrusted with responsibility for administering the institution in accordance with its stated purposes, which are frequently expressed in broad language. It has an obligation to plan the development of the institution, select and determine the tenure of its chief executive, hold assets of the institution in trust, act as a court of last resort, and play an important role in public relations.⁸ It may be called upon to interpret the institution to society or serve as a barrier to protect the academic community from that society.⁹ In theory, trustees have power to make almost all decisions affecting the institution: appointment, promotion, and conferral of tenure of faculty; commencement, modification, and termination of academic programs; establishment of standards for admission of students and requirements for degrees; approval of curricula; authorization of construction or renovation of buildings; approval of annual budgets; decisions concerning whether to borrow money and how to invest endowment; and long-range planning.

The extent to which a board delegates its responsibilities, and to whom, varies, depending in large part on historical factors, its confidence in its officers or faculty, and sometimes the political reality that delegating power to decide certain matters is advisable in order to assure tranquility on the campus. Boards in many universities delegate power broadly to the president and accept his or her decisions concerning what power should be entrusted to faculty, students, or other groups.

CENTRAL ADMINISTRATION

The central administration of a university is the chief executive (usually denominated "president") and her or his principal subordinate officers (usually denominated "vice presidents"), the chief academic officer (usually denominated "provost"), and their staffs.

Responsibilities of a central administration in one university may differ significantly from those in another. Some universities resemble a confederacy of schools. Power is highly centralized in others. In general, however, central administration is responsible for executing, implementing, and monitoring the policies of the board, proposing new ones, supervising investments, raising external support (other than grants to individual professors), relating to the community, providing support services, maintaining the physical plant, and developing an academic strategy for the institution as a whole.

President   The president is responsible for academic quality, athletic success, fundraising, public relations, financial management, and institutional integrity.[10] What he or she actually does personally depends upon the nature of the institution and the personality of the incumbent. Some presidents spend much of their time cultivating legislators, foundations, and private donors. All must represent the university in educational associations, before public bodies, and with alumni and other external constituencies. Some are personally involved in recruitment and promotion of senior faculty; others delegate such duties to their provosts. Some are intimately involved in business and investment issues; others leave such issues primarily to their boards and vice presidents for business affairs. Most have particular academic areas that they wish to emphasize and do so through control of the university budget.

A president's concept of the kind of leadership he or she should provide is of crucial importance to the nature of the participation expected from faculty. Presidential styles reflect different conditions, traditions, and personalities. Some presidents permit programs to develop and then administer them as ably as possible, regardless of the directions of such programs. Some take a more active role, serving first as a catalyst for development of a consensus concerning appropriate directions and then leading the university toward achievement of the goals so determined. Others are content with administering consensus policies. They consult with appropriate constituencies, determine personally the wisest directions, and lead the university toward their accomplishment. A few presidents act decisively with little prior faculty involvement.

Faculty have considerable power when a president sees his or her primary role as one of serving as a catalyst for developing a consensus. By definition, a consensus cannot be reached in the face of significant disagreement. In reality, such an approach may give the faculty a veto over fundamental initiatives for change.

Faculty obviously have a less dynamic role where the president is prepared to sponsor initiatives after consultation, even if no consensus emerges. The quality of the consultative process may be the key to the reality of faculty participation.

Few universities are committed to any single approach. Frequently, the issue under consideration will determine the relationship between a president and faculty if processes have not been formalized to such a degree that flexibility is no longer possible.

The real issue in many major institutions is the ethos of the presidential-faculty relationship and perceptions of the degree to which dynamic leadership is needed. Some universities, faced with inadequate resources, a significant legacy of deferred maintenance, inadequate salaries, noncompetitive financial aid, a need to reallocate funds and reorganize academic units to be on the cutting edge of newly emerging fields of knowledge, aging and overtenured faculty, and resistance to change, may conclude that a consensus on most significant issues is impossible, except on basic values that cannot be translated into effective initiatives. Faculty and presidents in some universities with such problems may be prepared to sacrifice faculty participation to permit presidents to deal with such issues decisively. Faculty and presidents in other institutions may conclude that no long-range progress is possible without faculty consensus in university initiatives, even if the price of faculty acquiescence may be action less responsible to perceived needs than some would desire.

Other University Officers   Universities usually have at least two senior officers directly under the president, a provost or vice president for academic affairs,

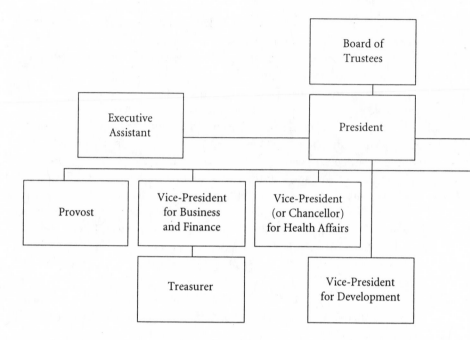

and a vice president for business and financial affairs. A university with an academic medical center normally has a vice president or chancellor for health affairs as well. Several other officers may exist, depending upon the complexity of the institution. A vice president for external relations or development is common, as are a vice president for student affairs, vice president for computer services, university counsel, secretary, and treasurer. The duties are suggested by their titles (see figure).

The exact authority of different vice presidents may be perplexing to them as well as to the faculty. For instance, the extent to which the vice president for business and finance has responsibility for business operations of hospitals or grant administration within a medical center, the extent to which a provost has responsibility for academic promotions within a school of medicine, or the division of responsibility between a provost and vice president for business and finance on budgetary matters may not always be clear.

Such issues obviously may have considerable importance for a junior faculty member who has a problem and doesn't understand to which officer he should turn for advice or decision. Sometimes, the answer can be determined by reference to a faculty manual, available in most institutions. A chairperson can often provide the answer, and, if not, usually the dean will be available to provide guidance.

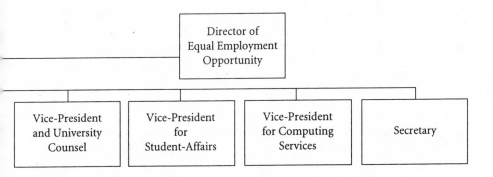

SCHOOLS

Deans, appointed by the president, provost, or a board of trustees, have general responsibility for operation of schools within a university. In some settings, deans function as chairpeople, a "first among equals" with faculty colleagues. In others they function more as an executive officer directly subordinate to the provost. Institutional history may determine which areas are appropriate for a decanal decision and which are appropriate for decision by a school faculty. For instance, allocation of financial aid may be a decanal prerogative in one school and determined by faculty in another.

Usually, a school develops its own academic programs within the framework of the university's overall academic plan. It determines its program of instruction and research, approves courses proposed by departments, establishes rules governing academic requirements, determines its priorities, and allocates revenue made available by central administration to carry out its programs. But universities differ concerning which matters a school decides for itself and which will be determined by a provost. An individual provost's conception of his or her job may be the decisive determinant. Some provosts see their job as one of strategic management of the overall academic programs of a university, delegating individual decisions to schools. Others feel the need to decide any issue that they consider important and do not hesitate to intervene in school decisions within the province of deans and schools elsewhere. Common techniques are enforcement of tight budgetary controls and active participation in faculty selection, promotion, and tenure.

Medical schools exercise much greater independence than other schools. Several factors contribute to their special status: size of sponsored research programs; broader base of federal support; mixture of research, patient care, and instruction; historic primacy of clinical departments; complexity of operating a university hospital; differences in sources of faculty salaries; and lengthy tenure of departmental chairs. Other professional schools enjoy a lesser degree of independence but tend to be more independent than arts and sciences. Most operate their own admissions, placement, and alumni affairs offices and maintain separate libraries. A higher degree of independence is most likely where a professional school generates income sufficient to cover most or all of its expenditures ("each tub on its own bottom") and has a reputation superior to that of most other schools within the university.

Departments   Departments presided over by chairpersons are common in large schools. The department has been the key academic unit over most of the past century.[11] Departments determine their curricula subject to school approval; they also make the initial recommendations for promotion and tenure; they admit and award financial aid to graduate students within rules and resources made available by a school; and they determine the requirements for their majors, subject to school approval.

The role of departmental chair (sometimes called head) also varies widely. The chair of a department within the arts and sciences commonly serves for a term of three to five years and may be reappointed. Frequently, his or her tenure and limited powers require reliance upon persuasion to lead.[12] Chairs of departments in a school of medicine sometimes serve indefinitely, basically at the pleasure of the vice president for health affairs or the dean. Decisions made by such chairs tend to encompass areas that would be reserved to faculty in an arts and sciences department.

FACULTY PARTICIPATION

Faculty participate in governance in different ways. They participate directly in departments. Junior faculty serve on committees and normally vote on all matters entrusted to a department other than promotion and tenure. Faculty also participate personally in the governance of some schools. Other schools function through a representative body, frequently denominated "senate" or "council," that normally conducts much of its business through committees.

Faculty from different schools may meet annually or semiannually in general faculty meetings, but university governance is usually entrusted to a faculty senate or council representing all faculties of the university and sometimes different ranks. Much of its business is also conducted through committees, and it may select faculty to represent it on a host of other committees that report to the board of trustees, the president, the provost, or others.

Powers of faculty bodies are normally the product of a long history of negotiation between faculty and administrators and boards. In general, most major universities entrust a significant role, if not virtually complete authority, to faculty to make decisions in three of the key areas of academic autonomy:[13] (1) admission and examination of students; (2) curricula and courses of study; (3) appointment, promotion, and tenuring of faculty. Central administration or a board may reserve a right to intervene in exceptional cases when it appears that a faculty is not proceeding along lines that best serve the purposes of the institution. Intervention occurs most often when a faculty decision has been made without adequate consideration of long-range financial implications or appropriate priorities.

Generally, however, administrators and boards acquiesce in faculty judgments of an academic nature. Differences concerning an appropriate faculty role occur more frequently when a faculty claims a right to influence decisions on other subjects.

Many faculty believe that faculty should be involved in all important decisions. Administrators and boards are sometimes reluctant to accept the need for faculty consultation on some matters that are not academic in nature. The following arguments are among those advanced for acting without submitting all matters to the faculty:

1. The faculty may have no special competence in many areas such as labor relations, investment policy, hiring and firing of coaches and senior administrators, tax policy, or whether the university should build a hotel or a student union.

2. Some faculty are preoccupied with the impact of decisions upon their own immediate work and welfare and are relatively uninformed or unconcerned with the big picture. Many issues in which faculty have an interest also affect students, alumni, nonacademic workers, and the public. Consulting with faculty alone may produce a distorted view of the best interests of the university. What is good for the faculty is not necessarily good for the university.

3. Involvement of faculty may cause delay that precludes administrators from meeting time schedules imposed by a board; issues raised by faculty may divert administrative resources from matters that administrators or boards think more important.

4. Relatively few of the most distinguished faculty participate in university senates or faculty committees outside their departments in many institutions. As a consequence, despite notable exceptions, faculty political leadership tends to fall more to people who devote more of their time to academic politics than to scholarship. The faculty participation process is also sometimes gerrymandered in such a way that faculty participation involves disproportionately high representation of the arts and sciences.

5. The faculty concept of "participation" often includes the notion that administrators should not take action without approval of representatives of the faculty. Participation is transformed into a veto power. Chief executives, who serve at the pleasure of boards that hold them personally responsible, may not be prepared to defer to faculty, most of whom will not occupy chairs or preside over a department or school and some of whom will not receive tenure or promotion.

6. Issues may arise at any time. Many faculty are not available during almost one-third of the year. Delay may result in loss of opportunity. Attempts to consult with individual faculty members who are available may result in recriminations that administrators bypassed appropriate channels of faculty participation.

Faculty, for their part, sometimes are understandably distrustful of administrative motives when issues of importance are not submitted for their advice. They offer the following arguments, among others, for greater participation:

1. Faculty are better qualified to reflect important educational values that may be shortchanged by administrators in the interest of expediency. Administrators may be too prone to react to more vocal or politically powerful constituencies that are less interested in research and teaching. They may tend to view the campus as a "multiversity," an indifferent amalgam of ideologies, constituencies, and pressures that require compromises "as an imperative rather than a reasoned choice among elegant alternatives,"[14] compromises that sacrifice principle and are inconsistent with faculty values. Administrators may be more concerned with balancing the budget than with how revenue is used.

2. Faculty are usually committed to the educational enterprise for life and have the most to lose from unwise decisions. Some administrators move freely among academia, business, and government and may have less commitment to the university and academic ideals.

3. A university faculty has broader areas of expertise than administrators admit, capabilities that could be directly of use in resolving issues a university must face.

4. Faculty councils or senates are rarely driven by parochial concerns. His-

torically, they have shown at least as great a concern as administrators have for broad social issues and the public interest.

5. Faculty must be regarded either as colleagues in policy making or as employees. If faculty are treated as employees, trade unions and confrontation rather than cooperation will likely result.

6. Any categorical separation of academic and nonacademic matters is necessarily artificial. Every important nonacademic matter has some impact on academic affairs.

These differences can easily be overestimated. Faculty and administrators share an essential community of interest in furthering the welfare of the institution they serve, although they may differ concerning which measures will best serve the common purpose. Furthermore, many, if not most, university administrators are tenured faculty who have devoted much of their academic lives to teaching and research and usually intend to return to those pursuits when they leave their administrative posts.

Faculty involvement tends to be less in institutions whose primary mission is teaching than in major research universities. There administrators, including departmental chairs, serve for longer periods. Boards, religious denominations, and local communities may exert greater influence on routine decisions. The perimeters within which policy is made may be greatly narrowed by economic realities.

AUTONOMY

There has been a consistent trend toward increased faculty participation in governance in major universities in recent years. Simultaneously, other trends have tended to reduce the real influence of faculty on decision making. Faculty gains in participation in governance have been offset in part by (1) greater participation by others in the decision-making process on the campus and (2) a trend toward overall loss of campus autonomy.

PARTICIPATION BY OTHERS

Faculty now share participation in governance on the campus with students and nonacademic staff. Student participation is a product of the late 1960s when students acquired the right to consult, usually in the form of service on joint committees, in most areas where faculty participate. Students sometimes sit on boards of trustees where there is no faculty representation.

The advent of collective bargaining on campus has provided a more significant role to nonacademic workers. Collective bargaining contracts often affect academic priorities. Funds made available to improve salaries and working conditions for staff are unavailable for faculty salaries, books, or financial assistance. A library may be required to close when the temperature-humidity ratio reaches a certain point; certain holidays may be required without regard to impact on academic operations.

Academic senates have been replaced by university senates in some universities. Such bodies may include faculty, administrators, nonacademic staff, students, and alumni, and frequently possess broader jurisdiction, but less power, than the faculty senates they supplanted. Creation of such an institution relegates the faculty to only one of many constituencies sharing in governance.

LOSS OF AUTONOMY

Little is gained by increased participation in decision making if important issues are decided outside the university. "Autonomy" in the sense of full self-governance—the ability of a university to govern itself without any outside control—does not now exist nor has it existed for a very long time, if ever.[15] Indeed, few in higher education would want autonomy if it involved full financial autonomy, that is, freedom from external support in any form. The real issue is not total freedom but a high degree of freedom from public or private control, particularly in certain areas. The major concern is that government, state and federal, and private bodies are imposing too many controls over the manner in which universities function. As Sir Zelman Cowen has noted, universities are "in danger of becoming utilities subject to general regulation in the public interest."[16]

Many once-independent state university campuses are now part of state systems governed by a "superboard." Others have been made subject to "coordinating boards" charged with responsibility to plan, budget, and program but without authority to "manage" or "govern" individual institutions within the system. Powers of a faculty to admit students, determine curricula, or appoint professors, or of a president or board to allocate income among various categories of expenditures, are much less important if a superboard or coordinating board has the authority to determine what programs will be offered on a campus, faculty size and student enrollment on a campus, funds that will be allocated to a campus, faculty salary scales, where buildings will be built, tuition rates, and similar matters.

Private universities likewise face significant external controls arising out of use of public funds. State boards sometimes attempt to exert control over them. Federal programs providing financial assistance to students and funding research in science, engineering, and medicine bring with them a host of regulations limiting university discretion.

General legislation also limits university autonomy. A national trend to regulate almost all forms of private activity to achieve important social goals is reflected in legislation not aimed specifically at universities but which does not exclude them from its scope. Such legislation often causes significant unintended problems because of essential differences between universities and private, profit-making organizations. Laws regulating minimum wages, health and safety, health insurance, and retirement programs are examples. Laws and regulations in the field of civil rights have special consequences for universities in hiring, promoting, firing, and compensating personnel.

There is nothing exceptional in these requirements. Problems, nonetheless, result from the manner in which statutes are interpreted by federal agencies, from the presence of trained bureaucracy within the university to assure compliance, and from costs in terms of formality and collegiality, as well as money, in proving compliance.

Faculty decisions on promotion or tenure and salary determinations are examples. Certainly universities should not discriminate, but a decision today must be reached in such a way that a faculty will be able to prove that it has not discriminated, as well as honestly decided each case on its merits. A decision to pay one faculty member a different salary from another involves judgments of quality of mind, promise of productivity, uniqueness of contributions to knowledge, and salaries paid by competitors. They are rarely quantifiable, but a decision of an administrator must be defensible in a court of law.

A different type of influence on university decision making is posed by legislation and administrative rules specifically aimed at universities. The federal government's experiments requiring medical schools to admit American students studying abroad as a condition to receipt of capitation grants, regulating in detail privacy and access to student records, and requiring universities to equalize per capita expenditures for men and women in intercollegiate athletics are examples.

Usually, extreme action is promptly modified. A year after the congressional intrusion into medical education, Congress restored at least the appearance of institutional autonomy. It amended the Privacy Act of 1974 within a year. Federal regulators ultimately retreated from their broad interpretation of what constitutes equality in intercollegiate athletics. All three examples, however, reflect areas that in an earlier era would have been a matter for unilateral university decision.

Similar direct intervention occurs at the state level, particularly when state legislatures or governors become upset about something happening on a public campus. "Speaker bans," efforts by legislatures to preclude speakers of certain political persuasions from speaking on a public campus, or dispatch of the National Guard to a campus to maintain order without request by a university president are examples.

Courts also limit university autonomy. Court decisions now recognize and enforce statutory and constitutional rights that either did not exist or previously had gone unnoticed. Issues of academic due process, academic freedom, and tenure are now frequently determined in courts rather than on campuses.

Governmental regulation obviously has justification. Governments have the right to determine whether public funds are being used for intended purposes and have a legitimate interest in efficient use of those funds. The size and influence of higher education is such that it cannot be permitted to ignore issues of importance to society as a whole because of more parochial interests. Constitutional and statutory rights are sometimes invaded by people and institutions of goodwill, and victims should not be without redress because an infraction occurred on a university campus. Occasionally, universities do make serious policy mistakes, and the people have a right in extreme cases to expect their elected public officials to act if the university is unresponsive to public concerns. Together, these limitations on autonomy reflect the reality that all institutions in a modern democratic society are accountable to the public.

Accrediting associations, particularly professional associations, also limit autonomy by imposing requirements as a condition of accreditation. A university may be forced to transfer resources from one school to another to assure continued accreditation of one of its components.

Often forgotten is the influence of donors and grantors. A private individual, a foundation, or a corporation may be prepared to provide a gift or grant or enter into a contract for a purpose that is low on a faculty priority list. Faculty may want money for faculty salaries, graduate student aid, or libraries; donors may wish to give it for organs, football, or an academic program in which they see great promise. A university may be forced to choose whether to forgo a gift or engage in an activity that it views skeptically. Whether to accept a gift or enter into a contract may produce acrimony when priorities differ within the university, particularly where the gift or contract in dispute would benefit one segment of the university at a potential long-range cost to another.

Many thoughtful observers are increasingly concerned that institutional autonomy is being endangered to such a degree that values implicit in such autonomy are in serious jeopardy. The battleground in the future may well be not the extent to which faculty participate in decision making within the university but what issues will be decided there.

ADVICE TO THE YOUNG SCHOLAR

The foregoing observations pose obvious issues for a young professor. Participation in governance will benefit not only a university but also a participant. Nevertheless, participation may require a significant expenditure of time, perhaps a scholar's most precious resource. Involvement may also lead to conflict with persons who have the power to affect your promotion, salary, and tenure.

Opportunities for service are almost endless. University standing committees, boards, or councils, such as academic affairs, student life, building and grounds, business and finance, the university press, long-range planning, faculty compensation and fringe benefits, interdisciplinary programs, faculty development, the library, university computing, alumni relations and fundraising, government-sponsored research, university-corporate relationships, intercollegiate athletics, social implications of investment policies, affirmative action, experimentation on human subjects, administrative oversight, research incentives, and community relations abound. School opportunities, normally in the form of membership on a governing council or committee, or participation in the work of subcommittees dealing with subjects such as admissions, financial aid, curriculum, scheduling, or undergraduate or graduate student life (housing, cocurricular activities, placement) need able people. Professional schools have additional committees that relate to particular professions and their concerns. A host of responsibilities, ranging from undergraduate and graduate studies to faculty appointments, require faculty involvement at the departmental level.

Some areas of possible participation are more likely to be rewarding than others. No firm rules can be laid down, but, on balance, work on committees or boards dealing with student life, building and grounds, financial or business issues, athletics, or the kind of committee that is likely to strain mightily and produce an ambiguous statement of philosophy to govern yet-unknown problems is likely to be less valuable to young scholars than service on committees that permit them to learn and contribute to solution of a concrete problem involving teaching or research. Service within a department where a young scholar's contribution may relate more directly to improvement of academic quality, and may be better appreciated by senior colleagues, may be especially desirable.

There are, of course, exceptions. It may be imprudent to decline an appointment by a provost or president. Service on a committee dealing with community relations may advance the young professor's professional career and benefit the institution in a small college where a tenure decision is less likely to depend upon research. In a professional school, service on a committee relating to the profession may not only serve the cause of the university but also fulfill a professional obligation, open up contacts, and suggest areas for useful research.

Some committees deal with issues that some regard as political and others as moral. Some faculty have deep beliefs that some things should or should not be done by or within a university — ROTC, government-supported military research, affirmative action, investment in companies doing business in some unsavory foreign nation, DNA research, research financed exclusively by private companies that retain patent rights, experiments upon animals, and so on. Obviously, faculty members with deep convictions should act according to the dictates of conscience and their concept of the purposes of the university.

A reasonable compromise may involve commitment of service in one important capacity during untenured years and budgeting time in a way to permit such service without detracting substantially from research and teaching. Simultaneously, a young faculty member can treat other areas as appropriate subjects of study during early years in a university. Valuable experience for future leadership can be gained vicariously without expenditure of time that can endanger a promising career.

Resolution of the issue of how much time should be devoted to participation in governance and the form such participation should take may be crucial to a young scholar. Conflict exists between values to which universities pay lip service and the reward system that is operative. Universities speak of the importance of teaching, research, public service, and service in university affairs, as if all were of equal value. Such statements may be believed by the public, trustees, legislators, alumni, and students but not by those who administer the rewards system. In many institutions, promotion and tenure are conferred only upon those who conduct research and publish work of high quality.

There is frequently a wide gap between such professed values and reality. Many senior faculty who assert the right to participate in governance, and the importance of such participation, neither wish to be involved personally nor place a high value upon contributions by those who are involved. Participation in governance is not discouraged but is given little weight in assessing a junior colleague's worth or promise. It may be even less significant than quality of teaching or public service, which are also regarded as inadequate substitutes for research. Furthermore, senior faculty may be unaware of governance participation outside a department.

Young professors who participate in governance extensively may do so at their peril. If they can do so without prejudice to their research, it will not be held against them. But every minute diverted from research is time not devoted to achievement of the primary requirement for advancement. Junior professors who participate excessively in university governance may find that they are unemployed faculty leaders.

NOTES

1. The literature on university governance and autonomy, the nature of universities, and relationships between universities and society is voluminous. A classic, although dated, is J. Barzun, *The American University* (New York: Harper and Row, 1968). A thoughtful study is W. H. Cowley, *Presidents, Professors, and Trustees: The Evolution of American Academic Government* (San Francisco: Jossey-Bass, 1980). Expressions of the theme that universities are controlled by a business/professional elite who use them to serve their own parochial purposes have appeared periodically from Upton Sinclair, *The Goose Step* (Pasadena, Calif., 1922), to David A. Smith, *Who Rules the Universities* (New York: Monthly Review Press, 1974), and B. A. Scott, *Crisis Management in Higher Education* (San Francisco: Jossey-Bass, 1983).

The thirteen-year period between 1967 and 1980 was an especially fertile period for studies of universities, only some of which related directly to governance or autonomy. The Carnegie Commission on Higher Education published twenty-two official policy reports and eighty commissioned research studies between 1967 and 1973, culminating in its final report, *Priorities for Action* (New York: McGraw-Hill, 1973). Its successor, the Carnegie Council on Policy Studies in Higher Education, published fifteen official policy studies, including its final report, *Three Thousand Futures: The Next Twenty Years in Education* (San Francisco: Jossey-Bass, 1980). The Sloan Commission on Government and Higher Education published fifty-five policy studies between 1977 and 1980, ending with *A Program for Renewed Partnership* (Cambridge, Mass.: Ballinger, 1980). The Carnegie Foundation for the Advancement of Teaching published *The Control of the Campus: A Report on the Governance of Higher Education* (Washington: Carnegie Foundation, 1982). Several other commission committees and task forces supported by government or foundation funding also made major contributions. Some of the major activities are summarized in Scott, *Crisis Management*. References will be made only to a few of the many books in the field.

2. Wolff listed four common concepts: the university as a sanctuary of scholarship; the university as a training camp for the professions; the university as a social services station; the university as an assembly line for the establishment of man, before proposing his own ideas of what a university should be (Robert P. Wolff, *The Ideal of the University* [Boston: Beacon Press, 1969]).

3. The Carnegie Commission on Higher Education noted five special features of governance of American educational institutions:

(1) Absence of centralized control by the national government—essential authority has rested with state governments and with boards of trustees.

(2) Concurrent existence of strong public and private segments.

(3) Trustee responsibility—basic responsibility to provide for governance of individual institutions has been in the hands of lay boards in both public and private institutions.

(4) Presidential authority—presidents have had substantial authority delegated to them by the lay board.

(5) Department authority—within the faculty the department has been the key unit of academic organization over most of the past century.

These characteristics contrast with the systems of some other nations in which "(1) the central government has had more control, (2) the private sector has not been as strong, (3) a council of deans or senior faculty members has performed many of the functions of the lay board in the United States, (4) the role of the president has been carried out more largely on a ceremonial level by a rector either elected for a short term by the senior faculty or appointed by the central government, and (5) faculty authority has rested with the chair 'professors who are arranged into central faculty groupings'" (The Carnegie Commission on Higher Education, *Governance of Higher Education* [1973], 5, 6).

4. S. V. Martorana, *College Boards of Trustees* (Washington: Center for Applied Research in Education, 1963), 8.

5. Ibid., 22–23.

6. Ibid., 40–47.

7. F. J. Atelsek and I. L. Gomberg, *Composition of College and University Governing Boards* (Washington: American Council on Education, 1977).

8. M. A. Rauh, *The Trusteeship of Colleges and Universities* (New York: McGraw-Hill, 1969), 5–9.

9. Perkins, *Conflicting Responsibilities of Governing Boards* (1973), 203–14.

10. J. L. Fisher, *Power of the Presidency* (New York: American Council on Education, 1984); *Presidents Make a Difference: A Report of the Commission on Strengthening Presidential Leadership* (Washington: The Association, 1984).

11. See n. 3 above.

12. See Allan Tucker, *Chairing the Academic Department: Leadership among Peers* (New York: American Council on Education, 1984).

13. The "key areas" are those so denominated by Sir Eric Ashby. E. Ashby, *Any Person, Any Study: An Essay on Higher Education in the United States* (New York: McGraw-Hill, 1971), summarized in L. B. Mayhew, *The Carnegie Commission on Higher Education* (San Francisco: Jossey-Bass, 1973), 278.

14. The concept of multiversity is that of Clark Kerr.

15. Carnegie Commission on Higher Education, *Governance of Higher Education*, 17.

16. Cowen, "The Governance of Universities," in *Universities in the Western World*, ed. Paul Seabury (New York: Free Press, 1975), 59, 62.

30

THE ROLE OF THE DEPARTMENT

IN THE GROVES OF ACADEME

JOEL COLTON

The Department — the living embodiment of the scholarly discipline in which one receives one's professional training — remains at the core of every academic's life and career. "History speaking," the young teacher in *Lucky Jim*, Kingsley Amis's academic novel, announces on the office telephone, and we know at once that he does not mean the voice of the past but his department. "Who are those two?" someone asks. "One is Political Science, the other is Sociology," comes the reply, and everyone understands perfectly. In an academic novel entitled *The Department*, the hero, a professor of English about to retire, looks back over the many years in which his personal and professional life has been intertwined with those of his colleagues. Or, in a real-life episode, a popular scholar-teacher delivers a talk to a group of students extolling at length the virtues of an academic career: the lifelong opportunity for intellectual growth, the chance to participate in the world of scholarship and learning through research and publishing, the continuing invitation to assist in the expansion of young minds, a more-often-than-not stimulating cultural and intellectual environment in which to live, the flexibility of the day-to-day and year-round work calendar, job security (compensating for lower material rewards than in other professions and business), sabbaticals and additional leaves for travel and research, and other tangible and intangible benefits. When queried about any disadvantages, our speaker hesitates momentarily and replies: "Yes, the colleagues in one's department!" The reply, intentionally facetious and good-humored, brings a smile but makes a point.

What is the department? What are its origins, functions, responsibilities, authority, and power, the limits to its jurisdiction and autonomy? How does it affect academic lives and careers? How does it administer its affairs? What is its internal governance like? What tensions and frictions lie beneath the surface? How does it attempt to administer individualistic scholar-teachers, all highly trained professionals with an adamant resistance to being managed? What tensions exist between it and something called the central administration? Young academics may not learn here everything that they have wished to know about the department from undergraduate days on and have been afraid to ask, but some information and enlightenment may be forthcoming.

THE DEPARTMENT AND SPECIALIZATION

The departments are at the heart of the teaching and research enterprise of the college and university precisely because they represent the disciplines, the specialized contributions to the perpetuation, dissemination, and advancement of knowledge that higher education is all about. These academic disciplines took shape in the last century. The liberal arts colleges, founded for the most part in the nineteenth century, believed that the goals of a liberal or general education were best accomplished through the teaching of specialized subjects. But even more so, the founders of the modern university at the end of the nineteenth century, borrowing from European prototypes, believed firmly in specialization in teaching and research. Specialization called for craftsmanship and expertise, to be perfected by young apprentices in the graduate programs and seminars offered in the departments of the major universities. From the 1870s to the present, graduate schools have demanded an "original contribution to knowledge," embodied in the doctoral dissertation, as part of one's research training and as a requirement for the Ph.D. degree, which, in turn, certifies and licenses the young scholar to become a full-fledged practitioner in the discipline, to "join" a department, and to embark on a career in teaching and research at a college or university. Specialization took on added reinforcement in this century, and especially after the Second World War, when science assumed so large a role in society and when all disciplines sought to emulate the prestige of the sciences.

It is because of the specialized disciplines that colleges and universities are divided into departments — not unlike, dare we say, Macy's or the Galeries Lafayette, where furniture, clothing, home accessories, garden equipment, and the like are all found on different floors. An institution on the average will run to about twenty-five departments, ranging alphabetically from art to zoology. In colleges, the traditional well-known arts and sciences disciplines are taught; in the universities (which by definition also have graduate M.A. and Ph.D. programs, as well as professional schools in engineering, law, medicine, theology, and other areas) there are more exotic units; there may be, for example, a department of Altaic and Uralic Languages. At times, loose groupings of departments, or divisions, are formed to correspond to the broader fields of scholarly inquiry, such as the humanities, the social sciences, the natural sciences. But these divisions are often employed for limited curricular and administrative purposes only and seldom impinge on the authority of the individual departments.

Specialization leads to its own problems. The discipline or department can become an end in itself. There is always the danger of lack of communication and cooperation at the expense of the broader institutional goals set by the administration and the faculty as a whole. At the very least, as a Darwinian fact of life, the departments will compete strenuously for what they consider their proper share of the college's or university's budgetary resources — and often for students because budgetary allocations (especially in public institutions) are often made in direct correlation with "full-time enrollments." Storm clouds gather when a department senses encroachment on its discipline, whether in the form of course offerings, joint faculty appointments, interdisciplinary programs, or budgetary allocations to new academic enterprises.

The picture does not end with simple specialization. Many disciplines, and hence the departments, break down further into subspecialties, so that it becomes difficult to define a faculty member simply as a professor of economics, or history, or physics; one is in economic theory or labor economics, medieval or Latin American history, low-temperature or high-energy physics. Geographical, topical, chronological, and methodological subspecialties have evolved, each with its own learned societies, annual conferences, publications. Within some larger departments these subdivisions can lead to internal competition for resources, and on occasion even to disagreement on the proper training of graduate students. The subspecialties often seek a critical mass of faculty appointments to guarantee their viability; non-Western components in history departments, always outnumbered by older areas of specialization, will often press for such appointments. In some departments, psychology as an example, experimental, clinical, and social psychology components often amount to three separate departments with separate outside grants, budgets, and administrative personnel for each.

If young academics do not know much about the external relations of departments, they already know a good deal about the internal workings of an academic department even before joining one. They have majored in a subject, and hence in a department, as undergraduates (and perhaps have had a second major or minor as well). Moreover, their graduate training has taken place almost exclusively within a department (with perhaps a few courses in a second discipline). Subject to overall institutional regulations (for example, length of residency, number of courses, language requirements), the department exercises virtual autonomy in determining the curriculum for the M.A. or Ph.D. degree in the discipline—the distribution of courses, the breadth and depth of knowledge to be examined in the Ph.D. general orals, the nature and quality of the dissertation. Once the new Ph.D.'s go job-hunting, moreover, they quickly learn how large a role the department plays in the appointment process, from advertising the vacancy to final selection; even the letter of appointment often comes from the department chair. Less visibly to the new faculty member, an administrative officer of the college or university (the dean—generally the dean of arts and sciences or dean of faculty, but sometimes the provost or president) has invariably authorized the appointment and approved or set the salary. Although the administrative officer, along with other administrative colleagues, may meet the candidate during the campus visit, the major contacts—interviews with individual faculty or groups of faculty, the seminar presentation, social gatherings—will be with the department and its members. For a junior appointment, the administration will generally accept the department's recommendations.

For all searches and appointments these days, however, the department may be reminded that it is no longer the independent agent that it once was. The dean may ask the department: How carefully did it search? Did it advertise the position adequately? Did it take care to track down minority candidates? Were there women candidates? Despite growing self-consciousness over the past several decades and conscious efforts to change matters, academic departments have remained notoriously male and white—before the Second World War they were overwhelmingly male, white, and Protestant—and the reminders are necessary. The former old-boy network of recruitment—the quick personal phone call by a department chair to a favored graduate department asking for a suitable, newly trained Ph.D. to fill a vacant slot—is less the practice and, at least in theory, no longer permissible. Moreover, since the 1960s, because of the expanded need for faculty at the time and the simultaneous emergence of many additional graduate departments offering the Ph.D. degree, colleges and universities now recruit more broadly geographically than ever in the past.

Subject to overall administrative controls—a phrase that inevitably appears frequently in these remarks—the department continues to play a major role in one's career after appointment: in the renewal of the appointment, the promotion from assistant to associate professor, the award of tenure (generally at the end of six or seven years), the promotion to full professor. (The old rank of instructor, incidentally, once the initial rank of appointment for the new Ph.D., went by the boards in the 1960s, although it is still retained for part-time or for non-tenure-track positions.)

Although new assistant professors become members of the faculty of the college or university to which they are appointed, and have a vague feeling of such faculty solidarity, they are immeasurably more closely identified with their department from the moment of their arrival on campus. In many career patterns they may remain members of that department for their entire career, with close professional and personal attachments to department colleagues, and even if one moves off to another institution, those bonds may last. Despite the jesting remarks cited about "colleagues" at the opening of this essay, some of one's closest friends will be members of the department that one has joined; common professional interests and personal attachments, despite frictions and tensions, bind members of a department with strong and lasting ties.

DEPARTMENTAL RESPONSIBILITIES

Not until one is a member of a department does one fully appreciate how much of a beehive of activity it is. Its responsibilities are many, whether it is small (two to six members, say in a college) or large (thirty to sixty or more in a university). Heading the department in all instances is the chair, whose special functions merit separate consideration below. The budget is central to the department's operations—and the most important limit on its autonomy. Annually, the chair submits a budget on behalf of the department with a supporting report and detailed documentation to the appropriate dean. Typically, the budget request seeks funding for new appointments, salary increments, secretarial support, office and laboratory space, supplies and equipment; a graduate department will also seek funds for graduate fellowships and assistantships. The dean and other central administrative officers must assess the competing budgetary requests that arrive from all departments, each couched in equally persuasive rhetoric and buttressed with equally convincing arguments and statistics. At the administrative level, decisions have to be made on the basis of the institution's goals, resources, and short- and long-term commitments, all of which are debated and set by the highest administrative echelons on up to the president and eventually by the trustees, who have the special responsibility to oversee the long-range welfare of the institution as they understand it. At that point, sometimes, one is far removed from the day-to-day frontline activities of departments and faculties. Among the faculty, especially in their role as members of departments, there is an inherent suspicion, half-jesting, half-earnest, about something called "the administration," and a tacit (or voiced) concern that it will subordinate educational goals and faculty needs to other objectives —buildings and grounds, athletics, public relations, additional administrative appointments, and the like. Tensions, in varying degrees and forms, between central administrations and departments are never absent from academic life; nothing unites a divided department like griping about the administration.

As to the budget, the departments bargain competitively, sometimes fever-ishly, for their share of the budgetary pie in a *bellum omnium contra omnes*. Without adequate resources, they argue, how does an ambitious department re-cruit and retain first-rate faculty? carry out its teaching responsibilities? encour-age research? or, if a graduate department, attract the most promising gradu-ate students? Some departments press their claims with self-confidence and aplomb; others follow the precept that the squeaky wheel gets the lubrication. But bargain competitively they all do, conceding only grudgingly the need for administrative allocation of limited institutional resources. In the natural sci-ences, more so than in other areas, it must be added, large outside grants from government and private funding sources are often available to supplement col-lege or university allocations.

No matter what their research concerns, a primary responsibility of the de-partments is to satisfy teaching demands. The department advises its majors and other students, disseminates information about courses and faculty, and responds to inquiries. Each semester the chair, with the help of selected associ-ates, determines teaching schedules, remembering (or being reminded of) each faculty member's foibles and other relevant factors: the owl who is of no use in the morning, the lark who chirps cheerfully only in the morning; the col-league who is willing to teach a section of introductory courses, the colleague who is not; the colleague willing to teach freshmen, and the colleague from whom freshmen must be protected. The department arranges coverage for fac-ulty members on sabbatical or other leaves, often not knowing the details of these leaves until the late spring, when many outside fellowships and grants are announced. Within the framework of the overall curriculum established by the faculty as a whole and the administration (and perennially reviewed), the de-partment shapes the requirements for the major, deciding on the number and sequence of courses to be taken, distribution among subdivisions within the department (organic, inorganic chemistry; English, American literature; and so on). It reviews and reorganizes the introductory courses. It tries not only to provide coverage of the subject matter but to offer also a variety of forms of instruction—lectures, discussion groups, seminars, colloquia, preceptorials, tutorials, honors programs, independent study. (Similarly, with variations, if a graduate department, it makes arrangements for its graduate program.) It also decides, on the basis of changes in faculty personnel or changing faculty inter-ests, on courses to be introduced, modified, or dropped. The faculty as a whole will exercise some jurisdiction over these courses—largely to avoid duplication and proliferation—but the principal initiative for course offerings and listings rests with the individual departments. The department, moreover, will gather statistics on course enrollments, students taught, full- and part-time instructional personnel, and other data, all of which are useful for historical reasons, for forecasting—and justifying—budgetary requests.

The department, principally through the chair, also carries on extensive day-to-day correspondence. As a communications link it represents the department to the profession as a whole; many of the professional organizations publish a directory of the larger departments in the discipline. It circulates to members of the department information about fellowships and grants and about conferences to be held. In graduate departments it circulates information to the graduate professor of vacancies in other institutions that might be filled by the department's new Ph.D.'s. It replies to letters from the public, or is called upon to assist in such replies by undergraduate and graduate admissions officers. The chair is in constant touch with officers of the central administration—the deans and the associate and assistant deans, the bursar's office, the registrar—and with other academic departments. All correspondence of individual faculty members with the administration, such as requests for leaves, is funneled through the department. The chair's mailbox is never empty.

THE DAY-TO-DAY OPERATIONS

How, then, are these extensive operations carried out? Obviously the magnitude of the operation varies with the size of the department and the number of students taught, and whether it is also a graduate program; but not surprisingly, many of the same functions are carried out even by small departments. Departments organize themselves to carry out these functions in a variety of ways but follow many common patterns. At the top of the structure, needless to say, is the chair. In larger departments, the chair may ask two or three faculty members to accept appointment for a period of time to assist in the administrative chores, say to supervise graduate studies or undergraduate studies or freshman instruction or to act as overall assistant chairpersons. In that way some of the duties are divided up, although the chair is never relieved of primary responsibility.

For its daily tasks a department almost invariably comes to depend upon the sine qua non of a well-run department—a long-term, experienced department secretary (or administrative assistant) who has lived through many incumbencies of the chair and from experience knows the administrative ropes about a multitude of matters—the budget, the mail, the never-ending paperwork, the files, statistics, and requisitioning of supplies. The department secretary keeps in constant touch with faculty members, undergraduates, graduate students, department alumni, the staff in other department and administrative offices, and with everyone else at the college or university in ways that are indispensable to the chair. Like a first sergeant in the army or a chief petty officer in the navy, the department secretary facilitates the work of the commanding officer in immeasurable ways. Woe to the young newly commissioned second lieutenant or ensign (read: newly commissioned Ph.D.-assistant professor) who fails to respect the authority of the office or does not quickly learn that courtesy and deference will accomplish more than pulling rank or throwing one's (not very substantial) weight around. In a good-size department a core of at least three or four additional secretaries will form part of the staff—and department family—and be available to provide secretarial assistance to the individual members of the faculty. No department, let it be noted, has ever been able to meet the secretarial needs of its faculty, especially when the demands converge, as they invariably do, at the same time. In this, as in other matters, the chair is called upon to use consummate skill in mediating conflicts and in sorting out priorities.

Democracy, in Winston Churchill's formula, is the worst form of government until one considers the alternatives. And democracy, in a department, works through committees. The chair will need and appoint faculty committees, standing (or continuing) and ad hoc. An executive committee, about which more will be said, is also often appointed or elected. The department may have among its standing committees a committee on courses (and a committee on the introductory course or courses), a library committee (to coordinate acquisitions and purchases), a committee on audiovisual materials or laboratory equipment or computer resources, a committee on outside lecturers, and many others. Ad hoc committees will be periodically appointed, such as a long-range planning committee to review the department's strengths and weaknesses at any given time and to help plan future development. A similar committee may prepare materials for outside evaluations requested by the administration or required by a state board or commission of higher education or in connection with a site visit by an accrediting or funding agency. Many ad hoc committees will be appointed for personnel matters. A search committee may help seek out candidates for an authorized vacancy (at any level) and do much of the preliminary sifting of credentials and interviewing before candidates are invited to the campus. An ad hoc committee may evaluate the file of a member of the department coming up for contract renewal or tenure or for promotion to associate or full professor and make a preliminary assessment for the department's consideration.

Although no alternative to committees has ever been invented, the consequence can be many committees, much committee work, and endless deliberations. Add in the college or university committees (again, standing and ad hoc) on which a faculty member is asked to serve (curriculum, courses, admissions, academic standards, the library, athletic policies, parking facilities, student publications, the United Way and other charities, the university press, personnel evaluations), and the burden visibly mounts. As time goes by, faculty members may expect more and more committee responsibilities, not fewer, both in the department and in the institution — with the exception of some colleagues who succeed in demonstrating or dramatizing their ineptitude for such assignments. Nor should one forget the time consumed (but not begrudged) when one is elected by department colleagues or by the faculty as a whole to such representative governing bodies as faculty senates and undergraduate or graduate faculty councils. Everyone is expected to play a role in "secondary management" in higher education.

The young faculty member may mercifully be spared many of these committee assignments, or a thoughtful chair may intervene to "protect" the young colleague if excessive requests are made outside the department. On the other hand, the junior faculty member can learn a good deal and gain valuable perspectives from working with faculty colleagues within the department and even more across the disciplines. The danger (for younger and older faculty alike) is that they may be distracted (or consciously or unconsciously seek distraction) from research responsibilities. When the times for tenure and promotion and other personnel decisions arrive, attention will be paid, to be sure, to institutional and departmental committee work, but no amount of "service" (or for that matter — in universities at least — even evidence of outstanding teaching) is likely to compensate for the absence of publications that signify a continuing commitment to research and scholarship. There are few exceptions to this rule at major universities, where the faculty enjoy reduced teaching loads (one, two, or three courses per semester, as against four or even more elsewhere) specifically to have time for research and writing. At the stronger liberal arts colleges, teaching and service components may be given significant weight in personnel decisions, but the research and publication record will not be ignored. On the other hand, in many small colleges where the faculty is small and the teaching load is heavy, and a diversity of courses remote from one's specialty are to be taught, teaching is often given the highest priority, and it is recognized that the kind of research that leads to publication is difficult to carry on. At some small colleges, one hears, publication and research may even be viewed negatively, interpreted as neglect of one's teaching responsibilities; one dean is reputed to have remarked: "If my faculty published, my college would perish."[1] The tensions between teaching and research are omnipresent, in every institution and every department, even if on different scales and in different ways. Few departments or institutions, however, no matter how eager they are to earn reputations for research and publication, will be sanguine about professors who cut corners on their teaching responsibilities and minimize the time and attention given to students in order to rush off to the library, laboratory, test tube, computer, or nuclear accelerator.

THE FUNCTIONS OF THE CHAIR

All this detail is by way of explaining how much goes on in a department. There is, however, another intriguing set of questions. How are decisions made? What forms of governance have evolved? What authority does the department possess?

For a long time, at least until the 1950s, the administration of academic departments remained an anachronism in a democratic society. The chair, either alone or with a small group of senior professors, ran the department's affairs under an authoritarian or at best an oligarchical regime. With the expansion of faculties after the Second World War, the pattern underwent initial change, and with further expansion and the campus upheavals of the late 1960s and early 1970s, it evolved in even more striking ways. From "prehistoric" times to this relatively recent past, the chair of the department, often called the "head," was generally appointed by the dean or other central administrative officer for an indefinite period of time and held office until retirement. It was tacitly understood that he or she—generally in those days, it was "she" only in women's colleges—represented the administration to the department. It is still possible to find a department head (and still called that) appointed by an administration in this same way for an indefinite period of time, but the practice is disappearing. This older pattern somewhat resembles the European and British model, where a single professor (Professor, capital P) often heads a large department, presiding over numerous senior lecturers, readers, assistants, fellows, and tutors. It remains the pattern in American schools of medicine where many departments are still run under long-term continuing appointments, with the chair exerting the predominant authority.

Under the newer scheme, in liberal arts and sciences departments at least, it has become increasingly common for the chair to be rotated, the term of office limited (two, three, or five years, with renewals possible), and the appointment based on close consultation with the departments through nominations to the administration or even election. Although debate may still continue about the primary allegiance of the chair, it is fair to say that with a strong department voice in the selection the incumbent tends to view the office as representing the department to the administration rather than vice versa—even though an astute department chair will quickly understand the need to reconcile department goals with those of the administration as skillfully as possible.

In the majority of cases, the chair is chosen from within the department (and administrations are generally relieved when this is possible). A 1984 survey of 323 history departments revealed that 94 percent of the chairs acquired the position from within the department.[2] An appointment from the outside, however, is not to be ruled out. If a department is perceived (sometimes by the department faculty members themselves) as weak or not living up to its potential, rent by factionalism (not unknown in departments), or thought to be in need of a major reorientation, the administration may select a head or chair from outside the institution. Even then, these days, the department generally participates in the search and meets with candidates before an appointment is made.

That the chair is now rotational and less powerful than previously, and departments more democratically run, does not mean that the office of the chair is unimportant. The incumbent is not likely any longer to be an autocrat, or even a benevolent despot; word of autocracy or despotism would quickly get around in the profession and make faculty recruitment (and retention) impossible. Under the new model, however, the chair need not be merely a presiding officer or convener. Even if decision making is shared with the department, much latitude remains for leadership, initiative, resourcefulness, and imagination on the part of an able incumbent.

About the office, past and present, few have written more perceptively or picturesquely than a seasoned former chair of a major university department of history. "There are many kinds of chairmen," he writes and proceeds to describe the most objectionable or least desirable:

> There is the enlightened despot. There is the unenlightened despot. There is the enlightened despot whose enlightenment is fading. There is the dean's viceroy, a Levantine opportunist who by deception and guile carries out the dean's intentions, which he can never disclose. There is the conscientious presiding officer, who rigorously executes the will of the majority, even when it is destructive or unjust. There is the party chieftain, ruling in the name of the dominant faction. There is the Phanariot hospodar [*sic*!], a Balkan carpetbagger who plunders the travel and entertainment funds and has his courses taught by the serfs of the junior faculty. There is the native son, custodian of those fashions called tradition, who tries to keep the future continuous with the fabled past. Finally, there is the manager, champion of accountability and productivity, who works under enrollment-driven budgets and labors to produce a healthy bottom line.[3]

The list, be it noted, is far from complete and does not rule out an overlapping of the categories. The usual disclaimers about resemblance to former or present holders of the office, living or dead, might be in order, but few incumbents these days would resemble any of these disagreeable portraits. A wise chair, in contemporary times, knows that authority must be exercised but also shared, a pattern that has increasingly become the rule.

The governance of departments varies with the history and traditions of departments. Generally, each department determines its own "constitution" and rules of procedure, sometimes as a matter of custom and tradition, sometimes in written bylaws. Many departments will have an executive committee to help in the governance of the department, consisting of two or three ex officio members (those assisting in the administrative chores of the department) and the remaining members elected by the department, with specific provision sometimes made for representation of junior, nontenured faculty. Like a presidential cabinet, an executive committee is generally advisory to the chair. It meets regularly, relieving the department of the need for overly frequent meetings—often a source of complaint and contention in a large department. The chair keeps the executive committee informed of negotiations with the administration and calls attention to pending or emerging issues, personnel and otherwise. The executive committee in turn keeps the chair enlightened on the tides of opinion within the department—in all ranks—on a variety of matters, nominates colleagues for committees, shares in preliminary discussions on personnel and other matters, and helps keep the lines of communication open between chair and department.

The chair's tasks remain formidable. It is a continuing challenge to administer a group of professionals, all of whom are rugged individualists, not readily amenable to direction or management and eager only to be left alone to carry out their professional and personal pursuits. Yet, if these individualists are not consulted or brought into the decision-making process when major departmental interests or concerns are involved, the reverberations will be consequential. Democracy or not, the senior professors remain self-consciously important, and a major problem for any chair is to keep the department's prima donnas happy—even if, as one chair noted testily, some of them cannot even carry a tune. The judicious chair, even if the office is construed as primus inter pares, can still be more primus than pares and can exercise genuine leadership, but only through consultation and consensus.

The everyday pressures on the chair itself are many. An industrious and efficient chair must foresee needs, keep ahead of deadlines, keep cool in the midst of friction, and head off gathering resentments and grievances. As part of the duties of the office, the chair guards the department's confidential records and correspondence, manages and evaluates the nonacademic secretarial and laboratory staff as well as academic colleagues, meets with students and student committees, listens to complaints of faculty and students, keeps colleagues informed about vital statistics in the department—marriages, births, illnesses, deaths—and keeps up with news of emeriti and alumni. The chair may preside over social gatherings of the department at his or her home or elsewhere or may organize dinners or receptions to welcome visiting lecturers or to honor retiring colleagues. (An alert chair keeps a ready list of the birth dates of members of the department to remind the department and the dean of retirement vacancies and replacements.) The chair may organize an all-day retreat to assess the strengths and weaknesses of the department and plan for the future. There are hospital or home visits to stricken colleagues and, on an even more somber note, memorial services to preside over or participate in for those who have died in retirement or in active service; at such services the department sits in a body in a final gesture of guildlike fraternity. (From Ph.D. sheepskin to terminal shroud the department will ever be with ye!) A proper chair will also preserve the traditions and memories of the department, keep confidential any skeletons in the departmental closet, and make every effort to see to it that humane relations are maintained in the department regardless of the deep political, intellectual, professional disagreements, and even factionalism that may exist.

The duties and responsibilities are many and tell something about the qualities called for in the ideal chair. A partial job description would read: mediator, negotiator, and arbitrator; budget, personnel, and recruiting officer; adviser on community housing and schooling, and on career opportunities for spouses; chief justice; pastor; parliamentarian; social director; lecture bureau director; team coach; Dutch uncle (or aunt); statistician; housekeeper; general office manager; and personal counselor and mentor. One could easily add to or amend the list; one former chair has included "jungle fighter" in his description. The seasoned observer quoted earlier, reinforcing the personal counseling duties mentioned above, reminds us that a chair must be concerned with many personal situations that may undermine the effectiveness of colleagues: "If Tacitus freezes at the sight of his typewriter, or Livy abuses the students, or Suetonius becomes enslaved to Bacchus, then the [chair] must consider how best to help them." And he concludes: "A department realizes its full potential when all its faculty members are achieving the highest quality of scholarship, teaching and service of which they are capable."[4]

This latter statement—to help a department realize its "full potential"—may explain why anyone accepts appointment to the chair. Why else would anyone be willing to take on the responsibilities and headaches? "I have no more taste for housekeeping than does my wife," said one chair.[5] The material rewards and perquisites are small—a reduction in teaching load, a modest stipend (described by one dispensing dean as "aspirin money"), some small travel and entertainment funds, a more commodious office (at least during the incumbency). One answer, of course, is that not many are asked—or chosen. Many (including some excellent scholars) are ruled out from consideration — by their colleagues or by administrators — for reasons of temperament or other personality factors. Many take the job precisely because it is on a rotational, limited-time basis and their turn has arrived, or they look to it as a change of pace; others may take it to head off a rival candidate considered undesirable. The time for choosing a chair, incidentally, can raise anxieties to a feverish pitch. One faculty member has remarked that it is more important to know who the next chair of one's department will be than to know who is to be the next president of the college or university.

Most frequently, those who accept the post see it as an opportunity to be of service in advancing the growth and development of the department by influencing appointments and other personnel decisions and by competing actively and successfully in the institution's budgetary politics. In larger departments in universities many believe that they can enhance the department's national stature and visibility, as mirrored in various professional ratings of departments (for example, those of the American Council on Education). To be rated among the top five (or even top ten or twenty) departments in one's discipline is a goal many departments believe worth striving for. These peer ratings are based on the reputation of the departments as measured by faculty publications, fellowships, grants, prizes, appointments to the boards of editors of professional journals, and election to national academies or to presidencies and other offices in leading professional associations. Although the ratings are sometimes subjective — they may reflect reputations from bygone days like the light from distant stars — there is generally a correlation between the ratings and achievement. The chair with ambitions for the department, like an athletic coach, brings the record of accomplishments to the attention of the department, boasts of or bemoans its national standing, and exhorts it to mightier efforts. The chair will also employ prestigious ratings as a bargaining chip with the administration.

One unenviable responsibility of the chair is to evaluate annually, in connection with the annual budget report and salary increases, each faculty member in the department, from the senior ranks to the most recent junior appointee, on the basis of their teaching, research, and service. No one has ever evaluated professional colleagues easily. What to do about the slow-publishing scholar who at the end of many years will produce a volume of lasting distinction or a few seminal articles, as against the colleague who publishes many articles or even books of lesser distinction? How to take into account a strong teaching record based on enthusiastic student teacher-course evaluations if unaccompanied by scholarly accomplishment? (How to evaluate student teacher-course evaluations in general?) What of the faithful committee member, and the faithful department servant, with minimal tangible evidence of research and publication? What of the faculty member who is sought elsewhere and must be given additional re-muneration and other blandishments to be retained? What of deserving col-leagues, solid and responsible scholar-teachers, whose real salary has become seriously eroded by inflation and in need of a major adjustment? The chair's judgments go forward to the administration which then translates them into annual merit increases (over and above any minimum cost-of-living increases). Be it noted that the departments (and the faculty as a whole) have little or no voice in the total sums set aside by the administration for salary increases. The departments, through their respective chairs, can only help the administration allocate the merit increases by assessing the professional contributions of the faculty in their departments. Although minimum and median salaries for fac-ulty at all ranks are available through the cooperation of college and university administrations in the annual reports published by the AAUP (American Asso-ciation of University Professors), individual salaries are another matter. They are often public knowledge at state and municipal institutions, or at least avail-able to those who seek them out. In private colleges and universities they are traditionally closely guarded state secrets kept confidential and locked away in the files of the department and administration. The secretiveness and confi-dentiality take on ironic dimensions when one realizes the limited range of all academic salaries; in the liberal arts and sciences, at least, from beginning as-sistant professor to retiring full professor, the spread is something like a factor of three, small indeed compared to other professions and occupations. But that does not make salaries, annual increments, and the modest differentials any less important nor the department chair's annual task any easier. With confidenti-ality the rule, one has to trust in the equity, fair-mindedness, professionalism, and sober judgment of the chair, and indeed of the administration.

Younger faculty members soon learn that another key responsibility of the conscientious chair is to serve as their chief mentor. By exercising the proper influence and leadership in the recruitment process, the chair can see to it from the beginning that only young persons of the highest promise are chosen. Then, by constant vigilance, tactful supervision, and frequent consultation, the chair, on behalf of the department, can make sure that the newly appointed faculty members understand the rules of the game, sharing with them any written or unwritten bylaws and procedures. The chair assists or should assist them in all ways possible to meet the teaching, research, and service criteria set up by the institution and the department for promotion and tenure. The chair may find it necessary to help them overcome problems of initial adjustment to teaching and should promptly share any adverse criticisms that may surface, perhaps in student evaluations of classroom performance. If necessary, the chair should protect the young faculty from excessive committee assignments or other administrative chores that might interfere with their research, and even seek released duties for them at critical junctures in their research and writing. In universities at least, the young faculty must be periodically reminded, if reminders are called for, that of the teaching, research, and service trinity, the most important remains research, as reflected in publication. In short, the chair should encourage, counsel, scold if necessary, and take all conceivable measures to nurture the young faculty—and help weed out the less-promising candidates for permanent appointments. Finally, the painful duty also devolves on the chair to break the news to the young colleague if the decision of the department or the administration on renewal or tenure is negative and share the reasons why, aware that such a decision in times of job scarcity can mean termination of an academic career in many disciplines. "Termination—always horrible," tersely commented one chair.[6]

A proper chair will oversee the department's personnel procedures and deliberations equitably and judiciously, appoint balanced and fair-minded ad hoc personnel committees, and present departmental recommendations to the administrative authorities effectively and persuasively. All personnel decisions, but especially tenure decisions, occasion soul-searching difficulties in a department (and in an institution). It falls to the responsibilities of the chair to oversee the entire, often tumultuous, process and to communicate its results—to the administration, to the university's tenure and promotion committee, and to the candidate (see Professor Goodwin's essay earlier in this volume). Some of these are pleasant chores; others are among any chair's most painful obligations.

LIMITS ON DEPARTMENTAL AUTONOMY

I have said much about the authority and autonomy of the department, and something of the limitations imposed upon it, but more needs to be said about the waning of departmental authority in recent years. College- and university-wide appointment, promotion, and tenure committees operate to curb the department's traditional power in personnel matters. On another front, administrations have tended to encourage interdisciplinary programs and interdepartmental coordination, partly for sound intellectual reasons, partly in times of inflation and slow faculty growth to maximize existing resources and effect necessary economies. Programs, institutes, and joint appointments have come into administrative favor, transcending the authority of the single department. Since the 1960s a number of inter- or codisciplinary fields of study have developed. These programs often represent cooperative endeavors arising out of the combined initiatives of several departments in which case there is no problem. But at other times programs, centers, and entire institutes emerge from student pressure or from administrative initiative or because they are part of the national academic scene. In other instances administrators (with the support of many faculty) will encourage curricular changes that the departments perceive as weakening their hold on courses that once met requirements for the degree and hence meant large student enrollments. Interdisciplinary courses in a core curriculum may replace older departmental offerings, or a writing program may be instituted quite separate from an English department. Many of these academic activities run counter to the disciplinary specialization embodied in the traditional departments and are viewed as threatening their autonomy or at least as diverting funds from them. Where opposition is impossible, departments will press, with varying success, to retain control over the faculty associated with these programs in order to have a voice in personnel decisions.

On still another front, differences emerge between departments and administrations over vacancies to be filled within departments. For budgetary or other institutional reasons administrations sometimes resist departmental requests for replacements when faculty retire or resign to go elsewhere, or at least replacements in the very same narrow specialty being vacated. (The art of the French baroque must be taught, the Art department will argue; the specialist in Kant must be replaced, Philosophy will contend.) For some vacancies administrators will approve replacements at a lower rank than the department seeks. At the other end of the spectrum some ambitious and energetic administrations will cajole or pressure departments into accepting high-priced luminary or "star" appointments in a search for "instant visibility." Departments are sometimes reluctant to turn down such appointments but are often apprehensive about the financial implications or the promotion opportunities for the present faculty or do not see the appointments as fitting the priorities they have themselves set.

Aware of the tender sensitivities of the departments, administrators impinge upon departmental autonomy as diplomatically as possible, but they do so nevertheless. When these administrative forays are made, many a department will forget its sharp internal divisions and draw together in a siege mentality to protect its territorial boundaries against the perceived threat. No matter what the philosophical and educational justification for the administrative initiatives, the departments will often adamantly resist them or accept them reluctantly when they are introduced. In the tensions that arise between departments and administrators it is not always the administrators who play the conservative role. The departments, it cannot be denied, represent a form of vested interest that it is difficult to dislodge. Although the conclusion may be contested by some, a scholar in his "biography" of a major university bluntly sums up the tug of war in a conclusion not flattering to the departments: "In a modern university the reformers, the idealists, even the would-be utopians, are most often administrators. . . . The resistance to change comes from the academic provinces, from the tough oligarchs that run departments, those who often are brilliant and innovative in their own scholarship, possibly leftist in their political leanings."[7] They are willing, he is saying, to challenge received truths in their scholarship and combat vested interests in society—but not in their universities.

The latent tensions between departments and central administrations can at times result in conflicted loyalties. Yet the tension should not be exaggerated. The faculty as a whole, through its representative bodies, and even departments, will often subordinate disciplinary and departmental interests to broader educational objectives in establishing or revising the curriculum and in other matters, or will demonstrate a sensitivity to budgetary stringencies that demand economies and limitations on expenditures. Moreover, there is tacit recognition that only through mutual cooperation of the department and the administration can the welfare of the institution be sustained. Administrators also recognize that the prestige and stature of the institution rest in the final analysis on the faculty, trained in specialized disciplines, and organized into departments, stubborn obstacles though they may be at times to the administrators' own agenda. Lastly, administrators know that their most productive faculty, despite institutional loyalties, can always be lured away by better opportunities elsewhere—to another department in another institution. In times of expansion and mobility such movements happen frequently, but even in times of reduced mobility "raiding" takes place, and invitations are based almost wholly on professional achievements and reputation within the discipline. It is a sign of a department's and institution's strength and prestige when its faculty are sought elsewhere. With the support of the administration, the department may seek to counter such outside offers, negotiating special salary increases or other emoluments, sometimes with success, sometimes without. At the same time, alert departments and supportive administrations will be out raiding other institutions and recruiting for their own faculty.

Throughout an academic career one remains as much a member of a department as of one's professional discipline. One is, to be sure, a professor at X College or Y University, but one is also a biologist, classicist, economist, geologist, mathematician, political scientist, sociologist, philologist, physicist. (Presumably, at least in theory, one could earn a living by practicing that profession — but try hanging out a shingle as Middle English scholar or French Revolution specialist.) Academics, whether they teach at small colleges or large universities, are also reminded of their discipline when each year they attend their professional meetings, or conventions, organized by the many alphabet-soup national learned societies (AEA, AHA, APA, MLA, PSA, and so on) or the even more subspecialized organizations. They meet at these annual meetings, discuss current research, read and debate each other's papers, participate in panel discussions, and listen to presidential and other addresses, but they also renew personal and professional ties — with old friends of graduate school days, with the older scholars under whom they once studied, and with the younger scholars whom they themselves have "trained" (perhaps as dissertation adviser, or Doktorvater, in the quaint German term). Invariably, conversation turns at some point to the departments in which they all teach and carry on their professional lives. The department, a corporate entity with its collective ego, represents on each campus the guild into which one is initiated for life upon receiving one's Ph.D. in a given branch of knowledge that we call a discipline.

If we learn anything from this essay, it is that the department remains at the center of one's academic life and career. We learn also that life within a department as a junior or senior faculty member bears little resemblance to life in the fabled ivory tower. The department, if it is ambitious, vigorous, aggressive, and competitive, is necessarily a focal point for continuing intellectual and political tensions and conflicts — within itself, with other departments, with administrations. Within the department, the clash of mind and will frequently matches the bitter battles of corporate boardrooms, even if the financial stakes are hardly comparable. Both in colleges and universities, in good times or bad, under able central administrative leadership or weak, with serious-minded students or frivolous, with more rigorous or more permissive curricula, in periods of growth or contraction, one's academic life and career are more linked to one's department (capital D) than to any other segment of the college or university campus.

NOTES

1. William Heywood, "Administering the History Department," *AHA [American Historical Association] Newsletter* 17, no. 4 (April 1979): 12.
2. John M. McGuire, "History Department Chairs: Characteristics, Influence, and Role," *AHA Newsletter* 23, no. 4 (April 1985): 13.
3. George P. Taylor, "Administration of Large Departments," *AHA Newsletter* 17, no. 5 (May 1979): 13.

4. Ibid., 15.

5. Samuel P. Hays, "On Having Been a Departmental Chairman," AHA *Newsletter* 17, no. 3 (March 1979): 12.

6. McGuire, "History Department Chairs," 14.

7. Paul K. Conkin, *Gone with the Ivy: A Biography of Vanderbilt University* (Knoxville: University of Tennessee Press, 1985), 395. The quotation first came to my attention in a review of the book by Thomas G. Dwyer in the *Journal of Southern History* 53 (August 1986): 499.

31

THE ACADEMIC COMMUNITY

PHILIP STEWART

Whatever the disparate paths that may lead them into the world of academia, scholars and teachers have in common an attraction to a lifestyle that, though surely no longer ascetic and seedy as it once appeared (at least in caricatures of it), has some faintly anachronistic charms. Not that the ivory tower notion survives intact, for we have had to learn that the university is not above or immune to society's ills. Nonetheless, the campus is, at least most of the time, a sort of haven where, despite the much-decried pressures of publishing and the rest, denizens enjoy broad flexibility in their use of time and, it is to be hoped, some leisure to indulge in thought for its own sake.

It would be nice to say that in this special world petty motives have no sway, that there are demonstrably fewer injustices or jealousies or even lawsuits. Still, short of statistical claims, experience tells me that academics figure most of their difficulties can be resolved internally, that the problems they are called upon to "solve" are largely of a contemplative nature not requiring immediate action, and that teaching others to think critically—and not forgetting in the process to think oneself—is what higher education is about. If we cannot expostulate absolutes, we can nonetheless claim and practice intellectual, moral, and humanitarian values. To the extent that we realize that ambition and embody that ideal, academia is a community of scholars.

Occasionally a scholar functions as an island, patiently spading through arcane archives or laboratory cultures for new finds of one kind or another. This is a faded but still honorable version of the profession. It is true that in many fields scholars still work most of the time by themselves, though they are likely to value if not require research or laboratory assistants and other amenities. By and large, however, the scholar is called upon more than ever to be a conscious part of a community, indeed of several communities. There are both external and internal kinds of solidarity that are important to the profession and the university in general.

As a professional, which means almost invariably as a specialist of sorts, one is most likely to nurture links to organizations within one's own discipline and particularly subdiscipline. It is reasonable to pursue both, within reason, as the occasions arise, since each relates to a differently defined collectivity. It is convenient for me to use my own case as an example, although it will apply in all points to no one else. (I teach literature, more specifically French literature, and more specifically still Enlightenment literature — in various combinations with other things.) You will likely find it essential to belong to at least one very broad-based disciplinary organization: in my case, that is the Modern Language Association. At one notch further definition, it is the American Association of Teachers of French, or an equivalent society. Cut chronologically rather than geographically, it involves the community of scholars in eighteenth-century studies as a whole (religion, history, art, and so on): for this there are regional societies, a national one, another in France; there is also an international society which holds large quadrennial congresses in widely scattered venues. As the focus narrows, there are many organizations devoted to the study of a single author or form of inquiry: I belong, for example, to societies for the study of the works of Challe, Marivaux, and Diderot, among others.

Attending meetings of such societies, giving papers, organizing panels, perhaps participating on editorial or advisory boards and writing book reviews: these are often described as "service to the profession" but this expression gets the point wrong. First of all, these organizations furnish the tools on which we all rely: bibliographies, directories, Web pages, job forums, and so forth. The umbrella societies often strive to help define national policy issues on which the discipline as a whole might or should take a public position. But more fundamentally, scholarly inquiry as an institution consists in dialogue; this applies in every discipline. While you could stay home and do all your communicating through articles or electronic bulletin boards, it is often more efficient, and is surely more stimulating and rewarding in human terms, to work the territory.

By attending such functions you learn more about people in the field, make acquaintance with others who share your research interests, maintain acquaintances previously established, see and are seen. This activity is as important to your institution as it is to you personally, since you inevitably contribute to others' perception of it and to its overall visibility. Many professional meetings also have an undeniable social aspect that is also constitutive, and rightly so, of the professional ethos. To benefit from regular contacts of this sort, which often quickly develop an international dimension, one need not be obsessed with jockeying for position. Many professional opportunities eventually develop from simple beginnings, not to mention long-term professional friendships between individuals who may meet only once a year or less, and more probably in a distant city (or country) than in either's home. For many, such regular contacts with colleagues in other institutions are the only direct form of reinforcement available that relates with any specificity to the research in which they spend the bulk of their own time engaged. They can also be stimulating, engrossing, and not infrequently pleasurable. It need hardly be stressed that meetings are also one of the most important ways for keeping current on what other specialists are thinking about. Even the teacher who is not inclined or expected to lead an intensely research-oriented life cannot well afford not to be plugged in to some such functions.

At the same time, single-minded specialization is neither the highest goal nor necessarily the most valuable personally. The process assumed above, by which through college, graduate school, dissertation, and employment you progressively restrict your focus, has to be counterbalanced in numerous ways and for numerous compelling reasons. It might be of dubious merit to become the profession's greatest expert in its most narrow, esoteric subject matter. Creative people often garner their most valuable insights from discussions with colleagues in other disciplines, and the academy is replete with examples of whole subject areas that have shifted under the influence of ideas imported from other disciplines. Some fields of study have spawned interdisciplinary associations dedicated to fostering such communication. Even so, you have to make it work for yourself. Interdisciplinary dialogue makes three essential kinds of input to your thinking: it gives you an outside view, helping to avoid the myopia of too intensely narrow research; it brings concepts and perspectives foreign to your own specialty to bear on your thinking; and it keeps you simultaneously conscious of and interested in the world of intellectual inquiry at large.

There is no way to generalize about the admixture of such participation that best serves each young scholar. There may be fields, and institutions, in which it is very nearly suicidal to branch out before achieving tenure, and you have every right to keep such practical considerations in mind. In such a situation, interdisciplinary curiosity will appear a luxury that must be postponed. On the other hand, the benefits of cross-fertilization may provide the spark that makes more original work possible — perhaps the very kind that would favor tenure prospects over more intense but less imaginative research. In other words, since you never really know what ideas will permit you to do your best work, you need to be on the lookout for challenging ones from the very start, and to be thinking of ways to apply them.

All such alliances, in any case, are subject to evolution. A teacher belongs to a number of different constituencies or communities; these may shift in their relative importance to the individual over time, just as one's role in and with them—from passive to active and vice versa—may change, according to one's own needs and theirs.

The community with which you are involved on your own campus also offers you this kind of cross-section. There the meaning and advantage of interrelations is to spread one's acquaintances into subject areas with which one has little or no previous experience and gain a better understanding of what an institution of learning is. That is also one of the main reasons for participating in its interior functions. You cannot, of course, avoid involvement with your own institution—though some try. Individual and entrepreneurial as the professoriate often is, you still, at a minimum, have to help other people design and administer courses and programs in your own department. This interaction is itself often rewarding and interesting despite the time it requires and the frequently repeated warning that "you don't get any tenure credit for it." But it is both part of the job and part of belonging to a collective enterprise. Besides, tenure should not be an encompassing obsession either: it is just as wrong to work doggedly and with single-minded ambition on research alone as it is to neglect research for camaraderie and good deeds.

To the degree you think of your fellow workers as the professoriate in general and your own college or university in particular, the issue of belonging is usually defined less in terms of joining organizations than in being available to serve and participate. An exception to this rule is the AAUP, which you may even be more or less obliged to join, nationally or locally, because of its role as faculty advocate, or informal or official faculty bargaining agent. Otherwise it is a matter of relative, personal priorities. Obviously there are also, on an utterly different level, civic involvements that some will elect and others not.

The best way to get a good overview of an institution is to serve on a variety of its committees. Nor is there a better way to get to know the breadth of its faculty, sometimes even beyond one's own division or school. A lot of disparaging witticisms have been spun at the expense of academic committees, reflecting the sad fact that they aren't always given important functions to fulfill or interesting assignments to complete—or they can just be poorly led. Similarly, if faculty (or council or senate) meetings are boring, it could be because they aren't organized right. Institutions that lack a process for regular faculty input inevitably foment a mentality that sets faculty against administration. They also lack an important control on the wisdom of decisions reached. The purpose of faculty participation in governance is to ensure that the principal educators have a systematic and reasoned role in the elaboration of institutional policies. To achieve this obviously requires administrative cooperation, which in turn is sometimes acquired only with some coercion; there is no general rule about how insistent or cooperative or militant one needs to be.

But more importantly, faculty input in policy is not achieved without considerable faculty commitment. Respect from administrators has to be earned: the right to influence decisions entails willingness to put time and thought into the process. A faculty that thinks of itself as the heart of an institution (as most do) must assume that function actively. Faculty representation should not and must not be left to a few stalwarts, for all kinds of perspectives, from every branch of the institution, are needed. It is the flourishing of the institution as a whole, not just the welfare of the faculty, that is at stake; indeed it is damaging for faculty to be perceived as pursuing their own self-interest foremost. At the same time, such involvement educates the faculty; and if its time is being squandered as a result, the best approach is to find ways to improve the process.

There are some things junior faculty members should not be asked to do. Department administrators should not inflict on them onerous functions such as director of undergraduate studies, even with a lightened teaching load, for the simple reason that while any kind of teaching may be found to abet research in some way, this simply cannot be said for filling out reports for the dean's office and putting together course schedules. Nor should they be placed in the position of arbitrating conflictual matters, and this includes service on committees charged with highly contentious problems such as—just one possible example—curricular reform. Tenured professors possess no necessary superiority on these or other matters, but they do have advantages; that is what tenure is about, and no one without it should be placed in undue jeopardy with respect to anyone who may later be in a position to weigh his or her scholarly accomplishments.

An institution of higher learning is a peculiar creature, a dynamic organism that cannot be adequately defined as the sum of its parts. People can get balkanized in departments and isolated, even lonely, in their offices just as they can in large cities. In the academy this can almost always be avoided with a little effort. It is not good to live entirely circumscribed by one's disciplinary apparatus and personnel, and it is not good for students to be taught by faculty whose focus is exceedingly narrow. Sometimes the discovery of problems in other departments will provide the relief of commiseration; sometimes learning about what another scholar is doing provides genuine insight and exhilaration. Joining a faculty is a lot like becoming a college freshman again. Ideally, it should present many opportunities for new human experiences and nondestructive experiments, for debates that don't turn into feuds. The ideal sometimes breaks down, to be sure, but it can be restored.

Just about all faculty bodies, even if elected, meet in sessions which are open to the faculty at large; it is worth attending them for a while, whether one is a voting member or not, just to get the feel of governance in the institution and to begin to recognize some of the players to whom others listen. Such people tend to be the ones who combine a certain degree of experience in faculty affairs, good judgment on matters of general concern, and a conviction of working for a common purpose that seems so self-evident it doesn't even need to be articulated. It is easy to be put off by procedures, particularly when they bog down in numbing routines; still, everything learned in such ways becomes useful input for some future assignment. And there is no hurry; it is fortunately not necessary to figure everything out right away. You do not suspect at first—and certainly you realized little if at all in those years you spent as a student—how complex a college or university is, how numerous its constituencies really are. As faculty you are not just members or employees but should rightfully consider yourselves in a real sense among the owners and managers. Educational institutions advance not just with faculty participation but usually under faculty initiative. You will have many chances to contribute and should take as many of them as you can.

From its earliest origins, the academic community has been defined by the co-presence of students and teachers, groups that were distinct in some ways but overlapped in others. One of the responsibilities you have to your students is to think of them genuinely as yours and to seek to learn from them as well as they from you. This is not always easy for professors to do. Not too many students respond fully to the intellectual challenge which you would like to present to them. In other words, it is in the nature of the situation that not all students are as good as you (and your graduate school classmates) were. There are still ways, if you are patient and adventurous enough, to find what is best in them, to try to stretch their limits, to establish something approaching genuine dialogue.

More broadly, you should try always to be aware that your institutions function with the daily help of many support groups: academic staff; counseling, food, and postal services; maintenance, physical plant, and so forth. It behooves you to be aware of their contribution, to be gracious in your interactions with them. They are in many ways the on-campus wing of our relations with the broader civic community in which the college or university—not, of course, to the neglect of its specific educational responsibilities—needs to be constructively engaged.

Like any polite society, the academy is held together in part by conventions of decency, honor, and mutual obligation. If occasionally they are breached, it is important to repair them quickly: any of us who really relished hand-to-hand combat would not, presumably, have elected this particular profession in the first place. I am not referring only to the strategic tact of treating one's elders with deference but of treating all one's colleagues with the reasonable measure of respect which you equally expect and deserve from them. Honest disagreements sometimes, of course, lead antagonists to feel untenderly toward each other, and that is where the mandates of civility come in. No one acquires an enviable reputation on a campus by loudly pointing out the shortcomings of other faculty members or even administrators. In days of contentiousness over freedom-of-speech, racial, or other issues, this admonition retains all of its importance. In the academy we try to avoid conflict wherever possible, except in the civilized form of reasoned debate. This instinct sometimes makes us appear pusillanimous to parts of the world at large, but it is central to the kind of ethos we value and advocate.

Such priorities do not have to be practiced to the point of quaintness, but it would be self-destructive for professors or their students to try to pretend that the academy is or should be value-free. When I was in college, a necktie was required for men in the dining hall, a rule that corresponded to a particular idea of what was minimal decency for the occasion; it is not perhaps a rule one would desire to bring back at a time when most teachers have long since left the necktie at home. It is not an inherently bad thing that classroom styles change over time, and that includes forms of courtesy and even rigidity of discipline. A great deal of intellectual endeavor, all the same, is based not just on civility but on mutual trust; if illustrations were needed, the scandals and controversies over plagiarism or imposture, or over cheating in scientific experimentation, would do quite well. How can inquiry be intelligently and efficiently advanced if you cannot trust implicitly what your colleagues, wherever they are, are asserting?

Indeed an awful lot in the academy as a whole depends on mutual reliance. Great confidence is placed in teachers: not just the awesome authority of judging others' performance if not intellect, but everyday prerogatives too. Colleges and universities place personal, sometimes intimate, knowledge of others virtually at teachers' discretion. They police them only very loosely if at all for the kinds of activities they carry on in the classroom and elsewhere on campus. Most campus libraries allow faculty extended borrowing privileges and often waive fines even when books are overdue. Such privileges certainly can be abused. A teacher may rarely be tempted to steal from the till, but there may be analogous temptations that are less pecuniary. Intellectual integrity is not negotiable; it is moral in essence, and you owe it to each other as well as to the world to consider it unconditional. The True and the Good may no longer constitute a wholly sufficient definition of your pursuits as scholars or individuals; but scholars who lose their commitment to truth, compassion, and even generosity have in a most unfortunate sense lost their souls.

The university is not, per se, a spiritual place; nor was it, in all likelihood, even in the early days when theology was its chief occupation. Its joys are not boundless, not to mention eternal, and they are, alas, not uninterrupted even in the here and now. Few people can really imagine it is nirvana. It is just a human community, but a particular sort of one. Although its attractions must be assumed to appeal to people with certain inclinations rather than others, its denizens, far from coming all from the same mold, are, in fact, spectacularly varied. As in other communities, they have to have numerous ways of getting along and getting their business done, and as elsewhere they have to provide their own particular forces of cohesion. Those who find these conditions congenial, and can negotiate their best place in such an environment, are likely to consider themselves part of a genuinely privileged profession.

SELECTED FURTHER READINGS

Issues of immediate concern to new (and not so new) academics are regularly covered in the primary journals devoted to higher education: *Academe*; *Change*; *Chronicle of Higher Education*; *Innovative Higher Education*; *Journal of General Education*; *Journal of Higher Education*; and *Liberal Education*.

Adams, Hazard. *The Academic Tribes*. New York: Liveright, 1976.

Adviser, Teacher, Role Model, Friend: On Being a Mentor to Students in Science and Engineering. Washington: National Academic Press, 1997.

Behling, J. H. *Guidelines for Preparing the Research Proposal*. Lanham, Md.: University Press of America, 1984.

Boice, Robert. *The New Faculty Member*. San Francisco: Jossey-Bass, 1992.

Bower, Howard, and Jack H. Schuster. *American Professors*. New York: McGraw-Hill, 1996.

Brodhead, Richard H. *The Good of This Place: Values and Challenges in College Education*. New Haven, Conn.: Yale University Press, 2004.

Cahn, Steven M. *Saints and Scamps: Ethics in Academia*. Totowa, N.J.: Rowman and Littlefield, 1986.

Caplan, Theodore, and Reece McGee. *The Academic Marketplace*. New York: Ayer, 1972.

The Chicago Manual of Style. 15th ed. Chicago: University of Chicago Press, 2003.

Conrad, D. L. *The Quick Proposal Workbook*. San Francisco: Public Management Institute, 1980.

Cook, Clair Kehrwald. *Line by Line: How to Edit Your Own Writing*. Boston: Houghton Mifflin, 1985.

Day, Robert, and Barbara Gastel. *How to Write and Publish a Scientific Paper*. 6th ed. Westport, Conn.: Greenwood, 2006.

DeSole, Gloria, and Leonore Hoffmann, eds. *Rocking the Boat: Academic Women and Academic Processes*. New York: Modern Language Association, 1981.

Dowell, Walter W. *Getting into Print: The Decision Making Process in Scholarly Publishing*. Chicago: University of Chicago Press, 1985.

Dudovitz, Resa L., ed. *Women in Academe*. New York: Pergamon, 1985.

Fish, Stanley Eugene. *There's No Such Thing as Free Speech, and It's a Good Thing Too*. New York: Oxford University Press, 1994.

Gibson, Gerald W. *Good Start: A Guidebook for New Faculty in Liberal Arts Colleges.* Boston: Anker Publishing, 1992.

Gless, Darryl, and Barbara Herrnstein Smith. *The Politics of Liberal Education.* Durham, N.C.: Duke University Press, 1992.

Gullett, Margaret M., ed. *The Art and Craft of Teaching.* Cambridge, Mass.: Harvard University Press: Harvard-Danforth Center for Teaching, 1984.

Hall, Roberta, and Bernice R. Sandler. *The Classroom Climate: A Chilly One for Women?* Washington: Project on the Status and Education of Women, 1982.

Heiberger, Mary Morris, and Julia Miller Vick. *The Academic Job Search Handbook.* 3rd ed. Philadelphia: University of Pennsylvania Press, 2001.

Higham, Robin. *The Compleat Academic.* New York: St. Martin's, 1974.

How to Get the Mentoring You Want. Ann Arbor: University of Michigan Press, 1999.

How to Mentor Graduate Students: A Guide for Faculty at a Diverse University. Ann Arbor: University of Michigan Press, 1999.

Ikenberry, Stanley O., and Renee C. Friedman. *Beyond Academic Departments.* San Francisco: Jossey-Bass, 1972.

Keohane, Nannerl. *Higher Ground: Ethics and Leadership in the Modern University.* Durham, N.C.: Duke University Press, 2006.

King, Margaret F. *On the Right Track: A Manual for Research Mentors.* Washington: Council of Graduate Schools, 2003.

Literary Market Place 2006. Medford, N.J., 2006.

Lucy, Beth. *Handbook for Academic Authors.* Rev. ed. Cambridge: Cambridge University Press, 1990.

Mason, Mary Ann, and Marc Goulden, "Do Babies Matter: The Effect of Family Formation on the Lifelong Careers of Academic Men and Women." *Academe.* November-December 2002.

Mason, Mary Ann, and Marc Goulden, "Do Babies Matter (Part II): Closing the Gender Gap." *Academe*, November-December 2004.

Rishel, Thomas W. *The Academic Job Search in Mathematics.* Providence: American Mathematical Society, 1998.

Schuster, Jack H. *Enhancing Faculty Careers.* San Francisco: Jossey-Bass, 1990.

Schuster, Marilyn R., and Susan R. Van Dyne. *Women's Place in the Academy.* Totowa: Rowman and Littlefield, 1985.

Scientific Style and Format: The CBE Manual for Authors, Editors, and Publishers. 6th ed. Cambridge: Cambridge University Press, 1994.

Seldin, Peter. *Changing Practices in Faculty Evaluation.* San Francisco: Jossey-Bass. 1984.

Shils, Edward. *The Academic Ethic.* Chicago: University of Chicago Press, 1983.

Smelser, Neil J., and Robin Content. *The Changing Academic Market.* Berkeley: University of California Press, 1980.

Strunk, William Jr., and E. B. White. *The Elements of Style.* 4th ed. New York: Longman, 2000.

The Teaching of Values in Higher Education: A Seminar. Washington: Woodrow Wilson International Center for Scholars, 1986.

Theodora, Athena. *The Campus Troublemakers: Academic Women in Protest.* Houston: Cap and Gown Press, 1986.

Touraine, Alain. *The Academic System in American Society.* New York: McGraw-Hill, 1974.

Ulich, Robert. *Three Thousand Years of Educational Wisdom*. Cambridge, Mass.: Harvard University Press, 1954.

Valvoord, Barbara, ed. *Academic Departments: How They Work, How They Change*. San Francisco: Jossey-Bass, 2000.

Veysey, Lawrence R. *The Emergence of the American University*. Chicago: University of Chicago Press, 1965.

Whitehead, Alfred North. *Aims of Education and Other Essays*. New York: Macmillan, 1929.

CONTRIBUTORS

JUDITH K. ARGON is the vice president of research administration at the Joseph Stokes Jr. Research Institute at the Children's Hospital of Philadelphia. She has also served as a research administrator at Duke University and the B. S. D. Pritzker School of Medicine at the University of Chicago.

LOUIS J. BUDD is James B. Duke Professor Emeritus at Duke University. Professor Budd served for several years as the managing editor of *American Literature*.

RONALD R. BUTTERS is a professor of English and the chair of the English department at Duke University. He has long served as editor of *American Speech*.

NORMAN L. CHRISTENSEN is the former dean of the Nicholas School of the Environment at Duke University. He is a professor of biology and environmental studies.

JOEL COLTON is a professor emeritus of history at Duke University. Professor Colton also served as director for the humanities at the Rockefeller Foundation.

PAUL L. CONWAY is the director of Information Technical Services for Duke's Perkins Library System, as well as the director of Digital Asset Initiatives at the university.

JOHN G. CROSS is a professor emeritus of economics at the University of Michigan. He and Professor Goldenberg have been conducting a study of non-tenure-track hiring practices for the Andrew W. Mellon Foundation.

FRED E. CROSSLAND, currently retired, served for many years as a program officer for higher education and research at the Ford Foundation.

CATHY N. DAVIDSON is a professor of American literature and the vice provost for interdisciplinary studies at Duke University. Professor Davidson has also served as editor of *American Literature* and as the director of the John Hope Franklin Humanities Institute at Duke.

A. LEIGH DENEEF is a professor of English at Duke University. He served for many years as the associate dean of the Graduate School.

BETH A. EASTLICK is the associate director of foundation relations at Duke University.

MATTHEW W. FINKIN is a professor of law at the University of Illinois. Professor Finkin has also served on the professional staff of the American Association of University Professors.

JERRY G. GAFF served for many years as the senior vice president of the Association of American Colleges and Universities. He and Anne S. Pruitt were the founders of the Preparing Future Faculty project, on which they have published several monographs.

EDIE N. GOLDENBERG is a professor of political science and public policy at the University of Michigan. She and Professor Cross have been researching non-tenure-track hiring practices for the Andrew W. Mellon Foundation.

CRAUFURD D. GOODWIN is James B. Duke Professor of Economics at Duke University. Professor Goodwin has also served as the dean of the Graduate School and the vice provost for research, as well as the chair of the university's Appointment, Promotion, and Tenure Committee.

STANLEY M. HAUERWAS is Gilbert T. Rowe Professor of Theological Ethics at the Duke Divinity School. He has also served as the director of graduate studies for the Ph.D. program in religion.

DEBORAH L. JAKUBS is Rita DiGiallonardo Holloway University Librarian and the vice provost for library affairs at Duke University. She has also served as director of the Latin American Studies program at the university.

L. GREGORY JONES was among the initial group of graduate students whose discussions culminated in the first edition of this handbook. After some time in other academic venues away from Duke, Professor Jones returned to the campus as the dean of the Divinity School.

NELLIE Y. MCKAY was a professor of American and Afro-American literatures at the University of Wisconsin, Madison. She served on a number of advisory boards and commissions studying the status of women and black women in the academy. Professor McKay died in January 2006.

PATRICK M. MURPHY served as an education technologist specialist with the Office of Instructional Technology at Duke University. He developed a series of workshops for the Graduate School on the instructional uses of technology.

ELIZABETH STUDLEY NATHANS is the dean of freshmen at Harvard University. Dean Nathans developed the Pre-Major Advising Center at Duke University before moving to Harvard.

A. KENNETH PYE died in 1994 after a distinguished career at Duke University, where he served as dean of the Law School, Samuel Fox Mordecai Professor of Law, and chancellor of the university; and at Southern Methodist University, where he served as president.

ZACHARY B. ROBBINS is the associate director of corporate relations at Duke University.

SAMUEL SCHUMAN has had a distinguished career in a number of liberal arts colleges. He served as the vice president for academic affairs at Guilford College and the chancellor of the University of North Carolina, Asheville, before assuming his present position as the chancellor of the University of Minnesota, Morris.

ANNE FIROR SCOTT is William K. Boyd Professor Emeritus of History at Duke, where she had a distinguished career as both a scholar of the history of American women and a challenging teacher.

SUDHIR SHETTY works with the World Bank, where he is currently the sector manager of the Poverty Reduction and Economic Reduction Group and the vice president of economic management. Prior to joining the World Bank, Dr. Shetty was an assistant professor of public policy studies and economics at Duke University.

PHILIP STEWART is a professor of French in the Duke Department of Romance Studies. Professor Stewart has served in many administrative positions within the university, including department chair and chair of the University Academic Council.

BOYD R. STRAIN is a professor emeritus of botany at Duke University.

EMILY TOTH is a professor of English and women's studies at Louisiana State University. Her previous academic home was at Pennsylvania State University, where she directed the graduate program in women's studies. Professor Toth is perhaps best known for her ongoing column "Ms. Mentor," which she writes for the *Chronicle of Higher Education*.

P. AARNE VESILIND is a professor of civil and environmental engineering at Bucknell University. He has long been active in the development of programs in the responsible conduct of research.

JUDITH S. WHITE is the executive director of Higher Education Resource Services at the University of Denver. She served as an assistant vice president of Duke University and assistant director of campus services. Dr. White was also sexual harassment prevention coordinator and special assistant to the president at Duke.

HENRY M. WILBUR is B. F. D. Runk Professor of Biology at the University of Virginia and director of the Mountain Ridge Biological Station.

KEN WISSOKER is editorial director of the Duke University Press. He has written and spoken widely on issues related to book publishing today.

A. LEIGH DENEEF is a professor of English and the former associate dean of the Graduate School at Duke University.

CRAUFURD D. GOODWIN is James B. Duke Professor of Economics at Duke University. He has also served as the dean of the Graduate School (1980–87) and the vice provost for research.

Library of Congress Cataloging-in-Publication Data

The academic's handbook / edited by
A. Leigh DeNeef and Craufurd D. Goodwin. — 3rd ed.
p. cm.   Includes bibliographical references and index.
ISBN-13: 978-0-8223-3883-3 (cloth : alk. paper)
ISBN-10: 0-8223-3883-1 (cloth : alk. paper)
ISBN-13: 978-0-8223-3874-1 (pbk. : alk. paper)
ISBN-10: 0-8223-3874-2 (pbk. : alk. paper)
1. College teachers — United States. 2. Universities and colleges
— United States. I. DeNeef, A. Leigh. II. Goodwin, Craufurd D. W.
LB1778.2.A24 2006   378.1′2 — dc22
2006020430